Ben Riley-Smith is the *Daily Telegraph*'s Political Editor. He has spent a decade at the paper covering politics in the Scottish Parliament, Westminster and Washington, DC. He has interviewed the last six prime ministers and covered the elections and referendums that have shaped recent British politics first hand. He has been shortlisted twice for political journalism at the British Journalism Awards and once at the Press Awards.

Praise for *Blue Murder*

'A rather brilliant attempt to encapsulate fourteen years of zigzagging, fast-changing and often melodramatic leadership by one of the world's most successful parties. Riley-Smith has excellent, garrulous sources, produces plenty of fresh stories, and writes entertainingly and very lucidly about some of the most remarkable characters modern Britain has seen; and their feuds. This book provides strong lessons from (recent) history for the modern Tories; and plenty of ammunition for their foes'   Andrew Marr

'Not only a fascinating dissection of the Conservative Party, but a wonderfully written canter through an extraordinary decade and a bit. Highly recommended'   Chris Mason

'A majestic, digested read of the last fourteen years of Tory leadership, drawing together the threads of [five] premierships each defined by Brexit'   *Guardian*

'Insightful, authoritative and incredibly readable, this is an essential account of the last fourteen years of Conservative rule, which lays bare the rivalries and betrayals, mistakes and misunderstandings, naivety and mendacity, which have characterised this chaotic and tumultuous era, all delivered with wit and panache by one of Westminster's best-connected journalists. It had me open-mouthed with amazement one minute and shaking my head in bewilderment the next'   Ed Balls

T0301222

'The essential anatomy of the modern, occasionally mad and often maddening Conservative Party. You see the political body with its faults and fault-lines, skullduggery and scheming, big ideas and petty jealousies . . . I hugely enjoyed the small detail and the first-rate analysis of the bigger picture'   Jon Sopel

'Filled with chaos, rebellion, in-fighting, backbiting and catastrophe . . . A cracking read'   *Financial Times*

'A grippingly written, detailed book that answers so many questions about why the Tories have ended up how they are today. Journalism is the first draft of history, but this is the proper version'
                                    Isabel Hardman

'A sharp insider account of the long Tory reign'   *New Statesman*

'Gripping and insightful . . . What a tumultuous period in British political history it has been . . . and what a brilliant account of it – is there anyone Riley-Smith hasn't spoken to?'   Evan Davis

'Engaging . . . an exhaustively researched history . . . every one of its chapters manages to throw up nuggets for political historians and general readers alike . . . Riley-Smith is an excellent, pithy writer with a knack for a telling phrase . . . among the best books written about the chaos and carnage of the past fourteen years'
                                    Sunday Telegraph

'Terrific . . . I can't recommend highly enough . . . Not all political books are page-turners. This really is'   Matthew d'Ancona

'Packed with insight, gossip and candid reflections from the major players, [*Blue Murder*] illuminates and expands our understanding of a vital chapter in recent political history'   Stephen Bush

'Riley-Smith expertly explains how a governing party mainly skilled in backstabbing survived in power despite a series of catastrophic policy decisions: mainly by repeatedly heaving its leader overboard . . . A good but saddening read'   Michael Portillo

'Future historians, keen to attribute a sense of purpose to the last fourteen chaotic years of Conservative government will take Riley-Smith's lucid and riveting book as their guide'   Alan Johnson

'Colourful and richly researched . . . will engage today's readers and serve as a valuable resource for future historians interested in an extraordinary era of British politics'   Rafael Behr

'The last fourteen years have been a tumultuous period for British politics in general and the Conservative Party in particular. Riley-Smith has brought this to life in his fast-paced account of the key moments and personalities, full of new revelations on what was really happening'   David Gauke

Blue Murder

The Rise and Fall of the Conservative Government,
2010–2024

BEN RILEY-SMITH

JOHN MURRAY

First published in Great Britain as *The Right to Rule* in 2023
by John Murray (Publishers)

This paperback edition published in 2024

2

Copyright © Ben Riley-Smith 2023, 2024

The right of Ben Riley-Smith to be identified as the
Author of the Work has been asserted by him in accordance
with the Copyright, Designs and Patents Act 1988.

A CIP catalogue record for this title is available from the British Library

Paperback ISBN 9781399810319
ebook ISBN 9781399810326

Typeset in Bembo MT Pro by
Palimpsest Book Production Ltd, Falkirk, Stirlingshire

Printed and bound in Great Britain by Clays Ltd, Elcograf S.p.A.

John Murray policy is to use papers that are natural, renewable and
recyclable products and made from wood grown in sustainable forests.
The logging and manufacturing processes are expected to conform
to the environmental regulations of the country of origin.

Carmelite House
50 Victoria Embankment
London EC4Y 0DZ

www.johnmurraypress.co.uk

John Murray Press, part of Hodder & Stoughton Limited
An Hachette UK company

The authorised representative in the EEA is Hachette Ireland, 8 Castlecourt Centre,
Castleknock Road, Castleknock, Dublin 15, D15 YF6A, Ireland

To Louisa and Tristram,
to whom I owe everything.

And to Agnes,
with whom I will share everything ahead.

Contents

Author's Note

POLITICAL REPORTING IS a messy business. Trying to carve out facts from the maelstrom of claims, spin, deception and obfuscation can be much harder than critics sometimes suggest, especially with the passing of time. It is, then, perhaps worth a brief note on my approach.

I am a reporter rather than an opinion writer. That means personal views are very deliberately left at the door. While no correspondent is naive enough to think that their upbringing and outlook do not shape their journalism, a conscious effort has been made to strive for impartiality. That means removing the prism of personal politics, trying to ascertain what is accurate and following the path from there. Shortcomings, which are inevitable, are not for want of trying.

Claims can be corroborated by those who were present. Contemporary notes, recordings, text exchanges and emails can back up accounts. Extra sources to deepen reporting have been sought out as much as possible within the time limit set for the project. Less tangible things, such as a portrait of a prime minister's character and approach to power, have been built up by gathering many views from those – both allies and critics – with first-hand experience. Eye-catching or jaw-dropping claims that could not be stacked up have been left out. Scepticism rather than cynicism has been a watchword. The harshest interpretation of a politician's motives – on whichever side – almost always over-simplifies the facts and is rarely illuminating.

The core new material for the book comes from interviews. More than 120 people were interviewed between November 2022 and July 2023, plus I arranged twenty-five further chats in June and July 2024 for the extra chapter on the 2024 election campaign. The audio recordings last longer than a hundred hours, the transcripts go beyond a million words. Most of those conversations were conducted off the record, which means that the information and quotes generated could be used but not attributed by name to the person speaking. However, it was agreed that I could double-back afterwards and request interviewees to put certain remarks on the record. I tried to do this wherever possible, given that it is so much better for the reader to know explicitly who is speaking. The vast majority of interviewees put at least some remarks on the record. Some made tweaks to wording before signing them off. A list of some one hundred people who were interviewed is provided below, which will give the reader a sense of the breadth of sources. A good many asked to remain anonymous, especially those until recently inside the government; they are not named on the list. Other briefer, more casual conversations that fed into the book are also not captured here.

At many points in the narrative, comments are shared in an off-the-record capacity. To me this is justifiable and serves a vital purpose. Being able to provide direct accounts by those who witnessed critical moments themselves is of real value. Interviewees speak more freely when they know that what they say will not automatically appear in public under their name. There are downsides to that too – a lower bar for passing on deceptions, perhaps. Hence the drive to corroborate as much as possible. I have sought to be as specific as circumstances allow about the role, position or faction of the individual speaking. At times these descriptions have been kept vague to protect source identities. Beware guessing – it is rarely the obvious person.

The endnotes – more than a thousand of them – provide a guide for those curious about where information has come from. On-the-record comments from new interviews are explicitly flagged there. So too are references to some of the books that already cover aspects of this period in great detail, as well as newspaper articles, speeches and other material. Direct quotations from conversations that appear in the narrative came via sources who participated in them, or were reported by someone who did, or other well-placed figures.

Finally, two quick apologies. The first, for the use of 'the author' at points during the book when indicating where information came from. It is a cumbersome, pretentious phrase – but better than the alternative of 'me' or 'I', which thrusts the reporter personally into the story.

And, secondly, for the swearing. Profanities are a daily occurrence in politics. There is a reason Theresa May's aides and colleagues pointed to the fact she never swore as a defining feature. In Westminster, it is the absence of expletives that really shocks.

Ben Riley-Smith
Haggerston, London, July 2024

Interviewees

Adam Jones, Alex Dawson, Baroness (Alison) Suttie, Ameet Gill, Dame Andrea Leadsom, Lord (Andrew) Feldman, Ben Gummer, Bob Blackman, Boris Johnson, Brandon Lewis, Chris Grayling, Chris Philp, Chris Wilkins, Cleo Watson, Craig Elder, Sir Craig Oliver, Craig Whittaker, Damian Green, Daniel Korski, Sir Danny Alexander, Lord (David) Cameron, David Canzini, David Davis, Lord (David) Frost, David Laws, Sir David Lidington, Dominic Raab, Ed Miliband, Lord (Eddie) Udny-Lister, Lord (Eric) Pickles, Fiona Hill, Lord (Gavin) Barwell, Sir Gavin Williamson, George Osborne, Giles Kenningham, Baroness (Gisela) Stuart, Sir Graham Brady, Graham Stuart, Grant Shapps, Greg Swift, Guto Harri, Henry Cook, Iain Carter, Sir Iain Duncan Smith, Isaac Levido, Sir Ivan Rogers, Sir Jacob Rees-Mogg, Sir Jake Berry, James Schneider, Jamie Hope, Jason Stein, Jeremy Corbyn, Sir John Hayes, Baroness (JoJo) Penn, Julian Smith, Baroness (Kate) Fall, Katie Perrior, Kwasi Kwarteng, Baroness (Liz) Sanderson, Baroness (Liz) Sugg, Liz Truss, Lizzie Loudon, Lucia Hodgson, Sir Lynton Crosby, Mark Francois, Mark Fullbrook, Lord (Mark) Sedwill, Matthew Elliott, Mats Persson, Michael Gove, Lord (Michael) Howard, Nadhim Zahawi, Baroness (Natalie) Evans, Nick Timothy, Baroness (Nicky) Morgan, Nigel Adams, Nigel Farage, Nikki da Costa, Norman Baker, Sir Oliver Letwin, Oliver Lewis, Patrick Heneghan, Paul Harrison, Paul Stephenson, Lord (Philip) Hammond, Dame Priti Patel, Ranil Jayawardena, Raoul Ruparel, Richard Jackson, Sir Robert Buckland, Robert Colvile, Rory Stewart, Ross Kempsell, Ruth Porter, Ryan Coetzee, Sajid Javid, Seumas Milne, Sir Simon Clarke, Lord (Spencer) Livermore, Lord (Stephen) Gilbert, Lord (Stephen) Parkinson, Steve Baker, Sir Steve Webb, Theresa Villiers, Sir Vince Cable, Wendy Morton, Will Walden, Lord (William) Hague, Sir William Lewis.

The Conservative Party is like an absolute monarchy, moderated by regicide.

William Hague, coalition talks, 2010

A Conservative government always eventually falls because they believe themselves *entitled* to power. And Labour governments always fall . . . because they don't.

James Graham, *This House*, 2012

When the herd moves, it moves.

Boris Johnson, resignation speech, 7 July 2022

Introduction

LARRY THE CAT could be forgiven for his nonchalance. As Rishi Sunak, all immaculate suit and immaculate hair, breezed up Downing Street for the first time as prime minister, there was barely a look from the Number 10 chief mouser as he passed.

The scene was by now all too familiar. Overhead buzzed a helicopter beaming footage of the arrival to the nation. Off to the side, dispersed and stern-faced, were members of the security detail. Ahead, to Sunak's left: the press pack, reporters huddled close together and crouched low so that the cameras could capture his approach. Falling further behind with each step was the throng of protesters gathered beyond the gates.

Leaves peppered the ground that morning, 25 October 2022, just as they had when Liz Truss made the same walk only seven weeks earlier. There had been two new prime ministers in the autumn alone, Truss crashing out with the economic warning lights flashing and into the history books for the shortest ever tenure in Number 10. There had been three new prime ministers in little more than three years; four in just over six. Upheaval had become the norm.

Reaching the wooden podium outside the black front door, Sunak opened the folder he was carrying and looked into the cameras. There would be echoes of the man who had kicked off this long Conservative Party run, David Cameron, in the message that followed. Debt was a vice that should not be forced upon 'the next generation'. Politics was about 'professionalism and accountability'. And, critically, errors had occurred under his predecessor that must be put right. 'Some mistakes were made,' Sunak said. 'Not born of ill will, or bad intentions. Quite the opposite, in fact. But mistakes, nonetheless.' There was a difference this time, though. The mess Sunak was vowing to clear up had been left by his own party.

Before entering his new home, where officials and advisers were lined up waiting to burst into applause, the Tory leader paused for the photographers and raised a solitary hand. Back in 2010 when Cameron had been on this spot, Sunak was not even an MP. Indeed, he was still in his twenties and living on the other side of the world.[1] Yet here he was now, approaching thirteen years on, being handed the torch of power. So frequently had it been passed of late from Conservative to Conservative, it had begun to feel like an inheritance.

There would be no customary smile offered up by Sunak. Instead there was a furrowed brow and impassiveness – a serious politician for sober times. And with that, he turned and headed in, the Number 10 door closing behind another Tory prime minister.

For all its familiarity, the moment was also extraordinary. David Cameron, Theresa May, Boris Johnson, Liz Truss, Rishi Sunak – five Conservatives back to back running the country. No political party had pulled off that feat for almost two centuries. It was the Tories then too, a six-prime-minister streak that stretched from William Cavendish-Bentinck in 1807 to Arthur Wellesley in 1830. The latest feat spoke to the party's ruthless pursuit of power and its ability to shape-shift to meet the public mood. It spoke, too, of deep turbulence, of an instinct for regicide and how, when the itch had been scratched once, it proved harder to resist doing it again (and again).

All shades of Tory blue had been on display: the Cameroon modernisation project, merging fiscal prudence with patrician responsibility and enough New Labour continuity to bring the public on side; May's dutiful determination to deliver a Brexit she never voted for, while smoothing the sharper edges of the free market; Johnson's big-tent, big-spending Conservatism that shuddered under the weight of its own contradictions; Truss's primary-colours vision of low taxes and turbocharged growth, cheered on by the base but less so by the markets; and then Sunak's 'take your medicine' economics, grounded in theory and pursued with a dogged work ethic. At times directly opposed positions had been adopted, Cameron's portrayal of government borrowing as the root of all evil versus Truss's embrace of debt to deliver a tax-slashing mini-Budget. Yet the through-line of Tory rule had remained.

Nor had the churn of historic events been enough to persuade the public to kick them out. There had been the patch-up job when inheriting the aftermath of the 2007–8 financial crash, a biting austerity programme that markedly shrank the size of the state. There had been an unanticipated Brexit, throwing the UK's economic and foreign policy strategy into the air against the will of the government. A once-in-a-century pandemic had struck, resulting in a once-in-three-centuries economic contraction via a nationwide lockdown. War had returned to the European continent. And yet, still, there they were: the Conservatives at the centre of government.

How? That is the question this book attempts to examine. To do so, rather than offer an encyclopaedic cataloguing of what happened, it will zoom in on ten critical moments or parts of the story, the pivotal points that explain the wider whole. One will show how David Cameron, coming up short in the 2010 general election, exhibited flexibility and nous in striking a deal with another party to end the Tories' wilderness years. Another will detail the way in which, with brutal clarity, the Conservatives then turned on their coalition partners, decimating the Liberal Democrats to secure a shock House of Commons majority in 2015. The sliding-doors moments on the long road to the 2016 EU referendum, a mix of politicking and risk-taking propelling Cameron towards the very destination he was determined to avoid, will be explored. So too the first year of a new prime minister, Theresa May, picking up the pieces of the government implosion while leaning on two dominant co-chiefs of staff.

There will be the inside story of the calamitous 2017 Tory election campaign, retold courtesy of more than five hundred pages of leaked documents, which saw the certainty of a knock-out victory proved illusory and the country plunged back into the Brexit battles. And how Johnson rose from backbench alienation in late 2018 to all-powerful election conqueror by the end of 2019, via the toppling of a prime minister when all the dark arts were on display from the party's mini-Machiavellis. Boris's approach to office and whether the biggest Tory majority since Margaret Thatcher was squandered will be scrutinised, with more than twenty of his Cabinet ministers giving insights. So too will the fall of Johnson, an extraordinary nine-month slide that involved the total disintegration of his relationship with then-chancellor Rishi Sunak. Insiders at the top of the Liz Truss premiership – forty-nine days and out – will reveal why the mini-Budget swelled and what made her sack Kwasi Kwarteng. And then there is comeback kid Sunak's leadership victory the month after his defeat and the rescue mission launched thereafter from Downing Street.

An eleventh chapter has been added for the paperback edition of this book, completing the story by retelling the Tory wipeout of the 2024 general election, with insiders in all the main party campaigns revealing how it really played out.

Key players in each of those moments have been interviewed to understand the real dynamics at play – the core material for what follows. Conversations with all five prime ministers have fed into the reporting. David Cameron, Boris Johnson and Liz Truss gave interviews for the book in 2023. Rishi Sunak was interviewed four times by the author for the *Daily Telegraph*, once during the Tory leadership race in July 2022 and again when prime minister in June 2023, April 2024 and June 2024, with full transcripts providing previously unpublished comments. Theresa May did not talk for the book, but previous *Telegraph* interviews with the author during her premiership in May and September 2017 offered insights into her thinking. So too did off-the-record conversations, press conference questions and foreign trip huddles with all five over the years. Former chancellors gave their views: George Osborne, Philip Hammond, Sajid Javid, Nadhim Zahawi and Kwasi Kwarteng were all interviewed. Scores of other government ministers, MPs, Downing Street insiders, civil servants, special advisers, Treasury officials and wider political players helped flesh out the picture, some choosing to remain off-record. Key rival party figures during this time also talked: Ed Miliband, Jeremy Corbyn, Nigel Farage, Danny Alexander, David Laws and Vince Cable among them. In total, more than 120 people were interviewed.

As a reporter with the *Telegraph* for more than a decade on a variety of political beats, the author has also been lucky enough to cover many of the critical moments first-hand: witnessing the scramble to save the Union in the 2014 Scottish independence referendum; riding the battle buses of the 2015 general election; tracking Boris as he waved Cornish pasties and kippers for Brexit in 2016; questioning May during her misfiring 2017 election campaign; documenting the decline and fall of Johnson; grilling Truss publicly after she sacked her chancellor and ditched her tax cuts; analysing the rise of Rishi. Such glimpses behind the curtain helped construct a fuller picture.

The story that emerges is one of a party built to rule. Time and again, the same message was echoed by interviewees: what must be understood is that the Conservatives are not an 'ideological party' but a 'power party'. Labour was formed to represent a demographic, the working class, and to bring about a vision: democratic socialism. The Tories have never been as anchored on either point. There are values or principles that carry through: free enterprise, individual responsibility, the importance of the nation-state, a suspicion of big government, a defence of tradition. But there is an inherent flexibility that, when fused with a clear-eyed determination to be in power, can prove remarkably effective. The Conservatives are the world's most successful party in modern democratic history, as their MPs often like to note.

The clearest manifestation of the party's ability to adapt comes in the system for removing leaders. The Labour Party does not have a formal 'no confidence' mechanism. The Conservative Party does, with each MP able to submit a letter declaring as much to the 1922 Committee. In Labour, a rival candidate has to gather signatures from 20 per cent of the party's MPs to trigger a challenge. For the Tories, the bar is lower: just 15 per cent of MPs need to submit a letter to force a no-confidence vote. With Labour, those rebel MPs expect to be named. With the Tories, the opposite is true: Brutuses are granted the cloak of anonymity.

The inbuilt trigger system can reap electoral rewards: Theresa May was replaced with Boris Johnson in 2019 to smash through the Brexit impasse, see off Jeremy Corbyn and secure a Tory majority. All three boxes were comprehensively ticked. For the Conservatives to go from leading a government determined to defeat Brexit to one determined to deliver Brexit, all the while continuing their unbroken period in power, takes some political alchemy. The inability of Labour MPs to oust Corbyn, despite the vast majority of them voting to get rid of him in 2016, is the flip side of the same coin.[2] The Tory rules create a need for the party's leader to look constantly over their shoulder. David Cameron once wrote that 'never for a minute' did he forget the all-important 15 per cent figure. He added: 'Not once during eleven years as Conservative leader did I feel secure for any length of time.'[3]

Which leads to another theme: one of unchained ambition and bitter feuds. What drove the Tory shape-shifting from 2010 was not just changes in public opinion, the idiosyncrasies of circumstances and the difficulty of matching ideals to realities, but also the decisions of the individuals involved. Egotism, jealousy, determination, skul-duggery, vanity, vengeance and greed all played their part. At moments the personal rivalries of a handful of people, as much as their political visions for Britain, had a defining role in the course of history. Such tussles can be found in all political parties. But it was the Tories who were in government, meaning the impact was outsized. As time went on and new ways to regenerate were sought, the lever marked 'regicide' would be pulled again and again. Where once it had led to political salvation, what instead followed were vast opinion poll drops, contributing to the kind of spiralling of the party's fortunes that such mechanisms were designed to stop. It ended in blue murder, the biggest Tory defeat in modern history inflicted by a public sick of all the in-fighting.

This book is not a deep dive into how Conservative policies have shaped Britain, though such works no doubt are needed. Nor is it a forensic account of each year in office or an assessment of the party's record of governance. Instead, it is an attempt to understand how the Conservative Party kept changing, kept revolting and kept winning. To Tories delighted by the run, it will offer clues as to how it might be repeated. To Labour supporters horrified by fourteen years of Conservative rule, it will offer an explanation of how it was achieved. To everyone else, hopefully, it will bring a better understanding of the forces that have changed lives and the country for ever.

I

A Lighter Shade of Blue

DAVID CAMERON TOOK a breath as eight million people watched.[1] Standing at the podium, a long shadow stretching behind him from the studio lights, he tried to hide his nerves.[2] Never before in British politics had the party leaders agreed to a televised election debate. Conscious of the risks, the frontrunner had always said no. But Cameron, the favourite in 2010, had broken the trend. His five-year modernisation drive had brought the Conservative Party to the brink of power. With Number 10 in touching distance, he had gambled, believing debates were in the country's interest and, all being well, his own. Now it was time to discover how the dice would fall.

To the Conservative leader's left on the ITV set was the man who stood between him and Downing Street. Gordon Brown, the prime minister, was overseeing the fag end of the New Labour government. His attempt to rejuvenate the project after ousting Tony Blair had hit the buffers with the 2007–8 financial crash, meaning election defeat was expected. The Tories had led Labour in the opinion polls for years. Cameron was younger and a smoother performer. The match-up looked favourable.

To his right was a relative unknown: the leader of Britain's third political party. Nick Clegg was only two and a bit years into his tenure as leader of the Liberal Democrats and had no realistic prospect of becoming prime minister. Indeed, even making it into a three-way debate was a win, giving him level pegging with more established politicians. Brown had been Labour's leader or Treasury lead for eighteen years. Cameron had led his party for half a decade. Voters knew little of Clegg.

In ninety minutes of prime-time TV on 15 April 2010, that

I

changed. On a set whose decor screamed nineties quiz show, Cameron tried to land his message about the need for financial restraint after Labour's profligacy. Brown dialled up the 'Tory cuts' narrative that would be his core campaign theme. But it was Clegg who cut through. Time and again he would step away from his two rivals, waving a hand towards them and declaring a plague on both their houses. 'The more they attack each other, the more they sound exactly the same,' he quipped, neatly tying Labour and the Tories together as a single failed establishment. 'I hear the words, they sound great, but it's not just what you say, it's what you do,' he said, tapping into the public discontent with governing parties. He even wore a contrasting suit – navy blue to the black of Cameron and Brown.

Clegg addressed audience members by their first names: a human touch. He stared into the camera when speaking, making eye contact with the nation. Even better, he seemed relaxed.

Cameron soon felt the debate slipping away. 'This is not going in the way I want it to go,' he thought to himself.[3] He had known what strategy Clegg would deploy – fellow Tory MP Jeremy Hunt had predicted the attacks almost word for word while playing the Lib Dem leader in debate prep. But countering the moves was easier said than done. Both Cameron and Brown were courting Lib Dem voters, so both deployed 'I agree with Nick' messages – inadvertently elevating the Lib Dem appeal. 'It's difficult because they're not really debates. They are mechanisms for delivering a message,' Cameron recalled. 'You've got to make your point in answer very briefly and then go down the barrel of the camera to the folks back at home. And I was still trying to think: "No, no, it's a debate." So it was frustrating at times.'[4]

That frustration was compounded once he stepped off stage. Snap polls universally gave Clegg the victory. Worse, in the days ahead, the proportion of people saying they would vote Lib Dem soared. Soon the phenomenon had a moniker – Cleggmania. And it was bleeding Tory support.

Cameron had always known that getting the Conservatives a majority in the 2010 election would be a tall order. The magic number was 326, one seat more than half of the 650 available in the

House of Commons. The last general election, in 2005, had left the Tories on just 198. Cameron liked to call the mountain of extra seats needed his 'Everest'.[5] With Clegg's breakout debate performance, the chances of winning Lib–Con marginals were fading, and with them hopes of a Tory majority.

At home after the debate Cameron found little comfort. 'You were hopeless' was the blunt assessment of his wife, Samantha Cameron.[6] Lying in bed, he thought of Tory MP friends now facing defeat in their seats to Lib Dems. 'The feeling was worse than fear or disappointment,' recalled the man responsible for the debates even happening. 'It was guilt.'[7]

And then there was action. In the six weeks that remained until voting day on 6 May, Cameron would continue to project optimism that victory was just around the corner. Privately, however, his inner circle changed tack. The pivot was done in secret, hidden from the press, but was no less significant for that. It was time, they concluded, to think about coalition talks.

Days after the first debate, George Osborne, the Tory shadow chancellor and Cameron's sidekick in his party overhaul, discussed this shift in tactics with the Tory leader in Notting Hill, the cushy west London borough where they both lived. 'I think we're going to have to think about a coalition,' Cameron told him.[8] Osborne agreed. Cameron did not want to be directly involved – it would be a distraction and leave him without plausible deniability if journalists asked about planning. Yet the approval was given for preparations to be made.

For five years, Cameron, Osborne and a tight-knit group of allies had tried to drag the Tories back to electability after successive defeats to New Labour. Every move had been considered through the prism of whether it would help them return to government. 'Change to win' had been the slogan of Cameron's 2005 leadership pitch, his political North Star. And now, with the finishing line in sight, came the gut punch of clarity: it looked as though they were going to come up short.

Starting coalition planning was an admission of failure of sorts. But it spoke, too, of a visceral yearning for power – something that would become a defining feature in the Tories' twists and turns in the years ahead. If a deal was needed to reach Downing Street, they wanted to be ready.

It should be no surprise that Osborne got the call-up. The Cameroonian project was as much a two-man job as Blair and Brown's overhaul of the Labour Party – just without the bitterness and perception of betrayal.

Cameron and Osborne, like so many of their Tory frontbench predecessors, had entered the world of Westminster via the Conservative Research Department. Both were privately schooled, Cameron at Eton and Gideon, as Osborne was christened, at St Paul's. Both went to Oxford University – Cameron studying Philosophy, Politics and Economics, Osborne History – where they were members of the tailcoat-wearing, room-wrecking Bullingdon Club.

But they were not direct contemporaries in Conservative circles. Cameron was five years the senior and rapidly climbing the ladder when Osborne got on the first rung in 1994. Indeed, Cameron was already being tipped for the top job. 'Everyone said he was the next Tory leader but three,' Osborne recalled.[9] Back then, they knew of each other but were not friends.

Both, however, did have a front-row seat at the death of a once-dominant Tory government, an experience central to shaping their political instincts. Cameron was special adviser (spad) to Norman Lamont, the chancellor, on Black Wednesday, when Britain crashed out of the European Exchange Rate Mechanism in September 1992, sending interest rates soaring.

Battling for his employer's career, Cameron would later recount the phone call he received one night from a deputy editor at the *Sun*. 'The good news is that your boss's picture is on the front page of tomorrow's newspaper,' the voice down the line explained. 'The bad news is that his head is in the middle of a cut-out-and-keep dartboard.'[10] Lamont was gone by the following spring, with Cameron learning how hard it can be to counter a press narrative.

Osborne's insights into John Major's crumbling premiership came at the hands of the man himself. During the 1997 election campaign, it was the job of Osborne, then in his mid-twenties, to brief the prime minister on media developments. Every morning he would pick up the newspapers from King's Cross station around 2 a.m., cut out any problematic articles at Tory HQ and then head to Major's Downing Street flat to update him around 6 a.m. Some of the most bruising headlines can still be recalled by Osborne, not least among them Major's own sister telling a tabloid that he could not beat Tony Blair. But the starkest moment came in the prime ministerial flat just before election day. 'It was all packed up,' Osborne said. 'I was like: "Oh, right, we really are going to lose."'[11]

The story of the Conservative Party from 2010 can be told in many ways. It is a tale of votes, gambles, miscalculations, mixed in with global trends, party management and electoral shifts. But it is also a story of a tiny number of individuals – perhaps a dozen – and of how their principles, biases, egos, loyalties and at times fiercely pursued rivalries shaped the nation. The Cameron–Osborne axis defines the first half of that story, though the characters who dominate the second half are already present: Boris Johnson, Theresa May and Michael Gove in particular. Tracking these political relationships – some of which would be tested to destruction – is key to understanding the decisions that changed Britain. It shows how the biggest political developments can be shaped by the pettiest of clashes.

Cameron and Osborne only really became friends after the 2001 election, when both entered Parliament for the first time, Cameron representing the constituency of Witney, Osborne Tatton. Just twenty-six new Tory MPs were elected that year, leaving a small group of newbies. (Another was Boris Johnson. All three men were taking their first joint steps on a path that would lead to one destroying the other two's political careers.)

These were the days of deepest, darkest opposition. William Hague's attempt to return the Tory Party to electability in a single term after Major's blowout defeat was a dismal failure. Blair's majority in 2001 was almost as big as in 1997. Out went Hague, in came grassroots' favourite Iain Duncan Smith and on went the party's struggles to reconnect with the wider electorate.

Osborne and Cameron were both feeling their way into a parliamentary career, finding themselves for the first time on the front line rather than behind the scenes. Osborne remembered noticing

that in a debate about emergency security legislation being pushed
through after the 9/11 terror attacks by David Blunkett, then home
secretary, Cameron was the only other Tory MP who sat listening
in the Commons throughout.

'We went from companions to friends,' Osborne said of those
years, a transition helped by the fact they lived close to each other.
'I would give him a lift to and from home in my car. Then I decided
I needed to get fitter so I took up cycling. I said, "Oh, I'm really
sorry, David, I can't give you a lift anymore to Parliament." And he
said, "Well, I'll take up cycling." So we used to then cycle together.
On those journeys to and from Notting Hill we just had lots of
conversations about what had gone wrong with the Tory Party, why
the Hague thing hadn't worked and why Iain Duncan Smith wasn't
working.'

He went on: 'We were desperate to try and find answers to how
to get the Conservative Party back into a place where it might win.
All the talk at the time was there will never be another Conservative
government.'[12]

They were both also rising in prominence. Come the 2005 general
election, Duncan Smith had fallen as leader. His embattled declaration to the 2003 Tory conference hall that the 'quiet man' was
'turning up the volume' had been met by a mass reach for the mute
button, with colleagues installing the experienced Michael Howard
in his place. Cameron had been elevated to oversee the party's election manifesto. Osborne was chief secretary to the Treasury – a
shadow cabinet job. Their comparative youth ensured that they were
often seen on TV during the campaign. Yet, despite the unpopularity
of the Iraq War, the result was similar. A third Tony Blair win, a
third New Labour term, a third defeat for the Tories.

Cameron and Osborne by now had something of a political mind
meld as well as a deep personal friendship. Both would become
godparents to one of the other's children. And both harboured
ambitions for the top job. There took place between them, like
Brown and Blair a decade before, a discussion about who was best
placed to seek the leadership on a modernisation ticket. In contrast
to the Labour pair's infamous 'Granita pact', struck in an Islington
restaurant which saw Blair emerge as the candidate and Brown

harbouring resentments, the conversation between Cameron and Osborne left no bitter taste – at least none detectable in public.

Osborne, to his surprise, had already been approached by the departing Howard about going for leader. Aged only thirty-three, he was wavering over whether to launch a bid. Cameron, however, was determined to run – as became apparent when the pair discussed the matter. Osborne agreed that Cameron should join the race. He would chair his friend's campaign instead.

Victory looked unlikely as the contest began that summer. Just a handful of Tory MPs backed Cameron's bid at first, with numbers stalling as David Davis cemented his status as the early favourite. But a no-notes speech at the 2005 Tory conference changed the dynamic, Cameron projecting energy and optimism in contrast to Davis's more staid Toryism. From there the momentum switched, support ebbing away from Davis. On 6 December, the results were announced. With 68 per cent of the members' vote, Cameron, aged just thirty-nine, was elected the Conservative Party leader.

The central themes in the long slog from that moment to the 2010 general election help explain what followed during the coalition talks. There was a push to detoxify the Tory brand. One of the few times Cameron and Osborne rebelled was when Tory MPs were ordered under Duncan Smith to oppose same-sex adoption. Now in leadership roles – Osborne was made Cameron's shadow chancellor – they updated policy to be more in line with the public mood.

The party became softer on social justice. Hence the infamous 'hug a hoodie' stance, words Cameron never actually uttered but which was the press distillation of his less punitive approach. Likewise 'hug a husky', Fleet Street's shorthand for his photoshoot sledding in the Arctic – a push to make the Tories appear more environ-mentally friendly, which included changing the party's torch logo to an oak tree. There was a diversity drive to find Tory candidates more representative of modern Britain and not just middle-aged white men.

Cameron also surrounded himself with a trusted group of fellow MPs, advisers and aides, many of whom would remain by his side throughout the next decade.

Osborne was Cameron's 'partner in politics'.[13] 'With his understanding of politics, and the dynamics of the Conservative Party and the media and what needed to be done, he provided very clear thinking,' Cameron summed up Osborne's qualities in an interview. 'He thinks about politics, people and policy all the time. He is always on, always thinking around the next corner. He was a brilliant person to be working with.'[14] Osborne saw himself as Cameron's 'shadow chancellor, chief of staff and chief whip' all in one.[15] (And, he would go on to hope, successor as party leader and prime minister.)

There was supposedly a moment when the partnership almost cracked – a story told, but never shared publicly, by a Cameron inner-circle member. Whenever considering sacking a shadow cabinet minister, the then leader of the opposition would request to see any letters and emails that had been received relating to the subject from his private office. Only the aide who dealt with correspondence and the chief of staff would know that the evidence had been called for. In autumn 2008, Osborne was under fierce press scrutiny over claims – always denied – that he had sought a donation from the Russian billionaire Oleg Deripaska. Cameron, unbeknown to the wider office, summoned the correspondence for that evening. 'Cameron was very close to firing him,' the source said. The next morning, placated by whatever had been read, he decided not to act.[16]

But that incident was a real outlier. 'David and George were very much a double-headed leadership,' said Kate Fall, another central member of the Cameron team who would become his Downing Street deputy chief of staff. 'George was definitely the more bumptious, slightly like the younger brother. David was more the decision-maker. People used to say that George was intensely strategic and I think that's fair. If David would ask, "What's the right thing to do?", George would say, "Yes, what's the right thing but also how is it going to be difficult for Labour if we go here?"'[17]

A second key figure in the Cameron clan was William Hague. Hague was Osborne and Cameron's senior in age, and, as a former party leader, in position for much of their early careers. In 2005, Cameron brought Hague back onto the Tory frontbench, ending his years in the wilderness after losing the 2001 election by making him shadow foreign secretary. Considered by some of his peers the best prime minister the Tories never had, having suffered the misfortune of leading the party during Blair's prime, Hague had political instincts that were valued by Cameron. Osborne, once Hague's political secretary and speech-writer, was also a fan. Throughout the next decade Hague would be part of Cameron's 'special inner grouping', in his own words, often meeting at Cameron's house with both men on Sunday nights to chew over the week ahead.[18]

A third was Oliver Letwin. Ten years older than Cameron, though also Eton-educated, the MP for West Dorset had risen from being a brilliant History student at Cambridge University to becoming a Margaret Thatcher policy thinker – his fingerprints were on the imploding Poll Tax which hastened her political demise – and eventually a shadow cabinet minister. A run in the top posts of shadow home secretary and shadow chancellor ended in 2005, when he became one of the few Tory MPs to back Cameron's leadership bid at the outset.

His intellect sat at the heart of the Cameron project. 'Oliver was kind, endearing and clever,' as Cameron put it. 'He may have looked like an old-fashioned Tory MP, with red corduroy trousers and matching complexion, but no one had been more influential in helping me develop my brand of "modern, compassionate Conservatism" over the past five years [before the 2010 election].'[19]

The fourth key member of the Cameron inner circle was the bespectacled Ed Llewellyn. Another old Etonian – he had been in the year above Cameron – Llewellyn had taken a route through Westminster that had begun in party politics but crossed into the civil service. He served in Hong Kong as Governor Chris Patten's personal adviser and in Bosnia and Herzegovina under then-High Representative Paddy Ashdown. Llewellyn became Cameron's chief of staff in 2005, a role he would keep both in opposition and government. 'Diminutive and quietly spoken, Ed derived his authority from his intellect, decency and experience,' as his boss put it in his memoir, *For the Record*.[20]

There were others, too, at the heart of the Cameron project. Steve Hilton, the bald, blue-sky thinker who as director of strategy was instrumental in shaping the softer, kinder Tory brand both men envisaged. Andy Coulson, the plain-speaking former *News of the*

World editor who ran the communications team. Michael Gove, the *Times* journalist turned Tory MP moderniser who helped with the intellectual underpinning.

But it was Osborne, Hague, Letwin and Llewellyn to whom Cameron turned in his moment of weakness as election day neared in 2010. Publicly, he was declaring that victory was around the corner. Privately, his most trusted allies were preparing for something quite different.

On successive weekends after that tricky first conversation between Cameron and Osborne in which they admitted their fears, a gathering was held at the latter's Notting Hill townhouse. The small group scoured the Lib Dem manifesto, dug out Clegg's past stances on deal-making and mapped out options. Come election day, the plan was drafted – if it was needed. Now it was over to the public.

Chilli con carne was on the menu on election night at David Cameron's constituency home in Dean, a village in West Oxfordshire.[21] A handful of the Tory leader's closest advisers had gathered to watch the results come in, Kate Fall among them. MP allies were in their own constituencies, nervously awaiting count announcements.

Election day is universally described by politicians as the oddest of experiences. There is nothing left to do, other than vote and perhaps knock on some doors to boost turnout. The campaign has been run, the big decisions are now in the past. As the tectonic plates of politics shift, party leaders twiddle their thumbs, their careers hanging in the balance as they await the reveal.

Earlier in the day Cameron and his inner circle had been chewing things over at Steve Hilton's nearby house. All the opinion polls were telling a similar story: the Conservatives ahead, but not by enough to avoid a hung parliament, the term for when no party has the overall Commons majority needed to pass laws alone. Hopes remained – pre-election polls had proved wrong before – but they were slim.

In Dean, Cameron passed the time chopping logs.[22] With faded brick walls covered in green vines, the house was a quintessential Cotswolds cottage. Cosy and homely, it was the base away from London for the Camerons and their two children, Nancy and Elwen. Samantha Cameron was pregnant with a third, to be named Florence.

The couple had also had another child, Ivan, who had a rare form of epilepsy and died aged six in 2009. The tragedy had affected Cameron deeply. After the news broke of Ivan's passing, Brown cancelled Prime Minister's Questions and made time for Commons tributes instead – an act of kindness Cameron never forgot.

Preparing the chilli in the kitchen, the group tried to take their minds off the forthcoming results. After dinner they moved through to the living room, anxiety rising as they sat on sofas waiting for the BBC's election night exit poll. In the end, they got a tip-off – Ameet Gill, an aide who would become Cameron's speech-writer, got the intel from a source at the Beeb ten minutes before the broadcast.[23] The exit poll had the Conservatives in the lead on 307 seats, followed by Labour on 255 and the Lib Dems on 59.[24] (This proved quite accurate: the final result would turn out to be 306 for the Tories, 258 for Labour and 57 for the Lib Dems.)

Some conclusions were obvious. The Conservatives would have the most seats – a victory of sorts. Labour, after thirteen years in power, had plummeted, losing close to a hundred MPs. And the Lib Dems had not made the breakthrough they wanted. But equally obvious was another reality: the Tories had indeed come up short. They did not have the majority needed to govern alone.

The mood in Dean reflected the split verdict. Fall was 'thrilled', then gripped by 'anxiety' as the results slowly confirmed they had not got across the line.[25] Another present felt 'jubilation' and 'fucking relief' that the party was top, but 'a bit gutted' at missing the majority.[26] Cameron appeared less downbeat, having expected a hung parliament.[27] 'Deep in my soul, I think I thought this was always going to be difficult to do in one go,' he recalled.[28]

Some history had been made. At the final count, the Tories had increased their seat total by ninety-six from the 2005 election – the biggest rise the party had enjoyed since 1931, with a swing that would be unmatched even by Boris Johnson's 2019 triumph. They had broken the run of victories of the most electable incarnation of the Labour Party ever, denying them a fourth term in office. But still, against an unpopular prime minister who had overseen the start of one of the deepest recessions in a century, they had failed to win outright.

Within minutes, the spinning began. Brown's team viewed the better-than-expected result as a vindication of their campaign ruthlessly targeting Tory spending cuts. Peter Mandelson, the 'third man' of Blair and Brown's New Labour project, hit the airwaves arguing his party had the right to try to form a government first.[29] Theresa May, then shadow work and pensions secretary, was on TV for the Tories but struck a downbeat tone, saying it had not been an easy night. 'What the fuck? We've won the fucking election!' reacted Osborne, who raced to his own count early to get on the broadcasts himself.[30]

For Cameron, the long night had surreal moments. While he was awaiting his own seat's result at the Windrush Leisure Centre in Witney, a call came through from Arnold Schwarzenegger, the actor turned governor of California. Congratulations on the victory, Arnie told Cameron. But I have not quite won, Cameron had to respond. 'There I was, in a leisure centre, in the middle of the night, explaining the first-past-the-post election system to the Terminator,' he recalled.[31]

If Cameron's emotions were mixed, Nick Clegg's were much bleaker. The Liberal Democrat leader's chief of staff and fellow MP, Danny Alexander, a flame-haired and softly spoken Scot, had breezily predicted on election day that the party was heading for '85-plus seats'.[32] The optimism was understandable – Clegg, it appeared, had clearly enjoyed the best campaign, with a boosted Lib Dem polling position to prove it. But the party got nowhere near 85. Their 57-seat haul was, unthinkably for Clegg's team, actually five lower than that secured in the 2005 election.

Today his allies believe a sharper-than-expected vote squeeze is to blame, minds focusing in voting booths on the fact that the prime minister would ultimately be either Tory or Labour. The heightened press scrutiny after the first debate may also have played a part. And, as Clegg would later note, the margins were so fine: 4,000 extra votes in the right places would have won his party another eleven seats.[33] It was not to be. Cleggmania may still have had an impact – the squeeze began when the party was enjoying a higher level of support – but it failed to result in gains.

'I felt bruised, disappointed on all sorts of levels,' Clegg said.[34] David Laws, the Lib Dem education spokesman who would play a central role in coalition talks, said the party leader almost cried when he addressed staff back in London. 'Nick was actually extremely demotivated and upset about the results,' Laws said. 'He was pretty much on the edge of tears when he came back and spoke to party staff.'[35]

There was little time for recriminations, however. The governorship of Britain hung in the balance.

In politics there are moments when a handful of people in a short space of time make decisions with outsized consequences. The five days beginning on Friday, 7 May 2010 represented such a moment. The lack of a recent precedent − not since February 1974 had one party failed to win an outright majority at a UK general election − ramped up the pressure. Clues as to how the Tory Party's future would play out in the decade ahead can be found in those dramatic few days. The political dexterity deployed when the chance to take power was sensed is one; the relative freedom from party bureaucracy in order to act decisively is another. There would be clandestine meetings, bluffs and counterbluffs, the quiet shelving of priorities and the willing embrace of old foes. Gordon Brown, Nick Clegg and David Cameron would all attempt to plot a route to government. The electoral realities framed the discussions, of course, but individual judgement calls drove them. Only one party could end up with their man leading the country.

For Cameron, back in London after election night and lying in bed in the gleaming glass-fronted Park Plaza hotel, which faces the Houses of Parliament across the Thames, different paths sketched themselves out before him in his mind. One, perhaps the easiest for the party to swallow, was minority government. The Tories could seek to rule without an out-and-out majority, challenging opposition MPs to vote against measures which the government would argue were critical. Yet without any kind of agreement in place with some rivals this would be precarious. Every vote risked toppling the government. Perhaps if it was felled and a speedy second election called, the Tories would triumph. Perhaps not. In the meantime, few concrete reforms could be implemented.

Another was a so-called 'confidence and supply' agreement. That would see the Tories enter government alone, but a second party would agree to vote for key policies and support it in any confidence motions, bringing a degree of stability. The other party would have to be the Liberal Democrats, given the numbers. In return, a number of Lib Dem policies would be implemented, sweetening the deal and allowing the party to claim some wins while holding the Tories at arm's length, since their MPs would not become ministers.

In their pre-election coalition preparations, both the Tories and the Lib Dems considered this the most likely outcome in the event of a hung parliament.[36] Indeed, a written confidence and supply deal had even been drafted by Cameron's secret group of planners before polling day.[37] The Tories thought the Lib Dems would never want to join a Tory government fully, given the history of smaller parties being wiped out after such deals on the Continent. Clegg's team thought Cameron would never offer the electoral reform that was their requirement for any more ambitious pact.

There was a third option: a full-blown coalition. Government would become a shared endeavour between the Tories and the Lib Dems, with the latter getting ministerial posts – including in the Cabinet – and a beefed-up set of policy promises. There were risks. The Tories would have to ditch parts of their promised programme and some of their MPs would miss out on ministerial roles. The Lib Dems would have to back much of the Tory agenda, including spending cuts, and become the joint face of the project. But there were upsides, too – most obviously, stability at a time of deep financial uncertainty as a credit crisis crippled Greece and risked spreading. Yet it would be a step into the unknown – no coalition had been formed in the UK for seventy years, and then only during a world war.

And then there was another path not open to Cameron but which haunted his thoughts – a Labour–Lib Dem deal. On the numbers it looked extremely difficult. Add together the two parties' MPs and they were still short of the majority needed to pass laws, meaning agreements with smaller parties would also have to be reached. A so-called 'rainbow coalition' – perhaps including the Northern Irish Democratic Unionist Party (DUP) – was possible, however. And Labour and the Lib Dems were historically much more closely aligned in terms of outlook. Many of their grandees had dreamed of a great realignment of the Left to lock the Conservatives out of Downing Street for good. It was tricky – not least the idea of Brown staying on as prime minister after his party had failed to come first in the election – but it was theoretically doable.

For a few short hours Cameron slept as the options turned themselves over in his mind. When he woke, he had his answer. Given the gravity of the economic situation and the ambiguity of the election result, there was one path that had to be tried. 'I saw with complete lucidity what needed to happen,' he wrote in his memoirs – and those close to him agree he awoke with a clarity of vision that in the post-election fog surprised them. 'It wasn't the obvious thing to do, but it was the right thing to do,'[38] Cameron said. He would be going for a coalition.

'The election result didn't feel like an accident,' Cameron would explain. 'Something different had happened, because people wanted something different. Parliament hadn't been hung for 36 years. I was advocating something that hadn't been done in peacetime for 150 years: forming a full coalition.'[39]

A connection teeing up some form of discussions had already been made, with Ed Llewellyn, Cameron's chief of staff, pre-emptively texting Danny Alexander, his opposite number in the Lib Dems, at 4 a.m. that morning.[40] The key moment, making public Cameron's instinct, would come later that day when the Tory leader addressed the cameras from St Stephen's Club, a Westminster private members' club.

'I want to make a big, open and comprehensive offer to the Liberal Democrats,' Cameron told the country, speaking from a room in which hung a portrait of Winston Churchill, the last Tory to lead a coalition. 'I want us to work together in tackling our country's big and urgent problems – the debt crisis, our deep social problems and our broken political system.'

Such a move would be in the 'national interest', Cameron said. Coalition would offer 'a strong basis for a strong government'. There were also 'many areas of common ground'. Given that Cameron and Clegg had been tearing chunks out of each other for weeks in the campaign, the comments may have jarred with some listeners.

But little known to the public was a realisation which had already struck the Cameron team in private – one that made a coalition all the more likely.

Oliver Letwin was not just an MP, he was a policy wonk. Hearing him speak, a stranger could be forgiven for believing Letwin an academic, his cerebral prose being distinct from the usual partisan point-scoring in Westminster. In 2005, with the Tories' election defeat, he had lost his job as shadow chancellor. With the Cameron modernisation, Letwin had found a new intellectual as well as political project to pour his efforts into.

It was not just the Conservatives who had switched leaders since 2005. All three major parties had done so – a rarity between election cycles. Blair, of course, had been forced out by Brown, the fearsome former chancellor and Church of Scotland minister's son who tried to fashion his own brand of New Labour. The Liberal Democrats had changed leaders twice. Charles Kennedy, who oversaw a party revival, stepped down in 2006 after revealing his alcoholism. Menzies Campbell succeeded him but was forced out a year later over concerns that at sixty-six a fresher face was needed for the approaching election.

Nick Clegg was still relatively new to Parliament when he won the leadership in December 2007. He had become an MP just two years earlier, elected to represent Sheffield Hallam after spending five years in Brussels as a Lib Dem MEP. His youth – he was forty – belied his determination. As leader, Clegg began moving the party, with little fanfare, towards the Tories and away from Labour.

The critical text in this manoeuvre had appeared three years earlier. It was called *The Orange Book: Reclaiming Liberalism* and was the most important publication in the coalition's origin story. Its cover depicted a girl on a step ladder painting a wall a new shade of orange – a not-so-subtle hint at the themes of change and renewal within, given that the party's official colour was yellow.

David Laws co-edited the book. 'It was to try to bring the Lib Dems back to liberal traditions in which free markets, competition and choice did have a central role,' Laws said. Its enemy was 'the assumption that the state can always do things best'.[41] On economics in particular it represented a move away from Labour's belief in the power of 'big government'. Laws summed up the shift in approach as trying to show that 'social liberal' ends could be delivered by 'economically liberal' means.[42]

The Lib Dem old guard was suspicious; Laws remembered a mauling at the next parliamentary party gathering he attended.[43] Others were struck by the change too. Osborne, convinced that Laws at heart was a Tory, actually attempted to get him to switch parties in 2006. The offer was rebuffed. But among the book's chapter authors were many who would go on to serve as coalition ministers: Ed Davey, Chris Huhne, Steve Webb, plus Laws and Clegg himself. Come 2010, they were the party's senior players.

Ideological manoeuvring within Britain's third political party would not get most people's hearts racing. Letwin, however, took a keen interest. In an interview, he recalled:

> Most people are much too busy with their ordinary lives, even when in politics, to worry about what others are doing, especially if they are minority parties and therefore won't govern anytime soon. Very few people in politics had any sense of what the Orange Lib Dem group was doing. But I read every morsel of what was written and went to various events and talked to academics who helped them come up with it. What became clear to me was this extraordinary similitude between what I thought, what David and George thought, and what the *Orange Book* people thought.[44]

Michael Howard's Conservatives and Charles Kennedy's Lib Dems had been miles apart at the 2005 election. But with Cameron pushing the Tories towards the centre ground, and Clegg doing the same to his own party, the gap had been narrowing and narrowing.

'Both parties had been sensibly reformed – others would have said they had been appallingly hijacked,' Letwin explained, nodding to the protests from traditionalists. 'You had these two broadly liberal, broadly progressive groupings. If you asked them what they thought about sound money or gay rights or green energy, there wasn't much to choose from.'[45]

In the weeks of secret planning during the 2010 election campaign, it was Letwin who was tasked with going through the Lib Dem manifesto with a fine-tooth comb, working out how an agreement could be reached. The exercise confirmed what had long been his hunch: it would be much simpler than people assumed. 'The two programmes were 90 per cent similar, 70–80 per cent identical,' he concluded. 'So it was easy to put together in the end.'[46]

The confidence and supply document he drafted for Cameron ahead of election night focused on the points of difference. Electoral reform was an obvious one, with the Lib Dems favouring a form of proportional representation, by which a party wins seats according to overall vote share rather than just who comes top in each constituency. Nuclear power was another: the Lib Dems were dead set against it. The parties also differed starkly on the European Union. But, to Letwin, these were not insurmountable hurdles.

Figures in both leaders' inner camps today believe that without the *Orange Book* push and Clegg in charge no coalition deal would have been struck. Laws said that 'more likely' the Tories would have ruled in a minority government.[47] William Hague said that 'any other Liberal leader before Clegg would not have made this deal'.[48] Charles Kennedy, Clegg's predecessor but one, said so explicitly at the time: 'I would not have formed a coalition with the Conservatives had I been leader.'[49]

There was, however, another overlap that proved just as significant, one not of ideologies, but personalities. Whichever deal was made, Tories and Lib Dems or Labour and Lib Dems, the two party leaders would have to work closely together. That meant either Cameron and Clegg or Brown and Clegg. And it was here, in another quirk of circumstance, that the Tories had an advantage. The former pairing, similar in age, life experiences and temperaments, just clicked. The latter – to put it mildly – did not.

Strip out the names and Cameron's and Clegg's CVs would look remarkably similar. Instead of Eton and Oxford, Clegg's education read Westminster and Cambridge – albeit split by a gap year spent teaching skiing in Austria. Both grew up in the South-East of England: Clegg was born in Buckinghamshire, Cameron was raised in the adjacent county of Berkshire. Clegg, with more continental ancestors, developed from an adviser into a politician in Brussels, while Cameron did so in London. Born three months apart, both men by 2010 were married with young children.

They did not know each other well, though there had been early signs of seeing eye-to-eye. Waiting at the opening of the Supreme Court in 2009 as Brown and the Queen dealt with formalities, the two men exchanged small talk but ended up chatting for forty-five minutes. 'Nick and I talked politics, families and life,' Cameron recalled. 'We shared a liberal outlook and an easy manner. I left thinking, what a reasonable, rational, decent guy.'[50]

Brown, sixteen years Clegg's senior, enjoyed no such bonhomie. The prime minister was not known as the easiest of partners, as the litany of feuds in the New Labour years attested. (At the height of their internecine war, Brown refused to share details of his Budget with Blair until it was about to go off to the printers and could no longer be changed.) One rare meeting between all three leaders had come in 2009 in an attempt to agree reforms after the expenses scandal exposed by the *Daily Telegraph*. Brown reportedly viewed Clegg as being 'unhelpful', 'obstructive' and 'holier-than-thou' on the issue.[51] In turn Brown, according to one onlooker, was accused of behaving like an 'obnoxious bastard'.[52] A match made for coalition this was not.

The different party leader dynamics were underscored on that Friday, the afternoon following the election. Clegg throughout the campaign had promised to talk first to the leader whose party won most seats, and he stuck to his word. But Brown, keen to grasp his one remaining hope of staying in Downing Street, was pushing hard to open channels too. One after the other, with an hour's gap in between, Clegg talked to both men down the line from his home in Putney, south-west London, where he was mulling over the options.

Cameron led with the pair's similarities. 'I believe that you and I can get on,' he said, according to rough transcripts taken at the time.[53] 'I believe that this is doable and good for the country.' The men agreed their negotiating teams should meet that evening, ran through the broad approach and touched on their red lines. 'I enter this in a genuine spirit of compromise,' said Clegg.[54] The call was over in twelve minutes.

Next came Brown. 'Nick, well done, this was a triumph for you. You got your message across,' began the prime minister, according to the transcripts.[55] A smooth start. Then came the one-way traffic.

'Whatever the Conservatives are offering on policy, I am sure we could match them immediately'; 'We have so much in common on the constitutional reform agenda'; 'There is also Europe.' Each statement was reasonable enough; together the barrage became jarring. The call lasted twenty-three minutes, almost twice as long as the one with Cameron.

Alison Suttie, a senior Clegg aide who sat in on both calls and made the transcripts, attested to the difference in an interview. 'It was slightly painful to listen to,' Suttie said of the Brown conversation.[56] 'He talked at Nick rather than listened. Nick tried and failed on several occasions to interrupt.' The Cameron call, by contrast, was 'an instant "we could do business"', said Suttie. 'It just sort of worked. The personalities gelled. It was a surprise.'

When Clegg put down the phone after Brown's monologue, he turned to Suttie. 'That sounded like a 25-minute lecture!' she declared. 'Well, it certainly wasn't much of a conversation,' Clegg replied.[57] The personal dynamics were set.

The first formal talks happened that evening. The site selected was the Cabinet Office at 70 Whitehall. This was neutral territory. It was also 'tantalisingly, tauntingly close to 10 Downing Street', as Cameron put it.[58] The two buildings are actually connected. Osborne favoured the location to either the grand Admiralty House or Portcullis House, where many MPs had offices, believing the proximity to the nation's power centre would focus minds.

Cameron had selected four close allies – the ones tasked with planning during the campaign – as his negotiating team. Hague, with his deep Tory experience, would lead. Letwin was the details man (a running joke would be that he knew the Lib Dem manifesto better than them). Osborne was the political brain. Llewellyn was Cameron's eyes and ears in the room.

For Clegg, Danny Alexander was in charge. The pair had been close since meeting in Brussels as pro-European youngsters and shared a similar political outlook. Also in the room would be Laws, the *Orange Book* co-editor, who bore the scars of earlier coalition talks in the Scottish and Welsh parliaments. Joining them would be Chris Huhne, narrowly defeated by Clegg in the last leadership race,

and Andrew Stunell, a former chief whip schooled in local government power-sharing.

Throughout the talks the leaders themselves would be hands off,
having direct conversations only when sticking points arose or to
decide politically sensitive issues like Cabinet appointments.

The Lib Dems had also been doing their prep. In late 2009, a
deal-making taskforce was set up by Clegg to explore the avenues
potentially available. For them, the only way into government would
be through a pact, meaning there was little to be lost by starting early.

The civil service, too, had been preparing for the best part of a
year. Hung-parliament scenarios had been war-gamed, with officials
playing the leaders. Gus O'Donnell, then the Cabinet secretary –
Britain's top civil servant – later admitted that the real-life maths of
the 2010 election was almost identical to an option they had played
out, the 'infamous' scenario four. The problem? The negotiators
then had failed to reach a 'good conclusion'.[59]

At the first meeting after the election, the teams agreed the chat
would be a scoping exercise. They started with a topic that would
underpin the talks to come, one that would play a key role in shaping
the Tories' long stretch in government: the internal rules binding a
party leader.

Danny Alexander began. 'Look, perhaps we should each share our
internal procedures so that we both understand what we have to do
in order to get agreement,' he said. At the core of what he needed to
share was what the Lib Dems grandly termed their 'triple lock'. The
device had been forced on Paddy Ashdown by members when it
looked as though Blair might tempt the Lib Dem leader into a pact.[60]
It dictated that any coalition deal could only proceed with approval
from the party's MPs, its federal executive and the members themselves.

'So, I spent five or ten minutes explaining the triple lock and the
different layers within the party,' Alexander recalled. 'The people
we'd have to brief and get on side in the parliamentary party, and
the federal executive, and then eventually the special conference of
the party. William Hague just laughed at the end of it and said:
"Yes, for us it's much simpler. We'll go and tell David Cameron and
if he agrees, we'll do it."'[61]

Hague himself confirmed the story. 'It was horrendous,' he joked of the hoops his opposite number had to jump through. 'They said: "What are your procedures?" So I explained it was very simple. Policy-making is entirely vested in the leader, and if we don't like it, we get rid of the leader. But that's it. And they couldn't believe it, they sat there absolutely staggered.'[62]

Hague would boil it down into a neat phrase: the Conservative Party is 'an absolute monarchy, moderated by regicide'.[63] Even with his decades of political experience, Hague could not have predicted how prescient the words would prove in the coming years. Some would eventually pray for a little more moderation when it came to acts of regicide.

At the heart of the talks that day and throughout the weekend was, naturally, policy. Despite the wide areas of overlap – as identified by Letwin – there were also sharp points of difference. It was agreed the potential roadblocks would be discussed first.

Front and centre was the economy. The 2010 election campaign had been fought in the ruins of the British economy after the 2007–8 financial crisis, with the central tussle being which party could secure the recovery.

One of the defining decisions for the campaign had been taken during the crash, with Cameron and Osborne abandoning a promise to match Labour's spending plans for their first two years in office. The initial pledge had been an attempt to neutralise Labour's classic spending cuts attacks – the inversion of Blair and Brown's promise to stick to Tory spending plans before the 1997 election to prove they could be trusted with the economy. Instead, Cameron and Osborne made bringing down government debt the priority, eventually proposing £6 billion of spending cuts in the first year if they won the election.

The Lib Dems, like Labour, had fiercely opposed the cuts. But in the negotiations their opposition melted away. Partly, this was the result of the firmness of the Tories' stance: they had come first in the election and, in their eyes, secured backing for their debt-slashing approach. Clegg and Laws, explaining why they rowed in behind the Tories, would later argue that the financial situation had worsened during the campaign. Just days before the vote, Greece, teetering in a debt crisis, secured a EU–IMF bailout of almost £100 billion.[64] Concern that the

Greek meltdown could spread was shared by Gus O'Donnell, who pressed all negotiating teams for a swift resolution to reassure markets.

On tax and spend, though, there were Lib Dem wins. Osborne agreed to raise the amount someone could earn before paying income tax to £10,000, a Lib Dem manifesto promise. State pensions would also be protected by a 'triple guarantee', rising by the greatest of three measures: average earnings, prices as measured by the CPI or 2.5 per cent. (The Conservatives would come to steal and champion both policies as their own – a reminder of how close the parties had drifted to one another in policy, and of the lack of Tory scruples in the quest for votes.)

A capital gains tax increase was agreed, another Lib Dem policy. The Conservatives also dropped their promise to cut inheritance tax. The latter policy had mythical status in some Tory circles, having been announced at the 2007 party conference in a successful attempt to bounce Prime Minister Brown off calling a snap election – one that many in Cameron's team believe the Tories would have lost given the poll bounce Labour was enjoying after switching leaders. But the policy was more beloved by Tory hardliners than Cameroons, so few tears were wept by the leadership over its loss.

Away from economics, the Lib Dems demanded and secured other promises. Page one of their election manifesto had laid out four areas of change: 'fair taxes that put money back in your pocket; a fair future creating jobs by making Britain greener; a fair chance for every child; a fair deal by cleaning up politics'.[65] They wanted policies in each area that they could hold up as proof of tangible wins despite evident compromises.

The first box was ticked in economic talks. The second was not hard, given the Cameron project's climate focus. The seven-page initial agreement would include eighteen bullet points on the environment, ranging from rolling out smart meters to creating a 'green investment bank'.[66] The third saw the adoption of what the Lib Dems had dubbed a 'pupil premium', meaning extra education spending for the most disadvantaged one million children. The fourth, political reform – including a specific manifesto call for a 'more proportional voting system' – would prove the thorniest issue on which to reach agreement.

Workarounds were also agreed for other points of principle. While renewal of the Trident nuclear deterrent would go ahead, the Lib Dems would be free to make the case for alternatives. Existing nuclear power stations would be replaced, but – to reflect their long-term opposition – the Lib Dems could argue against such moves and abstain in the parliamentary votes.

There was also another get-out, now often forgotten. The Lib Dems were given the right to abstain on the vote raising university tuition fees. Clegg and his colleagues had vowed to abolish such fees in the 2010 election campaign, going so far as to pose with signed promises to vote down any proposed rise. Yet the review into the matter – launched in November 2009 and led by Lord Browne of Madingley – was expected to propose just such an increase.

'If the response of the Government to Lord Browne's report is one that Liberal Democrats cannot accept, then arrangements will be made to enable Liberal Democrat MPs to abstain in any vote,' read the critical line in the initial agreement between the parties.[67] And yet, in December 2010, Clegg would vote for the rise and urge his MPs to do the same. He believed it was the right thing to do. The country appeared to think otherwise. This flip-flop would become the Lib Dems' defining coalition 'betrayal', hardening public sentiment against them.

By Sunday evening, the shape of the agreement was emerging. Electoral reform remained a sticking point – hence confidence and supply rather than full coalition was still a possibility – yet optimism was high in the Conservative camp. Tory policies such as the creation of Universal Credit and the capping of non-EU migration had made it into the agreement. Osborne was delighted. 'This should be the happiest day of our lives,' he told Cameron as the team debriefed. 'It's all our policy that's being agreed.'[68]

Such optimism, however, was to prove short-lived. Twenty-four hours later Cameron would be convinced he was doomed to remain in opposition.

Gordon Brown's team had reacted to Cameron's post-election pitch of a 'big, open and comprehensive offer' to the Lib Dems not with despondency but with something closer to glee. To most of them, long accustomed to power and still sitting in Downing Street, the Tory leader's failure to demand the prime minister's immediate departure was a 'mistaken show of weakness'. (Though the reaction was not universal: Peter Mandelson would later describe thinking Cameron's pitch 'sounded like the new politics' and would hasten his party's modernisation, which it did.)[69]

The election result had clearly been bad for Labour. It had been the dominant political force in Britain since the mid-1990s but secured just 29 per cent of the vote, closer to the Lib Dems' share than the Conservatives'. And yet, the electorate had not handed the Tories an outright win. Squint and it was possible to make out a 'rainbow coalition' on the horizon. Brown, acknowledged by friend and foe alike as a master political tactician, grasped at the opportunity.

Even the briefest scan of history underscores why Labour and the Liberal Democrats were more natural bedfellows. The latter owed their existence, in part, to the former. The Liberal Party, descendants of the Whigs, had in the late 1980s merged with the Social Democratic Party (SDP), a centrist splinter group from Labour when the left-wing Michael Foot was leader, forming what would become the Lib Dems. Indeed, for veterans of the battles against Margaret Thatcher, defeating the Conservatives came close to their defining goal. 'I hate the Tories,' the Lib Dem shadow chancellor Vince Cable, who would go on to serve in the coalition, once said. 'I spent my whole life fighting them.'[70] Many had dreamed of the Left reuniting as a single bloc.

There were also personal connections, links soon leant on as Brown and his allies pushed the case for a deal with Labour. For instance, Cable and Brown had a relationship that dated back to 1975, when Cable, then a Labour councillor in Glasgow, wrote an essay in a pamphlet edited by Brown. Brown also knew Menzies Campbell and Charles Kennedy, two fellow Scots with influence as former Lib Dem leaders. There were other connections. Paddy Ashdown, who instinctively favoured a Lib–Lab deal, enthusiastically pulled strings behind the scenes, including trying to get the help of Tony Blair, now on the political sidelines after leaving Downing Street and stepping down as an MP. Phone lines buzzed amid the uncertainty, often without Clegg's awareness or explicit approval.

The biggest problem was always the maths. Combined, the total number of Labour MPs (258) and Lib Dem MPs (57) still only added up to 315 – short of the magic 326 number which guaranteed being able to pass laws in the Commons. A deal with a mishmash of the smaller parties might get you there – probably the DUP (8), perhaps also Plaid Cymru (3), the SDLP (3) and the Greens (1), though hopefully not the pro-Scottish independence SNP (6). But at what price? Holding the balance of power, such parties could command an exorbitant fee. And would any such coalition be stable? The majority could be wiped out if just a handful of MPs rebelled, at a time when the country faced severe financial challenges that demanded swift action.

Clegg was sceptical from the start. 'I have to say that based on the existing arithmetic in the Commons I am incredibly dubious that a rainbow coalition can deliver,' the Lib Dem leader said to his team the day after the election, according to one present. 'I also think the markets would go nuts.'[71] (That sensitivity to how traders would react would be notably lacking more than a decade later, in autumn 2022, when Liz Truss sent the pound plummeting after her 'mini' Budget imploded upon contact with reality.) The fact that Clegg considered a Labour deal despite the daunting arithmetic – plus the pressure from grandees – is a reminder, though, of how another outcome might have emerged had the result of the election delivered Brown's party one or two dozen more MPs.

A second issue, trickier to quantify but consistently voiced on the Lib Dem side years later, was the approach of the Labour negotiating team. Put simply: it did not appear that they all wanted a deal. The Lib Dem negotiators met their Labour counterparts surreptitiously at first on the Saturday, with more substantial talks after that. Brown picked five for his team: two former Blairites back in the fold (Peter Mandelson and Andrew Adonis, the transport secretary); two ex-Treasury loyalists now in the Cabinet (Ed Balls and Ed Miliband); and Harriet Harman, Labour's deputy leader. During talks, the first two seemed enthused, the last three less so.

Policy agreements should have been easy to strike, even with the Lib Dems' shift to the centre. But did Labour really want to share power? 'With the Conservatives, there was a sense that both sides wanted to try to get this done,' recalled Danny Alexander, the lead Lib Dem negotiator, in an interview.

> Not at any price. There were some very serious issues but if we could solve these problems, then there was a real benefit to the country of trying to come to an agreement. With the discussions with the Labour Party, it was clear that some of them wanted to get it done and others didn't. I'd say that was, to me, the biggest difference.

When asked to name names, Alexander added: 'It seemed that Ed Balls and Ed Miliband really were not very interested.'[72]

David Laws, also in the room for talks with both sides, agreed:

> Labour were very tough and unhelpful to deal with. They were coming to it from the perspective of 'here's a party that we've previously been able to ignore, telling us to change all our policies, left, right and centre'. Whereas with the Tories, we were both united in having, until recently, opposed the governing party and merrily wanting to chuck lots of its agenda into the bin.[73]

There were proof points. Harman said that one issue would have to be discussed later with whoever the Lib Dems' Home Office spokesperson was. That person was actually sitting in the room – Chris Huhne.[74] Labour's team also consistently declined to make concessions on economic matters, saying approval would be needed from the then chancellor, Alistair Darling, which called into question whether they had a proper mandate to negotiate. It would later emerge that Darling, along with many other Labour stalwarts, had reservations about whether a pact was workable or wise.

And then there was the elephant in the room – Gordon Brown himself. Whichever way the results were spun, it was hard to deny he had been the loser. The sitting prime minister, defending a thirteen-year record of government, had overseen the loss of ninety seats. He was not even the leader of the largest party. Was it credible he could remain in the top job? Clegg thought not. The Lib Dems feared such a grouping would be dubbed a 'coalition of losers' –

even if, as Mandelson argued, the two parties' combined vote share (52 per cent) far exceeded that of the Tories (36 per cent), bringing some legitimacy to the proposed arrangement. So the Lib Dems pleaded, in ever more explicit ways, for Gordon to step down so talks could progress.

Brown's lack of legitimacy was certainly the mood music from parts of the press. 'Squatter Holed Up in No 10' shouted the *Sun*'s front page that Saturday, two days after the election. 'The squatter, named as Mr Gordon Brown from Scotland, was refusing to budge from the Georgian townhouse in Downing Street, central London – denying entry to its rightful tenant.' Rupert Murdoch's tabloid was, by then, Tory-supporting and did not hide its colours. Even if historically, as Labour argued, the sitting prime minister tended to have first try at forming a government, the line of attack still had potency.

As night fell on Sunday, 9 May 2010 – the third day of negotiations – Brown was still rebuffing Clegg's plea to fall on his sword to allow Lib–Lab talks to progress. An impasse had been reached.

There can have been few more consequential days in recent British political history than Monday, 10 May 2010. As dawn broke all four paths that Cameron had envisaged in his hotel bed remained possible – a Lib–Con coalition, a Lib–Con supply and confidence deal, a Lib–Lab coalition and, though deemed undesirable by now, a Tory minority government.

At the centre of all these paths lay a single issue: the Alternative Vote (AV). From the very start the Lib Dems had made reforming how Britain elects its MPs the critical demand in talks. Indeed, David Laws had told Osborne in passing many years earlier that the price for any coalition would be electoral reform.

The Lib Dems' preferred option was pure proportional representation, by which a party would receive its share of MPs based on overall votes. The Conservatives remained firm believers in the current system, 'first past the post', which essentially created 650 mini-elections, one in each UK constituency. The winner in each was the candidate who got the most votes. It was a system that favoured bigger parties. For example, if the Lib Dems came second in every constituency, accruing millions of votes in the process, they would still have zero MPs.

Given that the Tories opposed all-out proportional representation and Labour was lukewarm on the issue, the Lib Dems piled their chips on another idea: the Alternative Vote. The idea was complex. Instead of voters selecting just one candidate, they would give rankings: one for their preferred MP, two for their second favourite and so on. If nobody got more than half of the vote, the worst performer would be eliminated and their votes redistributed based on the second rankings. And so on, until one candidate got above 50 per cent and was declared the winner.

If the specifics were fiddly, the politics were simple. Here was a chance for the Lib Dems to break the two-party stranglehold on government. A new electoral system – one in which smaller parties fared better – could forever change the shape of British politics. It left the Tories with a choice: whether it was worth gambling long-term electability for immediate power.

Cameron was reluctant to agree to a referendum on AV, a position his negotiators had so far stuck to in talks. His party was dead set against such a reform, fearing a forever-weakened hand if it took effect and robbed them of seats. Instead Cameron had approved offers short of that, such as a free vote in the Commons on a referendum (which was unlikely to pass). Brown, for his part, was much more open. His 2010 manifesto had actually backed bringing in the Alternative Vote as part of his post-expenses reform package, gambling that the Tories would have more to lose – even though some of his own MPs remained unconvinced. All was to play for.

On the Monday morning, Clegg and Brown met up again. Party pressure explained the Lib Dem engagement to some degree; likewise an awareness that the leverage helped with the Tories. Brown, feeling time running out, upped his offer on a number of fronts. Clegg could have a 'complete free hand' running policy towards Europe, he said, according to one detailed contemporaneous account by Tory MP Rob Wilson. It was a bold promise, one that exploited the chasm on the topic with the Tories. Clegg was told it would be a 'balanced government', implying that the Lib Dems would, remarkably, get half of all Cabinet posts. He also proposed a 'jumbo' package of constitutional reforms.[75] It was too big an offer not to consider.

Clegg and Cameron talked a number of times in the hours that followed. The mood soured as the Lib Dem leader made clear that he would have to take Labour's offer seriously and allow their teams to talk further. 'You cannot go with the guy who's just been voted out!' pleaded Cameron, sensing his grip on the door handle of Number 10 slipping as Brown turned the lock from the inside. 'You know you can't work for him, but you know you can work with me.'[76] Cameron would later dub one Clegg chat that day an 'angry, bad conversation'.[77] The charm was fading.

The stand-off centred on the Alternative Vote. Clegg – to Cameron's ears – was hinting that Brown had gone further than a referendum promise and was now vowing to bring in AV by changing the law without a public vote. 'You can't possibly do AV without a referendum,' Cameron railed at Clegg. 'It would be indefensible.'[78] It would turn out that Labour had never made such an offer. How explicit was Clegg in any indications such a deal was on the table? It is unclear. But Cameron and his team insisted they believed it – the development chimed with snippets coming in from other Tories and press contacts.

The choice was clear now. If Cameron wanted to seal a coalition, he had to up his offer. He had to promise an AV referendum himself.

Throughout the days of negotiating, Cameron had only limited consultation with his party. Former leaders like John Major, Michael Howard and Iain Duncan Smith had been personally informed when Cameron decided to go for a coalition deal. There had been calls keeping the shadow cabinet in the loop. MPs had been able to pop in to see him over the weekend. But, by and large, his hand was kept free. A decision of this scale, however, needed proper buy-in.

A gathering of the shadow cabinet was ordered. There were some voices of dissent. Chris Grayling, the shadow home secretary, was one. 'My point was simple: I thought that we should govern as a minority for six months and then call another election and win,' Grayling recalled.[79] Theresa Villiers, the shadow transport secretary, was another: 'I thought we were in a relatively strong position, that we didn't have to give way on this. As a matter of principle I don't support a switch to a PR system and I thought referendums were very unpredictable.'[80] Mark Francois, the shadow Europe minister, was a third, raising a red flag about fixing in law that the next election would be a full five years away.[81] But others – many more – spoke out in favour.

Cameron kept a tally. Supporters vastly outnumbered critics, as the Tory leader likely knew before going into the shadow cabinet meeting. 'It was one of those ones where Cameron had made his mind up and had squared one or two people in advance,' Grayling said.[82] Francois felt the same: 'He could see the door on Number 10 and he just needed to drive this through the shadow cabinet. The other senior members of the shadow cabinet were clearly on board. It was effectively a done deal.'[83] For Cameron, the hurdles proved minimal. 'It was quite straightforward,' he told the author. 'I think there was a sense that we needed to get back into office, we needed to deal with the very difficult financial situation.'[84]

As the meeting neared its end, an urgent message was relayed: Brown was about to make a statement. A television was switched on, the shadow cabinet watching as one. And there he was, the prime minister, outside Number 10, rolling the dice one last time.

'The reason that we have a hung parliament is that no single party and no single leader was able to win the full support of the country,' Brown said. 'As leader of my party, I must accept that that is a judgement on me. I therefore intend to ask the Labour Party to set in train the processes needed for its own leadership election.'

The prime minister was resigning, or at least signalling his resignation. Brown had indeed fallen on his sword, in a final gamble to get a Lib–Lab deal over the line. He added that he would be gone by the Labour conference that autumn. Suddenly, a major obstacle in the route to a deal to lock Cameron out of Downing Street had been removed. Could it all be slipping away from the Tories?

The AV referendum offer had been signed off by the shadow cabinet. Next was a full meeting with Tory backbenchers, the so-called 1922 Committee. Cameron was pleading now: 'Look.

Brown's going. And they're offering a full coalition. And they'll go all the way on voting reform. The very least we can offer is a referendum on AV. It is the price of power. Are you willing to pay the price?'[85] Some of the Tory old guard spoke out against it. Others bit their tongues, while still preferring the option of forming a minority government. This was less high principle, more low politics – the ground MPs had to give up if they wanted to retake the levers of power. As one Tory MP put it, tweaking Blair's famous line from the Northern Ireland peace talks: 'We feel the hand of history on our gonads, squeezing very hard.'[86]

Cameron won, the party followed. His pitch for power had worked. William Hague then announced the offer. Clegg's demand had been met. Now it was time to wait, as the Lib Dems talked to Labour.

That night, Cameron feared it was over. His team was told to take the office items out of bubble wrap: there would be no big move after all. Back at home that evening, the Tory leader admitted his worst fears to his wife, Samantha. 'You know, it's not going to happen,' he said over dinner in the kitchen. 'That's it. I'm going to be in opposition for a couple more years.'[87]

He need not have worried. Cameron had given Clegg the 'bankable' offer on electoral reform he wanted. Privately the Lib Dem leader had been more sceptical of the Labour pitch than he let on to Cameron. The difficulty of achieving a majority in the Commons had not gone away. Brown's departure, it would turn out, removed the one thing still giving the fractious Labour top brass a semblance of unity. In formal Labour–Lib Dem talks that evening little progress was made. Deals on economic policy were still elusive, with Darling not present. Things that Brown had promised failed to materialise. Even the AV offer looked unstable, with a suggestion that there might not be enough Labour votes to pass it. And then there was the lack of interest from the two Eds, Balls and Miliband, both of whom would soon launch bids for the newly vacated Labour leadership.

Confirmation came as Cameron slept. Danny Alexander called Ed Llewellyn at 1.30 a.m., their roles reversed from the 4 a.m. election-night text initiating contact. The Labour talks had collapsed,

Alexander explained. The only deal left on the table was with the Tories.[88]

The sun was shining as David Cameron and Nick Clegg emerged together into Downing Street's Rose Garden on Wednesday, 12 May 2010. The preceding five days had been a blur of high-wire nego-tiations, the dynamics and calculations shifting with each step. Now, in front of an assorted group of political journalists and with the country looking on, the leaders had their chance to bathe in their triumph.

The final day of discussions, Tuesday, had been relatively straight-forward. The key items outstanding were finalised, though the complete coalition agreement would not be locked down until later that month. Gordon Brown, once it became apparent that Labour's always slim hopes of a deal had disappeared, called time on his party's period in office in a speech outside Number 10 and headed to Buckingham Palace. Cameron, swiftly following Brown in to see the Queen, then headed up Downing Street – a walk he had for so long envisaged.

It was a moment of vindication. Cameron may have fallen short in the election, but through nimble manoeuvring and quick decision-making, driven by a hunger to return to power shared by his inner circle, a pact had been secured. Joining with the Liberal Democrats in a full coalition brought a comfortable Commons majority to allow them to enact real reforms – providing everything held. Indeed, it left Cameron less dependent on a rump of Tory tradi-tionalists who had long eyed him with suspicion, and vice versa. There had been compromises. Five Lib Dems would get Cabinet roles, meaning some Tories expecting top jobs would miss out – including Grayling and Villiers, who had both spoken out over the coalition deal in the shadow cabinet. But Cameron had got the pact over the line. The Conservative Party was once again in government.

Speaking outdoors side by side in their first press conference as prime minister and deputy prime minister, Cameron and Clegg smiled and cooed. 'I'm off,' joked Clegg at one point, feigning horror at some past Cameron slight brought up by a reporter. 'Come back!' the new prime minister groaned as Clegg pretended to walk. All was sweetness and light.

There was an almost marital feel to the scene: springtime amid the flowers. 'It did look and feel a bit like a wedding,' Cameron later said. 'And, like a groom, I was nervous, aware of the immensity of the occasion and the need to rise to it.' He had urged Clegg beforehand to give '20 per cent' more than felt appropriate at the event, to reassure the public that this was a partnership that would last.[89] And they both did.

Little could either man have suspected how brutal the divorce to come would be – a split orchestrated and executed with ruthless efficiency by just one side.

2

Brothers in Arms

THE SIGNS WERE there. In retrospect, David Laws can identify three.[1]

The first was the envelope on the mat in his constituency home. It was autumn 2014. The coalition, now four years old, had defied the sceptics, holding together firmer and longer than predicted. But the general election of 7 May 2015 was looming into view.

Inside was a letter from David Cameron. Laws, the Liberal Democrat MP for Yeovil, knew the prime minister well enough. As one of the coalition negotiators, he had played a central role in bringing about the government and was a minister in the education department. The letter set out a concise argument for voting Conservative.

Such mailouts are the bread-and-butter of campaigns, so Laws thought little more about the missive. Yet almost every week when he returned to his constituency there would be another letter from Cameron extolling the virtues of the Tories. Similar ones were dropping onto the doormats of the voters Laws relied on for his House of Commons seat – a targeted air strike that would prove as deadly as it was under the radar.

The second giveaway was a bit of political gossip. Every Thursday, MPs leave Westminster and head back to their seats for voter engagement. But government ministers – those MPs with department jobs – can only go once their duties have been completed. Among the most tiresome of these was responding on behalf of the government in backbench debates in the Commons.

One Thursday such a debate was scheduled by the powers-that-be to be covered by Laws. He baulked and got another education minister, a Conservative, to take his place, prompting grumbling from some Tory insiders. It was only later that he learned the reason for his initial selection. 'The strategy had been to fill up his diary as much as possible,' one Conservative peer let slip to a Lib Dem counterpart.[2] If Laws was in London, stuck in a debate, he could not be in Yeovil campaigning for locals to re-elect him.

George Osborne was involved in the third. Laws and Osborne got on well. When the coalition talks had concluded in 2010, the former was sent to work in the latter's Treasury as chief secretary. So it was with raised eyebrows that Laws noticed that the chancellor had visited a depot in his constituency to hail the announcement of new funding to improve the A303.

A two-party government had led to a tussle over who should take credit for individual initiatives. And here was Osborne, never a stranger to a high-vis jacket, using the power of the Treasury to plant a flag in enemy territory. When the pair bumped into each other at the Downing Street canteen one breakfast time, Laws could not resist letting Osborne know his politicking had been noted. 'Oh, don't worry, David,' Osborne smiled. 'I intend to spend an awful lot of time in Somerset over the next few months.'[3]

So there were signs. What was hidden was the wider picture. Even with his awareness – and the Lib Dems' evident polling woes – Laws thought he had little to worry about. After all, he had won his seat with a 56 per cent share of the vote back in 2010, more than all the other candidates combined and way ahead of his Tory rival. Before him the seat's MP had been Paddy Ashdown, the charismatic former Lib Dem leader. Other party strongholds might fall at the forthcoming election, but surely not this one, in the Lib Dems' South-West heartland.

'I was in the joyous position of going into that day thinking I most likely would remain an MP,' Laws recalled.[4] Election night would disprove those expectations. His defeat was resounding. This time Laws got just 33 per cent of the vote, a huge drop. The Tories had leapfrogged him to victory. For thirty-two years the Lib Dems had held Yeovil, but no longer. 'It was very disappointing and instantly believable,' recalled Laws, realising too late he had been 'blindsided'.

He was not alone. Leading Lib Dems across the country were toppled. Vince Cable, the business secretary and one of the party's most famous names, was ousted in Twickenham. Steve Webb, the pensions minister, had invited his teenage children to watch his victory speech in Thornbury and Yate; instead they witnessed the end of their father's political career.[5] Norman Baker, another minister for much of the coalition, was dispatched in Lewes. All three lost to Tories. Baker was so physically exhausted by the election battle that he would take three months off just to recover.[6]

That night the Lib Dems were almost wiped out as a parliamentary force. Forty-nine of their fifty-seven sitting MPs were ousted, leaving just eight.[7] In the South-West every single one of their fifteen MPs had been defeated, every single one losing to the Conservatives.

Election campaigns and their results are multifaceted. There are plenty of reasons why David Cameron defied the near-universal expectation of a hung parliament to deliver the Tories their first majority government since 1992: Labour's struggles to convince the public they could be trusted with the economy; the electorate's lukewarm view of Labour leader Ed Miliband; the SNP's dominance in Scotland after the independence referendum defeat; Ukip's squeezed vote share.

But above all it was the Tories eating up their coalition partners that won Cameron his majority. The strategy was plotted with precision, executed with aplomb and largely hidden from view. It was as calculated as it was brutally effective. When it came to the Conservatives' appetite for office, not even five years of joint government could keep the Lib Dems off the menu.

It was not always meant to be so. Indeed, there was a moment when in secret an audacious political pact rather than all-out war had been considered. Quite how much consideration was given to the idea has been kept under wraps until now.

Austerity was the defining mission of the coalition: an attempt to bring down government debt and secure growth by slashing public spending. Within weeks of the Lib–Con pact, cuts worth £6.2 billion were announced. In the years ahead, spending as a percentage of GDP would continue to fall, reversing rises under Gordon Brown. The policy was fiercely debated then and still is today. For many Tories, the drive showed an admirable determination to take the tough decisions needed to stabilise the UK economy; for critics, it was an ideological push to reduce the size of the state dressed up in the rhetoric of necessity.

In the early years the coalition had proved, in governmental terms, surprisingly robust. The Tories and Lib Dems pushed through reforms without catastrophic splits. Predictions that the power-sharing deal would only last a few months proved incorrect. But politically, the toll was being felt. The Lib Dems' drop in the polls had been rapid, their support halving within nine months. The Tory slide was more gradual but became pronounced after the 'Omnishambles' Budget of March 2012, which was unpicked by some embarrassing reversals. That autumn, the government's unpopularity was captured in a few seconds at the London 2012 Paralympics, when Chancellor Osborne was roundly booed while handing out medals. The midterm blues had arrived.

Which is why, among the coalition's four central players, minds turned to the past. Specifically, the 1918 general election.

During the First World War, the Conservatives and the Liberals had been in coalition in various forms. Rather than return to political combat in the vote called right after peace was declared, the party leaders agreed to a joint ticket. A letter signed by both David Lloyd George, the prime minister and leader of the pro-coalition Liberals, and Bonar Law, the Conservative leader, would be issued endorsing each candidate who had backed the current government. Those candidates would thus have the support of two party leaders as well as – it was hoped – two parties' voters. The upshot was an electoral triumph, returning the coalition to power. Each letter of endorsement was dubbed a 'coupon' – hence the 1918 vote going down in history as the 'Coupon Election'.

Osborne, a keen reader of history, became fascinated by the idea. If both coalition parties were heading for defeat, why not team up? Tory MPs seeking election would be given a free run in their constituencies with the Lib Dems not entering a candidate, and vice versa. 'Vote for the coalition in your area' would be the message.[8]

Another member of the so-called 'Quad', the group of four senior Cabinet ministers, two Tories and two Lib Dems, by which all major coalition decisions had to be approved, was interested. Danny

Alexander, once Nick Clegg's chief of staff and now in the Treasury, could see the logic.[9] 'I remember some very specific conversations about this,' Alexander said. 'Purely from an electoral, arithmetical point of view, it could be a very attractive proposition. George and I discussed it a couple of times, and we could both see some advantages to both parties and also to the programme that we were pushing through on the economy.'[10]

At a private dinner held by the Quad in Downing Street, the idea was discussed with the two arbiters, David Cameron and Nick Clegg. Cameron saw the upsides too. 'The appeal was quite clear: this is a very big turnaround and recovery job for the country and it's going to take at least one parliament and maybe more,' he recalled in an interview with the author. 'This government seemed to be working. We were fulfilling a lot of their manifesto while fulfilling a lot of our manifesto. It seemed like this was a perfectly sensible conversation to have.'[11]

Ultimately, the politics did not add up. Announcing the Tories would not stand in Lib Dem seats, all but giving up on hopes of achieving a majority of their own, risked a fierce backbench backlash from the party. For the Lib Dems, vowing another term with the Conservatives would have been even more complicated, since a fervent anti-Tory wing remained in the party. 'I think it became politically untenable for them,' Cameron said.[12] Alexander likewise accepted the problems: 'You can see why it would be very unattractive to both parties, because it meant sacrificing your independent message, sacrificing your independent identity.'[13]

The idea died in its infancy. Today, George Osborne, knowing what came next – the Lib Dem wipeout, the Tory majority, the Brexit vote, the resignations – wonders about the path not taken. 'Within around a year of the 2015 election, Clegg had lost his job, Cameron had lost his job, and I'd lost my job,' Osborne recalled. 'Was there another way through? Potentially. I think being the re-elected coalition with the simple message "the job's not finished" would have worked. I think we would have held the Tory Party together.'[14]

It is an intriguing counterfactual. But in reality, an electoral fight was coming between the parties. And Cameron and Osborne both knew which battle-hardened commander they wanted calling the shots for them.

Lynton Crosby by now was well versed in British politics. An Australian with swept-across grey hair and a no-nonsense manner, he had experienced his first taste of UK general elections in 2005. It had not gone according to plan. Drafted in late as a campaign strategist to assist Michael Howard's faltering tilt for the top, he had helped refine the Tory messaging, honing in on immigration. 'Are you thinking what we're thinking?' voters were asked in the campaign's core slogan. As it turned out, they were not, handing Labour a third term instead, with Crosby getting some of the blame for the defeat.

But back-to-back victories in London changed all that. In 2008, Crosby was forced on Boris Johnson by Osborne and Cameron in an attempt to bring order to his chaotic bid to become the capital's mayor.[15] It worked. This first mayoral victory in Labour-leaning London was notable. The second in 2012, when the Tories were in charge and austerity was biting, was even more eye-catching. And it turned Johnson into a Crosby evangelist, reversing the 2008 dynamic, with him now pressing Cameron and Osborne to let the Aussie take charge of their 2015 election campaign.

In the story of the Conservatives' long run in Downing Street from 2010, Crosby is one of the two most influential, consequential figures who was not an MP. The other is Dominic Cummings, another self-assured and plain-speaking strategist who viewed the Westminster commentariat with contempt. Crosby worked with both Cameron and Johnson – a rarity, given the pair's competitive relationship. (He would end up closer to Boris, one ally said, with the former mayor becoming a friend as well as a colleague.[16]) After the 2015 campaign, he would be in the bunker for Theresa May's 2017 election, behind the scenes for Johnson's 2019 ascent to power and on call throughout the subsequent collapse. He sat out the 2016 EU referendum, which split his Tory clientele.

Born in Kadina, South Australia, Crosby liked to describe himself as 'just a Methodist farm boy from the middle of nowhere'.[17] After a brief dalliance with frontline politics – 'in hindsight I wouldn't have voted for me,' he would joke of his failed attempt to win a regional seat in 1982 – came his rise to prominence as a back-room operator.[18] He helped John Howard, leader of the centre-right Liberal Party, to remain in power as prime minister of Australia for eleven years.

Crosby gained a reputation for identifying and deploying 'wedge' issues, often emotive subjects that would appeal to voters who were otherwise supportive of a rival party. (Critics would at times give the tactic a more dismissive tag: 'dog whistle' campaigning.) 'In politics, when reason and emotion collide, emotion invariably wins,' Crosby explained.[19] He had other sayings: 'you cannot fatten a pig on market day' on the importance of consistent, long-term messaging; 'scrub the barnacles off the boat' on the need to drop peripheral issues that had become voter distractions; and 'throw a dead cat on the table' when a jaw-dropping move could switch the conversation topic in a campaign. As a result, he received a moniker of his own from the press: the Wizard of Oz.

Crosby was initially reluctant to join Cameron's re-election campaign, as described in journalist Tim Ross's comprehensive and compelling book on the 2015 race, *Why the Tories Won*. Osborne's misfiring 2012 Budget had risked costing Johnson his second London mayoral victory, while Crosby also reportedly at times questioned Cameron's drive.[20] But the pleas of Cameron's inner circle won him over. There had been one central demand: that he be given sole, total control of the campaign. The Cameroons, scarred by the 2010 campaign – when comms chief Andy Coulson and blue-sky thinker Steve Hilton clashed on direction – were happy to agree.

To Cameron, Crosby appeared to have a rare 360-degree view of electoral politics. 'Where Lynton is very effective is that there aren't enough people in British politics who combine an understanding of polling with an understanding of how to run a campaign,' Cameron said. 'We've got lots of pollsters, we've got lots of campaigners, but his brilliance is really bringing those two things together.'[21]

He could also be curt to the point of bluntness, even with superiors. Johnson told a story from the early stages of the 2008 mayoral campaign when they were working together for the first time. Addressing a group of London councillors, an exhausted Johnson had failed to prepare a speech and winged it. Johnson was rather pleased with the outcome, until his phone buzzed with a short text message from Crosby: 'Crap speech, mate.'[22] Swearing was not uncommon from Crosby. MPs who deviated from the 2015 message would get similar texts: 'What the fuck, mate?' or 'That's not fucking helpful, is it?'[23] Even with Cameron, Crosby would be familiar, calling him 'David' rather than the 'prime minister' almost everyone else used.

To one figure who worked closely with Crosby, his Australianness was key. 'He's a very hard taskmaster and doesn't take any bullshit and he's very happy to, if necessary, speak truth to power. I think Australians are maybe uniquely qualified to do that, particularly in the UK,' the source explained

> British politics is incestuous. Everyone's from the same school, everyone's got all these great, chin-scratching opinions. But Lynton couldn't be placed. Particularly with that cohort, Cameron and Osborne, who judge everyone by what school they went to and all that sort of stuff. And they didn't know what school Lynton went to. So when you bang the table and say, 'Shut the fuck up,' everyone's like, 'Oh, we'd better listen to this guy.'[24]

*

By late 2012, when Crosby joined the team, there was still a lot of road to run before election day. Unusually for British politics, the date of the vote – 7 May 2015 – was known well in advance thanks to the Fixed-term Parliaments Act 2011, which dictated that an election would be held every five years. The law had been brought in by the coalition to increase its chance of lasting the course by making it harder to call a snap election.

As the months ticked down, the Tory strategy morphed. A reality little noted outside political circles is that elections are not nationwide battles. Not really. Instead, it is a small fraction of the 650 seats – those not written off as all but guaranteed to go to a particular party – that become the focus for the party strategists, whose task is to work out which those seats are and how the results can be tilted their way.

Back in 2012, sinking in the polls, with a flourish the Tories had announced a plan to gee-up their side. It would be dubbed the 'forty/forty strategy', targeting the retention of forty Conservative seats that had enjoyed only a slim majority at the 2010 election and the taking of forty held by other parties in marginal constituencies. The list of targets was never made public but, according to those in the know, it contained few Lib Dem seats.[25] That was to change.

As workers at Conservative Campaign Headquarters (CCHQ) dug into the polling, it became clear that taking seats from Labour would be tricky. Stealing them from the Lib Dems, however, seemed much more achievable. Many Lib Dem voters in the rural south were more open to backing the Tories than Labour voters, especially those pleased with the coalition. They preferred David Cameron to Labour's Ed Miliband by quite a margin. The opportunity was there; it just needed sign-off from the top.

Stephen Gilbert, the Tory head of campaigning who designed the forty/forty strategy, had become convinced that adding most of the seats currently occupied by Lib Dem MPs to the target list was the best approach.

'All we had to do was to persuade David and George,' he recalled in an interview.[26] Gilbert adopted a tried-and-tested approach, getting Osborne's buy-in before going to Cameron. Given their closeness, winning over the former would help secure the latter's support. 'George was pretty easy to persuade. He kind of went "gulp", but he was ruthless,' Gilbert said.[27] Osborne's recollection is similar: 'I think we were a bit squeamish about it. We were, I guess, moths drawn to the flame. It was easy pickings. It was quite a straight-forward campaign you could run against them and we would win all these seats.'[28]

The timing was a factor too. Come 2014, there had been a notable cooling in relations between the parties. The government was still functioning smoothly, but the warmth of the Rose Garden love-in had faded. The biggest scar, senior figures on both sides agreed, was the Alternative Vote referendum campaign. The Lib Dems' big win in the coalition negotiations resulted in a big defeat as the Tories weaponised Nick Clegg's unpopularity to triumph in the 2011 vote. In one heated Cabinet meeting, Lib Dem MP Chris Huhne had furiously challenged Cameron and Osborne over their tactics; he had an anti-AV leaflet with Clegg's face on it in his hand to prove his point.[29] The Tories wanted to win and did what was necessary to ensure that happened. It worked. Just a third of the country voted for AV; the old electoral system would remain. There had been other ruptures, as when the Lib Dems blocked changes to constituency boundaries that would have benefitted the Tories after House of Lords reform stalled. On that occasion it was the blue side that took the hit.

One significant gathering came at Chequers, the prime minister's country retreat, in the spring of 2014. Lynton Crosby came armed with dozens of graphs, subsequently seen by this author. One showed that David Cameron had a better favourability rating in Lib Dem seats than Tory seats – remarkable, given he was the Tory leader.[30] It spoke to how some traditional Conservatives viewed him with suspicion. Others showed that voters in Lib Dem constituencies thought both the country and their local area were going in the right direction – a sign of contentment with those in charge. Plus, the polling made clear that Ed Miliband was viewed dimly in Lib Dem seats. It revealed that the opportunity was there, one which the prime minister was eager to grasp.

Cameron had a steeliness where elections were concerned, according to those who know him best. 'He was always quite ruthless when it came to trying to get his party to win elections, I think more than people often think,' said Kate Fall, a friend since they had met at Oxford.[31] Another Cameron inner-circle member said something similar:

There came a point, obviously, when the gloves were off and it was uncomfortable, but it was also not unexpected. The Lib Dems were seeing the same numbers as we were. And what were we going to do, not fight them because we'd been working with them for four years? We still wanted a Conservative majority government.[32]

This is, of course, the nature of politics, as Cameron pointed out. 'The Lib Dems were trying to clean the Conservatives out of the South and the South-West,' he told the author. 'So there was no quarter given in by-elections, in council elections, in campaigning.

I mean, it was hand-to-hand combat. It's not as if the Lib Dems were hanging back in any way.'[33]

And so the green light was given. Many more Lib Dem constituencies were quietly added to the target list. Clegg's seat was not on it, but for rational rather than sentimental reasons – Labour rather than the Tories were best placed to take Sheffield Hallam.[34] The new Lib Dem targets swelled the number of 'in-play' battleground seats on the list to around one hundred – more than the original forty/forty. The tactic was the political equivalent of the female praying mantis, which after mating eats her male partner, beginning with the head. The 'decapitation strategy' was under way.[35]

Gilbert was responsible for the planning on the ground. One focus was picking local candidates. The famed Lib Dem incumbency factor was real. The Tories' polling found that when the local MP's name was put to respondents, rather than just the party brand, the Lib Dem vote share would jump up by as much as 25 percentage points.[36] 'Their whole schtick is "strong local champion". If you import a candidate they wreck you, you're finished,' a senior Tory campaign source said. So no more 'candidate-list clones'.[37] Money was invested in proper local infrastructure. Every target seat would get a permanent campaign manager, trained at the centre.

Gilbert explained the approach:

> It was clear that most of the Lib Dems [i.e., their voters] in these seats really liked and trusted David Cameron, really didn't trust or like Ed Miliband or Labour, but valued their good, local Lib Dem MP. So we instructed our candidate to send two simultaneous messages. One: 'I'm going to be a really strong local champion.' And two: 'If you vote for me you're going to get David Cameron, not Ed Miliband, and you trust him.' So you will get the best of both worlds.[38]

Keeping the strategy totally secret was unrealistic – the Lib Dems noticed the uptick in focus. Nonetheless, efforts were made to keep it under wraps. The mutual suspicion between Tory and Lib Dem advisers was at times comical, as attested by one story that seems almost too ludicrous for the political satire *The Thick of It* and which can be told for the first time here. In the latter coalition years Clegg was deploying more special advisers across Whitehall to get a better grip of government movements. Two Tory advisers in one department, fearing that their new Lib Dem colleague would spy on them, took steps to make sure they would not be too closely shadowed. A spare desk in their room was thus moved out, only for the civil service to propose putting their rival in the room next door. 'No fucking way, they're going to hear everything we are saying,' complained one of the Tories. 'Oh, we'll put in some extra insulation,' came the response. 'Don't fucking do that, because that's going to be FOIed for the amount it costs!' the Tory shot back, referencing Freedom of Information laws. The Tories won the argument: the Lib Dem was installed further down the corridor and out of harm's way.[39]

Crosby was the fiercest defender of the plan's secrecy. He hated 'process' stories, those about the nuts and bolts of election planning, being briefed to the press, preferring the code of silence. One Tory insider remembers being tasked with carrying out the inquisition after the *Sun* revealed details of the push against the Lib Dems. 'You can fucking find who this was, and I'm going to fucking kill them, they're fucking sacked,' Crosby raged, or words to that effect. Progress was made, a few names were in the frame. Then Crosby suddenly backtracked. 'Don't worry about that,' he told the person leading the search. 'Just move on.' It turned out that David Cameron had shared lunch with a senior figure at the paper a few days earlier and blabbed.[40]

Elements of political campaign strategies often interweave. In 2015, there were two core strands to the Conservatives' election plan, produced early and deliberately, that were not Lib Dem-specific but had a major impact on the outcome.

One was the economy. Ever since the Tories had abandoned their promise to match Labour's spending plans and started to tout the need for cuts to bring the deficit down – a switch made ahead of the 2010 election after the 2007–8 financial crash – they had pinned the blame for the UK's economic woes on their rivals. The narrative that Labour carelessness was the cause of the nation's financial trials was a wilful simplification of a crisis that first emerged on Wall Street and impacted the world. But it had stuck. Crosby and his team boiled down the position to a soundbite so commonly repeated it would be mocked by politicos: the 'long-term economic plan'. It was a way to own the improving economy – Cameron would declare he had created one thousand jobs a day since taking office – and dial up the risks of letting Labour back in. Years later one innovation designed to underline the Tories' economic competence, the creation of the Office for Budget Responsibility charged with producing independent forecasts rather than relying on Treasury-massaged figures, would come back to bite the party when Liz Truss and Kwasi Kwarteng circumvented it with disastrous effects. But that was far in the future. Cameron and Osborne's attack line became 'don't give the keys back to the guys who crashed the car'. Victory in the fight for trust with the economy was critical.

Another was countering the UK Independence Party (Ukip). It is easy to forget what a potent political force Nigel Farage's band of right-wing Eurosceptic insurgents then was – and what a threat it posed to the Conservatives. Its blend of status quo-bashing, saying the 'unsayable' and tapping into concerns on immigration and crime was effective against a Tory Party that had been pushed towards the centre ground. In 2014, Ukip came top in the European Parliament elections, picking up one in every four votes. They were flipping Tory MPs too, with Douglas Carswell and Mark Reckless defecting to Ukip and winning the subsequent by-elections. Ukip would go on to get almost four million votes at the 2015 election, more than 12 per cent of the total, coming second in 120 seats, but getting across the line in just one: Carswell's Clacton. Farage called the result, a reflection of the old first-past-the-post rules that the Lib Dems had tried to ditch, 'very, very painful'. 'Never in the history of British politics has anybody got more votes with fewer seats,' Farage said in an interview.[41]

Back in 2006, Cameron had dubbed Ukip supporters 'a bunch of fruitcakes and loonies and closet racists'.[42] Come 2015, he was offering an olive branch to tempt 'my little purple friends' back to the blue side.[43] The major move here came in January 2013 with the promise of an in/out referendum on European Union membership – the starting gun on the race that would end with Brexit. The threat was less that of Ukip winning vast numbers of seats than of denying Tory victories by forcing down their vote totals, allowing another party to sneak in at the top. Isaac Levido, another Australian political strategist who is often seen as Crosby's protégé and who would lead Johnson's winning 2019 election campaign, was inside the Tory tent for 2015 and acknowledged the danger. 'Ukip were an existential threat to us getting into a majority government,' Levido said. 'They only needed to perform marginally better in a handful of seats and we wouldn't have won a majority.'[44]

As the Conservatives strategised, so too did the two next-biggest parties in the Commons, though with different ends envisaged. For Labour, the hope was to consign Cameron to a one-term premiership and pull off a swift return to power. For the Liberal Democrats, the focus was stemming the bleeding so that they would have enough MPs once again to hold the balance of power in any coalition talks.

Ed Miliband had won the Labour leadership shortly after the 2010 election defeat. An acolyte of Gordon Brown as a Treasury adviser turned Cabinet member, Miliband had signalled more of a willingness to move beyond the New Labour years than most of his rivals in the leadership race. His victory meant defeat for the centrist frontrunner, his brother David Miliband, whom he beat by just 1.3 percentage points. The result would strain their relationship and give Fleet Street a fratricide narrative that would regularly be repeated in the run-up to the 2015 election.

Outcomes colour posterity's view of the past but from 2010 to 2015 Labour's defeat looked anything but inevitable. Miliband had succeeded in keeping his party united – a rare feat in opposition, as the Jeremy Corbyn years would show. Labour skipped ahead of the Tories in the polls in late 2010 and stayed there, with variously sized leads, until things tightened near the end of the election campaign. The early optimism was captured in January 2013 when the then campaign coordinator, the MP Tom Watson, announced with a flourish that Labour would attempt to flip 106 seats, saying a 60-seat Labour majority was 'realistic'.[45]

Come 2014, there were two obvious challenges threatening Labour's poll lead: one concerned the economy; the other, Miliband's personal poll ratings. No political party in recent times had won a general election when behind both in polls asking 'Who do you trust more to run the economy?' and 'Who do you think would be the best prime minister?' For much of the run-up to election day, Labour was trailing in both.

Spencer Livermore, who had worked for Gordon Brown in government for a decade, much of the time alongside Miliband, was drafted in to help lead the Labour campaign as head of strategy in spring 2014 and could see both problems.

On the economy, the core tension was between going after the Tories' austerity spending cuts and accepting the need to bring government debt down after the financial crash. 'Osborne was a brilliant strategist, in the guise of Gordon Brown very much in terms of uniting the position of chancellor and chief election strategist,' said Livermore in an interview.

> He used the economy to paint dividing lines and paint your opponent into a corner. He weaponised the deficit. Despite the deficit numbers getting worse every year, despite him never meeting any of his goals, somehow that became Labour's problem, rather than his. The worse it got, the worse Labour's problem got.[46]

Slip-ups exacerbated the issue. Miliband's attempt at a no-notes conference speech in September 2014 backfired when he failed to deliver the section on bringing down debt. 'Fuck, fuck, fuck, fuck,' he reportedly muttered in his hotel room afterwards, furious with himself.[47] The gleeful Tories pounced on the blunder in briefings to the press pack that day and for many months to come, casting Miliband as the man who literally forgot the deficit. The misstep stoked talk among disaffected Labour MPs of a late leadership switch, one idea being that the Blairite Alan Johnson might step in. In the event Johnson proved uninterested in the role and the plotting never took off. Separately, the leadership's ties to the last Labour government – Ed Balls, another Brown devotee, was shadow chancellor – may have made it harder to criticise its economic approach openly.

One of Labour's most senior figures then acknowledged the effectiveness of the Tory framing: 'One of Cameron's strengths was he had a message which was about cleaning up Labour's so-called mess. He was just ruthless about prosecuting that. I think he had an eye for things that were problematic.'

The figure added: 'They falsely managed to somehow say that the deficit that arose from the massive financial crisis was a result of Labour overspending. I think the problem for us was that the financial crisis happened while we were in government, which means you're held responsible . . . I'm sure we could have handled it better, but it was always going to be very difficult for us.'[48]

Knowing now what would happen next, how Jeremy Corbyn's anti-austerity message and unrepentant socialism helped Labour surge in Theresa May's botched snap election of 2017, Miliband has regrets. 'I would've been better with a bolder message,' he told the author in an interview.

> In a way, on austerity I was slightly caught between two stools. I wasn't reassuring enough for the people who wanted reassurance and I wasn't sort of radical and galvanising enough for the people who wanted radicalism. I probably would have been better being bolder because lifting a government out after one term is hard. My best moments, like the energy price freeze, phone hacking, came when I was taking on quite big forces. Getting connection with the public is not easy. I think a greater degree of boldness might have been better. But who knows?[49]

The second issue was just as hard when it came to shifting public perceptions. To his inner circle, Miliband palpably had the leadership qualities needed for the top job: decision-making nous; empathy with voters' struggles; a moral code, Treasury brain and New Labour-honed political instincts. But convincing punters proved trickier. Cameron consistently beat Miliband in polls on who was more suited to be prime minister. Critics' jibes that Miliband was too geeky or 'weird' to be leader, and looked like Wallace from the claymation comedy *Wallace and Gromit*, never went away. The cruellest blow came in his struggles to eat a bacon sandwich during an early morning stop-off in the 2014 European parliamentary election campaign, with excruciating photos capturing his attempts to chew. It was a media management slip – any politician can pull faces as they eat food, which is why aides try to avoid them doing so in front of the cameras. But it was used against Miliband. The Rupert Murdoch-owned *Sun* splashed the photo on its front page the day before the 2015 election. 'SAVE OUR BACON' read the headline. 'Don't swallow his porkies and keep him OUT.'

The episode speaks to a wider theme throughout the Tories' long Downing Street run: the backing of right-leaning newspapers. Fleet Street has long tilted to the Right, but that became more pronounced with the Murdoch titles flipping on Labour after Tony Blair's departure. From 2010, more leading papers would generally declare for the Tories (*The Times*, *Sun*, *Daily Telegraph*, *Daily Mail*, *Daily Express*) than for Labour (*Daily Mirror*, *Guardian*, *Independent*). The relationship between the former group and Tory Downing Street occupants was more nuanced than the caricature might suggest. Between elections these papers were often the ones that most infuriated Conservative prime ministers. David Cameron would decry the 'fucking *Daily Telegraph*'; Boris Johnson would be driven into rages by his former employer.[50] During election campaigns, however, papers wear their political leanings much more on their sleeve, at times echoing the attacks and messages of the side they endorse – coverage the broadcasters then spin off. More right-leaning papers meant the Tories disproportionately benefitting. At the time of the EU referendum, Conservatives leading the Remain campaign would come to recognise the challenges posed by that reality since many Tory-backing papers supported Brexit. As one Cameron Number 10 insider would later lament, it was a case of 'chickens coming home to roost'.[51]

Miliband's team were all too aware of his awkward public image. So in the summer of 2014 they persuaded him to try to own it with a speech. 'I am not from central casting,' Miliband said. 'You can find people who are more square-jawed, more chiselled, look less like Wallace. You could probably even find people who look better eating a bacon sandwich. If you want the politician from central casting, it's just not me, it's the other guy.'[52]

Cameron was also happy to lean in with his own speech on the topic, though Wallace and bacon sarnies went unmentioned in favour of making a connection to policy. 'Some might say: "Don't make this personal,"' he said right before the election. 'But when it comes to who's prime minister, the personal is national. The guy who forgot to mention the deficit could be the one in charge of our whole economy. The man who is too weak to stand up to the trade unions at home could be the one facing down our enemies abroad.'[53]

The very fact that Miliband felt the need to address his image problem and Cameron to exploit the Labour leader's struggles connecting with voters was an indication that both sides believed it was significant. Lynton Crosby, for his part, believed people thought Miliband was 'weak'. He intended to use that to the Tories' advantage.

The Liberal Democrats were in an even trickier position. They knew from the opening months of the coalition just how hard it would be at the next election. Sometimes senior figures wondered if they should have made different demands for government jobs. They were in secondary positions in so many departments: Clegg was Cameron's deputy; Danny Alexander was number two in the Treasury; David Laws was not top dog in the education department. When preparing for potential coalition talks after 2015, they mulled over demanding that Clegg be made chancellor or education secretary, or that the party take all the ministerial posts in one department, thereby helping them own those accomplishments.[54] But those original calls were long in the past now.

So was another Lib Dem decision – to support a rise in tuition fees in 2010. It was a flagrant breach of their signed promises during the 2010 campaign. Years later senior Tories, including Cameron, were still bemused by why Clegg did not order his Lib Dem MPs to abstain, just as the coalition agreement explicitly allowed. Senior Lib Dems admitted regrets too. 'What we should simply have done is vetoed any increase in fees,' said Laws.

> Which would've been a bad policy choice but it would've been better politically. A difference between Nick and Cameron, a genuine one, is on some big issues during the coalition, when doing the right thing in policy terms collided with doing the right thing politically; we often chose the right policy and thought we could sort the politics out. Cameron, whenever there was that collision, always chose good politics.[55]

It was not the only time a more sensitive ear for politics helped the Tories in this period. The tuition fees decision underscored the perception among the Lib Dems' left-wing supporters that the party had sold out for power.

An electoral survival plan was needed. And like the Tories, the Lib Dems turned to a plain-speaking foreigner to find a solution. Ryan Coetzee hailed from South Africa, where he had been a strategist and parliamentary representative for the liberal Democratic Alliance. Clegg made him strategy director after Coetzee sent a memo following a UK trip that detailed his shock on discovering that so few Lib Dem senior figures could say why someone should vote for the party. Joining the team in autumn 2012, Coetzee carried out polling to assess the scale of the challenge, zooming in on the quarter of voters most likely to back the party. The results showed that, even among this group, there was not a single issue that the Lib Dems were deemed best on, except for House of Lords reform. 'I was kind of horrified,' said Coetzee, looking back in an interview. 'It was a shattered brand.'[56]

In the South African's view, the party leadership had made a fatal miscalculation early in the coalition. They had wanted to project stability, viewing their key task as being to prove to the electorate that the party could govern seriously. 'It was wrong. Just fundamentally catastrophic,' Coetzee said.[57] To Lib Dem voters the Rose Garden bonhomie, Clegg and Cameron side by side, shouted not good governance but a 'capitulation', Coetzee believed.[58] Instead the focus should be on differentiation, on showing supporters what the party was getting in return.

Shortly after entering Downing Street to be by Clegg's side, Coetzee attended a meeting of special advisers addressed by Cameron. 'It's very important that we are seen to be united,' the prime minister explained. Coetzee had a different interpretation. 'What is he on about? It's exactly the opposite of what we must look like,' he told a colleague afterwards. He vowed to do more to show voters how the 'sausage is made' inside the coalition.[59]

Yet come 2014, little had budged. The party got a taste of what was coming in the European Parliament elections that spring. Clegg had gambled by focusing on his pro-EU stance, agreeing to a head-to-head debate against Nigel Farage. It did not work. The party came fifth, behind not just Ukip, Labour and the Tories but also the Green

Party. That night Coetzee's wife urged him to quit. He vowed to carry on out of loyalty to his colleagues, but he was not blind to what was coming. Considering the prospect of the approaching general election, Coetzee told his wife: 'I feel like a man standing naked on a beach watching a tsunami come towards him.'[60]

There were still twists to come, however. The most consequential came on 18 September 2014. That was the most nerve-racking night of David Cameron's political career and had knock-on effects for Westminster election calculations that few foresaw.

To this day Cameron still believes he had no choice but to call the referendum on Scottish independence. The majority of seats that the Scottish National Party (SNP) secured in the 2011 Scottish Parliament elections was never meant to happen: the voting system adopted when the body was created in the late 1990s deliberately mixed first-past-the-post with proportional voting to ensure coalitions, not single-party rule. But when the SNP, a party created to deliver Scotland's exit from the United Kingdom, secured a majority, denying them a vote on that issue – a decision that rested with the UK prime minister – would be politically challenging. 'I never thought I had much of a choice of whether to have a Scottish referendum or not,' Cameron told the author. 'I took the view that if the Scots voted for an SNP-dominated majority Parliament and you didn't grant a referendum straightaway, you're just going to be permanently under the cosh. If I had acted differently the case for the Union would have become weaker.'[61]

The race was closer than he expected. For much of the long campaign – the referendum was formally agreed in October 2012 – support for independence in polls hovered in the low to mid-30s. That is, only around one in three Scots were saying they would vote for independence, a lowly figure in a straight yes/no shootout. But then it began to creep up and up, from the high 30s to low 40s to mid-40s. Then came the heart-attack moment: the first poll giving independence the lead, just two weeks before the vote. Was Cameron about to become the prime minister who lost Scotland?

Westminster politics was put on pause. Prime Minister's Questions was cancelled, the party leaders flocking north of the border, fearing they were sleepwalking into the disintegration of the three-centuries-old Union. The SNP, led by the pugnacious Alex Salmond, a political brawler who revelled in his role as a modern-day Robert the Bruce, appeared to be connecting with voters in a way the pro-UK Better Together campaign struggled to do. Cameron turned to self-flagellation in the scramble for votes. Do not vote yes just to give the 'effing Tories' a 'kick', he pleaded.[62]

The night of the referendum, Cameron watched on from Downing Street. In his head he had drafted the speech to be given if independence won – one, presumably, of resignation. 'I'm absolutely passionate about the United Kingdom and I couldn't bear the thought of that going the wrong way,' Cameron said, agreeing with allies who believed he was more on edge that results night than on any other.[63] He was, after all, the leader of the Conservative and Unionist Party, the Tories' full official title. At one point he tried to get some sleep, but struggled. When a text came through saying things were looking good, he rushed downstairs to watch. His children, up early, eventually joined him. 'It was a night when I was extremely nervous about what was going to happen,' Cameron said. 'And it was very joyful to see the results come in.'[64] The Union was safe, for the time being at least.

The victory – more comfortable than expected in the end, with 45 per cent voting yes to independence and 55 per cent voting no – had longer-term impacts for Cameron's Downing Street team. The relentless focus on the financial implications of independence, made more real in the final fortnight as Scots looked over the precipice thanks to the Yes poll lead, had cut through: a blueprint that would be readopted for the 2016 EU referendum. It also gave Cameron a played-two, won-two record on referendums after the earlier Alternative Vote rout, fuelling a belief that he knew how to win these battles. Neither the blueprint nor the self-belief would deliver a victory come the campaign against Brexit.

But there were two much more immediate consequences, both central to how the 2015 election campaign would play out. The first was an almighty SNP surge. In the aftermath of the independence defeat, support for the SNP rocketed, a phenomenon some psephologists thought was explained by 'buyer's remorse' at a historic option not chosen. The Labour vote share in Scotland correspondingly plummeted, the party seemingly punished for so publicly partnering with the Tories in the pro-Union campaign. Scotland had been a New Labour stronghold; now it became Ed Miliband's wasteland. Of Labour's forty-one Scottish seats, forty would be lost in 2015. The country would be painted SNP yellow, the party claiming fifty-six of the fifty-nine seats available.

Labour's collapse in Scotland all but ended their hopes of outright victory, but it does not explain Cameron's own majority. The Tories had one Scottish seat before the 2015 election and one after, so no boost to their total came from north of the border. It was a second, more subtle knock on effect of the 'indyref' that pushed them along the return path to Downing Street.

Back in Westminster, Lynton Crosby and the others in the Tory campaign bunker had been focus-grouping their battleground seats for months. They knew in the crucial Liberal Democrat targets that voters viewed Ed Miliband as weak, that they had a positive view of Cameron, that if they could be made to think nationally not locally things tilted towards the Conservatives. But they felt a clinching argument was lacking. Step forward Alex Salmond, bogeyman. The referendum had given Salmond, and to a lesser extent Nicola Sturgeon, who took over as SNP leader and Scottish first minister after the referendum defeat, a certain notoriety among Unionists down south. For some voters, they resembled an insurgent force hell-bent on destroying the country they loved. With all the polls pointing to a hung parliament again, meaning more coalition talks, respondents in focus groups began voicing a concern. What happened if Labour struck a pact with the SNP? Would Salmond and Sturgeon boss around Miliband, furthering their push for independence?

The minute Crosby heard the sentiment, he knew that he had found the spear point to his attack. Isaac Levido, by Crosby's side in CCHQ, explained in an interview:

> The threat of the SNP holding the balance of power in a Labour minority government put rocket boosters under our message. That gave consequence to all these perceptions people had about Miliband,

that he was weak and would not be a strong leader and prime minister. For a long time we struggled to figure it out, and then it emerged. The consequence of his weakness was, because he won't have a majority, he'd be relying on Alex Salmond who was strong, so [Salmond] would have Miliband over a barrel demanding all the money in favour of Scotland along with the SNP's other niche interests.[65]

The message was distilled into a no-holds-barred poster campaign designed by the advertising agency M&C Saatchi. One image provocatively showed Salmond pinching notes from someone's back pocket. Another had Miliband dancing wildly as Salmond played the tune. Other, even more controversial options were vetoed. But one image would become the defining poster of the 2015 campaign: Alex Salmond with a minute Ed Miliband poking out of his jacket pocket.

Crosby, in an interview with the author, explained why the attack worked: 'The consequence of Ed Miliband being perceived as weak, and the view that he couldn't win on his own right, was that he'd need the support of the SNP. That would mean the SNP would call the shots and the rest of us would pay the price, which was largely an economic price. By framing the choice that way it set up the risk of voting Labour.'[66]

Boris Johnson thought it was genius. 'What it did was it totally legitimated people's hesitations about Miliband,' he has said. 'Suddenly, with the whole Scottish thing, there was a public service reason for doing it [voting Tory]. You were actually voting for stable government for the country . . . It was a brilliant tactic. Absolutely brilliant.'[67]

The trap was set. Come the most intensive part of the campaign it would snap viciously around the legs of Miliband and the Labour team.

The starting gun for the final election sprint was fired on 30 March 2015. Parliament was dissolved, with MPs free to focus squarely on winning votes – what is traditionally known as the 'short campaign'. Up to that point the tensions of a looming election had not impacted the running of government, according to both senior Tory and Lib Dem ministers, with relations between the parties remaining cordial.[68]

A week earlier the final Cabinet meeting had been held, with bottles of commemorative 'Co-ale-ition' beer handed out whose labels showed Cameron and Clegg waving together before the black Number 10 door. It was a final snapshot of harmony before campaigning began.

The parties had had years to prepare for this moment. Arguments had been honed, messages road-tested and tinkered with. The state of the contest, however, would prove deceptive throughout. Obsessing the media was the prospect of further coalition talks, with almost every poll suggesting no overall winner. It shaped the entire narrative, in fact, with endless focus put on who would do deals with whom. Labour's weak point. (After the election pollsters would launch an inquiry into how they so underplayed the scale of Tory support.)

The CCHQ apparatus built under Crosby's watchful eye had strengths that became apparent during the six-week campaign. Cash was one. Fundraising had been led by Andrew Feldman, the Tory co-chairman and yet another Cameron pal from Oxford: they had helped organise Brasenose College's summer ball together and were paired in the college tennis team. Since 2005, Feldman had helped the party raise an eye-watering £250 million, first paying off debts and then building an election fighting fund.[69] One clear boost was to mail campaigning. By one estimate, the Tories became the country's biggest user of direct mail as voting day approached.[70] As reflected in David Laws's experience in Yeovil, a voter in a Lib Dem target seat may have got as many as nine tailored mailouts in the short campaign.[71] Tory sources believe their mail drive dwarfed Labour's efforts in both scale and precision.[72]

Another success were the ground and digital teams. The former had been built up by Grant Shapps, then Tory co-chairman with Feldman. Inspired by a trip to Washington, DC, where he met Barack Obama's successful 2012 re-election team, Shapps built an army of door-knockers. They were dubbed 'Team2015' and were mainly made up of youngsters deployed en masse to battleground seats by bus, with the prospect of a pub curry and a drink after campaigning. Come the election, 100,000 door-knockers had been signed up. A group of paid consultants in CCHQ would go through twenty-one steps of prompts – asking 'Are you coming? When? On what transport? Do you want lunch?' – before each 'Super Saturday' and 'Super Sunday' to make sure the volunteers turned up.[73] 'It was a phenomenal ground campaign,' Shapps recalled, suggesting that in a tight race it made a difference.[74]

The digital campaign was run by two thirtysomethings, Craig Elder and Tom Edmonds. They consciously moved away from online gimmicks that had been used before – such as 'WebCameron', the Tory leader's video diaries – and concentrated on effectiveness. Facebook was the focus rather than Twitter, which tended to obsess Westminster: 55 per cent of the population used the former but less than 20 per cent used the latter.[75] Facebook also allowed for a stark degree of specific targeting: not just a voter's age, sex and socio-economic status but also consumer habits such as favourite newspaper or car brand.[76] Not to mention the constituency they lived in, allowing for maximum focus on the one hundred key seats. Some eight hundred different versions of the same advert could be trialled, with the returning data indicating which worked best.[77] One success was an ad that told voters 'yours is one of twenty-three seats that will decide the election'. It was a clever gambit: it was true the Tories needed twenty-three extra seats for a majority but the message was deployed in many more constituencies than that.[78] It helped Lib Dem voters think nationally not locally, as Crosby wanted.

Other advantages were won thanks to seemingly mundane campaign minutiae. The first daily meeting in CCHQ's grand building just north of the Houses of Parliament was held at 5.45 a.m., when department heads would brief Crosby on the plan for the day. A second meeting followed at 6.30 a.m. with a wider team, then a third at 7.30 a.m., where Cameron and Osborne would sign off any major decisions. A few minutes' walk away at Labour head-quarters the day's first meeting had not even begun. This would start at 7.45 a.m.[79] Every day, the Tories were out of bed, plotting and reacting, before Labour even had their shoes on.

Success skews memories; the campaign was not without missteps. Cameron faced a lot of Tory grumbling about the repetitiveness of it all – ministers uttering 'long-term economic plan' over and over, while limiting the prime minister's spontaneous interaction with voters. One low point came when in an impromptu joke the prime minister mistakenly said his football team was West Ham rather than Aston Villa, leading to mockery of his 'man of the people' blunder. (Cameron put it down to referencing the West Indies cricket team moments before, plus exhaustion.) 'It was awful,' recalled one aide who was with him as they drove away from the speech. 'How bad was that?' Cameron asked. 'It was really bad,' came the response.[80]

The incident led to a weekend of handwringing and a change of tack. Cameron was becoming frustrated by the claims that he was not showing enough passion on the campaign trail. 'It was just really annoying,' he recalled.[81] In his view, he was working flat out. The polls were not budging, Tories were sniping. The critique was a familiar one: Eton-educated Cameron was 'too posh to push', as one ally phrased it.[82] He was urged to show more emotion. Feldman, leaning on Hollywood, told him to 'do a Rocky'.[83] And so at the next event Cameron removed his suit jacket, declaring he was 'pumped up' and 'bloody lively' in an exaggerated show of enthusiasm.[84] 'We just used the media narrative like some jujitsu move to accept there had been no energy and now there was going to be lots of energy, when the truth was a bit less dramatic,' Cameron said.[85] But it worked, generating the desired headlines.

Much of the kudos for the campaign should go to Crosby, colleagues in the Tory bunker argue. His electoral clear-sightedness was matched with a pally energy in headquarters. Crosby would hand out stuffed koalas to juniors who overperformed, randomly play music to lighten the mood, talk to everyone whatever rank and, on election night, toot a horn for notable constituency wins. 'I find it almost impossible to conceive there's somebody on the planet better at their job than Lynton Crosby. He's amazing,' gushed Elder, one of the two digital gurus.[86] 'Lynton should take credit for a lot of what happened, because he was brilliant,' said Giles Kenningham, the Tory director of communications.[87] One example cited is when Labour's promise to scrap the non-domiciled tax status was dominating the broadcast news. Crosby deployed one of his famed 'dead cats', convincing the defence secretary, Michael Fallon, to warn that Miliband would 'stab the United Kingdom in the back' by joining with the SNP in the same way he had his brother David to win the Labour leadership.[88] This provocative intervention was roundly condemned by rival politicians. But now the conversation was about Miliband's character and SNP pacts, not Labour's chosen topic, just as Crosby wanted.

There were other neat innovations. Cameron began to carry round a note written by outgoing Labour Treasury chief secretary Liam Byrne for his successor in 2010, which joked 'there is no money' left – the perfect distillation of Tory claims about Labour profligacy. The note achieved that rare and most sought-after thing in elections: cut-through into the wider public consciousness. Meanwhile, to 'squeeze' Ukip voters into returning to the Conservatives, they were warned: 'go to bed with Nigel Farage and wake up with Ed Miliband' – a reminder that in reality only Cameron or his Labour rival could be prime minister.

Above all there was a relentless punching of the bruise that was the spectre of a Labour–SNP 'coalition of chaos'. Tory aides scrambled to work out where Miliband was giving speeches so they could flock there with Salmond and Sturgeon face masks for the press cameras. A load of campaign juniors also combed through SNP YouTube feeds searching for lines that could be weaponised.[89] One was Salmond joking that he would soon be 'writing the Labour Party's Budget', grainy footage of which was shared with millions via Cameron's Twitter feed. The prime minister was so well drilled even his private jokes had a Scottish bent. As an interview on ITV's *This Morning* ended, host Phillip Schofield teed up the following segment: 'Up next, a man who can pinch your wallet, your watch and even your tie without you noticing.' Cameron, thinking he was off mic, was heard saying: 'Who is that? Alex Salmond?'[90]

In the Labour camp, there had been positivity in the early weeks of the short campaign. Miliband, his team felt, had coped well in the two election debates. (Cameron, stung in 2010, only took part in one: a seven-way party leader shoutathon which produced more heat than light.) Indeed, Miliband's personal ratings ticked up during the campaign, suggesting his team's attempts to underscore his prime-ministerial qualities – including the much-mocked trait of making him appear behind a lectern for events, even once in a back garden – had some impact.

As the Tories dialled up the Labour–SNP attacks late in the race, however, Miliband's team felt increasingly trapped. The problems compounded each other. At first, the Labour leadership was slow to rule out a coalition, heightening press interest in the issue. Then, when pushed to go further – what about a less formal deal, or a vote-by-vote arrangement? – answers were not forthcoming. The hesitations underscored the perception of weakness in some voters' minds. All the while, the one place Miliband needed to visit more, Scotland, where Gordon Brown was among those urging extra trips to counter the SNP surge, was becoming increasingly problematic as it would prompt more questions about a potential deal.[91]

In the words of Stephen Livermore, one of those leading Labour's campaign, it was a living nightmare:

> We were in a hideous position. We needed to go to Scotland and we couldn't. We needed to rule an SNP deal out and we weren't. We needed to deflect it and we didn't have anything to deflect it with. It was exactly what the media wanted to talk about because it seemed to play into where the polling was indicating. So we were just in this vice. Someone described us as like a boxer in the corner just being pummelled and we had nothing. It was awful. You just said: 'Oh good, another day of being beaten up.'[92]

The pressure would lead to one of the campaign's most memorable missteps. Seeking to return eyeballs back to Labour's chosen issues – especially the NHS, one of the party's strongest cards against the Tories – a cunning plan was conjured up. To show that Labour's six election pledges would be delivered, why not carve them into stone? And so Miliband found himself unveiling an 8 ft 6 in monolith in a school car park in Hastings, promising to install it in the Downing Street garden if he won. The image of Miliband standing under a blanket of cloud by a slab engraved with loosely worded promises – 'a strong economic foundation' was one; 'controls on immigration' another – triggered instant online mockery. It was swiftly dubbed the EdStone.

Labour insiders believe the blunder, while embarrassing, was of little consequence.[93] It was the SNP deal warnings that really helped bury the party.

It was not just Labour seeing the impact. Lib Dem MPs fighting for their political lives in the Tory target seats began to feel the ground moving beneath their feet. Vince Cable, trying to hold Twickenham, noticed the change late. 'I was surprised by the extent to which the SNP line started to come through because people certainly in my part of the world are not anti-Scottish,' Cable said.

> There's no antipathy to the Scottish people or anything, but for some reason it hit a visceral feeling. 'These people are trying to split up the country.' I think it was partly that, partly a fear of chaos . . . I still can't quite understand how many of my highly educated constituents were struck by it but it did work. It worked to perfection.[94]

Steve Webb, whose Thornbury and Yate constituency in South Gloucestershire was the location for some renowned horse trials, always knew Tory waverers were a key support bloc, but this time they did not want to risk Labour getting in. 'A soft Conservative would vote for me if they weren't afraid of the Labour Party. In 1997, they could say: "If Blair gets in, Blair gets in." In 2010, a soft Conservative didn't want the SNP running the country.'[95] With Norman Baker, looking to extend his run representing Lewes in East Sussex into a third decade, some constituents were even more explicit. 'There were quite a few people saying: "You've been a really good MP but we can't afford for Scotland to go independent,"' Baker said.[96]

Ryan Coetzee, the Lib Dems' director of strategy, could see the fires breaking out right across the electoral map. There had been a hope among senior Lib Dems that the party could hold onto twenty-five, perhaps thirty seats at the election: a halving of their numbers but not an apocalyptic wipeout.[97] A message of restraint was deployed, spinning off the assumption that coalition talks were inevitable. The Lib Dems would be the centrist counterweight to whichever party won, they argued: a heart to the Tories and a moderating force on Labour. It did not work.

Nick Clegg, as party leader, once again led the campaign, but this time there was no Cleggmania. The media strategy involved putting him in photogenic scenes to force a way into newspaper pages and broadcast packages: Clegg meeting poorly hedgehogs at an animal sanctuary; Clegg whizzing along a zipline at Go Ape. It also involved limiting spontaneous interactions with voters, a tactic whose justification was underscored when a student stepped forward for a selfie with Clegg and then dropped his trousers. At one point the Lib Dems' bright-yellow battle bus, deployed to the South-West as the Tories circled, thudded into a pigeon, which was killed on impact. It felt like a metaphor.

'We kept narrowing the defensive line,' said Coetzee. 'We were saying: "Well, can we fall back on twenty-five seats? Can we fall back on twenty? Can we fall back on fifteen?"'[98] One thing might have stemmed the bleeding, Coetzee later concluded: announcing the Lib Dems would only do a coalition deal with the Tories, accepting that left-leaning voters were gone and going all-in for Conservatives. But the party hierarchy rejected the idea when it was floated. 'It wasn't the most fun campaign of my life,' recalled Coetzee. 'I mean, it was awful actually.'[99]

And then it was over. The race was run, the competitors' political fates now with the electorate. Once again, David Cameron's inner circle gathered in his cosy family home in the West Oxfordshire village of Dean. With the opinion polls still overwhelmingly pointing to a hung parliament, and many giving Labour a lead over the Tories, there was no expectation of an outright Conservative victory. 'Did I think we were going to win an overall majority? I don't think I did,' said Cameron. 'I just kept looking at the figures and thinking: "I know we're going to win lots of Lib Dem seats, I know we're going to probably lose a few Labour ones. I just can't see us getting enough of the first to overtake the second."'[100] His personal prediction had been 293 Tory MPs, way short of a majority, but that sank lower as the 10 p.m. exit poll approached.[101] George Osborne, Cameron's political partner, had a similar hunch: 'We were not expecting to win outright.'[102] That afternoon, the chancellor attempted to get his old ally to suspend disbelief for a moment and muse on whom he would pick in an exclusively Tory Cabinet, according to one person present.[103] Cameron shut the conversation down.

A very different prospect formed the basis of conversations inside the Dean cottage. Ever the political professional, Cameron wanted a speech drafted for each of the three most likely outcomes.[104] Two were coalition scenarios: the first was getting enough MPs to form a new pact; the second, a situation where the numbers were touch and go. The third outcome weighed was not a Tory majority; it was Labour coming out with more MPs than the Conservatives. That draft was a resignation speech.

Sitting on the Camerons' back patio, before a backdrop of vines with yellow flowers blooming, the prime minister read out his would-be departure speech from a laptop. 'I'm leaving Downing Street for the last time,' he said. 'We wish Ed and Justine the best, they'll find behind that black door very professional people who will do everything.'[105] There were tears from the handful of close allies listening in as they contemplated their boss's political mortality. 'We're all sitting there slightly sobbing into our cups of tea,' recalled Kate Fall.[106] 'I personally found it quite upsetting,' said a second person there.[107] Cameron was moved too: 'It was quite emotional. It was like, "Oh my God, in a few hours' time this could be actually happening."'[108]

So when the reveal came, it was all the sweeter. The team crammed into the living room for the exit poll. The results flashed onto the screen: the Tories would be the largest party. And then the seat prediction: within touching distance of a majority. Cue jubilation. 'There was just this enormous cheer and celebration. People were literally flinging each other around as if in a ceilidh,' said Craig Oliver, Cameron's director of communications.[109] Fall remembered 'literal uproar' in the room: 'We just were completely over the moon. We were completely not expecting it.'[110] There were whoops, hugs, fist-bumps. At the final count the Conservatives would win 330 seats, up twenty-four from 2010 and – crucially – with a Commons majority of eleven.[111]

The inverse scenes were playing out in rival campaign headquarters. Labour had been hopeful of getting more seats than the Tories, giving them the upper hand in coalition talks. The press had been briefed accordingly about why they should be able to negotiate first. Spencer Livermore had allowed optimism to creep in. 'I suppose you do allow yourself to start to believe,' he said. When the exit poll appeared, his eyes met those of another senior aide sitting at the other end of the table. 'We looked at each other and we both knew,' he said, the penny dropping about what the Tories had pulled off. 'It was like, "This is going to be a long and awful night." We knew from that moment.'[112] Far from gaining seats, Labour won twenty-six fewer than in 2010, leaving 232. Just 30 per cent of voters backed them, only just up from 2010's 29 per cent.[113] The next day Miliband announced his resignation as Labour leader, saying he was 'truly sorry'.[114]

In the Liberal Democrat bunker, Ryan Coetzee had Nick Clegg straight on the phone. 'Is it true?' Clegg said of the exit poll, hoping the wipeout forecast was somehow wrong. 'Really, can't we get a few more?'[115] Coetzee feared not. His feelings were bleak. The South African had spent the best part of three years living abroad trying to save a political party; now came regret. 'I tell you what I really thought,' Coetzee said in an interview. 'Should I have come here?'[116] When the counting was done, just eight Lib Dem MPs were left standing. The party was decimated; its time in government over. 'They hammered us,' Clegg would later say.[117] Like Miliband, he announced his resignation as party leader the next day. So too did Nigel Farage: his failure to win South Thanet marked his seventh defeat as a Ukip candidate in bids to obtain a Commons seat.[118] Miliband, Clegg, Farage – three party heads gone within twenty-four hours. The 'decapitation strategy' had proved more successful than had ever been envisaged.

The feat that Cameron and Crosby pulled off was immense. A centre-right party that had implemented swingeing public sector cuts in five years of austerity economics had skipped free of the coalition's shackles, rewarded by the electorate with sole rule. Perceptions of weakness in Ed Miliband and menace from the SNP had been fashioned together to force open the seats of their coalition partners, in a strategy even opposition party rivals admit was brilliantly conceived. Yes, polling errors suggesting a neck-and-neck race had elevated the message. Labour's failure to win back trust on the economy, Ukip's shrinking vote share and the SNP rout in Scotland all played their part. But it was the Conservatives' electoral bloody-mindedness, having adopted the Lib Dems as their governing counterparts and not flinching in bringing about their destruction, that most stands out. In total, the Tories would overturn twenty-seven Lib Dem seats.[119] As a result, they could now govern alone.

'I am not an old man,' Cameron would tell a jubilant Tory head-quarters in the early hours of 8 May. He had voted in 1987, when Margaret Thatcher won a majority. He was working for the Tories in 1992, when John Major did likewise. He had led the party back into government in 2010. 'But I think this', Cameron told the room, 'is the sweetest victory of them all.'[120]

Yet in that victory the seeds of his destruction had been sown. For sole rule meant that total implementation of the Tory manifesto was now expected. And one item, little discussed during the election, would ensure that in just over a year Cameron would join his rivals on the political slag heap.

3

Sliding Doors

DAVID CAMERON REMEMBERS exactly where he was when the text arrived. The family cottage in Dean held some of his happiest political memories. But it was here, on a sofa in the living room, that Cameron's phone pinged with the message he dreaded.[1] Boris Johnson was backing Brexit.

The prime minister knew all too well what it could mean for the campaign ahead. Johnson had won Labour-loving London twice, capturing voters beyond those traditionally reachable by Tories. He was the only leading politician with a better favourability rating than Cameron.[2] And it was on the trail that Johnson, considered the most effective Tory campaigner of his generation, really excelled.

And yet Boris was not a Brexiteer – at least, not until that text late on Sunday afternoon, 21 February 2016, four months before the in/out referendum on UK membership of the European Union. He had long been a Eurosceptic, no doubt. His political reputation was built as the *Daily Telegraph*'s Brussels correspondent, 'chucking rocks' about the EU that would 'crash' into the 'greenhouse' of John Major's creaking government.[3] But until this time he had never explicitly advocated leaving the bloc – not publicly and, according to many close friends, not privately either.[4]

In pursuit of Boris's support, Cameron had pulled every lever. Bribery was one. At a hut beside the US ambassador to the UK's London tennis court Cameron had floated a plum Cabinet job. With the match complete – Johnson adopting his customary 'aggressive, wildly unorthodox and extremely competitive' playing style – the prime minister said a 'top five' job would follow the referendum if Johnson backed Remain. When Boris wondered aloud what that meant, Cameron made it explicit: 'Defence is a top five job.'[5]

Reform was another lever yanked, with the offer of a law change. Johnson, like many Eurosceptics, rankled at the European Court of Justice's reach in the UK. So legislation was drawn up just for Boris that declared the UK Supreme Court the ultimate arbiter of EU law in the country. The bid to change the law was ultimately dropped – it was feared impractical – but it was special treatment nonetheless.

There had been pleas for the greater good. 'Don't take the course that you fundamentally think is wrong for the country,' Cameron kept saying.[6] And appeals to his vanity: 'In three or four years' time you'll probably be prime minister and you can do a better deal [with the EU].'[7] Even that weekend Cameron had not given up hope, 'furiously' texting him.[8]

But the time for vacillation was over. The deadline was nigh – Johnson had agreed to make the big reveal in his column for the next day's *Daily Telegraph*. Two versions – one for staying in the EU, the other for quitting – had been drafted that weekend. This spoke to his hesitancy but also reflected the method by which he often reached decisions, playing out two arguments, then picking a side. By now others had made their move. Half a dozen Cabinet ministers had declared for Leave the day before. The press pack had gathered outside Johnson's five-storey Islington townhouse. The send button needed to be hit. And yet, still he hesitated.

'I was the only person with him. He was genuinely torn. It was touch and go,' recalled Will Walden, Johnson's chief communications adviser at the time. 'You could tell he was really feeling the pressure. This was Boris uncut. This was not an act.' Walden remembered thinking it was possible, despite whispers that Boris was leaning towards Leave, that his boss could 'drop the biggest bombshell imaginable' and declare for Remain.[9]

For the key moments Johnson was alone in his study at the back of the house overlooking Regent's Canal. Everywhere was clutter. The desk was covered with piles of newspapers, documents, letters: the telltale signs of life admin put on pause. There was barely space for the computer over which he was hunched, tapping and ruminating. The bookshelves were filled with the classics, modern and ancient: a reminder of the heroes of Antiquity that Boris held in such high regard. In the balance was a choice whose repercussions would rock the country for years to come. One, too, with consequences for his dream of becoming prime minister.

And then, at last, a decision. 'Right, we're done,' said Johnson. 'Are you sure?' asked Walden. 'Yes.'[10] Moments later, Boris would be out of the front door, declaring to the cameras gathered that he would be 'advocating Vote Leave'. 'The last thing I wanted was to go against David Cameron or the government. But after a great deal of heartache I don't think there's anything else I can do,' he would explain. Before that, there was time – just – to give Cameron a heads-up. The text came through just nine minutes before the public were told and was much more candid. Brexit would be crushed 'like the toad beneath the harrow', Johnson predicted. But he could not look himself in the mirror if he campaigned for Remain.[11]

'I just remember it so clearly,' Cameron said in an interview with the author. 'I had a sense it was going the wrong way and then I got that text.' There was frustration. 'Why would an intelligent person who's literally been writing about politics and thinking about politics all his life and never argued for leaving the EU suddenly want to do that?' There was a realisation, too, about what it meant for the vote. 'If Boris was on the wrong side of the argument, that was very, very bad news.'[12]

For eleven years Cameron had tried to stop the Conservative Party ripping itself apart over Europe. And yet, step by logical step, he had led them to this moment. At points, other paths had been open to him, other routes not taken. As he made each choice, alternative destinations faded from view. With Boris's declaration, a last critical uncertainty became known. The battle would tear the Tories in two – and leave Cameron's premiership shredded.

History is shaped not just by great forces and the randomness of events but, at points, by a handful of individuals with outsized influence whose rivalries, grievances and unchained ambition leave their mark. That is true of Brexit. So much has been written about the vote to quit the European Union. It is unquestionably the most significant moment in the Conservatives' run in Downing Street since 2010, with 23 June 2016 serving as the before-and-after date for this whole political period. Rather than retracing every step of the EU referendum campaign, ground that has already been thoroughly trodden elsewhere, there is more value in zooming out a little. What were the points when another outcome could have followed? And how can the riddle be explained of a politician who was determined to keep Britain in the EU ultimately delivering the opposite? It is a tale in which the personal – not least between the two effective leaders of the campaigns – played a defining role.

Boris Johnson was not a friend of David Cameron. The word is used by Cameron in his memoirs but, according to those by his side throughout his political career, it does not accurately capture the nature of their relationship. They were near-contemporaries, certainly. Johnson was two years ahead of Cameron at Eton and Oxford University. They became MPs, alongside George Osborne, in the same year – 2001 – and were on good terms for much of the following period. But not close. 'I never felt like Boris was in their gang,' Kate Fall, who was at Oxford with Cameron and by his side during his Tory leadership, said of their early days in national politics.[13] 'They were always friendly and matey with Boris and found him amusing and clever, which he is. But I would never sort of see Boris with them . . . I think they always knew that there was a bit of competitiveness around them right from the start.' Andrew Feldman, another Oxford contemporary, agreed: 'What you've got to understand is Boris was not David Cameron's friend. He was his rival.'[14] A third long-standing Cameron ally said: 'I don't think he and Boris have ever been friends.'[15] For Craig Oliver, Cameron's communications director, there was a 'strange respectful rivalry' between them.[16] Texts were frequently shared. There was mutual affection, a bemused raising of the eyebrows at the other's successes; mutual suspicion too.

The Conservative Party's annual autumn conference was where the rivalry would often play out. Johnson courted a 'king over the water' image as mayor of London, the darling of the delegates as Cameron spoon-fed the country his tough medicine of austerity. A glimpse into Johnson's psyche was offered in a BBC *Newsnight* interview recorded at the 2011 conference, the year after Cameron reached the summit of British politics. A teasing Jeremy Paxman tried to get Boris to bite on the fact that the man his junior at school and university had become top dog. Eleven minutes in, it finally worked. 'Is it true that you've always felt yourself slightly intellectually inferior?' asked Paxman. 'Inferior?' came the reply, prompting laughter behind the camera. Paxman noted Cameron got a first-class degree at Oxford, better than Johnson's 2:1 in Classics, and wondered if it still rankled. 'It would,' Johnson said, eyes narrowing, 'if it wasn't that his First was in PPE.'[17] Classics trumped Philosophy, Politics and Economics in the intellectual stakes, it appeared. Johnson's conference turns drew such attention that later in his premiership Cameron and his aides would wargame strategies for the London mayor's speech. It was dubbed 'Boris handling day'. 'It was always deep sighs and "What's he going to do? How can we manage it?"' recalled one involved.[18]

Away from the political arena their exchanges would feature the same public-school joshing. One day in July 2013 both men by chance went to watch the cricket at Lord's, where England were taking on Australia in the Ashes. Cameron sat in the cheap seats, jacket off and surrounded by advisers, while Johnson, tie on, watched from high above in the balcony of the Pavilion which would host visiting royals. 'Man of the people!' Cameron declared when they met later that afternoon, or words to that effect, according to one present.[19] Johnson countered by noting he had just enjoyed lunch with some of cricket's most famous names. Even the most mundane of activities could become an arena for their competition. 'Boris would walk faster, and then Cameron would walk faster, and then Boris would walk faster,' recalled Walden, who as Johnson's City Hall comms chief often had to try to keep up. 'It would get to the point where you were practically running. And it was unsaid. It was basically willy-waving.'[20] Another Tory rivalry, though, would be just as critical to understanding what came next.

How does a politician distinguish between personal interest, party interest and the national interest? That is one of the many questions that hang over the long run-up to Brexit. MPs have a knack of equating the first two kinds of interest with the third. Politicians tend to believe that, if they are in charge, good will be done since their solutions to the country's problems are better than those of other parties. But motivations swirl, merge, overlap, are dialled up and down. Separating and weighing them against each other is tricky. Layered on top of that, can any politician accurately recount their thinking years after an event? Memoirs of every ideological shade pull off the trick of lining up the facts in such a way that the protagonist is shown to be well intentioned, wiser than most and prone to magnanimity. Then there are the constraints of circumstance. Whatever ideals and ambitions an MP may have, they are bound by their times. Somehow the reality of such distant moments must be captured. The challenge is intensified for decisions that irrevocably changed the country and weigh heavily on the lead characters. Brexit has certainly done that. Which makes it all the more difficult – and important – to try to unpick the choices made by those in power.

Ask David Cameron's closest political friends to capture his character and instincts and they often come back to the centrality of family, mixed with a sense of duty. 'The reason he wanted to do everything he wanted to do was because of his family. I do think that is what drove him,' said one who worked with him during his Tory leadership.[21] Throughout this period Cameron's wife, Samantha, was by his side, the marriage displaying a durability not seen with every one of his successors. It is notable too how many figures who were in the bunker for his 2005 leadership bid were still there come his 2016 resignation; again, not a feature characteristic of all the prime ministers who followed.

Cameron credits his father with passing on to him many of the values he lived by. Ian Cameron was a stockbroker whose humour and eccentricities, and defiance at being born with physical disabilities, are recounted in his son's memoir. 'Family first, hard work, do the right thing, take responsibility,' Cameron writes of the mantras his father lived by – values that allies also ascribe to the former prime minister.[22] In the same book he describes the cruelty of the seizures his baby son Ivan would endure due to having a condition called Ohtahara syndrome.[23] Caring for Ivan and the devastation at his passing had a profound effect on Cameron the politician as well as Cameron the father, according to friends.[24]

One of Cameron's strengths was his intellect, unquestioned by his critics. Vernon Bogdanor, who as professor of government at Oxford University taught many future members of the political elite, said Cameron was among his 'ablest' students.[25] Officials recall how quickly the young prime minister grasped the facts and arguments set out in his red boxes containing ministerial documents. There was a similar clarity of thought when it came to politics. 'He's got an instinctive feel of what the country thinks and he's also just very good at creating big political arguments,' said one Cameron adviser.[26] The hallmark of his speeches was not rhetorical flights of fancy but the outlining of rational steps leading to a clear conclusion.

There was also an unmistakable self-confidence, bred, colleagues believed, in the same educational institutions that had honed his smarts: Eton and Oxford. Those still loyal to their old boss framed this trait as a sureness of foot, the ability to make a call and stick by it. In the years ahead it would provide a stark contrast to the hesitancy shown at times by Theresa May and the sensitivity to press coverage displayed by Boris Johnson. But critics had a harsher word for it: arrogance. Tory MPs not in the Notting Hill set could feel dismissed by the prime minister and his chancellor, George Osborne, believing them out of touch. 'Two posh boys who don't know the price of milk,' as fellow Tory Nadine Dorries once so memorably put it.[27] Journalists on the political beat would sometimes note that Osborne was more affable in private than his spiky public persona suggested, and vice versa for Cameron.

Barack Obama, the US president who had Cameron as an opposite number for six and a half years, captured this quality in his memoirs with a pithy summary:

> In his early forties, with a youthful appearance and a studied informality (at every international summit, the first thing he'd do was take off his jacket and loosen his tie), the Eton-educated Cameron possessed an impressive command of the issues, a facility with language, and the easy confidence of someone who'd never been pressed too hard by life.

Obama did add: 'I liked him personally, even when we butted heads.'[28]

The mix was also neatly distilled by Ivan Rogers, who was Britain's ambassador to the EU during Cameron's renegotiation drive. Rogers was a step removed from the Cameron inner circle, held a job dependent on taking accurate readings of politicians and had seen other prime ministers up close in a decades-long Whitehall career, leaving him a well-placed observer.

'His strengths are: he's a quick learner, he's very smart, he's much less idle than people allege. He's quite hard-working by the standards of prime ministers; I would say at least as hard-working as Blair. He's extremely economically literate as well,' Rogers said in an interview with the author.[29]

> Of course the weaknesses are very much the obvious ones. He can sometimes be a touch complacent with his smartness, a bit pleased with himself, a bit glib. He could be superficial where you'd say, 'No, it's actually more difficult than that. You have to go through it.' Because he and Osborne felt themselves to be the brightest boys in the class, much brighter than most of their colleagues.

Every prime minister sees their traits amplified by the power of Downing Street. Every politician, too, becomes a caricature in the public eye. But it was this blend of characteristics – not least the certainty in his own rightness – that would shape how Cameron acted at each of the many forks in the road on Europe.

David Cameron was never a devotee of the EU. Even in a Conservative Party whose centre of gravity on the issue shifted so much during his quarter of a century in Westminster, Cameron was never at the most pro-European end, where Ken Clarke and Michael Heseltine were to be found. His adviser days shaped that. Cameron watched Britain's chaotic crash out of the European Exchange Rate Mechanism from the Treasury. He had seen the complications that EU membership brought when it came to migration and justice from the vantage point of the Home Office. 'David was very much in the middle,' said Kate Fall, who was a fellow Tory adviser in the 1990s. 'So, small-e Eurosceptic, wanting to see reform in Europe.'[30] Cameron was critical of joining the euro in 1997, when the official party policy was 'wait and see'.[31] He helped draft a pamphlet with his boss Chancellor Norman Lamont in 1992 that included the line 'no one would die for the European Union', both men rejecting

Number 10's request to delete it.[32] Such stories, recounted by Cameron in his memoir, must be taken with a dose of salt, according to some reporters who covered his early leadership and recalled a dismissiveness towards hardline Eurosceptics.

Come the 2005 Tory leadership campaign, more clarity was needed. Cameron was the fresh-faced outsider to David Davis, a well-known EU critic. Liam Fox, another Europhobe, and Clarke, an EU evangelist, were also running. With positions on Europe bound to be a dividing line, Cameron, then only four years into his parliamentary career, needed to show where he stood. And here that mix of motivations – personal and political – was to be seen.

A group of Eurosceptic Tory MPs, led by John Hayes, had decided to put a single demand as the price for their support. It involved a seemingly obscure topic: how political parties were grouped in the European Parliament. Politicians ran to become MEPs under the banner of a party in their own member state. But, once elected, they would form together with like-minded parties to maximise their voting power in Strasbourg. The groupings could be a clumsy amalgam of differing views, with the Conservatives part of the European People's Party (EPP), which believed in the EU member states moving ever closer together. This grated on the Tory Eurosceptics. Hence their demand: Pull the party out of the EPP.

Davis, the most prominent Eurosceptic in the leadership race and the frontrunner at the start, rejected the demand, fearing it would reduce the Tories' ability to influence European partners. But Cameron did not. He and Osborne would meet Hayes to discuss how to answer the call. 'Europe even at that stage was seen as an emblematic issue which divided the party,' said Hayes, looking back. 'It's true that David Davis was a Eurosceptic. Cameron almost had to establish his credentials. He had to be clear about his commitment on that subject. He had to prove that he meant business.' The conversations were more nuanced than a quid pro quo, but politics was clearly a part. 'It wasn't a trade-off. It was much more subtle than that. It was a growing together, a moving together. We advised him that it was important totemically that he understood Eurosceptics, that he understood their sensibilities and preoccupations.'[33]

Davis at one point called Cameron to urge him against taking such a position. 'This is a bad idea,' Davis recalled telling his rival. 'I'm not going to do this, David. You don't need to do this. Don't do it.'[34] The plea went unheeded. Cameron did vow to pull the Tories out of the EPP and would deliver on the pledge in office, frustrating German chancellor Angela Merkel. In the campaign he elevated the promise with the help of Open Europe, a Eurosceptic think tank. One insider there remembers discussions about using the position to maximise votes: 'He was definitely doing it to win over Eurosceptic MPs. Definitely. It was a direct pitch and he wanted our help in order to do so.'[35] Davis also saw the move as a clear bid for the backing of Eurosceptic Tories. 'He was desperate to get them on board,' Davis claimed.[36]

Cameron rejected in categorical terms any suggestion that he did not believe in the position. 'I was in the room when we joined the EPP in the first place. I was against it then,' Cameron said in an interview with the author. 'My view was the Conservative Party had to be a Eurosceptic party. I was what I would term a moderate, sensible, practical Eurosceptic. I wanted us to reform the EU and our relationship with it and stay in – and the EPP decision was an important part of that.'[37] Others, not just allies like George Osborne but critics like Jacob Rees-Mogg, the Brexiteer Tory MP, believe the position was honestly held.[38] Supporting evidence comes from Cameron later pushing to opt the UK out of the EU's 'ever closer union' in his renegotiation.

So Cameron's opposition to being in the EPP appears to have been honestly held. What the episode illustrated was something subtler, a dynamic that would define the coming decade: how Tory Eurosceptics could rally around one demand; how Cameron could adopt a position that met the request and eased the pressure; how short-term political rewards could follow. It was a loop that would repeat itself again and again, until it snapped spectacularly in 2016.

The origins of Britain's standoffish approach to what became the European Union can be variously traced. Some believe it was somehow hardwired into the country's DNA as an island nation, physically separated from the Continent. Others see fundamentally different readings of the Second World War, based on experience, as central: the UK viewing the nation-state as the ultimate bastion of freedom, with Britain helping defeat Nazi Germany, while neighbouring countries saw first-hand the devastation if a state's sole power went unchecked.

Britain was certainly late to the table. The Treaty of Rome, which created the European Economic Community, was signed by Belgium, France, West Germany, Italy, Luxembourg and the Netherlands in 1957. Two British attempts to sign up in the 1960s were met with a 'non' from French President Charles de Gaulle. The UK only joined in 1973, with a confirmatory referendum two years later. The morphing of the Common Market – championed by a young Margaret Thatcher – into a power bloc that governed an increasing number of aspects of British life over time caused strains. Tensions over Europe within the Conservative Party burst into public in the 1990s over the Maastricht Treaty, which created the modern-day EU, and with it shared European citizenship, joined-up security and foreign policy, and a path to a single currency.

When those by David Cameron's side look back at the sliding-doors moments on Europe during his leadership from 2005, one in particular jumps out. It involved the prospect of a referendum, but not on EU membership.

The concept of holding a referendum when the EU's foundation treaties were changed had by then bedded into British political discourse. John Major considered one over Maastricht: a debate Cameron saw from the inside as a Tory adviser. Tony Blair, who wanted to centralise the UK's place in the EU, had announced a referendum on the EU Constitution in the House of Commons. 'Let the issue be put. Let the battle be joined,' he declared with a flourish in April 2004. It meant all three leading UK parties went into the 2005 election proposing referendums. (Labour and the Liberal Democrats actually proposed two each: not just on the EU Constitution but on adopting the euro, if the decision was made to join.) However, first the French and then the Dutch voted no in their own referendums, killing off the EU Constitution.

The crunch point came on the introduction of the Constitution's successor, the Lisbon Treaty. It was at its core the same in all but name, creating the role of European Council president, scrapping some member state vetoes and enshrining in law a Charter of Fundamental Rights, which would give all EU citizens certain protections. Labour, now under Gordon Brown's leadership, dropped its referendum promise in 2007. But the Tories doubled down, with Cameron in September of that year giving a 'cast-iron guarantee' to hold one.[39]

If there had been a vote on Lisbon, would an in/out referendum have ever happened subsequently? William Hague, the Tory shadow foreign secretary at the time, thinks not. 'Britain would have held a referendum on the Lisbon Treaty, voted against the Lisbon Treaty, we would have blocked European integration, but we would not have then embarked on trying to leave the EU,' Hague said in an interview.[40] The UK would have checked EU amalgamation. 'You couldn't say any longer that the British public hadn't been consulted,' said Hague, referencing an argument that Brexiteers would make.[41]

David Cameron thinks similarly, calling the lack of a vote on Lisbon 'absolutely crucial' to what came next. 'In understanding the Conservative psyche about the referendum, you have to understand there was such a sense of disappointment that we didn't get the referendum that we were promised and deserved on the Lisbon Treaty,' Cameron said. If there had been such a vote 'the world would be a very different place'.[42]

Chance played a part too. If the Conservatives took power when the Lisbon Treaty issue was still live, a referendum could be held. But if all member states had already ratified the deal, it would be much harder to hold such a vote. In 2009, the year before the election in which the Tories were frontrunners, there was a major roadblock in the path to ratification in the form of Václav Klaus, president of the Czech Republic and a staunch Eurosceptic. Almost every other member state had ratified Lisbon. The Czech Parliament had approved it. But Klaus was holding out.

That summer Hague went on a secret visit hoping to persuade Klaus not to sign. 'I sat alone with him in Prague Castle imploring him,' said Hague, whose message was 'hold out until the following May when we thought we'd win an election'.[43] Cameron tried too, writing Klaus a letter whose core message was: 'You've just got to cling on, the cavalry is coming.'[44] But the timings were just too tight. Klaus told Hague the Czech Parliament could impeach him before the UK election arrived. He ratified the deal in November 2009. Cameron dropped his Lisbon referendum promise, deeming it undeliverable, giving a promise of a vote on future treaty change instead. Just six months later, in May 2010, he became prime minister. The sliding door had slammed shut.

The road from this point to Cameron announcing the in/out referendum in January 2013 via the Bloomberg speech is a winding one. But, in retrospect, four driving forces stand out: two are party political, the others wider changes that went beyond Britain.

The influence of the Conservative Party's Eurosceptic hardliners, and Cameron's tendency to move towards their demands even while decrying them, runs through the Brexit story like letters through a stick of rock. And in the early coalition years, that group latched onto a new demand: a straight vote on EU membership. The years-long battle over the EU Constitution and the Lisbon Treaty was over. Cameron's 'referendum lock' promise of a vote when the treaties were changed next had no date attached. And so a crusade for an all-or-nothing moment was launched.

The critical point came in October 2011. The pressure had been building since the election, with twenty-two backbench rebellions over Europe involving sixty Tory MPs already seen.[45] It ratcheted up further with a petition for a referendum on EU membership which had secured 100,000 signatures. And then, with a House of Commons motion for a referendum from Tory backbencher David Nuttall, it came to a head. Backbench votes are not binding on government policy, but Cameron nonetheless tried to enforce his authority and ordered his whips to stop Tory MPs voting for it. Some were threatened with being locked out of ministerial office for four years or even deselection.[46] And yet eighty-one Tory MPs backed the motion – the biggest Commons rebellion on Europe since the Second World War. Such a large number of Tories had not defied the whip even at the nadir of John Major's Maastricht battles.

Jacob Rees-Mogg, only in his second year as an MP, was among the eighty-one. He believed Cameron's attempted show of strength was a miscalculation. 'They managed to turn it into a signal of whether or not you were a Eurosceptic,' Rees-Mogg said of that clash. 'They over-whipped it, so if you were a Eurosceptic you couldn't not be part of the eighty-one.'[47]

The shock waves were felt throughout government. 'What the hell,' David Lidington, the Europe minister, thought when he heard the number.[48] Cameron believed as many as 120 Tory MPs would have backed the motion proposing a referendum without a whipping operation, though later admitted his tactics had been 'cack-handed'.[49] For him, it underscored how the appeal of an in/out vote had grown beyond the 'usual suspects', with even 'younger, liberal' Tory MPs feeling bound to the concept of a referendum after the Lisbon debacle. 'It showed the extent to which the ground was moving beneath us,' Cameron said.[50] Tim Shipman, the political journalist whose book *All Out War* is the definitive account of the Brexit vote, called it 'the moment a referendum became inevitable'.[51]

That turbulence was exacerbated by another figure gleefully rocking the boat. Nigel Farage, the leader of Ukip, revelled in his role as the Tories' tormentor-in-chief. With a clubbable 'man of the people' persona and a smoker's laugh, Farage presented himself as the politician with whom voters would most like to share a pint. His hard-right views on immigration and crime were condemned in Westminster but tapped into a resentment at the status quo which, in 2016, would prove much wider than the bubble realised. On the EU, his 'time to go' message had a simple appeal to Europhobes that Cameron's fudged compromise could not match.

In the UK result of the 2009 European Parliament elections Ukip had come second, winning almost one in six votes. The 2010 general election failed to deliver a breakthrough – Farage had briefly given up the leadership to Lord Pearson – but with the coalition's birth Ukip began to rise in the polls. By the autumn of 2012 it was the country's third most popular party, with the Lib Dems no longer getting protest votes after entering government. Ukip came second in by-elections in Rotherham and Middlesbrough that November. The Tories came fourth and fifth respectively.

The surge set nerves jangling in Downing Street. Cameron's pollster Andrew Cooper believed it was likely Ukip would win the 2014 European Parliament elections in the UK – which they did – at which time a referendum would be forced upon the prime minister. 'Since it is a question of when, not if, let's do it now, let's do it calmly and set out a proper argument,' Cooper recalled telling Cameron.[52] The prime minister's aides feared that without a referendum promise Cameron would have faced a leadership challenge when Ukip won in 2014.[53]

Farage believes he cornered Cameron. 'He had no choice, the insurgency was on. It was happening,' the former Ukip leader said in an interview. 'We professionalised the party, we were coming second in every by-election, we were absolutely on the march. Tory Association chairmen, current and ex, were joining us all over the country.' He added: 'We terrorised the Conservative Party.'[54] Every party leader likes to inflate their own influence. But the facts do suggest that no politician, barring perhaps Cameron, can claim more direct credit for bringing about the referendum than Farage.

Those two party-political realities – the fracturing of the Tories over a referendum and Ukip's momentum – were entwined with two wider developments. One was the surge in immigration. Cameron had vowed to get net migration – the number of people moving to the UK each year minus the total of those moving abroad – into the 'tens of thousands' in his 2010 election manifesto. Yet the numbers were going in the other direction. Official net migration rose from 177,000 in 2012 to 209,000 in 2013 and then 318,000 in 2014 – three times higher than the target of below 100,000.[55]

The problem was not just the erosion of trust in Cameron and his promises. It shone a light on what many Leave and Remain campaign figures years later would still see as the key issue that led to Brexit: frustration at EU free movement rules. These meant that every EU citizen had the right to move to Britain. Tony Blair's decision not to adopt transitional controls to limit access to the UK labour market temporarily when eight nations, many from Eastern Europe, joined the EU in 2004 sent immigration soaring in the years that followed. Mats Persson, then the Open Europe director who would go on to advise Cameron on the issue, believed the Brexit vote could best be explained by two numbers: thirteen thousand a year, the Blair government's net immigration estimate from the accession countries; and a million, the number of people who actually came in the decade that followed.[56] Migration would rise up the news agenda in the years leading up to the referendum, especially when the Syrian civil war triggered the flight of refugees towards Europe. Before that, though, concerns about immigration were driving support for Ukip and raising tricky questions about EU membership.

The second force beyond Cameron's control was the eurozone debt crisis, which struck in 2009. It too fed into migration, with the relative success of the UK economy afterwards acting as a pull factor. To Eurosceptic eyes, the problems appeared to confirm everything they had claimed about the inherent weakness of the single currency, the folly of 'ever closer union' and how other members were supposedly holding Britain back.

It also led to a moment of intense disillusionment for David Cameron. Attempts to secure assurances that Britain would not be disadvantaged by moves to bail out struggling eurozone countries came to a head in a European Council meeting in December 2011. With his vows to oppose treaty change being ignored as the leaders debated late into the night, Cameron, at some point between 3 a.m. and 5 a.m., made clear he would veto the move. At home, he was hailed as a conquering hero by the Tory Eurosceptics. In reality, he had been outmanoeuvred: the other EU leaders simply delivered the same outcome outside the EU treaties. It showed UK opposition could be ignored, just as the critics claimed. 'The volcano had erupted,' Cameron realised. 'All I could see ahead of me was the magma of chaos.'[57]

Christmas followed, and then New Year. Recording thoughts in January 2012 on tape – a practice Cameron adopted with a future memoir in mind – an idea was beginning to take root. The words are quoted in his book, *For the Record*. Cameron considers them among the most important in that text for understanding what came next. 'My long-term view is that Europe is changing and Britain is changing in its relationship to Europe because of the creation of the euro and a multi-speed Europe,' Cameron said. He went on: 'At some stage, altering Britain's relationship with the European Union in some regards and then putting it to a referendum I think would be good Conservative policy for the next Parliament.'[58] It would be a year before the idea would be fully formed, ready to be unveiled to the public. But the seed had been planted.

★

Throughout 2012 Cameron would mull over what to do. The considerations swirled: the pressure from Tory rebels, the electoral threat from Ukip, the risks and rewards of an in/out vote, all tied up with the more immediate challenge of winning the 2015 general election. By the end of the year the circle in the know would widen, but at first it was just his core team, including those who had struck the Liberal Democrat deal that handed him power in the first place.

William Hague, the foreign secretary, had wrestled the Tories' Europe alligator for four long years as party leader and was firmly in the yes camp when it came to calling a referendum. 'I thought there was electoral calculation,' Hague said, acknowledging that the need to win votes from Ukip was a factor. 'I wasn't a candidate in the 2015 election but I campaigned as an outgoing Cabinet minister. I was basically deployed to all those east coast seats. Kent, Lincolnshire. Pitched battles with Ukip, all of which we won except for one [Clacton]. And we would've lost them, though, without the referendum.' Secondly, he could see the party management point. 'It was, ironically, trying to keep the Conservative family together because it was going to fracture internally seriously without a referendum. Thirdly, and here we were wrong, we thought we could get some actual, meaningful concessions from the EU.'[59]

That meant one inner-circle member was on board. So too was another: Ed Llewellyn, Cameron's trusted chief of staff. A conversation the trio had together at a pizza restaurant at Chicago's O'Hare International Airport in May 2012, returning from a Nato summit, has entered the history books as a key moment when Cameron's mind began to set.

But not everyone was supportive. George Osborne, Cameron's closest friend and ally in the Commons, the co-author of his modernisation project, was against the move. 'What's true is that the Conservative Party had been feeding this narrative of betrayal by Europe for some time and this idea of a referendum had entered the bloodstream,' Osborne said in an interview. 'But [referendums] had become a device that both parties had used to say something instead of having an argument on the substance.'[60] Osborne, whom Cameron has called unrivalled as a Tory 'master tactician' and 'strategic' thinker, saw pitfalls in such a black and white choice.[61] 'My argument was that it would put the business community offside, it would split our party and we might lose,' Osborne said.[62] It was the most significant clash of the pair's time in government and testament to the strength of their friendship that it remained private.

Another Cameroon was also against – though, unlike Osborne, one drawn to Brexit. Michael Gove was then a political confidant of the prime minister, among the few who would often gather at Cameron's flat on Sunday nights to talk through the week ahead. 'I did think that the referendum would be a bad idea,' Gove told the author.

> There were several reasons for that. One of them was I thought, 'If there is a referendum I'll almost certainly if put to the test have to say no, i.e., that we should leave. And that means that I will almost certainly be on the opposite side to David and to others, which is something which I personally wish to avoid.' Also, I was not certain that a referendum was the answer.[63]

So warnings were delivered, but ultimately rejected. On the morning of 23 January 2013 Cameron rose to give the speech that would bind his hands. 'This morning I want to talk about the future of Europe,' the prime minister began, addressing an audience in the London headquarters of financial news service Bloomberg. What followed across 5,700 words displayed Cameron's logical way of thinking: a tightly constructed argument, carefully worded and leading remorselessly to the conclusion that he believed, with typical self-assurance, to be the right one.

The key section of the speech read:

> The next Conservative manifesto in 2015 will ask for a mandate from the British people for a Conservative government to negotiate a new settlement with our European partners in the next parliament. It will be a relationship with the single market at its heart.
>
> And when we have negotiated that new settlement, we will give the British people a referendum with a very simple in or out choice. To stay in the EU on these new terms; or come out altogether. It will be an in/out referendum.
>
> Legislation will be drafted before the next election. And if a Conservative government is elected we will introduce the enabling

legislation immediately and pass it by the end of that year. And we will complete this negotiation and hold this referendum within the first half of the next parliament.

He added, with a rhetorical flourish not unlike that deployed by Tony Blair all those years ago: 'It is time for the British people to have their say. It is time to settle this European question in British politics.'

So there it was. The Eurosceptics' demand had been met: a straight in/out referendum. There was a time limit: a vote by the end of 2017 if the Tories won a majority in the 2015 election. There would also be a chance to renegotiate the UK's terms of membership first. The prime minister made clear which way he leaned, saying he wanted a deal that 'keeps us in'. But every Tory politician would have to pick a side. The question was asked – coming up with an answer, when the time came, could not be dodged. Cameron had once told his party to stop 'banging on about Europe'. Now he was handing out megaphones.[64]

Could another decision have been taken? Cameron defended his call:

If you posit a world in which there was no referendum pledge in 2013, do you really think we would have got to the 2015 election without one? No. And even if we did, the next leader of the Conservative Party would have had a referendum pledge probably supporting 'out' in an in/out referendum. It wasn't just the way the Conservative Party was going, it was the way Europe was going. These two things in my view argue for that policy.[65]

But Osborne, Cameron's right-hand man, disagreed:

There was no doubt that Europe was going to be messy, but it didn't mean we had to concede a referendum. We were very powerful, at that point, in terms of leading our party. You could have just played it long . . . I'm not saying any of it was easy to deal with. But you could have gone on managing it, rather than saying: 'OK, let's have a fight.'[66]

★

Even with the decision taken, there were countless other forks in the road to Brexit. Some saw Cameron pushed along one way by forces beyond his full control. At others, choices were made knowingly and deliberately, whether or not the consequences were correctly weighed. These are moments that still replay over and over in the heads of those in Number 10 at the time. There are no definitive answers to their ifs and maybes, but they are important to the wider picture.

For starters, there was the 2015 general election. A Conservative majority was no certainty – in fact, all sides were braced for a hung parliament. Cameron and Nick Clegg had both thought through the possibility of the coalition's continuation. So if there had been another Tory–Lib Dem pact, would Cameron's promise of an in/ out referendum have survived?

Some key players believe not. Oliver Letwin, who was central to the 2010 coalition talks, is one. 'There would not have been a referendum,' he said of a 2015 Tory–Lib Dem coalition, noting potential get-outs such as holding a free MP vote on a referendum which would likely have fallen short.[67] Another figure in Cameron's Cabinet believed the Lib Dems would have been used by the leadership as cover for dropping the promise. Senior Lib Dems also insisted they would have blocked the pledge. 'We wouldn't have gone in unless it had been dropped,' said Danny Alexander, one of the four most senior coalition figures as a member of the 'Quad'.[68] Donald Tusk, the European Council president, even claimed Cameron had said likewise. 'He felt really safe, because he thought at the same time that there's no risk of a referendum, because his coalition partner, the Liberals, would block this idea of a referendum,' Tusk said in a 2019 documentary – an allegation flatly denied by Cameron's team.[69]

Cameron, however, dismissed the suggestions, noting that he repeatedly said the vote was a red line for talks during the 2015 election campaign. 'This couldn't have been dropped unless I was dropped,' he told the author.

Everyone's forgotten the 'red line' nature of my pledge, which is very important. I said before the election that there were certain things that had to happen, or I would not be prime minister. So the idea that we made the pledge thinking we would have a coalition, so it wouldn't happen, is clearly not true.[70]

Osborne echoed this position, saying Cameron was 'not looking for a way out'.[71]

In the event, it did not matter: the Tories won their majority. At which point other decisions loomed.

One was firmly in Cameron's gift: the date of the referendum. He had a two-and-a-half-year period to choose from, between the May 2015 election and the end of 2017. That was the deadline outlined in the Bloomberg speech, one adopted primarily to make voters believe in the promise. In the end, 23 June 2016 was selected. Members of Cameron's Downing Street have long mulled over the call. A snap referendum was out of the question. Cameron had committed to a renegotiation first and for a reason – a status quo EU was even more likely to be rejected by Britons, according to the polling; moreover, Cameron genuinely believed in the need for reform. But would going later have been wiser? The migration crisis triggered by the Syrian civil war forced the issue up the news agenda as the vote approached. One million migrants arrived in Europe in 2015, according to International Organization for Migration (IOM) estimates: three to four times more than the year before.[72] Thousands of people lost their lives crossing the Mediterranean, tragedies told on nightly news broadcasts and in the pages of daily newspapers. In March 2016, three months before the referendum, the EU struck a deal for asylum-seekers to remain in Turkey. A stark drop in the numbers would follow – but only after voters had already picked Brexit.

But there were also reasons not to wait until 2017. The French presidential elections and German federal elections were both due to take place that year, and the political space for EU compromises was always squeezed as leaders fought for re-election. The danger was that Cameron's renegotiation would get stuck in the slowdown: a possibility the UK's man in Brussels, Ivan Rogers, made plain in his advice.[73] And then there was the spectre of the midterm blues. Would Cameron, sure to be Remain's lead voice, really be more popular a year further away from his election win?

Cameron, looking back, remained open-minded:

There's a perfectly good case for saying, well, maybe we should have held it in 2017 rather than 2016. It didn't feel like that at the time. How is your authority going to be better? The economy was doing well in 2016. What was going to happen in 2017? But there's no point, if you lose a referendum, saying: 'I got all the decisions right.' It's worth thinking about these things.[74]

Another idea was pushed by some Tories: why not do a Harold Wilson? The Labour prime minister had made a show of stepping back in the 1975 referendum to confirm UK membership of the European Community and limiting his personal campaigning, despite wanting a Yes vote. Gavin Williamson, Cameron's eyes and ears in the Commons as his parliamentary private secretary, suggested this approach, believing it would help his boss's 'survival' chances whatever the result. But Cameron waved it away: 'Something as significant as this, you can't be a prime minister without an opinion.'[75] Iain Duncan Smith, the former Tory leader, was another who suggested the idea.[76] Copying Wilson might have helped Cameron stay on after the Brexit vote, whatever the outcome, but proving that it would have boosted the Remain cause is much trickier.

And then there were the 'what ifs' of the renegotiation itself. Cameron launched into a tour of European capitals almost straight after his triumphant 2015 re-election, determined to win over his counterparts one-to-one in the scramble for concessions. The talks would come to a head in a European Council meeting in February 2016. He was pushing for items in four 'baskets': sovereignty, competitiveness, protection from the eurozone and immigration. It was the fourth issue that was most closely tracked by politicians and the press.

The broad approach had been laid out back in the Bloomberg speech. And yet immigration had not even been mentioned in that text – an error Cameron later conceded, and a reminder of how sharply the issue rose up the political agenda as the Syrian civil war dragged on.[77] To make amends, Cameron delivered a speech on immigration in November 2014, triggering a heated Whitehall clash. Theresa May's Home Office initially wanted quotas: that is, a cap on how many EU citizens could move to the UK each year. But that was a clear breach of the so-called 'four freedoms' on which the bloc was founded: the free movement of goods, capital, services and people. So it morphed into an 'emergency brake', a temporary limit on numbers if immigration hit a certain level. Downing Street endlessly debated adopting this alternative policy. Would the EU agree to it? Instinctively it would not, but was it worth going all in for such a deal anyway?

Cameron decided not after personally sounding out Angela Merkel, the German chancellor, whose support his entire renegotiation strategy was pinned on, in late 2014. 'She goes sort of purple in the face,' recalled Ivan Rogers, Britain's EU ambassador who was in the room for the meeting. 'This is like swearing in church. This is an East German woman who's lived behind the Iron Curtain for the first thirty-five years of her life. There are some things she has a very, very fundamental belief in. Free movement is one of them.' Her response, in Rogers's retelling, was categorical: 'No, no, no. No way, David. Never.'[78] The emergency brake was dropped from the November 2014 speech, replaced by a variety of more limited demands to scale back EU migrant access to benefits from the UK welfare state – which, in turn, would get watered down in the talks.

Would an emergency brake have helped win over Eurosceptics? To a degree. Cameron was left exposed to the realities of free movement in the campaign. More EU critics waited until the renegotiation played out before making a call than is commonly remembered. Rees-Mogg, who would become one of the best-known Brexiteers, was among them: 'It was totemic. If he could have got some change in free movement of people, then the EU was reformable and we could stay in it. If he couldn't get anything, then actually it was a behemoth that was not going to change.'[79] But was it even achievable? David Lidington, the Remain-backing Europe minister, who pushed again at the 2015 Tory conference for the idea to be adopted, thought possibly so: 'I've always held to the view that the emergency brake we perhaps could have had in our initial negotiating position. I thought it was at the outer limit of what might be attainable.'[80] Cameron has argued that the gamble of betting everything on getting an emergency brake, then failing, was too great. A lunch in Florence in the summer of 2022 with Matteo Renzi, Italy's prime minister during the talks, eased his mind. 'If you think you could have got anything more out of the EU Council in your referendum, you are completely wrong,' Renzi said, in Cameron's retelling.[81]

Other ideas were floated. What if Cameron had stormed out of the renegotiation altogether? That was what Lynton Crosby, the strategist who masterminded his 2015 election success, recommended, both to get a better deal and to show the country he was playing hardball. 'If you don't ever fight, people don't notice,' Crosby argued at the time. But the prime minister bristled and waved it away: 'That's not me, I'm a reasonable person.'[82] Instead he declared victory at the February 2016 European Council, striding into a press conference beamed live to the nation via the *BBC News at Ten* to reveal that a deal had been struck. It had, indeed – and it was brutally panned by the Eurosceptic press in the days that followed as much too little, far too late.

The renegotiation was meant to be a strength, the ace up Cameron's sleeve that he could produce to convince voters that Britain's place in the EU had changed. Instead, it turned out to be a joker, ridiculed and all but discarded by the prime minister as an argument when the campaign began in earnest. To some, the process appeared counterproductive, reminding many Britons why they disliked the bloc. Voters saw a prime minister go to European leaders with a begging bowl and get precious little, the argument went. Every EU citizen could still move to the UK under the new deal, just like before. Brexiteers came to see the deal as strengthening not Cameron's hand but their own.

Looking back in interviews with the author, Osborne and Cameron, Remain's joint chiefs, have one specific renegotiation regret: raising expectations. 'We should have done a much better job at laying the ground,' said Osborne.

> We set on this idea that we would negotiate a better deal out of Europe. I actually think we got quite a lot out of that negotiation but it obviously didn't satisfy anyone. And then we went into the referendum campaign not having really made the argument consistently for Europe for more than about two or three weeks. We had to switch from 'these bastards aren't giving us what we want' to 'oh yes, we've got to stay, really'.[83]

Cameron said the same thing. 'I didn't do enough to keep expectations under control. We needed to do a better job of saying, "We're
having this renegotiation. Let's be clear about what is completely
not achievable."'[84]

But such hand-wringing was for later. The referendum campaign
proper had arrived, and it was time to pick a side. All eyes were on
two well-known Tories whose decisions were still hanging in the
balance.

There is near-unanimity from figures who ran both the Remain
and Leave campaigns that the two most consequential endorsements
were from Michael Gove and Boris Johnson. In the forty-eight hours
after Cameron's EU deal reveal on 19 February 2016, both men
would declare for out. Gove brought an intellectual heft and ministerial clout that gave permission to fellow Tories to step into the
Leave camp, plus strategic nous. Boris was to be the campaign star,
hoisting Cornish pasties aloft and touring Midlands knicker factories
with a Brexit bravado that warmed wavering voters. These qualities
explain why Cameron and Osborne poured their efforts into trying
to win both men to their side. Osborne later concluded that one
of their great strategic blunders was scheduling the vote before Gove
and Johnson were locked in for Remain. 'We should never have
pushed the button on the referendum without knowing where they
were,' he said.[85]

Johnson and Gove held different positions in the Cameron orbit
then. Appreciating such nuances is critical when weighing the significance of their decisions and motivations. Gove, unlike Boris, was
considered by David Cameron to be one of his 'best friends'.[86] Their
wives, Samantha Cameron and Sarah Vine, had a strong bond too.
Vine was godmother to the Camerons' daughter Florence, with the
families' children growing up in each other's houses. The political
links were just as strong. Cameron had helped persuade Gove to
leave *The Times* and enter the arena as an MP. Gove had a seat at
the top table for the Cameron modernisation project in opposition,
both men like-minded about how the party had to change. In office,
Cameron had Gove attend Prime Minister's Questions briefings,
trusting his political instincts and one-liners. It made the split, when

it came, all the more brutal. 'Betrayal' was the word long used by some Cameron loyalists.[87]

Their relationship had already taken a major dent before the referendum. It came in July 2014, with the next year's general election getting closer. Lynton Crosby, of 'scrape the barnacles off the boat' fame, had concerns. Downing Street thought the free school reforms Gove pushed through as education secretary should have been one of their crown-jewel reforms, but his unpopularity turned parents against them. Crosby spelled out to Cameron how bad the polling numbers were, the indication being it was time for the chop. Gove was summoned for a drink with Cameron and told he would be moved to chief whip, which had no public-facing duties. Gove was not 'overjoyed' but accepted at first, only to try to walk it back the next morning. 'No, that's it. It's done' was the thrust of Cameron's response.[88] Anger was captured in a tweet from Gove's wife Sarah Vine, who shared a *Daily Mail* article which declared: 'A shabby day's work which Cameron will live to regret.'

There was another difference between Gove and Boris: the former had long indicated that if push came to shove he would side with quitting the EU. Gove traced his Euroscepticism back to his upbringing in Aberdeen and its declining fishing industry. In 1983, as a teenager, he had supported Michael Foot's Labour, which called for withdrawal from the European Community, while at *The Times* he called Britain's place in the EU a 'historical aberration'. As a minister he would oppose policy changes flagged in 'write-rounds', only to be told that EU membership meant they must happen. Indeed, he had warned Cameron against holding a referendum, knowing his own instincts.

But Cameron still deemed him persuadable. 'The most difficult thing was knowing that it would cause a rupture,' Gove said in an interview. 'I remember turning over in my mind whether or not it would be possible to secure the sort of deal that would allow us to say: "Well, this is the best of all worlds." I allowed myself to think that it was possible.' There were other factors.

> The other fear very much in my mind was that once you've had a referendum and said, 'Yes,' then that's it, you've played your cards.

You may have been stroppy, you may have made certain demands, but at that point, once a referendum is concluded, then the EU could then say: 'Right, that's it.'[89]

So when the deal was done, without an emergency brake on immigration or anything curbing the reach of the European Court of Justice, Gove joined Vote Leave, which would be the official Brexit campaign.

According to his friends, Cameron had always suspected Johnson might come out for Brexit given the potential career benefits. But the Gove defection triggered cold rage. 'I always knew Boris was a shit, but I didn't realise Gove was a shit,' two sources remember Cameron saying at one point.[90] 'I just can't believe he did it. I can't believe he did it,' Cameron would repeat like a mantra, a friend recalled.[91] A fellow minister said it was 'very obvious' the 'blow' the news had caused, describing Cameron as looking more 'downbeat' and 'careworn' afterwards.[92] Even the Gove and Cameron family play dates were cancelled, according to a Downing Street insider.[93]

The anger would be fuelled by what the prime minister perceived as misdirection on the part of Gove and his wife. Cameron believed Vine had indicated when they all shared New Year's Eve together in 2015 that her husband would end up backing Remain.[94] Gove, warned by other Cameron friends that he would be locking arms with Nigel Farage if he advocated Brexit, reassured them that he would not play a central role in the campaign. Looking back, Gove said that he can understand that perception of his intentions, but he argued it was only when Vote Leave senior figures pleaded with him to play a more central role that he agreed. 'I can entirely understand they'd be frustrated,' he said. 'I didn't make any promise or pledge but they were entirely within their rights to think that I wasn't going to be particularly active during the campaign because I'd shown no inclination.'[95]

Gove also acknowledged the impact his decision had on his friendship with Cameron. 'Initially it was a bit difficult, but it just got more and more difficult during the course of the campaign,' he said.[96] Cameron hinted as much, saying Gove had been 'not just a friend but he was very much part of the internal working of the government' too.[97] Neither man, in their interviews with the author, appeared keen to dwell on the topic. But one of Cameron's closest political friends, speaking off the record, was more candid. Gove going against Cameron was 'devastating', the source said. 'It's deep. It hurts.' Time has since done much to heal the rift in the friendship their wives shared but not their own. 'They were really close and they're not now in the same way,' the source said. 'It's civil, but not more than that.'[98]

If the personal pain was stronger with Gove, politically it was Johnson who really cut through. The prize for Boris beyond the referendum – the one he had longed for after giving up his child-hood dreams of being 'world king' – was becoming prime minister. Cameron had upped the ante in his 2015 election campaign, casually telling BBC journalist James Lansdale that he would not seek a third term in Number 10 if he was successful. The remark, cursed by his friends as a blunder, put potential successors on notice after Cameron's win returned him to Downing Street. A new Conservative leader would thus be in place before the next election. The contest was coming. And in this prism, it is not Johnson's rivalry with Cameron that really matters, but that with the man to his right: George Osborne. Cameron, after all, had already beaten Johnson in the race to the top. He was the prime minister, regardless of Boris's head-scratching about how he had been leapfrogged by an underling. The competition with real bite, Cameroons of all shades agree, was with Osborne. It was an issue of succession – of who would follow Dave.

Those who saw the relationship up close recall verbal jousting, often tongue-in-cheek and never with any direct reference made to the leadership question. It could take place in front of almost any backdrop. A familiar one was in the Treasury. During the coalition, Osborne undoubtedly had more power. He was ensconced in a great office of state, with easy access to the prime minister's ear and his hands on the money, while Boris was away from the Commons. Twice a year, as the chancellor prepared his fiscal statements, the London mayor would come looking for cash. 'It was hilarious,' recalled one Treasury insider who sat in on the meetings.

> Boris would turn up on his bike, a bit of a mess. He wouldn't be
> with his aides, because obviously they'd come on the Tube. He'd get

out a scrumpled bit of briefing note that he had been given, but he'd never really get to it. Osborne was always really well prepared. He already knew what he was going to give Boris, but he enjoyed the game of running rings around him.[99]

Osborne would mock Johnson's pet projects, like the money spent on the little-used cable car across the Thames or the ArcelorMittal Orbit sculpture in the Olympic Park. Eddie Lister, Johnson's deputy mayor, who would later follow him to Downing Street, said his boss actually dedicated much time to determining what demands he should make, but recalled the same joshing. 'I found them highly entertaining,' Lister said. 'It would always be about thirty minutes of real knockabout. Then we'd settle down, and usually we won a couple of items that were on the shopping list. George always gave him something.'[100]

A similar scene would play out at Davos, the Alpine retreat that every year hosts the great and the good of business and politics for the World Economic Forum. At one masters-of-the-universe drinks do at a vast villa on the town's outskirts, Osborne was already inside when Johnson arrived. 'Everybody, here comes the leader of the municipal government in the United Kingdom!' Osborne declared with faux-fanfare, according to Will Walden, who was present. Boris roared with laughter, slapped his fellow Tory on the back and offered to get him a glass of wine. Osborne accepted, Johnson scurried off but returned with just one drink in hand, which he proceeded to sip. 'It was a riposte,' said Walden.[101] On another occasion, in January 2015, Johnson was frustrated at having been snubbed by Davos, with mayors left off the invitation list. His pleading with the organisers fell on deaf ears. And so a plan was cooked up to steal the headlines from Osborne and Cameron, who were of course on the list. 'We had a week,' recalled Lister. 'We thought: "Well, what are we going to do?" because there was always rivalry between him and George and Dave. So we said: "We've got to find somewhere to go, to do something." And, of course, that's when he went off to northern Iraq.' A photograph of Johnson, squinting down the barrel of an AK-47 during his visit to see British troops, was splashed across the front pages of the papers. The Foreign Office was 'furious', Lister said.[102] But the Davos pics of a besuited Osborne had been trumped.

No space was too small or remote for their ego-sniping, or worse. For example, a lift in Hong Kong. The pair were on a trade-boosting trip to China – these were the days of Osborne's self-proclaimed 'golden era' in Sino-British relations – and had ended up at a private dining club. It had been back-and-forth all night, according to Walden. Osborne would mock the 'Boris Island' plan for an airport on the Thames estuary; Johnson would counter: 'They're going to land on the sea, matey!' And on and on. As the night wound up, the two men and their two aides headed out. 'For some reason another quip was made about the airport and they ended up having a wrestling match in the lift,' Walden recalled. He and his counterpart watched in astonishment as the two men grappled like teenagers in a play fight. 'And then the lift hit zero and went "ping". The doors opened and literally they walked straight out.'[103]

Their bickering could even reach the subterranean. When they visited a Battle of Britain bunker together in Uxbridge, Johnson's parliamentary constituency, a project to which Osborne had given £1 million of new investment, the pair spent their time pushing military units around with long wooden sticks on a huge battlefield map. The scene spoke to Osborne's mischievous side – the press had been invited – but things were getting serious now. It was September 2015: after the Tory victory, after Cameron's revelation he would not seek a third term and at a point when Johnson and Osborne were seen as the two most likely successors. 'They were shoving military pieces around and playing emperor,' recalled one who was present.[104] 'The whole thing in the bunker was very quippy,' said a second.[105]

Such antics made for wonderful copy for the hacks. But the wisecracks belied a race for the top that became tied up with a matter of critical importance to the country – the Brexit debate. As the vote approached, every politician was forced to make a choice. Osborne had already picked his side. He would not just be for Remain but would be leading the charge, dropping bombs from the Treasury to secure a win. Yet Tory members, polls suggested, were clearly leaning towards Leave. Going that way gave leadership hopefuls – say, Boris Johnson – the chance to become the hero of the grassroots, regardless of whether the referendum was ultimately won or lost. And it was the members who would pick Cameron's successor.

Five months after that scene of bunker bonhomie, Johnson came out for Brexit. On the political battlefield, Boris and Osborne – for the first time in their careers – were now fighting on opposite sides.

The decision would have mattered little if Boris had not played a central role in the campaign. Or if one side had won by a mile. But neither was the case. Johnson became the face of Brexit and Leave won by a nose: 51.9 per cent of the vote to 48.1 per cent, a gap of less than 4 percentage points. If 635,000 Leave voters (out of 33.6 million people who cast a ballot) had ticked the box for Remain, Brexit would have been quashed. It is in that context that Johnson's choice – that swirl of ambition and rivalry and belief and calculation – gets its significance.

Which begs a question. If Johnson had backed and campaigned for Remain, would Remain have won? It is impossible to know. And yet a remarkable number of senior politicians, strategists and advisers on either side of the debate believe the answer is yes. Step back and consider the significance of that. The biggest change in direction for the UK in more than forty years, an outcome with incalculable consequences for the country's 67 million people, may have come down to which way just one man decided to jump.

Some of those who think the Brexit vote might have turned out differently if Boris had gone the other way are leading Remainers. David Cameron for one: 'That's unknowable, but I think there's a case for saying yes.'[106] William Hague: 'I think it's a given. How narrow it was and how much he energised that campaign.'[107] Ivan Rogers, Britain's EU ambassador: 'He's got charisma, he cuts through to people'; 'Boris coming out against them was crucial.'[108] Andrew Feldman, the Conservative Party chairman: 'One hundred per cent. Who was going to be the standard-bearer? Farage was a marginal figure.'[109]

Leading Brexiteers have also reached the same conclusion. Michael Gove: 'He sent a 4,000-volt charge through the campaign. It's difficult to know but I suspect we probably wouldn't have won if Boris hadn't endorsed Leave.'[110] Jacob Rees-Mogg: 'Yes, I think Boris made the difference'; 'he brought popular appeal and he appealed to voters who wouldn't open the door to Nigel Farage.'[111] Matthew Elliott, the Vote Leave chief executive: 'Boris's net worth is way more than

2 percentage points for sure'; 'he could sell Brexit like nobody else could and paint that sunny, optimistic picture of what Britain would be like outside the EU.'[112] Eddie Lister, Johnson's mayoral deputy: 'Yes, totally convinced about it.'[113] Paul Stephenson, the Vote Leave communications director: 'People loved Boris. He was a rock star.'[114]

Some do disagree. David Davis, the former Brexit secretary, is one: 'I don't think it made any difference.'[115] Theresa Villiers, one of six members of Cameron's Cabinet to back Brexit, is another.[116] Lynton Crosby also doubts the claim.[117] But even Farage, who would have reasons of vanity for playing Johnson's influence down, is open to the idea that Brexit might not have happened with Boris on the other side. 'It would have been a lot closer and possibly against,' Farage told the author. 'I've never, ever denied that it was important that he came on board.'[118]

Which leads to a second question, the answer to which is also unknowable but is much more pointed. Did Johnson really believe leaving the EU was the best outcome for the country when he campaigned for it? Or, put another way: did he declare for Brexit to boost his chances of winning the looming Tory leadership race, rather than for the good of the UK? Here views are split much more neatly along the referendum dividing lines.

One of the half dozen most senior Remain figures is convinced:

I would happily bet anything, including my life, that Boris Johnson didn't want to leave the EU and is not somebody who believes we should have left the EU. He may be rationalising that now, but that was absolutely not his position in 2016. As people who had been ruthlessly focused on power for all those years, we had forgotten someone else might be ruthlessly focused on power.

William Hague agreed when the words were put to him. 'Yes. I subscribe to that view,' he said, adding: 'Boris calculated the ideal thing was if David Cameron won the referendum and he had been prominent in the opposition to it, and then he'd be superbly placed for the future leadership.'[119]

Cameron's view is already on record. He writes in his memoir that Johnson's worries about the reach of European courts in Britain was secondary to another concern – 'what was the best outcome for him'. His account continues:

> I could almost see his thought process take shape. Whichever senior Tory politician took the lead on the Brexit side – so loaded with images of patriotism, independence and romance – would become the darling of the party. He didn't want to risk allowing someone else with a high profile – Michael Gove in particular – to win that crown.[120]

Others echo Cameron's claim off the record. One minister involved in Remain efforts who is now deeply disillusioned with Johnson and his role in the debate had a particularly strong view on the matter: 'Whether a policy is in the national interest or not is of little importance to Boris I think the only abiding principle that he has followed is that of how to advance his own destiny.'[121] Johnson picked his side the day after Gove went public.

Brexiteers reject the accusation in equally strident terms. Rees-Mogg called the suggestion 'absolute nonsense', adding: 'He'd spent twenty years pointing out how ridiculous the EU was.'[122] Elliott said he was '100 per cent' certain Johnson thought Brexit was the right decision for Britain.[123] Gove thought similarly:

> He believed it and believes it. Now, was it the case that he may have thought that he had a better chance becoming prime minister one day if he backed Leave whether or not Leave won? I'm sure he did. However, the act of writing two articles, which people are cynical about, I can completely understand. That's one of the ways in which he makes up his mind . . . I'm sure that he felt that making the argument to stay was not where his heart was.[124]

Two further realities add weight to that case. Many Eurosceptics did leave it late to pick a side, including those who, like Johnson, had previously never publicly called for the UK to leave the EU. They include some high-profile Brexiteers such as Rees-Mogg and Iain Duncan Smith, who only declared their views when the renegotiation stalled.[125] A second was the stance of Johnson's then-wife, Marina Wheeler, who backed Leave. One friend of his said the influence she had on his thinking, noting how often he would reference her comments while weighing up his own view, has been underappreciated.[126]

In the end, Cameron would come to rue not just Johnson's decision but how many other Tories backed Brexit having never spoken up for it in the years before. 'It was my biggest miscalculation,' Cameron said. 'I just simply didn't see it. I'm too logical, I thought: if you've never argued for Brexit, why would you argue for it when there's a better deal on the table?'[127] But he had asked the question. He had forced the point. And now, with only a short campaigning period before the vote, the calls had been made.

During the years that Cameron and Osborne had toiled to keep Britain inside the European Union, there had, of course, been figures trying to achieve the opposite. The Leave campaign's story is more diffuse than that of Remain. Over the preceding twenty years Tory Euroscepticism had manifested itself in various guises: campaign bodies formed to oppose the euro or to force referendums on treaty change, or with looser groups arguing against integration and making tactical plays. Figures floating in that world thought of themselves as the 'Eurosceptic mafia'.[128] It was only after the 2015 election, with Cameron's unexpected win making the in/out vote a certainty, that the anti-Remain ultras began to form up.

Matthew Elliott was the instigator. He had successfully led the campaign against the Alternative Vote, the great Lib Dem coalition prize crushed in a 2011 referendum. He also had a track record of raising money from EU critics for like-minded organisations. Elliott appreciated that his strengths lay in being a backroom operator, not a campaign leader. He also knew who he wanted for the latter role: Dominic Cummings.

As political advisers with a public profile and notoriety go, Cummings cannot be beaten. None of the thousands of aides and officials in successive Tory governments since 2010 comes even close to being as well known. His role leading Vote Leave – as Matthew Elliott's outfit would be called – has been portrayed on the screen by Benedict Cumberbatch, who captured Cummings's physicality right down to the balding pate, Durham accent and maverick energy in the TV drama *Brexit: The Uncivil War*. Dom would go on to help construct and then tear down Boris Johnson's premiership.

Part of the reason Elliott approached Cummings, a fellow

Eurosceptic mafia member who had been an effective if combative special adviser to Michael Gove before leaving government in disillusionment, was because he needed a no-holds-barred campaigner. 'Dominic has a single-minded purpose to achieving objectives that very few other campaigners have,' Elliott explained in an interview.

> When you run a campaign, you are, of course, constrained by the law, but beyond that it's got to be a battle without limits. In the EU referendum, we needed to say it as it was about Cameron and the government's track record on migration and other issues. We couldn't think what repercussions there might be down the line for the Conservative Party, or future elections.[129]

There were countless battles to be won even before the final campaign sprint began. Some were in the Commons, where supportive MPs forced changes – such as the requirement for a 'purdah' period that bound the government's hands on spending that would help the Brexiteers' cause. Another was bouncing Cameron into letting some of his Cabinet ministers campaign for Leave despite the government's official Remain stance – which he did in the end, agreeing with reluctance to waive collective responsibility after Eurosceptic pressure.

A third, the dominant focus in the early months, was to win Vote Leave the designation as the official Brexit campaign. The key rival was Farage and Ukip donor Arron Banks's group, Leave.EU. The Tory-focused Grassroots Out (GO) would emerge later too. The battle between the Faragists and Vote Leave was bloody and has its own history. Cummings had considered a two-referendum strategy, an attempt to de-risk going for Leave in the first by offering a vote on the terms of renegotiated membership in a second, but the idea was dropped when the Kippers, as Farage's gang was nicknamed, weaponised it.[130] In the end, two months before the referendum, Vote Leave won the official designation and with it a donor cash boost at just the right time.

Cummings was the brains behind many of the campaign's most memorable moves.[131] 'Take back control', the slogan which figures on both sides admitted brilliantly captured the anti-status quo mood, was his idea. It began as 'Take control' and emerged from the focus groups that Cummings would hold over and over again. So too was Cummings behind the infamous campaign bus claim that 'We send the EU £350 million a week', using the figure for money going to Brussels without deducting the amount sent back in the UK's rebate.

In the early weeks of 2016, as the government intensified its attacks on Brexit, those in the Vote Leave headquarters in Millbank Tower, down the river from the Houses of Parliament, remember Cummings uttering the same reassurance: 'Don't worry, the cavalry is coming.'[132] He meant Gove and Johnson, two men he was personally attempting to sway, just as Cameron and Osborne were for the other side. There was already a band of Tories involved in Vote Leave. Daniel Hannan, the Conservative MEP dubbed an unsung hero of the Brexit cause, was on board early. So too were Eurosceptic old hands like the Tory MP Bernard Jenkin. Cummings had kept control throughout the ups and downs of the campaign, including a plot from the parliamentary brigade to oust him, thwarted when Vote Leave staff threatened to quit if Cummings was pushed out. And then, at last, the cavalry arrived. Gove was joined by five other Cabinet ministers who had defied Cameron: Iain Duncan Smith, John Whittingdale, Chris Grayling, Theresa Villiers and Priti Patel. And, in Johnson, the group had its frontman.

The formal referendum campaign had all the usual features: debates watched by millions, including one at Wembley Stadium; campaign buses, the Leave one usually containing Boris; attempts to dominate the airwaves with hyperbolic claims. The Remain campaign's strategy was essentially the one that had worked in the 2014 Scottish independence referendum and the unexpected 2015 Tory election win – focus on and amplify the financial consequences of voting the other way. Lynton Crosby, the architect of the Conservatives' 2015 triumph, had told Cameron and his team at an informal gathering at Chequers not to repeat this approach for the EU referendum. 'Do not ever say that again,' he had snapped at one adviser who admitted they were planning to repeat 'Project Fear'. 'You will lose if you start saying things like that.'[133] And yet that was the lever that the Remain campaigners pulled, most notably late on when Osborne threatened a post-Brexit 'emergency Budget' of tax hikes and swingeing spending cuts.

The Leave campaign had another tactic for making the headlines: to lean in on the blue-on-blue attacks. Its strategists knew that Johnson and Gove would be wary of directly attacking Cameron, so they set about eroding their reluctance. One day, when claims of strains in Boris's marriage reached the tabloids, senior Vote Leave figures pointed the finger at Downing Street. 'These people are fucking coming for you and your family,' one remembered Johnson being told. 'Right,' came the response from Boris. 'Well, how do we win?'[134] At another moment David Cameron did their work for them. In a Commons debate the day after Johnson declared for Leave, the prime minister took a swipe at his opponent's reported interest in a two-referendum strategy. 'I have known a number of couples who have begun divorce proceedings,' Cameron said, as Johnson – whose relationship troubles were well documented – sat behind him. 'But I do not know any who have begun divorce proceedings in order to renew their marriage vows.' According to one senior Vote Leave source: 'Boris then picked up the phone to Dom straight after and said, "We need a council of war. We need to get these fuckers."'[135]

Playing on existing Tory rivalries and bitternesses had benefits for Vote Leave. It was the story the press was most interested in – a dispiriting reflection of how the political hack-pack can work. It also encouraged the protagonists to deliver fiercer attack lines that made the case for Brexit more succinctly. Leave campaigners recalled just that dynamic in the drafting of one of the most memorable broadsides against Cameron. It came four weeks before voting day and concerned immigration, the Remain campaign's weak spot. A letter was to be sent to the prime minister, signed by Gove and Johnson. One senior Vote Leave figure remembered watching wide-eyed as both men made online edits to the shared file. 'You'd see it on the Google Doc. Boris Johnson was working through, just adding bits of flair. Michael Gove was bashing away, writing whole paragraphs. They egged each other. We would write it very hard and then they would tone it down but then they would add extra bits.'[136] The final version was brutal. Cameron's failure to hit his 'tens of thousands' immigration target had been 'corrosive of public trust', it claimed. The attack fused two explosive elements – calling out the prime minister's personal credibility and exploiting the lack of immigration changes in his renegotiation – with brutal effectiveness.

The *Sunday Times* splashed the story. Craig Oliver, the Downing Street communications director seconded to the Remain campaign, had to break the news to his boss, who erupted in fury. 'I remember David Cameron being so upset that he basically put the phone down,' Oliver recalled.

> Then he called me back a few minutes later and said, 'I'm sorry, it's just that I can't quite believe that these people are questioning my integrity. This is below the belt, it's wrong.' Anybody who knows David Cameron should know how out of character that is for him . . . I think he was genuinely shocked by that.[137]

There was another critical element: what Tory Remainers saw as a huge, Labour-shaped hole in the campaign. Jeremy Corbyn, an uninhibited socialist, had seen his plucky tilt at the leadership after Ed Miliband's resignation snowball into unexpected victory. The Islington North MP had for decades espoused a Bennite form of Euroscepticism, viewing the bloc as something of a capitalist stitch-up. Indeed, Corbyn had voted no in the 1975 referendum on Britain's European Community membership. But now, as Labour leader, he was ostensibly one of the most important voices for Remain. Cummings had already sensed that traditional working-class Labour voters were just as critical to his side's success as countryside Tories. It was not by chance that Vote Leave's adopted colour was bright Labour red or that its bus vowed to pump Brexit cash back into the NHS. These were deliberate attempts to woo that chunk of the electorate.

Figures at the top of both campaigns believe Corbyn's at best luke-warm support for the EU was a major handicap to the Remain cause. 'Corbyn was huge in the fact that he essentially stood Labour down,' said Matthew Elliott.[138] Vote Leave had their own Labour MP front and centre: the German-born Gisela Stuart, who was much more prominent in the final stretch than is commonly remembered. Stuart recalled being surprised by the lack of pro-EU voices from her party on the airwaves: 'There was this silence from Labour.'[139] Craig Oliver, trying to rectify that problem, was exasperated. 'You can't discount the fact that the Labour Party didn't play,' he said. 'If you'd had somebody like Ed Miliband or Keir Starmer as leader of the Labour Party, I think they would have taken the campaign by the scruff of the neck.'[140]

Seumas Milne, Corbyn's communications director, pushed back on this narrative. He said the Labour leader did do extensive campaigning, focusing on rallies and events across the country rather than set-piece speeches. Corbyn's measured support – in one TV appearance he put his passion for remaining in the EU at 'seven or seven and a half' out of ten – was a more effective message for wavering voters than the New Labour-dominated Labour In campaign's passionate backing, Milne argued. 'Their line was "long live the EU and all its works", ours was to make the case for "Remain and Reform",' Milne recalled. 'They thought anything less than 100 per cent endorsement of the EU was treachery and bad for the campaign. But in reality, that wasn't a good message for our voters in particular.' He also rejected outright the speculation that Corbyn in the secrecy of the ballot box voted Brexit, calling it 'total fantasy'.[141]

Corbyn himself, speaking to the author, referenced how Labour had been burnt in the 2014 Scottish independence referendum when defending his approach. 'I was determined not to fall into the trap of Scottish Labour in the Better Together campaign, which did so much damage to Scottish Labour because it associated them with the Tories, and they've paid the price evermore,' said Corbyn. 'I was determined to try to straddle the divide within the party, so I said "remain and reform".' He also waved away loose speculation that he really voted for Brexit: 'I voted to remain. I voted Leave in 1975 [at the European Community membership referendum], but I freely admit that I did vote Remain.'[142]

And then, at long last, it was time for another results night. Rather than being in Dean, David Cameron and his team watched it all unfold from Downing Street, since he was not needed at a constituency count. A buffet was set out in the splendour of the Thatcher Room on the first floor. The irony of watching the results in a space named after a leader who decried referendums as 'a device of dictators and demagogues' appears to have gone unnoted.

The expectation among the most prominent politicians on both sides was a defeat for the Brexiteers. A conference call between Boris Johnson, Michael Gove, Dominic Cummings, Matthew Elliott and Gisela Stuart before the polls closed saw the first three discussing how to manage being beaten. 'All Boris, Michael and Dom would talk about was how to handle the fallout from losing,' Elliott said.[143] Stuart, attending the official Manchester count with Elliott, recalled piping up: 'Boys, what do I say when we win?!'[144] Johnson, who in typical fashion almost missed voting in person due to delays returning from his daughter's Edinburgh graduation, had admitted to a stranger on the train back from the airport he thought the Brexiteers would lose.[145] The punter turned out to be a Labour activist, the throwaway remark soon national news. Nigel Farage was also downbeat, saying when asked by a reporter just after voting ended that he thought Remain would win. The mood was the reverse in Number 10. Cameron was upbeat after his pollster Andrew Cooper reported a 10-point lead for Remain.[146] George Osborne, appearing confident of victory, went for drinks with the Remain team in the popular Blue Boar watering hole nearby.[147]

And then came the one-two punch. First Newcastle, a beneficiary of much EU cash, only backed Remain by 50.7 per cent. And then next-door Sunderland: 61.3 per cent for Leave, way higher than expected and far above what models suggested was needed for Remain to win overall. The pattern for the night was set: declaration after declaration better for Leave than expected, and again and again not just Tory shires but Labour heartlands in the North-East and Midlands voting for the exit door. Corbyn's message had not worked. The cities became the last hope – wait for them to come in, Remainers told themselves. It proved illusory.

For the Leavers, there was elation and disbelief. Boris Johnson, watching from his Islington home in shorts and a Brazilian football top, was getting 'more and more excited', according to one there – proof, in their eyes, that he really wanted Brexit to win. Only later did the 'fuck me, what are we going to do about all of this?' moment strike.[148] Nigel Farage, at Leave.EU's party in the opulent London restaurant Rules, tried to scramble a bet on Brexit when an internal pollster said victory was coming. It was more than £10,000, he told the author – 'I like a bet' – but the bookies, reading the wind, rejected it.[149] Farage's two sons were with him at the moment his political life's mission was completed. 'It was a crusade,' Farage said. 'You can't look at it any other way.' In Vote Leave towers, Dominic Cummings punched through the plasterboard ceiling in delight.[150]

For the Cameron team there was only despair. Osborne had slipped out of the Blue Boar drinks after the announcement of the early results, no longer expecting victory.[151] 'It was just like watching a slow car crash,' recalled Kate Fall. 'We just sort of sat there in silence.'[152] At around 3 a.m., Cameron motioned to a handful of his closest allies to join him in a smaller group. 'We've lost. I'm going to resign in the morning,' he told them.[153] There were pleas for him to reconsider, not to make a snap decision. He had after all repeatedly said he would not quit, but that had been a ploy to stop voters backing Brexit to oust him. 'My authority will be undermined and it will just become a nightmare,' one in the room remembered Cameron saying. 'The people that believe in this need to negotiate it. I don't believe in it, so how can I?'[154]

As a new dawn broke, Cameron addressed the nation. Speaking from behind a lectern outside Number 10, pale light filtering into the street, the prime minister called time on his premiership. 'The British people have voted to leave the European Union and their will must be respected,' he began. Cameron said he would attempt to steady the ship, but added: 'I do not think it would be right for me to try to be the captain that steers our country to its next destination.' The only glimpse of emotion came in the final lines uttered as Samantha Cameron watched on beside him, one arm crossed behind her back. 'I love this country and I feel honoured to have served it,' Cameron said, his voice catching on the last few words. 'And I will do everything I can in future to help this great country succeed.'

On a train back from Manchester, victory secured, a bleary-eyed Gisela Stuart's phone pinged with a text. It was from her son. 'Holy shit, mother. You've just removed the prime minister, taken us out of the EU and wiped trillions off the stock market. What are you planning for tomorrow?' She typed out a short response: 'Mowing the lawn.'[155]

It was the narrowness of the result that would come to haunt Cameron's team. Exactly 17,410,742 votes were cast for the UK to leave the European Union, 16,141,241 for Remain: rounded up and down, 52 per cent for Brexit and 48 per cent against. If Leave had won by a much greater margin that day, it would have been easier not just for the country but for those in Downing Street to digest the outcome and move on. Instead, the 'what ifs' still loop around their heads. What if the timings had meant there was a vote on the Lisbon Treaty? Or if Cameron had rejected the demands of the Tory Europhobes from the off? Could he have secured that emergency brake? Should he have held the referendum later? But the biggest 'what if' – the one still laced with animosity and suspicion of the real motives more than half a decade on – is to do with Cameron's Eton contemporary. What if Boris Johnson had backed Remain?

One person who has known the two men for decades, someone still in touch with them both, tells stories of the effect Johnson's decision had on them. They are stories that hint at regret. For Cameron, the months after the referendum were ones of despair. 'He was completely traumatised by the violence of it and the fact of it,' the source said. 'Of course he was. And he was embarrassed and he was upset and he was worried about the country.' Even half a decade on, he was still 'finding his way'.[156] There was an eventual return to the political arena for Cameron, a surprise stint as foreign secretary, but it would last just eight months.

Johnson, even in the wake of everything, still seeks the spotlight. But there has been soul-searching. One such moment came late at night, long after the referendum and after a few drinks, when he was foreign secretary. 'Sometimes,' Boris told the source, reflecting on that choice in his Islington study and the text to Cameron and all that followed, 'sometimes I think I just fucked all this up.'[157]

4

A New Sheriff

THERESA MAY'S FACE betrayed no obvious hint of what she had just learned. Stepping up to the podium at the Institute of Engineering and Technology in Birmingham, the home secretary gave nothing away. Greying hair in a neat bob and voice with all its customary steeliness, May outlined her pitch for the Conservative Party leadership, one she said would be taken to the country in the weeks ahead. It was 11 July 2016. David Cameron had revealed he was leaving Downing Street and the initial field of candidates scrambling to replace him had already been culled to just two: May and Andrea Leadsom. Now the party members would decide.

Neither could the change in circumstances be detected in the contents of May's address that morning, pages of promises of reform and renewal read out one after the other, the cameras rolling. Certainly the rows of seated supporters seemed none the wiser, listening in a polite silence broken only by the odd 'hear, hear'. But there was one woman watching on, Fiona Hill, who could tell. She was one half of May's pair of most trusted and influential advisers, along with Nick Timothy. It was in the eyes, open a little wider than usual. 'The minute I saw her face on the television I knew,' said Hill. 'I could see a slight look of shock.'[1]

May's speech was meant to fire the starting gun on a race that would finish in September. In fact, the race was already over – as May by then knew. A few hours earlier, she had received a text from Leadsom. 'Good morning, Theresa,' it read. 'Would it be possible to have a quick urgent phone call please?'[2] Hill and May had discussed what to do. Leadsom's campaign had certainly hit choppy waters. A media storm had erupted after she appeared to suggest in a *Times* interview that being a mother gave her an edge over the childless May, an implication Leadsom said she never intended.[3] Her lack of Cabinet experience – Leadsom had never made it to the top table, though she had been a minister for two years – was also causing consternation among some Tory MPs. But even so May and Hill had not predicted what was about to happen. 'I think it's in the country's interest for you to take on the job right now,' Leadsom said once the call was set up.[4] She was dropping out. An assurance was sought by Leadsom and given by May that Brexit would be delivered. Then Leadsom asked May to keep schtum. 'I would appreciate it if you don't tell anyone, please,' she said, asking for time to inform her own team of her decision. May agreed. The story told is that May did not even tell her husband, Philip, though one person in the room said glances shared and a kiss on both cheeks suggested he knew.[5] Everyone else was certainly kept in the dark. May delivered her speech that day knowing she would soon be prime minister – and knowing, too, the size of the task at hand.

Has an incoming prime minister faced such a daunting recalibration of Britain's approach to the rest of the globe since the Second World War? The country's entire economic and foreign policy had been tossed into the air, against the will of the government, with the vote to leave the European Union. All of the four biggest and most prominent political parties in the House of Commons had opposed Brexit. The civil service had done no detailed contingency planning for a Leave vote at the command of Downing Street, which feared leaks – a lack of preparation deemed scandalous by scores of ministers and advisers subsequently. Nor had any blueprint been produced by the Leave campaign, which disappeared in a puff of smoke after the referendum and had deliberately avoided specifics about the kind of post-membership deal the UK should strike with the EU. Now it fell to a Remainer to define and deliver Brexit.

The challenge was compounded by the pace of events. Just seventeen days separated the Brexit result (widely unexpected) and Cameron's resignation (previously ruled out) from Leadsom's sudden departure (catching Westminster off guard) which handed May the crown. Cameron had the best part of five years as opposition leader to think through what he believed, where he stood on policy and who he wanted delivering it before entering Downing Street.

Tony Blair had three years. Gordon Brown knew for months that he would be moving from Number 11 to Number 10, and had been plotting for years and dreaming for decades. It is true that, before them, John Major and James Callaghan had stepped in after speedy leadership contests, but were the circumstances as challenging? In terms of lack of preparation time plus scale of task at hand, arguably no post-war prime ministers can match May.

David Axelrod, Barack Obama's long-time political confidant, liked to say that US presidential campaigns are an 'MRI for the soul'. Something similar is true of the occupancy of Downing Street. A prime minister's instincts and personality traits are magnified through the power of the office. The intense scrutiny and decision-making demands winkle out weaknesses that increase in significance. Virtues as a Cabinet minister can transform into vices in the top role, where you cannot pick your battles. A prime minister must also be communicator-in-chief. When Theresa May walked through the door of Number 10, she did so with Nick Timothy and Fiona Hill by her side. She would use them like crutches, supporting her steps into the unknown in her first year in office. In the eyes of critics, May's co-chiefs of staff could lead as well as follow their boss. They wielded more political power than many Cabinet ministers, enforcing her will and, at times, their own. Capturing the true nature of that triumvirate is key to understanding the decisions taken in those unprecedented and uncertain months right after the referendum – calls that still fundamentally shape the country today.

That it was May who came to find herself with her hand on the tiller was in large part a consequence of the Brexiteers' spectacularly botched attempts to secure the role for themselves. The betrayal and egotism on display in the fraught early stages of the Tory leadership race attained Shakespearean levels, equal parts tragedy and farce. Or perhaps the final scene in *Reservoir Dogs* is a more apt comparison – the deliverers of Brexit pointing their guns at each other in a stand-off that became a mutual firing squad.

It had not started that way. Once the stunned reaction to exceeded expectations had been shaken off, Boris Johnson, Michael Gove and Andrea Leadsom had agreed to club together. The

'Dream Team', as those on board dubbed them, had Johnson as their candidate and, it was hoped, would become the rallying point for Leavers. As the Brexit campaign's leader in all but name, Johnson had captured the media spotlight, a reality that saw Gove initially forgo his own leadership hopes and become Johnson's campaign manager. The two men's teams merged with other senior Vote Leave figures, plotting a path to victory in what was already shaping up as a 'Boris' versus 'stop Boris' contest, with May the obvious pick for the latter camp.

But the early alliance would self-destruct over a thirty-six-hour period as consequential as it was laughable in its details. On Wednesday, 29 June, the day before the deadline for candidates to submit nomination papers, Leadsom was wavering. Meeting Johnson in his parliamentary office, she pushed for specifics about which Cabinet job might be on offer to her. He declined to engage – but made clear that Gove, who was present, would be chancellor, deputy prime minister and chief Brexit negotiator. 'Is this for real?' Leadsom thought, incredulous that one person could take on all three roles.[6] She pushed to secure one of the three for herself, Johnson resisted, she stormed out. Later in the day he relented. Yes, Leadsom could have a top-three job. She agreed, with one proviso – that he write as much in a letter to her and tweet something like 'I'm looking forward to announcing my top team with Michael and Andrea'.[7] Boris agreed.

The exact details of what followed remain a bone of contention. That evening, Tory MPs gathered first at the Saatchi Gallery and then at the Hurlingham Club for an annual donors' dinner. Johnson had drafted the letter but forgotten to bring it, so someone was dispatched to his office to fetch it. It never arrived. He had meant to send the tweet – in one account, he had ordered it to be issued.[8] But for much of the night his phone was in the possession of Nick Boles, one of Gove's best friends who was helping Johnson draft his launch speech for the following day. As the hours ticked by there was silence. Leadsom left the dinner to join supportive MPs urging her to launch a leadership bid of her own. As 10 p.m. approached, still nothing. 'I'm very sorry Boris and Michael,' she typed, delivering the news by text. She would run herself. 'No hard feelings!'[9]

The Dream Team tripod was now one leg down. A second would soon fall off in remarkable fashion. It was Gove, not Leadsom, who had been the central supporter of Johnson. But the events of that day – Boris pulling out of a pro-EU Tory MP hustings; Boris struggling to write his leadership launch address; a series of emotive speeches at the donors' dinner praising the departing Cameron, whom Gove had helped dispatch; and now Leadsom dropping out – brought his own growing doubts to a head. He held a conclave of his inner circle late that night for urgent discussions. Gove recalled his thinking in an interview:

> There was just an accumulation of things that made me think, 'Boris is about to take on the most important role in the country at a crucial time and he's just not ready. He's just not doing any of the things that you would expect someone to do if they were about to make that transition.'

He too had Shakespeare on his mind: 'I remember saying to myself and to others, "Prince Hal has become Henry the Fifth." But, in fact, he was behaving more like Falstaff.'[10]

The following morning, the day of Johnson's launch, Team Boris was still in the dark about Gove's misgivings. The first suspicion one Johnson adviser had was when Gove's aides suddenly went silent in an email chain about the event.[11] The bombshell finally dropped in a call to Lynton Crosby, Johnson's trusted election guru. 'I'm running,' Gove announced. 'Yes, I know, Michael. I'm happy to advise, but you're the campaign chairman,' Crosby replied, thinking he was talking about Johnson's bid. 'No, I'm running for prime minister,' Gove said. 'What?' exclaimed Crosby. 'No, Michael. Fuck me. Why?!'[12] The message had not been communicated to Johnson yet. It is said that Gove tried to ring him, although Johnson allies insist there was never a missed call.[13] Which left Crosby to break the news to the boss. 'Oh, matey, it's all over then,' said Johnson, distraught.[14] One close aide recalled Johnson having 'a real hangdog misery, he just couldn't believe Gove had done it'.[15] The final decision was held off for a huddle in campaign HQ. Senior advisers, including Crosby, urged him to pull out. Johnson, after talking it through with his wife Marina Wheeler, agreed.

The knife, when it was produced, was brutally wielded. 'I have come, reluctantly, to the conclusion that Boris cannot provide the leadership or build the team for the task ahead,' read the critical line in the statement declaring Gove's candidacy. It dropped around 9 a.m. on Thursday, 30 June. Two and a half hours later Johnson delivered his launch speech as written, save for a tweaked final few lines:

> That is the agenda for the next prime minister of this country. But I must tell you, my friends, you who have waited faithfully for the punchline of this speech, that having consulted colleagues and in view of the circumstances in Parliament I have concluded that person cannot be me.

As jaws dropped at the volte-face, one MP backer in the crowd, Nadine Dorries, appeared close to tears.

Boris was gone. Gove, facing a tidal wave of fury from Johnsonites – 'There is a very deep pit reserved in Hell' for Gove, tweeted Tory MP Jake Berry – was soon swept aside too. Leadsom was the last Brexiteer standing but fell on her own sword. Would Johnson have won if he had stayed in? Some allies believe so to this day. Leadsom is convinced the Brexit-backing Tory membership would have given her the victory if she had chosen to continue: 'It is unknowable, but yes, I do think I would've won.'[16] In the end it was May who secured the keys to Number 10. David Cameron, his own premiership ended by Boris's Brexit gamble, could barely contain his glee. He texted Johnson: 'You should have stuck with me mate.'[17]

Talk to those who have served Theresa May the longest and know best what really drives her and they point to one thing above all others. It was flagged up in the first words she uttered in public as prime minister. On the steps outside Number 10, having accepted Queen Elizabeth II's invitation to form a government, May used her podium address to vow to fight 'burning injustice'. 'If you're born poor, you will die on average nine years earlier than others. If you're black, you're treated more harshly by the criminal justice system than if you're white. If you're a white, working-class boy, you're less likely than anybody else in Britain to go to university,' she said.[18] Her mission would be to 'make Britain a country that works for everyone'.

High-flown rhetoric is a must for the Downing Street speeches that are now a tradition for incoming UK leaders. But for May, the words came from a deeper place. Some put it down to her upbringing as the only daughter of a vicar, Hubert Brasier. She lost both parents in her twenties. David Cameron once joked that his Anglican faith 'comes and goes' like Magic FM in the Chilterns, but for May it was a constant.[19] Every Sunday as prime minister she would take holy communion at St Andrew's Church in Sonning, a village in her Maidenhead constituency, her appearance each week so predictable that it became a stake-out for photographers. It led to reluctance to do *The Andrew Marr Show*, the BBC's Sunday morning political flagship programme.[20] Her faith, like so much with May, was a private matter, never mentioned in political discussions. She had a 'quiet sense of core Anglican public service', according to Ben Gummer, who led her Cabinet Office and himself had a grandfather who was a vicar.[21] David Lidington, seen as May's deputy in the second half of her premiership, said: 'Theresa is the closest thing to a Christian Democrat prime minister that we have ever had. Her approach to politics and public service is grounded in her religious faith.'[22]

Those who worked for May are quick to pick out moments that reflect her determination to right wrongs. For one special adviser it was when May, then home secretary, met the widow of Alexander Litvinenko after publicly pointing the finger at the Kremlin over his poisoning. She leaned in close as the pair talked in the sofa area of her office. 'It wasn't necessarily anything that she said, it was the way she said it. She wasn't bullshitting, she wasn't bluffing, she cared seriously and was resolved to take action,' said the adviser.[23] For Stephen Parkinson, another Home Office spad, it was a meeting with Alexander Paul, a black Londoner who by the time he was eighteen had been stopped and searched more than twenty times by police. 'She let him talk a lot,' said Parkinson. 'She was clearly moved and found his account powerful.'[24] May would scale back use of the power, later vowing to 'redouble our efforts to give a voice to the voiceless' when Paul died after developing brain cancer.

Katie Perrior, May's first Downing Street director of communications, recalled watching in tears as the prime minister embraced Margaret Aspinall, the chair of the Hillsborough Family Support Group, after giving her a Woman of the Year award. May praised the 'extra-ordinary dignity' of Aspinall, who lost her son in the tragedy. Aspinall said May, unlike other politicians, did what she promised.[25]

The trait can be traced through into May's policy agenda. She launched a 'racial disparity audit' aimed at mapping out how people from different ethnicities were treated in education, health services, the criminal justice system and the private sector. She pushed more companies to reveal their gender pay gap. Efforts to root out modern slavery became a thread that ran through her Home Office and Number 10 years. At points critics would argue that reality starkly failed to live up to the ideals May espoused. On her watch the Windrush scandal emerged, which saw scores of people who had long ago moved to Britain from the Caribbean wrongly detained and deported. The 'hostile environment' she had overseen as home secre-tary in a push to control illegal immigration was a contributing factor.

Inside government even critics, though, acknowledged the sincerity of her approach. One Cabinet minister who served under May and became disillusioned with her premiership summed it up:

> Theresa May is a fundamentally decent person. And decent is a double-edged word here. This is a very English term. I know lots of people like her. Do I necessarily like them? Not necessarily. Do I want to spend time with them? Probably not. But am I happy that a large part of our country is made up of people who are funda-mentally decent? Yes, I think probably I am.[26]

As well as her drive to right wrongs, allies often point to another fact central to understanding Theresa May as an MP and PM: the enduring connection with her constituency. May is the only repre-sentative the seat of Maidenhead, newly created in 1997, has ever had. She served it for nineteen years before becoming Conservative leader and had been a councillor for eight before that. Sir Keir Starmer and Rishi Sunak, in contrast, had only been MPs repre-senting constituents for five and seven years, respectively, before becoming party leaders. Nor would she cut and run from the House of Commons once her Downing Street days were done, unlike David Cameron and Tony Blair. 'I don't think there's been a prime minister in modern British political history who's been as devoted a constituency MP,' said Gavin Barwell, who was May's chief of staff from 2017 to 2019.[27] When she was not travelling abroad May liked to return to her constituency home on Thursday nights and only go back to London on Monday morning, meaning close to half the week was spent away from Number 10. One adviser said she rarely used Chequers, the prime minister's grace-and-favour country residence, and if she went there for dinner would sometimes be driven home to Maidenhead rather than stay over.[28] Another recalled dreading the task of telling May that there was a London meeting on Friday which meant she had to miss constituency duties.[29] There was the day each year, around Easter, when the prime minister acted as marshal for a Maidenhead 10-mile race. Or the time, remembered by an adviser from her previous job, when the US Department of Homeland Security called seeking her out: 'We had to explain that the home secretary was at a cake sale in Woodley.'[30]

Maidenhead was home for the Mays. Theresa had met her future husband, Philip, in the late 1970s at Oxford University, where she studied Geography and they shared an interest in Conservative student politics. The bespectacled Mr May had a warm smile and a softly spoken manner, glimpsed in joint interviews. On Saturdays, Prime Minister May would slip into old habits: drop by the dry cleaner's with Philip's clothes, have a drink at the same café, visit the butcher's and stop off at Waitrose. On Sundays, there was church. At some point before the return to London there would be a gym session with a personal trainer. Her Maidenhead life offered a slice of normality, one that sometimes jarred with her new job.[31] 'There was a whole thing about Special Branch digging a trench in the garden and putting a fence in,' one member of May's inner circle recalled. 'Now you had to get to the compost bin by going through a gate. She would say: "It's just so annoying. Why did they have to do this?"'[32] Another remembered watching in bemusement one day as May put the alarm on and double-locked the front door as if, even with a round-the-clock security detail provided by the state, the risk from burglars remained.[33]

Maidenhead was not just a personal anchoring for May; the

constituency also shaped her political antennae. She would go door-knocking at least once a month as prime minister – she treated Maidenhead as a marginal, having seen her majority drop to just 3,300 votes in the 2001 election – and feed back what she heard. 'She would go out canvassing all year round and often would bring it up in meetings with officials,' recalled Stephen Parkinson, who followed her into Number 10. 'She would say, "No, that won't wash," "No, somebody raised this with me." She knew what was cutting through.'[34] It led to frustration with Sajid Javid, her communities secretary, whose attempts to loosen planning rules to kick-start house building were kiboshed by May. 'The first thing she did was go to the annexe and look at what his formula meant for Maidenhead,' one senior Number 10 figure said of her actions when she got the proposals. 'She is an absolute NIMBY,' said another.[35]

Her normality was Home Counties humdrum, with an eyebrow raised at prime ministerial excess. One adviser remembered the look on her face when told by party chiefs that she could access a clothing allowance, as David and Samantha Cameron had. 'I won't be needing that. Philip can buy his own suits,' came the retort.[36] Diary managers who tried to schedule the 'down time' on foreign trips her predecessor had enjoyed were given short shrift; the sections were expunged from future visit itineraries.[37] She was a rarity among modern politicians in some respects. 'I never, ever, ever in my whole entire career heard her swear,' said Perrior, who first worked with her in the early 2000s – an irony given senior aides could turn the air blue.[38] She was allergic to the palace intrigue that Westminster thrives on. 'She's the only politician I've ever known who actively stopped people repeating gossip in front of her,' said Damian Green, who first met May at Oxford and served as her de facto deputy prime minister before Lidington.[39]

Which is not to say she could not relax. 'She does like crap TV,' said one who knows her well.[40] *Line of Duty*, *Homeland* and *NCIS* are all on her watch list – ever the home secretary. The *Slough House* series of spy books is a recent favourite, one of which features a female prime minister blighted by a haystack-haired Brexiteer rival, and she is well read in the English classics. Agatha Christie made the list when the *Daily Telegraph* asked her for dream dinner-party guests, along with the explorer Edward Whymper, horticulturalist Gertrude Jekyll, travel writer Wilfred Thesiger, painter of eye-catching Christian scenes Sir Stanley Spencer and aviator Lettice Curtis.[41] Four of the six were born in the 1800s; none was a politician. On foreign trips a game of cards would pass the time, or the devouring of a sudoku (always from *The Times*). Lent would bring the giving-up of crisps. Special treats included classical concerts, the Henley Regatta, her favourite posh Italian in London. Wine at dinner; the odd whisky after a late-night summit.[42] Such snippets paint a picture of a prime minister as much as flagship policy speeches. Boris Johnson was not known to forgo crisps during religious holidays or dedicate hours to sudokus.

There were other character traits, however, that had a more direct impact on her ability to govern. She had gained a reputation, rightly, as a forensic scrutineer of detail. At the Home Office, the great killer of ministerial careers under New Labour, this had served her brilliantly for six years. But Number 10 was different. 'Being prime minister you have to be on top of fifty different things at once,' said Ivan Rogers, Britain's EU ambassador under May who had seen many Downing Street occupants in his long Whitehall career. 'Theresa had a Gordon problem, without his genuine brilliance on some economic issues. She can only focus on a very limited number of things at the same time. Then she gets to the bottom of it and likes to go over and over and over it and take too long in reaching final decisions'[43] Other top mandarins also saw echoes of Gordon Brown's granular, controlling approach. One recalled how May and her team naturally gathered with the Brownites at the funeral of Cabinet secretary Jeremy Heywood, while Cameron's and Nick Clegg's teams grouped together.[44] Stephen Parkinson, an adviser who saw her up close in both Cabinet roles, said:

> At the Home Office you have levers that you can pull. If you've got strikes at the border, you can get the army in or relax checks, for instance . . . But being prime minister it is all soft power. You have got to persuade the Cabinet and the rest of government and your party to go along with you. And that is hard to do at the best of times.[45]

Her tendency to hold on tightly to things was compounded by another character trait: Theresa May is an introvert. Allies put it in different ways: shyness; being quite a private person; a reserved quality; an unwillingness to open up. Such attributes could help around the negotiating table in Whitehall, where her inscrutability would give nothing away to colleagues. 'She'd be a brilliant poker player,' said one long-time aide.[46] But in a political system built on the ability to twist arms and keep ministerial colleagues on side it had downsides too. 'She's not a back-slapping bon viveur,' said Ben Gummer, one of her Cabinet ministers.[47] Another said: 'On a couple of occasions she invited me up to the flat for a drink, for a chat. It was quite hard work. At least on one occasion I made my excuses after forty-five minutes and left.'[48] Her lack of small talk was famous across Westminster. At one Tory conference meal with the *Daily Mail* political team, endless questioning had failed to generate anything newsworthy. An exasperated reporter eventually piped up: 'Have you read *Fifty Shades of Grey*?' 'Certainly not!' glowered May.[49]

Where the trait became a real political problem was in communication. Behind closed doors May could display a dry wit. In constituency settings or on the doorstep she could connect with a handful of voters. But in the set pieces of the twenty-first-century media landscape – grillings under the lights of TV studios; press conferences where every question has a sting in the tail; glitzy policy launches on the campaign trail – May could be stilted. The stiff responses and lack of rhetorical dexterity, with emotions hidden, would see her dubbed the Maybot by the *Guardian*'s perceptive parliamentary sketch writer John Crace. It was a weakness that would be exposed brutally when she headed up her first general election campaign in 2017.

The standoffishness was heightened when she faced journalists. On foreign trips prime ministers would always head to the back of the plane for a question-and-answer session with travelling reporters, dubbed the 'huddle'. Johnson, a journalist at heart, relished the sparring; Cameron would glide through unfazed. But May beforehand would be anxious. 'It was painful, the whole thing. We did hours of prep in the front of the plane,' recalled Perrior, the comms chief whose job it was to get May ready. 'She would be nervous.

She would be snappy. She looked at me like I was asking silly questions.' The huddle itself would be strictly time-limited, endured not enjoyed.[50]

May's team would try different tricks to get her to emote in public. 'Today you've got to be outraged on behalf of the public,' Fiona Hill would urge her, introducing a framing that sometimes worked.[51] Before one interview with the *Sun on Sunday*, May and her team discussed an expected question about what her departed parents would have thought about their daughter becoming prime minister. Lizzie Loudon, May's press secretary, who had lost her own father years earlier, offered thoughts about her own position: 'I feel like in some way he would know that this was where I was going to end up and of course he would be hugely proud of me. I take comfort in that.' She was left wide-eyed when May repeated the line almost word for word.[52]

Some saw strategy behind the unwillingness to show the world emotion. May co-founded the Women2Win group to improve the gender balance on the Tory benches and knew how female MPs could be depicted in the press. Early in her political career May 'was conscious not to let her voice go too high' when she spoke in the Commons, according to her close aide Liz Sanderson.[53] Her team was frustrated by what they saw as a media obsession with whether she cried at trying moments. When her voice did wobble once in public, in her farewell speech outside Downing Street, she apologised to her inner circle. Gavin Barwell, who as her chief of staff tried to loosen her up in front of the electorate, let out his frustration: 'Who is going to think worse of you as a person that you're upset because you're standing down as prime minister? Why is this a bad thing?' May listened patiently before responding: 'The papers will use those images differently because I'm female.'[54] Avoiding the sexist trope of a woman swayed by her emotions mattered.

It is in the context of these strengths and weaknesses that two central characters in the first year of the May premiership must be placed and understood. Nick Timothy and Fiona Hill had more raw power than any other political advisers in Number 10 during the long stretch of Tory government from 2010. Dominic Cummings is the only other who comes close, but he was not woven into the fabric of Boris Johnson's leadership in quite the same way. Some lasted much longer – Ed Llewellyn under David Cameron, for example. But none had the breadth of influence of Nick and Fi.

Timothy had met May in the noughties as he rose through the ranks of the Conservative Research Department, a well-trodden path for young Tories destined for greater things. He was born in Birmingham and his political idol was the city's mayor Joseph Chamberlain, whose big-tent Liberalism inspired his own ideological outlook. Timothy's brand of Conservatism with the sharp edges smoothed down chimed with May's own leanings towards a patrician Toryism. The label of Theresa May's 'policy brain' would be attached to Timothy, who was seen by his peers as one of their intake's brightest Conservative thinkers. The interplay between the pair, though, was subtler than that suggests, with May's moral framework being coloured in and brought to life by her adviser. 'Rasputin' would be another tag given by the tabloids when his influence in Number 10 became clear. He certainly had the beard for it, a thick thatch straight out of tsarist Russia.

Fiona Hill, a determined Glaswegian with a backbone of steel, had been a journalist, working her way up from the *Daily Record* to the *Scotsman* and eventually Sky News, before first crossing into the Conservative press operation in 2006. She got to know May when they were paired up for the TV debate spin rooms in the 2010 election. She joined Timothy as a special adviser at the Home Office when May, who had been shadowing the work and pensions brief, got the surprise appointment after Cameron became prime minister. Hill had a knack for predicting the political weather – an uncanny foresight that saw Timothy and May nickname her 'the witch'.[55] Over the years, a depth of relationship would develop between Hill and May far beyond that between most spads and their bosses, covering not just policy and media advice but fashion tips and life reassurances. One Cabinet minister called it a 'strange' mother–daughter bond.[56]

Allies and critics alike do not doubt just how central Nick and Fi were to May's Cabinet career. 'They were incredibly important to her in the Home Office. They were integral to her becoming prime minister,' said a senior Downing Street colleague who remains on good terms with both advisers.[57] Paul Harrison, who saw their work from afar as a Health Department special adviser before later becoming May's press secretary, said: 'They operated with Theresa's complete trust and complete licence. That is important. They understood her really well, they knew her mind and they were able to represent that around Whitehall to significant effect.'[58] Critics go a step further, portraying May's position as one of dependence. 'I think they filled bits of her personality or gaps that she would have,' said one Downing Street adviser. 'So Nick articulated a whole political philosophy that she could not . . . Fiona could be hugely outwardly charismatic and sociable and warm and would get cosy with people in a way that Theresa couldn't really'[59] Another adviser, disillusioned with their reign, went further: 'At the worst points I would call her [May] a victim, that's how bad it was. A victim of their meddling, their puppet-mastery.'[60] Boris Johnson once returned from a trying meeting with the dominant pair and, referencing a Theresa May policy, joked: 'That's modern slavery right there.'[61] A minister who served in senior roles under Cameron, May and Johnson said it was her deficiencies that left space to be filled by the two advisers:

> No prime minister is 100 per cent of what you need. That was the case with David, with Boris, with Theresa. I would argue with David and with Boris they were 65 per cent of what you needed and then they buttressed themselves up with the other people that can fill the rest . . . Theresa would have been about 40 per cent.[62]

The perception that Timothy did the policy and Hill the comms was never quite right, even in their Home Office days. Legislation on modern slavery was the brainchild of Hill, with May needing to be convinced before adopting the cause that would become a central plank of her legacy. The co-chiefs, firm friends as well as colleagues, would divide work by projects, not disciplines. The problem, to critics, was that in the early months in Number 10 they hoarded power and held a tight grip on decision-making. Policy matters were certainly in their domain; so too media strategy and Downing Street staffing. But sometimes items of little consequence were held up awaiting their approval, according to one insider, such as whether a department could tweet a particular message or what the press spokesperson's exact script should be for the twice-daily Lobby journalist briefings.[63]

For some working under 'the chiefs' their behaviour crossed a line. 'I found it absolutely extraordinary the way that they ran Downing Street and the way that they played or treated other special advisers or civil servants,' said one Number 10 insider.[64] The press dubbed the pair the 'terrible twins' and the 'gruesome twosome' when negative stories eventually leaked.[65] The most public bust-up came with Katie Perrior. She was brought in as Downing Street director of communications but felt her job of a lifetime was undercut by Hill's hostility. Perrior went all guns blazing after leaving at the 2017 election, writing in *The Times*:

> What I could never work out was whether Mrs May condoned their behaviour and turned a blind eye or didn't understand how destructive they both were. For all the love of a hierarchy, the chiefs treated Cabinet members exactly the same – rude, abusive, childish behaviour. For two people who have never achieved elected office, I was staggered at the disrespect they showed on a daily basis.[66]

The attacks were countered at the time by claims that Perrior was not up to the job. One May adviser without a firm foot in either camp insisted the critical portrayals of the pair's behaviour were 'overblown'.

Personalities matter in politics. So do rivalries. Theresa May, Nick Timothy and Fiona Hill were all shaped not just by the different paths that had led them to Number 10 but by the years they spent side by side in the Whitehall trenches. In that first year in Downing Street the confluence of their values, instincts, motivations and peculiarities, the better angels of their ideals and the fires stoked by slights, real or imagined, would play an outsized role in how Britain was governed. That significance can be especially detected in three areas.

The first concerned a question faced not just by Theresa May but by the next three Tory leaders too: how far to diverge from the course set by one's predecessor? Just like Boris Johnson, Liz Truss and Rishi Sunak, May was only prime minister thanks to past leaders' electoral successes. It was David Cameron who had won the Conservatives their shock majority in 2015, one handed on via an unanticipated Brexit. That too meant an inherited manifesto packed with his policy priorities. May, just like her successors, naturally wanted to stamp her own authority on the office. But there was an extra animus between her and the old guard not present with all the others.

May always got on well with Cameron, according to ministerial colleagues. They both embodied a rustic Conservatism of village greens and looking after your neighbour. Cameron valued his home secretary's tenacity and attention to detail. But May took a dimmer view of George Osborne, who used the long arm of the Treasury to further his hopes of getting the crown. 'She hated Osborne. There was a visceral dislike,' one Cabinet colleague of both claimed.[67] 'Don't mention that man to me,' she would mutter, with the pair squaring off over Home Office budget demands or measures to deliver the Tories' fabled – and always missed – target of reducing net migration to below 100,000 a year.[68] A Number 10 adviser said she 'struggled' with Osborne, fifteen years her junior, and his 'cock of the walk' act.[69] David Lidington, who served under May in the Home Office, said there was 'no doubt' she felt 'patronised' by the Cameroons. 'There was palpable, simmering anger and resentment there. She had never been treated as one of the inner circle at Number 10 and really trusted by them. There's something about what she saw as the "posh boys' club" that just really jarred with her.'[70] One senior mandarin recalled: 'She was always treated like dirt by both Cameron and Osborne as a kind of boring grammar school girl.'[71]

For Timothy and Hill, there were more tangible reasons to be disillusioned: both had been denied jobs by the Ancien Régime. Hill's sacking in 2014 had been ordered by David Cameron in order to end an escalating briefing war between May and Michael Gove, then education secretary, over how to counter extremism in schools. 'She was very hurt,' recalled Timothy of her removal.[72] Timothy's own slight came later that year. He and fellow Home Office spad Stephen Parkinson were banished from the list of approved Tory candidates to run to become MPs owing to their refusal to campaign in a by-election. They insisted it breached their government contracts; Tory chairman Grant Shapps saw advisers too big-headed to do the hard yards. May pleaded their case over the phone. Shapps checked twice with Cameron, who backed him. The decision stood. The aides suspected an Osborne ploy to deny May supporters in the coming Commons contest over the Cameron succession – a claim denied by Shapps. Timothy would vow 'revenge'. Eventually Shapps would find himself locked out of government under May.[73]

Osborne was in for even more brutal treatment. As a lead protagonist in 'Project Fear' – the nickname given by critics to the Remain campaign – the chancellor was not flavour of the month with Tory Eurosceptics. He had not run for the Tory leadership after the Brexit vote, accepting the political reality, but as second in command for six years he expected a Cabinet job from May, according to one ally.[74] Instead came humiliation. Usually Cabinet ministers are sacked in the privacy of the prime minister's parliamentary office, away from TV cameras, while only those with new jobs are paraded up Downing Street. So Osborne's spirits must have been raised as he entered through the Number 10 front door in full view of the press pack. Alone with May those hopes were dashed. Sitting a few floors below the flat where Osborne was still living, May fired him. She finished with a sting: 'Go away and get to know the Conservative Party better.'[75] The words would soon make their way into the press. Was the public staging deliberate? 'It was a definite calculated decision to humiliate,' said one Number 10 insider – a view widely held among May advisers and ministers. Some May allies, though, insist it was not premeditated. Either way, when the Sky News ticker announced that Osborne had quit the government, Hill, according to one witness, demanded a change in the wording: 'He didn't quit. She fired him. Correct it.'[76] A fuming Osborne would leave the Commons within a year, become *Evening Standard* editor and launch repeated attacks on a Tory government only in place thanks to the election he had helped win. In one infamous leaked comment, Osborne told senior editorial staff he would not stop until May was 'chopped up in bags in my freezer'.[77]

The degree to which personal gripes drove the reframing of

Conservatism under May is tough to ascertain. The change in emphasis was clear from her speech on the steps of Downing Street. It was the JAMs, as they would be dubbed – those 'just about managing' – who would become the focus of her policy interventions. 'If you're one of those families, if you're just managing, I want to address you directly,' May said. 'I know you're working around the clock, I know you're doing your best, and I know that sometimes life can be a struggle. The government I lead will be driven not by the interests of the privileged few, but by yours.'[78] Chris Wilkins, May's director of strategy and chief speech-writer who did much to flesh out her thinking, saw clear distinctions with her predecessor. 'It was much more about communitarianism,' he said. 'What she saw in Cameron and Osborne's style was a very metropolitan, liberal, globalised view of the world. She was much more concerned about the detail of people's lives here and the way people lived in communities, this sense of the importance of belonging.'[79]

That played through into the policy agenda. May and Timothy had a more relaxed view about the state stepping in when the free market misfired. Big business was viewed with hesitancy. 'She is suspicious of very large corporations,' said her chancellor, Philip Hammond.[80] May wanted worker representatives on company boards. The Brexit vote was seen as a 'cry of pain' from a public disillusioned with the status quo in Team May's analysis – one similar to that of her successor, Boris Johnson.[81] Policies had to match the moment. 'If you believe you're a citizen of the world, you're a citizen of nowhere,' May told the Tory conference three months after taking office – a Nick Timothy phrase that triggered a backlash from those who saw it as a rejection of open, outward-facing Britain.[82] Some on the inside, including Wilkins, came to regret its use.[83]

One policy volte-face would come to define the break with Dave and George. Grammar schools were back. The Cameron era ban on new grammars was to be scrapped, the *Daily Telegraph* revealed a month after May took office.[84] It split the Tory backbench, meaning a parliamentary battle was inevitable. But it was a fight the Mayites wanted. The rule of the 'privileged few' was indeed over. Out had gone Cameron's public school set, the end of the 'chumocracy' embodied by the removal of sofas from the prime minister's office.[85] In power now were two children of grammar schools: May and Timothy.

The second area shaped profoundly by the new power axis was also the most important: the approach to leaving the European Union.

May was no Brexiteer. She had declared for Remain, albeit in lukewarm fashion. As the referendum approached May had kept her cards close to her chest. The question split her advisers: Timothy was a committed Leaver whereas Hill favoured continued membership. Timothy, on the outside since the 2015 election after his path to becoming an MP was blocked, had sent May a note spelling out the arguments for Leave, though he never believed she was persuadable.[86] When she delivered a speech coming out for Remain her message was much more nuanced than the official campaign lines, with May noting it was not true 'the sky will fall in' if Brexit won.[87] David Cameron's team were infuriated that she did not do more to deliver victory, one member dubbing her 'Submarine May' for disappearing when she was most needed.[88] But Cameron saw how the strategy of not playing a highly visible role in the referendum could help her reach Number 10 if the country voted for Brexit.[89]

In the result's immediate aftermath there was disappointment and, if Timothy is to be believed, tears from May. 'She was concerned that the people who'd voted for it were going to lose out the most,' Timothy said of their phone call after the result was announced.[90] He was in Italy on holiday but jetted back to help her leadership campaign. Scores of MPs rallied to May's side as she portrayed herself as the grown-up in the room, a serious politician for serious times – a theme that would be echoed years later come Rishi Sunak's clean-up job after Liz Truss. When the Vote Leavers self-destructed, the premiership – and the fate of Brexit – fell into her hands.

A phrase that had echoed through the campaign would be deployed as a fig leaf in the early months of her premiership while May considered her options: 'Brexit means Brexit.' Its simplicity was laughed off by cynics as lacking any meaning, but for May's team it sent an important signal to the public – and colleagues – that she would not try to unpick the result. '"Brexit means Brexit" changed in meaning over time,' said Timothy. 'It was first to reassure the party that she understood what Brexit means. Then it came to mean "leaving the institutions and structures in full". And then it became a way to lecture people: "It has to mean Brexit."[91] Other signals that she could be trusted were sent. The 'three Brexiteers' were appointed to outward-facing departments, in what could be dubbed a 'you Brexit, you pays for it' approach. Boris Johnson got the Foreign Office. 'Oh wow!' he exclaimed, according to one present, in genuine shock at being handed a great office of state and a lifeline after his political assassination by Gove.[92] Thanks for the generosity would eventually fade, with Johnson going on to play a central part in the fall of May when it came. David Davis went to the Department for Exiting the European Union while Liam Fox got the Department for International Trade. The latter two departments were newly created, essentially carved out of the first.

It is important to remember just how undefined the shape of Britain's exit from the EU still was that summer and autumn of 2016. No single vision of post-Brexit relations with the Continent had been spelled out by Vote Leave, deliberately – the lack of specificity made attacking the consequences trickier. That left vast space for interpretation. Would the Norway model be best, outside the bloc but with full access to the single market? Or something like Turkey, with its own customs arrangement but no financial contributions? Or Switzerland, which had a unique patchwork of negotiated deals? Brexit was in the eye of the beholder, yet nobody knew what May was seeing as she peered ahead.

The day the building blocks of a hard Brexit began to emerge from the fog was 2 October 2016. At the Conservative Party conference in Birmingham May would break with tradition by delivering two speeches; the first, on that date, would be all about Brexit. Amid growing Eurosceptic grumbling about wasted time, May announced that formal exit talks would be triggered via the Article 50 mechanism no later than the end of March 2017. She also unveiled the Great Repeal Bill, promising to scrap the European Communities Act which had taken the country into the EU – although in reality it also copied and pasted vast swathes of EU law onto the UK statute book.

The real significance of the speech lay not in the two flagged announcements but the words used to detail her vision of the future relationship with the EU. 'Let me be clear. We are not leaving the European Union only to give up control of immigration again,' May said, all but ruling out full single market membership given that free movement was one of the EU's four freedoms. 'Our laws will be made not in Brussels but in Westminster. The judges interpreting those laws will sit not in Luxembourg but in courts in this country. The authority of EU law in Britain will end,' she also declared, calling time on oversight from the European Court of Justice – a necessity for staying in the customs union. Any copycat deals were also waved away: 'It is not going to be a "Norway model". It's not going to be a "Switzerland model". It is going to be an agreement between an independent, sovereign United Kingdom and the European Union.'[93] In a few sentences, the doors to countless negotiating possibilities were slammed shut.

Philip Hammond, the Remain-voting chancellor watching from the audience as the cameras rolled, attempted to hide his shock. 'I was sitting there in the hall trying to keep a poker face, which was very difficult because this was extremely provocative stuff,' Hammond said.

> I was pretty horrified by what I was hearing because I could see immediately that we were boxing ourselves into the hardest possible Brexit corner. She hadn't discussed that with me or, so far as I know, anyone else in the Cabinet. With that speech, she condemned herself to fighting a rear-guard action for the next three years as she gradually embraced the need for a more practical Brexit that reduced the economic fallout.[94]

David Davis, the Brexit secretary, was also apparently kept in the dark. 'I'm not even sure if I saw that speech,' he said, though he could not be categorical.[95] A third key figure out of the loop was Ivan Rogers, the UK's man in Brussels, who watched aghast. He was soon hauled in to see Jean-Claude Juncker, the European Commission president. 'What the bloody hell is this? Why has she said that? She didn't need to say that, she's gone so far. This is a ridiculous position! I fear it will damage her and make things harder,' fumed Juncker, who had read the speech three times and still could not get his head around it.[96] Rogers tried to bat away concerns, explaining that May just needed to convince her Brexit-backing base she was not a 'counter-revolutionary'. But he too was put out and in turn called Jeremy Heywood, the Cabinet secretary: 'What the fuck is this? This is a disaster out in Brussels. It will really weaken her position at her debut European Council [due within days]. People are just talking about nothing else. Did you see the speech before it was delivered?' The response from Heywood, according to Rogers, was in the negative: 'No, I didn't see it. None of us saw it.'[97]

So the men responsible for protecting the UK economy, negotiating the country's EU exit, liaising with Brussels and heading up the civil service had all been cut out from work on the speech which defined the Brexit approach. Just two people, it appears, had made the calls: May and Timothy.

Chris Wilkins, May's speech-writer who was focusing on her second conference address, thinks the intervention was never intended to be that definitive: 'I don't know if anyone really grasped the magnitude of what she was saying in that speech at the time.'[98] Hammond detected the fingerprints of May's right-hand man: 'I think Nick Timothy was over-zealous on her behalf to prove her credentials to Brexiteers by going way over the top.'[99] Timothy has always rejected the suggestion that he bounced May into adopting the approach. To her, he said, the positions set out – leaving the single market, leaving the customs union – were the obvious extrapolations of the Leave vote.[100] What was implicit in the speech became explicit three months later in the Lancaster House address of January 2017. But the flag was first planted at the party conference.

The third striking way in which the realities of the new leadership played out was also the most personally fraught: the near-total disintegration of the most important relationship in Cabinet.

Why Theresa May picked Philip Hammond as her chancellor even Nick and Fi do not know. Certainly the MPs had known each other for decades – he was another Oxford University contemporary May turned to once at the top. They had fought neighbouring East London by-elections in 1994, with Hammond's first ever TV broadcast appearance being made alongside May. They had similar temperaments and sober public images, both positioned in the party's pragmatic centre-right. They were also both holders of great offices of state, with Hammond serving as foreign secretary, leading some to see his selection as fitting the 'time for the grown-ups' message of May's leadership campaign. But they were not bosom buddies.

Pulling together a Cabinet is a headache for any prime minister, even more so for one who had not expected to be in the role three weeks earlier. Looking back, there were peculiarities in the choices made. The time pressure of those heady post-Brexit days was surely a factor. Greg Clark was handed a newly beefed-up business department, only to discover that his vision for the industrial strategy fundamentally differed from that of the co-chiefs. Amber Rudd, a leading liberal Tory, was put in the Home Office and made to continue May's tough-on-immigration stance under the watchful eye of the boss. An education secretary, Justine Greening, was picked who was uncomfortable with Downing Street's core demand of scrapping the grammar schools ban.

The unpredictability of May's promotions is captured in one particular reshuffle anecdote. Health Minister Ben Gummer was so certain a Cabinet post would not be coming his way that he spent the day at Lord's enjoying the cricket over multiple refreshments with friends. It was only a 5 p.m. call from the Number 10 switchboard, picked up while at the gents urinal, that informed him otherwise. Having sprinted to the Tube, a flushed Gummer spent most of the meeting with the prime minister, in which he was made a minister in the Cabinet Office, trying to hide the effects of a day's drinking.[101]

For Hammond, the appointment was no surprise. May was meant to tap him for the role during the leadership race, but at an awkward dinner at The Adjournment restaurant in Portcullis House she failed to make the offer explicit – despite her guest having already been tipped off. Hammond suspected that Hill, his spinner a decade earlier when he was shadow chief secretary to the Treasury, had put him forward. The formal approach, when it came, was brief. 'Theresa really didn't have anything to say other than "I'd like you to be my chancellor",' recalled Hammond.[102] Critically, to Hammond's mind, no parameters were laid out. 'She didn't set out any conditions and she didn't set out any agenda, which was a massive mistake,' Hammond said. 'Because almost certainly, if she had, I would have said, "OK, I understand," and I would have felt somewhat bound by that. But she didn't.'[103]

The differences did not take long to emerge. Most fundamental was the schism on Brexit. Despite both being Remainers, May rapidly came to terms with the result, according to members of her inner circle who said she never considered a second referendum throughout the ups and downs of the years ahead. By contrast, Hammond, once viewed by colleagues as a solid Eurosceptic, was contemptuous of Brexiteer claims that sunlit economic uplands were just around the corner and wanted to do everything to protect British businesses from what was coming. He pushed to stay as close economically to the EU as possible, then championed 'transition periods' to protect firms from a cliff-edge departure, while arguing that the Treasury should keep back extra cash in case of Brexit turbulence. To one May adviser, Hammond was 'stubborn' and ignorant of what Tory MPs would stomach: 'When it came to party management, it just seemed like someone had forgotten to put the batteries in.'[104] Another said: 'He could start a fight in a paper bag.'[105] Hammond allies would counter by saying he was a Brexit realist. In turn, Hammond liked to joke about May's authoritarian streak. Driving through the Chinese city of Hangzhou during a G20 joint visit he looked out at the empty streets with a policeman every ten metres and joked: 'I can't help thinking she'll be deeply, deeply impressed by this.'[106] The chancellor believed the prime minister neither understood nor was comfortable with economics – a charge that, when reflected in anonymous Treasury source quotes in the papers, caused uproar in Downing Street. May loyalists point to her decade at the Bank of England by way of rebuttal. 'It was never very apparent to the outside world at the time how dysfunctional their relationship was,' said a Treasury insider who saw it first-hand.[107] A Cabinet colleague put it more bluntly: 'She and Philip Hammond grew to loathe each other quite quickly.'[108]

However, it was with Nick Timothy, who was two decades younger than Hammond but had the ear of his boss, that the fiercest clashes played out. Timothy, 'a man not short of evangelism' as one friend puts it, had a vision for a more interventionist form of Tory economics.[109] The chancellor, it is safe to say, did not share the outlook. 'Nick Timothy is to taste,' Hammond said. 'But he's a deeply opinionated person with a pretty radical view of the world and a very significant anti-establishment streak in him, which is really not Theresa at all.'[110] Timothy thought Hammond 'quite sneery' in meetings.[111] Hill too found him intransigent: 'His behaviour was really bad. I will never quite forgive Philip, I'm afraid.'[112] Timothy and Hammond would clash over the best way to fund new grammar schools, over plans for a 'modern industrial strategy', over countless other policy drives. Their visceral dislike of each other was captured in an extraordinary leak when it was suggested that Timothy had often referred to Hammond as 'the cunt' in Downing Street. The chancellor, fuming, phoned a senior Number 10 figure. 'I want you to tell me the truth, yes or no. Am I referred to as "the cunt" in the private office?' Caught in the headlights, the adviser replied: 'Chancellor, I can't comment.'[113] Timothy would later deny to friends he had called Hammond 'the cunt', but rather, in one moment of exasperation, 'a cunt'.[114]

If tensions over Brexit and Timothy stretched Hammond's relationship with May to breaking point, the Spring Budget debacle of March 2017 was the moment it snapped. The chancellor announced that the self-employed – a growing chunk of the workforce – would start paying National Insurance rates closer to those of fully employed workers. Hammond saw fairness in the policy, ending a quirk in the system that benefited rich one-man bands, and believes to this day that it was the right approach. The problem: it was an explicit breach of the party's election manifesto promise not to raise the rate of income tax, VAT or National Insurance. One Treasury insider viewed the blunder as symptomatic of an approach that saw the chancellor dubbed 'Spreadsheet Phil' by the tabloids, fixating on small details and missing the wider picture.[115] Hammond pointed the finger at a raft of aides and officials in Number 10 and Number 11 whose job it was to spot the political dangers. Either way, after days of prevarication – technically the manifesto promise had already been breached in the fine print of a law nobody noticed passed during George Osborne's time as chancellor, but the argument did not wash – Hammond was ordered to U-turn. He offered his resignation, May waved it away, but the damage was done.[116] 'He was embarrassed and humiliated by it,' said one Cabinet colleague. 'They stopped having a functioning relationship post-Budget.'[117]

Political actions are the products of their times. The intensity and uncertainty of the months after the EU referendum can be hard to recapture now. Ben Gummer, the youngest member of the Cabinet tasked with overseeing government business in a Whitehall reeling from the Brexit vote, summed it up best. 'I really want to impress on you that there was a real sense of making sure that the country didn't collapse. The markets were holding their breath and saying: "If you make the wrong calls now, this is going to be a disaster,"' Gummer said. 'We felt personal jeopardy in those first few months – it felt like standing on a tightrope.'[118] This is the context in which Nick and Fi's instinct to grip hard must be seen.

Nor, indeed, should their influence be interpreted as inherently misfiring. Politically, it was the reverse. Theresa May's 'politics isn't a game' mantra, the image of a 'bloody difficult woman' – to borrow a Ken Clarke phrase – standing up to Brussels and acting in the national interest, resonated with the public. The Conservative poll lead over Labour hit double digits, then soared past 20 percentage points. So too did May's personal ratings skyrocket, reaching Margaret Thatcher levels and leading some Tory MPs only half in jest to dub her 'Mummy'. If inside the government there was dysfunction, the prevailing mood beyond Westminster appeared to be that, given everything, things were going swimmingly.

Instead, different insights into the nature of political power emerge from that first year – about how proximity to the leader can trump the hierarchy of an organisational chart, how the idiosyncrasies of a prime minister's character can determine how the country is run. Would Theresa May have recast Conservatism as she did without Timothy and Hill? Would she have picked such a hard Brexit on her own? Or fallen out so spectacularly with her chancellor? Perhaps. But, at the very least, not in the same way.

Nick Timothy spent years playing down claims about his outsized influence on the early May premiership. But now, many years on, he has come to accept some of what was said. It is true May was not a 'creative' thinker, Timothy agreed in an interview, relying on others for that.[119] She could be impenetrable. 'I think I knew her less well than I thought I did,' he admitted.[120] And then there was the dominance of the co-chiefs. As they dreamed in the Home Office of their boss reaching Number 10, Nick and Fi had always vowed never to become chiefs of staff. Simon King, the department's director of strategy, had been earmarked for the role by the pair, but at the time of the Brexit vote he was in Japan. And so in the maelstrom of Cameron's resignation and the snap leadership race and Leadsom's sudden withdrawal and the need for a plan, they had stepped into the void. 'Arguably we were too powerful,' said Timothy in a moment of candour. 'That was partly a reflection of the fact that Theresa lets her advisers decide who she is pretty much, to be honest. It's something I always denied to myself. But I think, on reflection, there's truth in it.'[121]

One critical call was still to be taken, however. It would end up stripping the co-chiefs of every shred of political power they had and dooming their boss's premiership.

5

Mayday

THE CALL THAT plunged Theresa May's premiership into peril was just as short as the one that had handed her power eleven months earlier. It was not May herself who received the news this time but her adviser Fiona Hill. It was a few minutes before 10 p.m. on 8 June 2017, results night for the snap election May had called to increase her House of Commons majority. Inside the Conservative Campaign Headquarters (CCHQ) the BBC's exit poll was awaited with a near-universal expectation of sizable gains. The voice on the phone, however, suggested otherwise.

'It's a hung parliament, Fiona,' said Andrew Marr, the BBC's veteran political correspondent, tipping off Hill.[1] Not only would the Tories fail to increase their number of MPs, they were forecast to fall back. It was a staggering prediction. When the Conservatives triggered the race, they had been 20 percentage points ahead of Jeremy Corbyn's Labour in the opinion polls. Now, it appeared that David Cameron's slim 2015 majority was gone. Hill rushed to Nick Timothy, her fellow Downing Street co-chief of staff and confidant, to break the news. 'Don't joke,' he said. But no one was laughing. To Timothy, it felt like 'the end of the world'.[2]

Colleagues watching the pair through the glass walls of their private room were beginning to twig. 'This doesn't look good, something's up,' thought one.[3] More caught on as Nick and Fi marched through CCHQ's open-plan office, packed with staffers, to the back room where the campaign leaders were housed. The news was met with disbelief. 'This is bullshit,' said Lynton Crosby, the mastermind of the 2015 victory who had been brought in to secure another win.[4] One late internal projection had pointed to a Tory majority of ninety-two seats.[5] It would prove illusory.

Come 10 p.m., when TV screens revealed the exit poll to the rest of the building, there was an 'intake of breath', then 'absolute silence'.[6] Darren Mott, the party's long-serving director of campaigning, would later collapse, slumping to the floor. An ambulance's blue flashing lights would add to the sense of emergency.[7] May had never wanted an election: it was others who persuaded her to act. Now dread filled those who had done the lobbying. Timothy was in a 'total daze'.[8] Hill was 'walking around from one room to another, not quite knowing where to go or what to do', getting looks of 'sheer hatred' from donors in the VIP area.[9] JoJo Penn, May's deputy chief of staff, would refer to the exit poll as 'the moment I found out we were screwed', according to a Tory source.[10] For Chris Wilkins, May's director of strategy, it led to the 'worst night of my life'.[11]

And then came May's reaction. In public, the prime minister had built a reputation as a leader with a dogged determination and an iron will. In private, too, she usually gave little away. But tonight there were tears. 'They're saying it's a hung parliament!' said May, watching on from her Maidenhead constituency home, down the line to Timothy.[12] He heard the emotion as he reached to offer reassurance: 'She was properly crying.'[13] Hill too could tell her boss had been 'in tears' when May called: 'I need you here.'[14] She jumped in a car.

The exit poll, in the end, would prove right. Calling the snap election had been the biggest gamble of Theresa May's political career and it had backfired in spectacular fashion. As Conservatives across the country reeled, one would allow himself a smile, revenge being a dish best served at the ballot box. George Osborne would declare later: 'Theresa May is a dead woman walking.'[15]

Theresa May would, in fact, cling on. A deal was stitched together with Northern Ireland's Democratic Unionist Party (DUP), bringing enough votes to keep government business ticking over. The lack of a Cabinet putsch, not least from Boris Johnson who withheld his knife, was critical too. In the end May's premiership would last another two years – much longer than most predicted that night. But Osborne's analysis, ultimately, would prove correct. Without a Commons majority it would be impossible to secure approval for a Brexit deal, the most important policy issue of the day. Months would be spent cutting and recutting the terms of the UK's departure with Brussels, only to fall short of the MP votes needed for them to be passed.

The stand-off would lead to declarations of a crisis in British parliamentary democracy, but in truth there was a simpler explanation: May had simply failed to get the numbers. When Boris Johnson eventually succeeded her, turning up the dial on 'no deal' fears and romping home to an eighty-seat majority at his own snap election, a deal that was not too different would pass with ease. Which is why the 2017 election matters so much. It was the pivotal moment in the May premiership but was also critical for the country in a way that has faded too quickly in the collective memory. If May had increased the Tory majority, as many in her camp still believe she should have done, a Brexit deal would likely have passed Parliament. Her authority with colleagues, already strong, would have been enhanced, making rebellions more challenging for Tory MPs just re-elected on a mandate to deliver Brexit. The House of Lords would have found it trickier to unpick her Brexit deal given the Salisbury Convention, which protects government legislation promised in its election manifesto. She would have returned to Brussels with a fresh mandate.

Instead, the hubris of trying to bank a huge opinion poll lead resulted in a hung parliament, a backwards step not just for May but for those hoping to move on from Brexit. The country was plunged into a doom loop of trying, again and again, to plot a course out of the EU which could unite a Commons evenly split by the 2017 result. One figure who helped run the Tory campaign likened it to an aeroplane crash, when twenty-odd different errors have to happen one after the other to result in disaster. 'Basically, that was what fucking happened,' the source said. 'Everything went wrong.' With the help of more than five hundred pages of leaked documents from both Tory and Labour camps – election memos, polling trackers, private emails, messaging scripts, campaign timetables – the story of that disaster can now be told.

*

Nick Timothy was the first across the Rubicon. During the short leadership race in the summer of 2016, before Theresa May had even reached Number 10, he suspected a general election would be needed if Brexit was ever going to be delivered. 'It was really obvious that there was never going to be a majority in the Commons for any particular outcome,' Timothy recalled.[16] He urged May not to rule out an early vote categorically, but she did just that, preferring to deliver a message of 'real certainty' – an assurance many Tory MPs at the time were demanding.[17] The explicit denials of a looming election would continue all the way to the sudden pivot.

Fiona Hill was next. She had waved away Timothy's arguments during the leadership contest but, looking back, thought that 'deep down' she knew it was needed.[18] With summer passed and May settled into the role, Timothy tried again. 'It wasn't a difficult conversation because the first thing I said to him was "I know",' said Hill.[19] So, from autumn 2016, the two brightest stars in May's orbit were indicating the same way forward.

Brexit delivery was the obvious reason. May had inherited a Commons majority of eleven from the last election, meaning if all opposition party MPs voted against a measure just six Tories had to join them to force defeat on the government.[20] Given that most Conservative MPs had backed Remain, exceeding that bar was not hard to imagine, even amid the rhetoric of needing to respect the referendum result.

There were other reasons too. May was hamstrung by David Cameron's manifesto. The reimagining of Conservatism dreamed of by Timothy was butting up against political reality. Any policy change not in the 2015 election prospectus could be voted down in the House of Lords, where the Tories had no majority, since the so-called Salisbury Convention only protected manifesto promises. Ending the new grammar school ban was one flagship plan that looked destined to be put through the shredder by peers. In addition, of course, there was the opinion poll lead, blinking its 'come get me' eyes at the new leadership as it grew in size each month. How long would it stay this big? Gordon Brown had baulked at the chance to bank an early poll lead with a quick election after taking over from Tony

Blair. His team lived to regret not seizing the moment, as May's advisers knew.

And so more members of May's inner circle made the crossing too. Chris Wilkins, her chief speech-writer and director of strategy, was one. 'If you think Brexit really is this key moment of change and we need to do things differently, then you need your own mandate,' Wilkins argued. 'You're tied to David Cameron's election manifesto, which was obviously written before Brexit and no longer holds.'[21] JoJo Penn, the Downing Street deputy chief of staff, was another: 'It didn't look like a crazy idea to have an election because we were very far ahead very consistently in the polls.'[22] By early 2017, two senior Cabinet ministers had joined them: Philip Hammond, still chancellor despite falling out with May, and David Davis, the Brexit secretary. Both feared the timing of a 2020 election, Hammond believing it would undercut his push for transition periods, Davis fearing Brussels would exploit the looming vote in negotiations.[23]

For months and months, Theresa May held out. The battle over Article 50 weakened her resolve. The legal fight had been lost, the Supreme Court ordering her to get Parliament's approval for triggering the process of leaving the EU. On the face of it, the Commons appeared a doddle, 498 MPs voting to use Article 50 compared to 114 voting against on 1 February 2017, but behind the scenes there was much Tory arm-twisting. 'She came back from the Commons and said: "Well, that was more difficult than I thought, I can begin to see it now,"' said Hill.[24] There was another temptation. The Conservative victory in the Copeland by-election later that month sent records tumbling. Labour had held the Cumbrian constituency and its predecessors since 1924. No governing party had flipped an opposition party seat in a by-election for thirty-five years. May's electoral magic, it appeared, was real.

As winter turned to spring, May was warming to the idea. But she was not there yet. Over wine and crisps in her Downing Street flat one night after work, four members of May's inner circle – Timothy, Hill, Wilkins and Penn – pushed their case. May and, significantly, her husband, Philip, were still resistant. How would we get round previously ruling out a snap election, May asked. Voters would get over that, she was assured. 'What happens if I come back and I've only got the same majority?' May asked. 'The key thing is it will be your majority,' argued Wilkins.[25] Philip May, believing his wife's premiership was at stake, pushed back the hardest. 'You're asking us to risk the whole thing? That's a massive decision for us to take,' he said, or similar words, according to two people there.[26] This argument was trickier to counter.

The idea that the Mays decided to call the election during a five-day walking holiday in Snowdonia, North Wales, in early April – one pushed by Downing Street at the time – is only half-true, according to insiders.[27] Plans were already being put in place before the break. The green light was finally given after the Easter break. May had decided: she wanted an election. The prime minister too was now over the Rubicon, not looking back. The discussions had been kept so tight that even senior Number 10 figures were blind-sided when brought into the loop. 'What are you doing on 8 June?' Timothy would say teasingly, delivering the punchline as diaries were reached for: 'Voting in a general election.'[28] When the nation was told on 18 April, the Westminster bubble, taken in by the endless denials, was just as stunned.

Looking back, May's allies see two early mistakes. Not in calling the election itself – the key Tory players still think trying to convert the giant poll lead into more seats was the right decision. Rather, the missteps were in how they did it. One was the wavering. If May had decided earlier, the general election could have been timed to coincide with the locals on 4 May, when, it turned out, the Tories would trounce Labour. Instead, voters would be made to go to the ballot box twice in two months at Downing Street's insistence. The other was the campaign's length. The Fixed-term Parliaments Act had been created by the coalition to schedule general elections every five years, robbing the prime minister of the power to trigger an early vote without the support of other parties. This race proved that was a fallacy – the official opposition in reality would always find it hard to keep saying no to an election indefinitely – but complications from the law, plus May's wish to pass some outstanding pieces of legislation, meant the campaign would last over seven weeks. That was longer than usual and would exacerbate the late

Tory slump. All seemed fine as the Conservative campaign band-wagon got up and running, but the first errors in a fateful journey had already been made.

Everything that followed must be seen through the prism of the intense time pressure that a snap election creates. Theresa May's team had avoided pitfalls tumbled into by Gordon Brown: failing to go for it when the opportunity arose; and letting discussions leak into the media before a call was made. But in doing so, the chal-lenges of launching a nationwide campaign from a standing start were underestimated. There had been at least three years of plotting for the Tories' triumphant 2015 election bid, allowing for the messages to be fine tuned and politics to be picked for an agreed campaign framing. This time there were barely three weeks of proper prepar ation and even that was only for the tiny handful of people in the know. Others – grassroots strategists and candidate selectors, for example, and almost every single Tory MP – had to begin from scratch. So too did Labour, of course – which was part of the calculation. But many of the errors that followed must be seen in that context. Everyone was making calls on the hoof.

Lynton Crosby had not been expecting an early election. He was in Fiji for his wife Dawn's sixtieth birthday when a call came in from Stephen Gilbert, a CCHQ veteran. 'The prime minister's going to ring you, she wants to put a proposition to you,' Gilbert explained. 'She's not going for an election? I thought she ruled it out?' replied Crosby.[29] May was indeed going for one and Crosby's involvement was wanted. Nick Timothy had already decided he and Fi were not best placed to lead the election push. 'We've never run a national election campaign,' he had told Gilbert, which led them to Crosby.[30] The 'Wizard of Oz' still carried his halo from the shock 2015 win. Crosby did not know May well, not compared to David Cameron and Boris Johnson, but the polls pointed to another Tory victory. He would say yes, though he would not join the team for two weeks, completing the holiday commitment to his family first. Other members of his team were sent scrambling to CCHQ: Isaac Levido, another Aussie strategist, was switching flights in Dallas when word arrived, forcing him to abandon the second leg of his planned journey and head for London instead. Gilbert, not Crosby, would be campaign director. An email from Gilbert on 17 April confirmed the terms: Crosby and his colleague Mark Textor, the research brains of the operation, would be described as 'playing leading roles in the campaign'.[31] Their firm's work came at a considerable price – more than half a million pounds, according to one Tory campaign source.[32]

Their plan was captured in three memos, seen by this author, compiled by Crosby and Textor and shared with Team May. Dating from early April, before the election was announced, risks were flagged up. One memo downloaded views from four focus groups, two in London and one each in Bury and Bolton. 'Voters have a strong desire for certainty and do *not* want an election now,' read the opening words.[33] A second memo, laying out the findings of a 'benchmark' opinion poll, gave a similar conclusion: 'The research shows there is clearly a lot of risk involved with going for an early election – and there is a real need to nail down the "why" for doing so now.'[34] Crosby and Textor tied together what they had found in a 'Strategic Note', the third memo. 'Our research shows that this election can be won,' read one part. 'A good campaign could deliver an increased majority for the Conservatives, but there is also a clear risk that the party could end up with fewer seats than it has currently if the campaign is not framed in the correct way.'[35] So the warning was explicit, though so too was the talk of potential success.

As it transpired the big clash would not be over differing expectations but how to run the race. In 2015, Crosby had been handed sole power over the Tory campaign, and everyone in the bunker, David Cameron included, had agreed on the approach. In 2017, that never happened. There were two power bases: Theresa May's Downing Street insiders, headed by Nick and Fi; and the outside professionals, led by Crosby and Textor. There were two contradictory visions too. The stand-off would never be resolved, with a clumsy mix of the approaches adopted. As the blame game that exploded in public after the result would show, these fault lines had been there all the while.

One difference of approach came over campaign nuts and bolts.

Theresa May polled better than the Conservative Party brand and way better than her direct rival, Labour leader Jeremy Corbyn. To the election pros, pinning the pitch on May therefore made sense. May versus Corbyn brought a better chance of victory than Tories versus Labour, in theory. May's set accepted the analysis of the situation but favoured a different approach, one truer to the prime minister. They wanted daily press conferences as there had been in the 1980s and 1990s, when each campaign day would begin with leading party figures taking questions from the press in London, hoping that this approach would put more of a focus on substance rather than on style. Some days May would be joined by other Cabinet ministers, sometimes she would not be there in person at all.

The 'presidential' approach won out.[36] It was visible in its purest form when the blue battle bus was unveiled. 'THERESA MAY: FOR BRITAIN' read the words on its side in huge lettering, with a vast scrawled signature nearby. Squint and the 'Conservatives' tag on the door could just about be seen. This framing meant that when May wilted under the pressure of her first general election campaign as leader the impact was all the more consequential.

However, the most fundamental clash came over the different camps' 'big picture' vision. For Nick Timothy, as well as those alongside him like Chris Wilkins and Fiona Hill, the election was about embodying the change May had promised to deliver after Brexit, meeting that 'cry of pain' from the country.[37] But for Crosby, Textor and the election specialists it was continuity after a referendum which had brought great uncertainty that voters craved. The difference is laid bare most starkly in the documents over which Timothy and Crosby had most control.

For Crosby, it was the memos of secret campaign advice. There were many, but that 'Strategic Note' delivered before the election was announced distilled his advice to its essence. Nine 'critical' points for success were spelled out on its first page. One talked about 'framing the election as a chance to achieve stability, security and continuity which the other parties and politicians threaten'. Another stressed 'understanding that this is not an "ordinary election" where a focus on policies, manifesto and what the Tory Party might do are the central element'. A third read: 'Recognising this is not about change but continuity.'[38]

The message was made even more explicit in a later section:

> Voters do not want change. They believe they secured change at last year's EU referendum, and now they want that change to be implemented. They are broadly happy with the direction the country is going, and are desperate to avoid further uncertainty.
>
> Voters are looking for stability and certainty after a period of instability and uncertainty. These are key equities of Theresa May. Thus the Conservatives must show how in the long-term holding an election now will actually reduce uncertainty and is a way of getting on with Brexit.
>
> This is not an election about changing social policy, or changing the way the economy works as that will come from implementing Brexit. Rather, this election is about securing the best leadership to make Brexit work and see the UK through the uncertainty that lies ahead.[39]

Nick Timothy was pushing the opposite approach. That much is clear from a document he co-wrote and for which he held responsibility: the Conservative Party election manifesto. Far from playing it dull, Timothy produced a manifesto that was vaulting in its ambition to redefine what Conservatism meant and how it would be applied to the twenty-first century. 'This manifesto sets out a vision for Britain's future – not just for the next five years, but beyond,' it read. Five 'giant challenges' were identified to be addressed, riffing off the 'five evils' of the 1942 Beveridge Report that were the launchpad for Labour's vision of a welfare state after the Second World War.[40]

Its bold attempt to change what the party stood for was captured in one eye-catching passage:

> We will need to govern in the manner established by Theresa May since she became prime minister last year. We must reject the ideological templates provided by the socialist left and the libertarian right and instead embrace the mainstream view that recognises the good that government can do. Rather than pursue an agenda based on a supposed centre ground defined and established by elites in Westminster, we will govern in the interests of the mainstream of

the British public . . . Under the strong and stable leadership of Theresa May, there will be no ideological crusades. The government's agenda will not be allowed to drift to the right. Our starting point is that we should take decisions on the basis of what works. And we will always be guided by what matters to the ordinary, working families of this nation.[41]

Lynton Crosby thought manifestos were for 'ideologues and wankers' and had floated not having one at all; Timothy had used it to reshape the party in his and May's image.[42] Crosby wanted the core message to be one of 'continuity'; Timothy's manifesto was so driven by 'change' the word was used thirty-nine times, more than in the Tory re-election bids in 2015 (twenty-four) and 2019 (fourteen).[43] Crosby had explicitly warned against floating new policies; Timothy's blueprint for government would be packed with them.

One would prove devastating in its impact.

Yet the Tory divisions were dwarfed by those of their great election rival. Since 2015, the Labour Party had been going through one of its periodic bouts of factional warring, prompted by the rise to the top of one man: Jeremy Corbyn.

Corbyn was the accidental Labour leader. In the three decades he had been the MP for Islington North, Corbyn, mild-mannered and idealistic, had never lusted after his party's leadership and showed no sign of doing so when it became vacant with Ed Miliband's resignation after the May 2015 election. That his name was even put forward was a quirk of fate. At a gathering of Labour MP members of the Socialist Campaign Group other candidates were considered and dismissed – some, like John McDonnell, because they had tried and failed in the past – before eyes fell on the bearded sexagenarian.[44] Corbyn then only made the ballot, securing the thirty-five MP nominations needed with two minutes to spare before the deadline, thanks to 'lent' votes. Dame Margaret Beckett, the New Labour grandee who gave Corbyn her signature to widen the debate, would later call the decision 'one of the biggest political mistakes I've ever made'.[45]

But, once through, he electrified the contest. At hustings audience members would burst into applause as Corbyn condemned the Iraq invasion or called for mass renationalisation. His straight answers and clear convictions contrasted with the triangulation of centrist rivals Yvette Cooper, Andy Burnham and Liz Kendall, tapping into a weariness at the compromises of the New Labour era. Fuelling it all was a surge of new left-wing party members, able to sign up for just £3 thanks to Miliband's 2014 leadership election reforms – still considered by Labour moderates a misjudgement of epic proportions. The changes were meant to minimise trade union influence. In fact, they handed power to the hard Left that first Neil Kinnock and then Tony Blair and Gordon Brown had spent the 1980s and 1990s marginalising. That the reforms were even adopted was the result of another quirk of fate: a drunken brawl in a Commons bar that saw Labour MP Eric Joyce resign, triggering a by-election in Falkirk, in turn leading to alleged meddling by unions that forced Miliband's hands. It was one of the great 'butterfly wing' moments of this period of British politics. A direct line can be drawn from Joyce's headbutt to Corbyn taking to a stage in Parliament Square in September 2015, his leadership having just been secured, and blasting out 'The Red Flag' across Westminster with joyous supporters.

By the time of the snap election of 2017, Corbyn had already seen off one attempted coup. In the wake of the Brexit vote, Labour MPs had overwhelmingly called on their leader to go, 172 voting for a no-confidence motion and just forty voting against, but party members simply re-elected him in the leadership race that followed, with Owen Smith defeated. Another coup had threatened after the Copeland by-election loss which helped persuade May to call the vote. As a result, when the snap election was triggered there were differing responses. Corbyn, not a politician easily fazed, appeared upbeat. The Labour leader insisted on diving straight into campaigning, sticking to a scheduled Birmingham visit. 'I never felt terrible about it. Jeremy clearly didn't because he was happy to get out on the road,' said one senior adviser who was with him in Parliament when the election was called.[46] But a few minutes' walk away in the Labour Party headquarters at Southside, where many senior officials long predated the Corbyn takeover, there was despondency. 'We thought we were going to get wiped out,' said one, recalling early internal predictions that just one hundred MPs would survive. 'This is a fucking lost hope, there's absolutely no point.'[47]

Seumas Milne was among the optimists. The *Guardian* political correspondent and columnist had crossed over to become Corbyn's executive director of strategy and communications in 2015. He was not blind to the scale of the challenge, having been privately predicting a snap election as May's opinion poll lead soared, but found reasons to be upbeat. One was that campaigns brought strict broadcasting rules which Milne believed would allow Corbyn's message to reach voters in a more objective fashion than the coverage to date. A second was that the post-referendum coup had actually tightened Corbyn's grip on the party allowing him to fill the shadow cabinet with loyalists and secure sign-off for left-wing policies that his team was convinced were popular. A third came from a deliberate reframing of Corbyn as a left-wing populist leader. Donald Trump in America, Syriza in Greece, Marine Le Pen in France and the pro-independence push in Scotland had all tapped into a form of anti-status quo populism in the preceding few years. Milne hoped for something similar and picked an election slogan with that in mind: 'For the Many, Not the Few'. 'It was explicitly an anti-establishment, anti-elite, pro-popular majority politics, feeding off the kind of progressive populism that had shown itself to be successful in different ways, in different countries,' said Milne.[48] A 'narrative arc' for the campaign, captured in an internal document, would speak to this populist drive. 'Jeremy Corbyn – the Man, the Politician, the Leader' was the theme for week one; 'Rigged System – Holding People Back' was week two. Focuses on the economy, healthcare and education followed before rallying back around the 'For the Many, Not the Few' theme in the closing days.[49]

Usually Team Corbyn was based in the leader's suite of offices in Parliament's Norman Shaw South building. But for the campaign, they were in with the moderates of Southside. The tensions were real: aides recall factions sitting separately, high-school rivalries played out in the battle for the governorship of Britain. One tussle that would be seen throughout was whether to put the focus on 'defensive' seats, that is, those held by the party already, or 'offensive' ones held by others. A strategy document signed off by Milne showed the Corbynistas' ambitions: 'We are fighting this election to win. Nothing less will do.' Another part read: 'Jeremy's tour is central to the campaign, both for direct contact with campaigners and voters and for media relations. It should include offensive and defensive seats, roughly in equal measure.'[50] But in Labour HQ, it was defensive seats that were made the focus – resulting in two competing strategies that echoed the Tories' own splits. Patrick Heneghan, Labour's executive director in charge of elections who had served the party for the best part of two decades, was one who made the defensive call. 'I was still looking at the polling numbers, listening to what the MPs were saying to us here and felt that we still needed to run a by-and-large defensive campaign.'[51] At times the clashes could be jaw-dropping. At one point Heneghan was given a list by a senior Corbyn figure of moderate MPs and told to scale back funding from their campaigns. The MPs in question were Tom Watson in West Bromwich East, Yvette Cooper in Normanton, Pontefract and Castleford, Caroline Flint in Don Valley, Dan Jarvis in Barnsley Central, Kate Green in Stretford and Urmston, Bridget Phillipson in Houghton and Sunderland South, Rachel Reeves in Leeds West, Chris Bryant in Rhondda, Seema Malhotra in Feltham and Heston, Angela Eagle in Wallasey, Kevan Jones in North Durham, John Healey in Wentworth and Dearne, Phil Wilson in Sedgefield, and Neil Coyle in Bermondsey and Old Southwark. Perceived Corbyn critics were being singled out for punishment. A contemporary scribbled note seen by the author backs up Heneghan's account. The request was rejected but it showed the depths to which relations between the two sides had sunk. Corbyn allies, it should be noted, had long complained of the opposite, claiming it was moderate Labour MPs who received favourable funding from HQ.

The story of 2017 is at its core a tale of two manifestos – one leaked, the other vilified.

For the first three weeks the Conservative campaign ran just as Lynton Crosby had hoped. While not the campaign manager, he was still a dominant force in the CCHQ bunker, according to Tory insiders. It was his framing that was used in Theresa May's early interventions.

The prime minister's Downing Street speech announcing the election had put Brexit front and centre. 'Our opponents believe because the government's majority is so small that our resolve will weaken and that they can force us to change course,' she said, trying to justify her 180-degree spin in announcing the election by pointing to the need to strengthen her hand for Brussels negotiations. 'They are wrong.'[52] Tory-backing papers applauded the news, the *Daily Mail* declaring 'CRUSH THE SABOTEURS' on its front page with a photograph of an icy May stare. Early responses from voters were mixed. 'You're joking? Not another one?!' declared Brenda from Bristol in a BBC clip that went viral.[53] The flip-flop on calling the election soon faded from the headlines, however. May would repeat the Brexit trick two weeks later, giving another Number 10 speech, this time accusing the EU of interfering in the vote.[54] The flimsy proof points included a critical media briefing about a lunch she had with two senior European politicians and a warning that Britain must pay its debts before departure. But Brexit was back in the spotlight the day before the local elections. The result: the Tories stormed to 38 per cent, way ahead of Labour on 27 per cent.[55] These were real votes, not the theoreticals of opinion polls. Tory spirits were high.

So when James Schneider, Corbyn's director of strategic communications, got back-to-back bombshell phone calls from political reporters on 10 May he could be forgiven for feeling the fates aligning. 'Hello, mate, I've got the manifesto,' said Jack Blanchard from the *Mirror*. 'What, all of it?' joked Schneider. 'Yes, I've got all of it,' came the response. Schneider played for time, scrambling for answers after hanging up, but then a second call dropped from Kate McCann of the *Daily Telegraph*. She too had it. 'Of course you do,' said Schneider, exasperated.[56] For the first time in modern British history a political party's entire manifesto had leaked. Coming right before Labour's National Executive Committee was due to debate and approve the package, it seemed to Schneider a deliberate attempt by moderates to force late changes to the avowedly left-wing platform. The apparent reasoning: get the policies in the public domain before they are locked down, trigger a backlash and hope they are watered down. 'It was awful,' Schneider recalled.

Corbyn's manifesto had been packed with left-wing retail offers, matching his new populist position. Tuition fees would be scrapped under a Labour government. The railways, water companies, energy firms and Royal Mail would be nationalised. The 50p top rate of income tax would come back and more people would pay the 45p rate. The thirty hours of free childcare offer would be expanded to cover two-year-olds. The *Telegraph*'s splash decried 'Corbyn's manifesto to take Britain back to 1970s'; the *Mirror* went with 'Corbyn will nationalise energy, rail and mail'. The leaks jumped to the top of the broadcast bulletins and would dominate election coverage for days, then return there again come the official manifesto launch on 16 May.

Yet from the jaws of seeming disaster came a Labour victory in the form of a poll surge. A hole had been punched through the Tories' Brexit framing, the spotlight suddenly falling instead on tax, spending and the domestic policy agenda. Many of the individual policies, such as renationalising the railways, proved popular according to polling – as the Corbyn camp knew they would after carrying out rounds of testing. The Tory line that the measures were financially reckless, an attack that would have cut through in 2019, was blunted by the assumption among voters that May's victory was already a given. 'It was fantastic because it gave lots of oxygen and airtime to our policies,' Schneider said, his fears over the leak long gone.[57] Jeremy Corbyn thinks the same. 'I was really annoyed,' he said of his initial reaction. 'But then, actually, in a funny kind of way it helped . . . it started getting quite an interesting write-up by a lot of people.'[58] Seamus Milne joked: 'It worked so well for us that then everyone thought that we had done it ourselves.'[59] That was not the case – an informal Labour leak investigation and other well-placed sources suggest as much, though no culprit has ever been named – but it might as well have been. The Corbyn campaign had its first big win.

Ask Conservative MPs about their 2017 manifesto and two words are usually spat back: social care. It exists like a scar on the collective consciousness of those who fought the election. Was there a single Tory policy in the five general elections in this period that had a greater impact on the final result? The EU referendum promise in 2015 ultimately proved more consequential, but senior Tories who led that campaign are split about just how many voters it persuaded to switch parties.

That Nick Timothy and Ben Gummer, the Cabinet Office minister and manifesto co-author, wanted to tackle one of the great overlooked issues in recent British policy-making was admirable. An ageing population had forced the spotlight onto a quirk of the UK healthcare system: while the state picked up 100 per cent of the cost of NHS treatment, families were largely left to pay the bills for social care themselves. The costs could be crippling if an elderly parent was unlucky enough to develop a debilitating illness, such as dementia, sometimes forcing the sale of homes to finance treatment. It was a structural problem that successive sets of government ministers had dodged – and one that May's policy team wanted to fix.

A proposed solution had emerged thanks to Sir Andrew Dilnot. The former director of the Institute for Fiscal Studies, a leading Westminster think tank, had been tasked by David Cameron to find answers. His proposal had two elements: a floor and a cap. The floor was linked to a person's assets. It set a level below which the state would step in and pick up the tab, meaning a chunk of inheritance would be protected whatever happened. The cap was to do with social care costs. It named a top limit on the lifetime amount one person could pay for social care, after which the state would cover costs. The concepts worked in tandem. The floor made sure someone would never be left with nothing; the cap meant no one would have to pay hundreds of thousands of pounds for treatment.

Cameron had accepted Dilnot's plan but effectively parked it, with no date for implementation announced. Theresa May's policy team, away from the limelight, had quietly gone cold on one particular element: the cap. In their eyes, rich families were unfairly among the big beneficiaries of the cap. Millionaires could have the state pay for their social care once they hit the lifetime care cost total, with the poor helping fund their support through taxes. Thinking about what should be done instead was already under way. A green paper floating ideas was due that summer. So why not just be specific in the manifesto in May?

Trying to make a merit out of being straight with the British people, Timothy and Gummer – assisted by Will Tanner, who would go on to become Rishi Sunak's Number 10 deputy chief of staff – picked 'an ageing society' as one of the five great challenges to be addressed by the manifesto. 'We must admit that the solidarity that binds generations is under strain in our country,' a line in the relevant section of the document read, followed by policies to deal with the problem.[60] Many had a sting in the tail for older Britons. The triple lock on state pensions would in 2020 become a double lock, with pensions still rising in line with inflation or average wages, whichever might be higher, but no longer by a guaranteed 2.5 per cent, meaning potentially lower increases. The winter fuel payment would stop being given to all pensioners and would be means-tested instead, meaning wealthy older people lost out. The sweetener in the deal was meant to be the new social care proposal. The state would step in if someone's assets dwindled below £100,000 as they paid for social care: the new 'floor'. It was four times more generous than the version of a floor which existed for some judged to need care, set at £23,250. What was left unsaid was the abandonment of the cap, conspicuous by its absence.

The idea that Lynton Crosby's team never knew of the policy is wide of the mark, as email exchanges seen by the author show. On 25 April, twenty-three days before the manifesto was unveiled, Mark Textor was sent summaries of a dozen potentially controversial manifesto policies for testing. Among them was an early version of the social care idea when the floor was set at £50,000.[61] Nor is it correct to suggest that all the feedback was negative. Textor's note two days later distilling the findings had the social care plan among the six policies which 'on balance' were 'a good idea . . . on the face of it'.[62] But, lower down the same note, there were also clear warning signs. 'This social care policy is very confusing to voters, they don't understand it and therefore are divided over its merits,' read one line.[63] Another quoted a respondent saying, 'so they're going to take everything from me' except for the amount protected – the exact attack line that would prove so devastating when deployed in the campaign.[64] The sentences undercut any suggestion that the policies were waved through without hesitation. Crosby had explicitly warned against an 'ordinary election' focused on manifestos and policies. Yet that is what was coming.

When the circle of trust widened, the alarm bells rang louder. Gummer and Timothy had been closely concealing their manifesto work, as is normal. What was unusual this time round was the intense time pressure – the document was essentially pulled together in three weeks. 'We were working at such speed,' recalled Gummer.[65] When Fiona Hill, in charge of election comms, saw the social care proposal just days before it went to the printers she baulked. The split was the most fundamental in the year of Nick–Fi dominance over Downing Street. She had always trusted Timothy's judgement '100 per cent' but her instinct – the one that had proved so prescient she had been nicknamed 'the witch' – sensed a misstep. 'This policy is crap. I know it's crap. I'm going over to see Theresa to tell her that it's crap,' Hill thought.[66] JoJo Penn, May's deputy chief of staff, also eventually got cold feet. She did not think a campaign was the right time to float such a knotty new policy. 'It's hard to explain, it's complicated, you don't get that time or space in a campaign to put something like that forward,' said a Tory source.[67] Jeremy Hunt, the health secretary, was also unsure. He had been involved for months in social care discussions but, when shown relevant sections of the manifesto just before launch, he was surprised to see such a detailed new policy being put forward. 'He was really very worried about it,' said Paul Harrison, Hunt's special adviser, who recalled that his boss – a loyalist by instinct – pushed to rework the plan.[68] Harrison also voiced concerns, telling Hill: 'I am really worried about this.'[69] Gummer insisted the only person who flagged their unhappiness to him was Hill.[70] In the end, Hill and Penn took their concerns directly to the prime minister, moving a National Security Council meeting in order to see May in Downing Street and plead for a last-minute removal of the measure from the manifesto.[71] 'Theresa said, "No, I want it in. It's a bold thing, it's important to do,"' recalled Timothy, who sat in on the encounter.[72] The decision had been made.

On the morning of 18 May, manifesto day, Cabinet ministers

finally got to read the full document on the train to Halifax for the launch event. Sajid Javid, who as the Cabinet minister overseeing local government was involved in social care policy, was furious. He had deliberately not been shown the relevant section of the manifesto, according to two sources familiar with what happened – a sign of the distrust between May's inner circle and some senior ministers.[73] Education secretary Justine Greening discovered that free school lunches would become means-tested: another policy that caused anger, despite a new promise of free primary school breakfasts.[74] One Cabinet minister recalled the chancellor, Philip Hammond, crying out about one part: 'Hang on, that's not what I agreed!'[75] David Davis, already in Yorkshire and due to chair the event, did not even have a copy and was going spare. 'I never saw it until twenty minutes before the actual launch,' Davis said.[76] The manifesto team has argued that the process was no different from usual. Cabinet ministers contest this, insisting that there was less time for input and deliberation due to such tight timings. 'In the end, the Cabinet was bounced,' said one minister around the top table. There was 'huge arrogance' hidden behind the boldness of the manifesto – the 'foolish' assumption that a 'big win' was coming.[77]

Initially the social care policy, briefed into the day's newspapers, got the soft landing desired. 'YOU WON'T HAVE TO SELL HOME TO PAY FOR CARE,' shouted the *Daily Mail* front page. But before the launch had even taken place, the spin began to unravel. Sir Andrew Dilnot, fuming at the abandonment of his cap after being warned by Hunt, took to Radio 4's *Today* programme to castigate the plan. Elderly people who racked up huge social care costs would be 'helpless' to stop most of their assets being sold, he warned. The new proposal was like dodgy house insurance that stipulated: 'If it does burn down then you're completely on your own, you have to pay for all of it until you're down to the last £100,000.'[78] Far from protecting the homes of rich Tory voters, the proposal left them still exposed.

The blowback was fierce. Quite who coined the phrase 'dementia tax' is contested but both Labour and the Lib Dems pounced on the tag. The attack had the sting of truth to it: if someone was unlucky enough to get dementia the state would not pick up the bill except for the least well-off. The nuance – that that was the case already; indeed, the policy provided some extra protection by raising the asset floor – was lost. The scrapping of the cap was ruthlessly weaponised and aimed at a core Tory support group: elderly moneyed homeowners. 'We've taken leave of our fucking senses!' one backbencher in a marginal seat hollered down the phone at Davis.[79] Even Ben Gummer, one of the policy's co-authors, said its political impact was 'pretty nuclear'.[80] He would be blown away with other Tory MPs come election day, losing the battleground seat of Ipswich.

A council of war was called the following Sunday, with the campaign chiefs and Jeremy Hunt gathering in Tory HQ as the party's poll rating sank lower. Rather than a counteroffensive being plotted, there was an admission of defeat. May was told to ditch the policy. It was an attempt to 'stem the blood', one involved said.[81] The get-out was a passing manifesto mention of a green paper consulting on the changes. On Monday, 22 May, the prime minister performed the U-turn at the Tories' Welsh manifesto launch. 'I want to make a further point clear,' May said, noting the green paper reference and saying that 'consultation will include an absolute limit on the amount people have to pay for their care costs'. The cap was back. But as reporters pounced in the Q&A that followed, May compounded the problem. Number 10 advisers had suggested the change in position be played down, according to one account.[82] The fig leaf May used was that the 'principles' of the manifesto had not changed. Christopher Hope, the *Daily Telegraph*'s tenacious political hack, got the crucial soundbite, asking her what would change next. 'Nothing has changed!' May exclaimed in response, spreading her arms wide with open palms chopping like guillotines. 'Nothing. Has. Changed.' No longer was she 'strong and stable', to quote the words of Theresa May's presidential branding. She had, as Channel 4's Michael Crick put it in the press conference, become 'weak and wobbly'.

The social care debacle would leave Crosby exasperated. 'The first rule of politics is you have to secure your base. We scared our base, we undermined our base, that was the problem,' he later complained to others.[83] The Tory manifesto turned the campaign into a policy battle – not one defined by Brexit – and zoomed in not on sweets that the Conservatives were handing out but on tough medicine. Nick Timothy has since accepted that the social care policy should have had a cap: 'The absence of the cap meant that people who had more could be led to believe that they would lose absolutely everything, even if they wouldn't.'[84] Ben Gummer spent years thinking over the call and remains conflicted, still seeing a cap as flawed.[85] One senior Tory insider concluded that May's approach ended up doubling the pain:

> She picked the absolute worst of both worlds. She would've been better either saying, 'Yes, I've listened. It was the wrong decision and therefore I'm changing,' or saying, 'I know this isn't popular but it's the right thing to do, and I'm sticking by it.' By saying, 'Nothing has changed,' when something clearly had, she completely lost any of that equity about being strong and stable.[86]

★

By now it was clear the Tory campaign juggernaut was malfunctioning. Smoke was billowing from the engine; the speed was dropping alarmingly. But there were fresh setbacks to come.

With the narrative inverted, developments were viewed through a different lens. The first of two tragedies struck on the evening of Theresa May's social care about-turn. An Islamist suicide bomber detonated an explosion at the Manchester Arena as young fans and parents left an Ariana Grande concert, killing twenty-two people and injuring more than a thousand. Campaigning was cancelled as the hunt for co-conspirators was launched. Twelve days later another terror attack was launched on London Bridge, three radicals smashing into people with a van before going on a stabbing frenzy. Eight people were killed and forty-eight injured. With election day approaching, both events fed into the political debate. For May, who had spent six years heading up the Home Office, the developments could have put the focus on her perceived strengths on security issues. Instead it was the fall in armed police officer numbers on her watch – a reality focused on by Labour in its anti-austerity drive – that featured more prominently in the public debate.

Another problem was May's stilted media appearances. 'Her idea of campaigning is knocking on doors in Maidenhead. Being honest, she was terrified and quite wooden in her engagement with people beyond her patch,' said one Tory campaign chief.[87] In May's defence, she had not designed the presidential-style theme that pinned so much on her personal brand. A May ally recalled her saying one day in CCHQ: 'I hate this campaign. They're telling me what to do and where to stand and what to wear and I absolutely hate it.'[88] Another said the prime minister grew 'very tired and ratty'.[89] The media narrative of May fearing spontaneity was fuelled by a refusal to take part in TV debates, the caution of a frontrunner on display. 'If you're up against Tony Blair, maybe it would be the smart strategy. If you're up against Corbyn? Bonkers,' said David Davis.[90] David Cameron, watching from afar, thought the decision not to do debates as he had done caused real political damage.[91]

Pressure had even led to the brief and ill-staged return of an outcast. Philip Hammond had been summoned to St Ermin's Hotel near CCHQ when the race began, informed by the Aussie professionals that he would play no part in the campaign despite being chancellor.[92] But after Labour's manifesto dominance and reports that Hammond would be sacked post-election, a joint event with May was scheduled. In it, she repeatedly declined to promise that the chancellor would keep his job – another misfiring campaign moment. Hammond was so certain he would be gone that before election day he took photos of his Treasury office, pocketed some artefacts, sounded out other job opportunities and prepared his family's move out of Downing Street.[93] The disastrous result would leave May too weakened to sack him.

As May faltered, Jeremy Corbyn soared. A lifetime of addresses to protest movements was serving the Labour leader well, his rosy rhetoric of a shared struggle and common good showing up the prime minister's heavy-handed efforts at message discipline. The thousands who turned out for some rallies contrasted with the Tories' controlled invitation-only events, encapsulating Labour's 'For the Many' theme. The numbers and the energy that Corbyn drew for stump speeches astonished even his own most loyal advisers. 'It was pretty extraordinary,' recalled Milne, who saw the reaction as 'unprecedented' in modern

British election campaigns.[94] The chant that came to embody the excitement Corbyn engendered in his fans may never have come about but for the tardiness of Pete Doherty. Corbyn's team was in two minds about dropping into a music festival at the Tranmere Rovers football stadium, seeing risk in the former Libertines frontman's presence. 'I was very worried that Pete Doherty might be drunk, jump on Jeremy – the thing could go very wrong,' said James Schneider.[95] On hearing that Doherty was running late, they took a gamble, however, breaking away from campaigning nearby to deliver a quick Corbyn address to the festival crowd. Midway through his speech the audience suddenly started chanting. It was to the tune of 'Seven Nation Army' by The White Stripes. 'Oh, Jeremy Corbyn! Oh, Jeremy Corbyn!' The Labour leader himself was bemused at first, unable to hear the words. 'Oh, God! We've lost the crowd, they want me off,' Corbyn recalled thinking. 'Then I looked at the crowd and they were all smiling.'[96] Schneider, watching from the stage, burst into laughter. The populist framing was working. Labour's summer anthem was born.

Why did Corbyn appear to connect in 2017 in a way not replicated in 2019, when Labour would slump to its lowest seat total since 1935? The Tories who led the 2017 campaign have theories. Low expectations is one. Corbyn had not led a general election bid before and his jovial manner defied the portrayal of a terrorist-sympathising radical pushed by his political foes.

'Even though some people might not like him they did admire that he stuck to his guns and stood up for some things,' said one of the most senior figures in the Tory campaign.[97] Problems landing the Brexit attack was another. In 2017, it was much harder to show that Parliament had thwarted Brexit than it would be in 2019, masking Labour's deep split on the issue. Campaigns are also matters of comparative strengths and weaknesses, and the Maybot accentuated Corbyn's relaxed style in a way Boris Johnson's campaign razzmatazz would not two years later. One London School of Economics analysis found that Labour seats in which Corbyn held events saw their vote share jump almost 9 percentage points higher than those he missed on the campaign. There was no corresponding difference between Tory seats Theresa May did and did not visit.[98]

All Tory election gurus agree, however, on one key reason: the electorate did not think Labour would win. 'Corbyn did not seem like a credible threat because he appeared so unbelievable. Voters thought: "Is he ever really going to become prime minister?" And because so many people expected the Conservatives to run away with the election, they could be lazy with their vote,' said Isaac Levido, who worked with Crosby on the campaign.[99] Critical to the Tories' 2015 victory were polls showing a hung parliament and the real concerns that that possibility heightened for wavering voters. In 2017, a Tory triumph was baked in. Nick Timothy said:

> I've been through a lot of election campaigns and it's like a heavy-weight boxing contest, you are punching the shit out of one another every day and then eventually you stagger to your corners at the end of the rounds, you're exhausted and broken, and then somebody decides whether you won or not. There was none of the slugfest, because the media, the broadcasters treated it like it was going to be a coronation. If you started to do an attack on Labour they would be like, 'Yes, so what?'[100]

Labour staffers in Southside, too, were aware of this dynamic. Quietly, some moderates, doubtful of the Corbyn hype, were telling constituents that May would win but that having a local Labour champion would put a check on her government. 'Far more MPs than people realise' were deploying this message, according to one senior Labour official, who put the figure at thirty.[101]

The full scale of the slide would be captured most dramatically in one particular set of memos.[102] There were thirty of these in total during the campaign, all produced by Crosby and Textor's company and addressed to Theresa May and Stephen Gilbert. They were called 'Marginal Seats Track' reports, a summary of polling in fifty tightly contested constituencies, nineteen held by the Tories and thirty-one by Labour. In the evening some five hundred people spread across the seats would be called and asked a set of questions, with the results fed back to the centre in the memos with advice woven in. These were the battleground seats – the ones that would determine whether May would expand her majority.

At the start the numbers looked rosy. The Conservatives had a

50 per cent vote share to Labour's 33 per cent. Theresa May's personal figures were even better: 67 per cent of respondents said she would make a better prime minister than Jeremy Corbyn, who was down on 26 per cent. In the 'key strategic imperatives' listed at the end of each memo the early suggestions chimed with the original Crosby and Textor plan. May was urged to 'frame the campaign nationally around leadership and securing stability' and focus on 'issues that benefit the Conservatives', specifically Brexit and the economy.

But then the numbers changed. One big drop in Tory support came in May, just after the Labour manifesto leaked. A second stark slump followed the publication of the Tory manifesto. Suddenly new messages appeared at the top of the memos' points of advice. 'Urgently implement the agreed speech and "ring fence" the social care issue,' read the memo on 22 May, the day of May's U-turn. By early June, after the two terror attacks, the messages were urging campaigners to criticise Corbyn's lack of support for the 'shoot to kill' police policy and the perceived 'incompetence' of his shadow home secretary, Diane Abbott. Pleas to reframe the race around Brexit no longer appeared high up in the list of advice contained in many of the final memos. The public had moved on.

In the last of the thirty tracker polls, May's lead over Corbyn on the question of who would make the best prime minister had dwindled. She was still ahead, but barely, by 49 per cent to 40 per cent. Worse still, Labour had actually jumped ahead on vote share, at 45 per cent to the Tories' 38 per cent. In the battleground seats that would define the race, the Conservatives were now behind. It was a jaw-dropping turnaround. One truism often trumpeted in Westminster is that campaigns rarely make a difference in elections, but not here. Those Tory blunders had racked up one after the other, each compounding the last, sending its campaign into a nosedive.

The scale of the fall was laid bare come polling day. The Conservative and Labour vote shares were actually both up, to 42 per cent and 40 per cent respectively, thanks in large part to the collapse of Ukip after the 2016 EU referendum. But in a parliamentary democracy it is seats that matter. Labour had 262 MPs, a rise of thirty. The Tories had 317 MPs, still in first place, but that was down thirteen. Even worse, it was short of an overall majority. May, cautious and calculating by nature, had been bounced into rolling the dice. It had backfired. Far from increasing the Tory majority, she had seen the one inherited from Cameron turn to dust.

Today, the two Tory camps still point fingers at each other as they wonder what might have been. Chris Wilkins, sidelined in the race, said of the Aussie professionals: 'We had a 20-point lead going into it. We knew exactly, critically, what Theresa May's brand was and they then ran a campaign which was completely contrary to all of it and which drove a coach and horses through this carefully cultivated brand.'[103] Timothy wrote in a *Spectator* piece after the election that it was 'wrong' to build the campaign so much around May's image. He added. 'My biggest regret, however, is that we did not campaign in accordance with the insight that took Theresa to Downing Street in the first place.'[104] Fiona Hill said: 'With the benefit of hindsight I actually think if Nick and I had just run the campaign it would have been better.'[105]

The professionals brought in for the race rejected these critiques. There are 'what ifs' on their side too. What if the Brexit framing had been stuck to, as Boris Johnson would do in 2019? What if May had proved a better campaigner, avoiding the collapse in her favourability ratings? What if the social care policy had never been in the manifesto, which they wanted to be bland? A final memo, featuring an analysis run by Crosby and Textor's firm for internal use after the election, looked at various reasons for the disaster. It concluded that 'the parties' manifestos are the most important factor in explaining the result'.[106] Crosby, according to one ally, now considers his involvement in the race 'one of the biggest regrets of his career'.[107]

As for the careers of Theresa May's co-chiefs, they would not last the weekend. When the prime minister arrived at CCHQ in the early hours after election night she gave a pep talk to the distraught staffers, then called Timothy and Hill into the boardroom. Already May's phone had lit up with Cabinet minister demands for the heads of the all-powerful advisers, not least from Hammond, who told her: 'Get rid of them or you're toast.'[108] The three Tories sat in 'awkward silence', the triumvirate that had governed Britain stunned by what had just happened and weighing up what was to follow.[109] Timothy offered his resignation. Hill was uncertain. May's phone was buzzing with demands. She glanced at the screen and said: 'The donors think you need to go.'[110] On 10 June, two days after the election, the pair resigned.

May would stagger on, the electoral wound cauterised with the double departure and a deal with the DUP. Time, however, would not heal all the scars. Nick and Fi had been May's closest advisers for seven years. To some, she owed her premiership to them. To others, she had relied on them too much. Their visions and ambitions had merged and overlapped, feeding off each other with mutual benefits as they closed in on the centre of power. But now, the prime minister decided they were no longer part of her life. It would be half a decade before May and Hill would sit down alone together again.[111] Timothy, six years on, had still not got the call.[112]

6

Regicide and Renewal

I T WAS THE scene of a dream realised. Boris Johnson's hands were scrunched into fists, punching the air in celebration like a boxer after a knockout. His mouth was open and jutting forward, releasing a roar of triumph. The head was bowed a little, eyes fixed on the TV screen announcing the victory. Boris was out of his chair, leaping in jubilation. 'It was one of those total unadulterated moments of joy,' recalled one by his side that night, 12 December 2019. 'It was like he almost forgot himself. He was absolutely ecstatic, jumping around the place.'[1]

The moment Johnson learned that he was heading for the Conservative Party's biggest House of Commons majority since Margaret Thatcher was shared with just a handful of allies. Carrie Symonds, then his girlfriend, dressed in black for results night, grinned in amazement. Dominic Cummings, architect of the Brexit-at-all-costs strategy, appeared stunned, laptop in hand and scarf around his neck. Others there whooped and embraced. The location, fittingly enough, was Thatcher's old study on the first floor of Downing Street.

Bottles of Budweiser and pots of Co-op pasta provided the sustenance that evening, giving the vibe of 'a bad New Year's Eve party'.[2] When the group had gathered around 9 p.m. gentlemen's bets had been placed on what the Tory majority would be. A Tory win was expected, though the 2016 and 2017 votes served as a reminder that forecasts could be wrong. Johnson, the most cautious, plumped for a majority of around twenty seats. Lee Cain, his communications chief, went for thirty.[3] Cummings picked sixty-eight, the highest of anyone – though that number was lower than the modelling on his computer showed, Dom disbelieving the statistics for once. The exit poll, when it dropped, exceeded all the predictions: eighty-six. Cue delirium. A few hundred yards away, in Conservative Campaign Headquarters (CCHQ), the reaction of those watching on a big screen resembled a football crowd celebrating a World Cup final winner. Campaign chiefs bear-hugged, activists squealed in delight. Chants of 'five more years' rang out. 'The only thing missing was some idiot throwing their pint in the air,' said one present.[4]

Johnson's delight matched his character: he had always been an obsessive competitor. When playing one Cabinet minister's nine-year-old son at tennis he insisted on marking the score after every point.[5] Aides who had played in matches on Johnson's court at his Oxfordshire cottage joked that he used old balls scrubbed of fuzz to obtain an advantage.[6] Boris had once been so determined to gain the upper hand that he snatched David Cameron's notes off the table during talks when he was London mayor, prompting a schoolboy-like tussle.[7] Johnson even had a ping-pong table in his Downing Street flat and would invite aides up for a game when he was home alone.[8]

At the time of the 2019 vote, the first winter general election in eighty-four years, Johnson was already prime minister, but one handcuffed by the lack of a majority.[9] He had gone all out on Brexit, facing down his party's Remainers and the nation's top judges in an attempt to force a deal through. Blocked, he had turned to the people – and won the ultimate prize. Once the counting was done, the Tory majority would be eighty. Johnson was now king of all he surveyed, backed by the public and with the numbers to reshape Britain in his image. Cause indeed for fist-pumping. The victory was vindication.

The triumph was not his alone, however. The painting of the Iron Lady hanging above as Boris punched the air was a reminder of another, less palatable truth – that he was the beneficiary of a political assassination. Not since Maggie had a Tory prime minister been ousted by their own MPs. John Major was crushed at the ballot box. David Cameron fell on his own sword after the Brexit blunder. For Theresa May, Boris's predecessor, it had been death by a thousand cuts at the hands of colleagues. Those rebels had played their part.

The story of Johnson's rise to the top is one of how a leader can be felled. On display are all of Westminster's dark arts: secret whipping operations, letters of no confidence, dinner-party plotting, leadership deal-making, voting skulduggery. The Conservatives pride themselves on being the most successful political party in democratic history. By toppling one leader and appointing another who then crushed Labour, the Tories had underscored their capacity for the ruthless pursuit of power, eventually extending their Downing Street run into a second decade. But other forces had also been unleashed. It was a reminder: no Conservative leader was untouchable. Johnson, one day, would come to understand that too.

That Theresa May survived the immediate aftermath of her disastrous 2017 election owes much itself to political deal-making. Distraught in her Downing Street flat and soon to be detached from her closest advisers, Nick Timothy and Fiona Hill, May was propped up by two Cabinet ministers. David Davis, the Brexit secretary, and Gavin Williamson, the chief whip, rushed to her side the morning after results night to work out a survival plan. 'She looked pretty shaken. I would guess she'd been in tears at some point,' said Davis.[10] The co-chiefs of staff would go, that much was clear. The Cabinet had to be secured – May soon hit the phone. And to get the numbers needed to win votes in the Commons, a deal with the Democratic Unionist Party (DUP) was needed. So Williamson got on the plane to Northern Ireland.

'Speak softly and carry a big stick,' goes one proverb beloved of US presidents. It could describe Gavin Williamson's style. A former fireplace salesman, Williamson's polite manner and Scarborough accent masked an iron will, glimpsed sometimes in a flash of the eyes. He had become a reader of Tory MPs par excellence, first as a trusted parliamentary aide to Cameron, and then as May's discipline enforcer, having helped her obtain the crown. To the ears of some colleagues, his urgings could tilt into menaces: he would leave Rishi Sunak's Cabinet in November 2022 when forthright texts he had sent to a colleague emerged. His choice of pet – a tarantula called Cronus, named after the Greek god who castrated his father to take power and ate his children to retain it – did little to soften the image. But his skills at securing votes were much sought after by Tory leadership hopefuls.

The weekend after the election, Williamson held talks first at the Northern Ireland Office and then at DUP MP Sir Jeffrey Donaldson's rural house. It was not revealed at the time, but a full coalition was on the table. The offer would have seen Nigel Dodds, another DUP MP, enter the Cabinet as international trade secretary, with another junior ministerial post being given to the party.[11] May at one point wobbled, attempting to retract the offer as Tories muttered about the DUP being awkward bedfellows, but Williamson waved away her doubts. In the end a confidence and supply deal was struck, the DUP favouring a more hands-off arrangement that kept its MPs on the backbenches but secured £1 billion extra funding for Northern Ireland.

That was only half of the solution, however. Potential rebels had to be locked in behind May, most significantly her foreign secretary, Boris Johnson. Williamson, arriving back in London on Sunday, met Johnson in an empty Foreign Office. Unable to talk in Johnson's own office – the keys had been misplaced – they chatted in the ornate Locarno Suite, more often used for hosting press conferences with world leaders. There was a warning that instability could topple the government and let in Labour, but also a more pointed plea. 'I was very clear to him,' Williamson recalled in an interview. 'I said, "If everyone goes on massive leadership manoeuvres, right here and right now, it will pull down the ability to deliver a Brexit deal."' Then the message got blunter.

> If you do that then it's going to have enormous consequences. You're marking your card with an awful lot of people. If you do the right thing to give that stability, then ultimately she will be replaced at a different moment. It will be the right thing for the country and the party.[12]

The implications were clear. Act now and Tories will not forgive you. Hold fire and the chance to lead will come later. Johnson was persuaded. The prime minister, for now, was safe.

The relationship between Theresa May and Boris Johnson in the Cabinet was always fraught. He had been astonished to be handed the Foreign Office by May, who aides said felt some pity for the way Michael Gove had undercut his leadership hopes. But the conversation outlining his appointment had come with a sting in the tail.

'I've always thought there were two Borises,' May told him, according to Nick Timothy, who was in the room. 'There's the fun Boris, entertaining Boris, fundamentally unserious Boris, and then there's the Boris who ran London successfully.' The country, she added, wanted to see the latter. Timothy thought the remark 'patronising'.[13]

Ostensibly Boris had been handed a plum role, one of the great offices of state. But the department's power had been diluted. The job of delivering Brexit, Johnson's legacy and the most pressing foreign policy issue of the day, had been carved out and turned into its own department. Trade deal strategy had also become a standalone department headed up by a different minister. 'We'd stripped the Foreign Office back quite a bit,' recalled Timothy.[14] In addition, overseas aid spending had long been removed from the department. So the train set handed to Johnson was already depleted. Even then, some hoped he would mess up as conductor. 'We put him in the Foreign Office to keep him busy and hopefully distract him from trying to replace Theresa as prime minister from the sidelines. We also wanted to give him a job big enough to expose his operational and policy limitations,' said Fiona Hill with bluntness as she looked back. 'He can be a useful show pony, he's happy being a show pony and he's good at being one. We made the calculation that his show-pony ways might come in handy at the right political moments.'[15]

As politicians, May and Johnson were wired differently. The prime minister had little interest in drafting speeches, sometimes reading chunks prepared for her with minimal thought. At one donors' dinner after a trip to see Donald Trump, she joked, 'I don't think I have received such a big hand since I walked down the colonnade at the White House.'[16] The line, referencing Trump's supposed small hands, was crafted by speech-writer Chris Wilkins. May later told him she had no idea why everyone laughed.[17] Johnson was the opposite, a rhetorician by trade who even after he became prime minister bristled at having words written for him. On the details they were different too. May was a forensic reader of ministerial submissions; Johnson a conjurer of the big picture.

These differences in approach would play out around the Cabinet table. Johnson would at times 'audibly be drumming his fingers' as others spoke.[18] 'Boris used to behave like the boy at the back of the

The nerves before battle in the first TV debate, 15 April 2010.

Nick Clegg, David Cameron and Gordon Brown with the election in the balance.

William Hague and George Osborne were trusted enough by Cameron to secretly prepare for power-sharing talks with the Liberal Democrats.

Smiles and a show in the Downing Street Rose Garden to christen the coalition, 12 May 2010.

Samantha and David Cameron behind the door of Number 10 five years later, after securing sole Tory rule thanks to a shock House of Commons majority at the 2015 general election.

Ed Miliband's geeky public image was brutally weaponised by the Conservatives in the 2015 campaign, with the help of supportive newspapers . . .

. . but it was the spectre of the SNP calling the shots in a weak Labour government that created a critical call to action for voters.

It was Boris Johnson's rivalry with George Osborne, rather than David Cameron, that most shaped Brexit referendum calculations, both men manoeuvring to be the next prime minister.

Moments before Johnson declared for Brexit outside his home in Islington, North London, in February 2016, he was still considering backing Remain, according to the one aide by his side.

Many of the most senior Remain and Leave campaign figures still believe that without Boris, seen here waving a Cornish pasty with Labour's Gisela Stuart, the UK would not have voted for Brexit.

The cat that got the cream: Nigel Farage on EU referendum results night.

Farewell to eleven years as Tory leader and six as prime minister, 24 June 2016.

Strong, stable and severe, Theresa May took the Tory crown with a 'time for the grown-ups' message after the Brexiteers imploded in the race to replace Cameron.

Campaign guru Lynton Crosby, the 'Wizard of Oz', had guided the Conservatives to triumph in 2015, but the electoral magic went missing in a divided and malfunctioning 2017 campaign.

Powerful co-chiefs of staff Nick Timothy and Fiona Hill helped persuade Theresa May to gamble everything on the 2017 election, then paid the price when it backfired.

Gavin Williamson, whose pet tarantula Cronus was named after a Greek god who castrated his father to take power, helped successive Tory hopefuls to become leader via the dark arts.

aham Brady, keeper of the ry no-confidence letters as airman of the backbench 22 Committee, built a utation on remaining ht-lipped about numbers.

Grant Shapps's vote-counting of Tory colleagues via a spreadsheet, inspired by US President Lyndon B. Johnson, helped win Boris Johnson the leadership and keep him there.

Steve Baker (left) and Mark Francois used the European Research Group, and its secret 'Buddies' whipping system, to thwart Theresa May's Brexit deal and eventually topple her.

Jeremy Corbyn's relaxed campaigning style and the crowds he drew in the run-up to the 2017 election were in sharp contrast to Theresa May's stilted public appearances, helping him exceed expectations.

The grand backdrop of Chequers was not enough to persuade all of May's Cabinet to back her Brexit deal in July 2018, with David Davis, followed by Boris Johnson, quitting within days.

Scribbled signatures in Jacob Rees-Mogg's visitors' book capture attendees at rounds of dinner-party plotting explicitly designed to push Boris Johnson as the next Tory leader in early 2019.

class,' said Damian Green, a Cabinet colleague. There would be 'chuntering' as others voiced opposing views, May sometimes urging him to listen.[19] Johnson was once spotted firing off texts below the table, despite phones being banned.[20] David Lidington, another Cabinet contemporary, recalled one exchange where Johnson, just returned from Singapore, suggested that the UK copy its approach of removing an old regulation every time a new one was adopted. 'Boris, we've had that policy for at least the last six years,' shot back May.[21] The foreign secretary did try to strike up a connection with his prime minister. 'What can I do to make her like me? Why doesn't she like me? Everyone likes me,' he would sigh to Katie Perrior, May's comms chief who would act as envoy, having worked with Johnson in the past.[22] But at points the prime minister would appear to relish her superior status. At one *Spectator* magazine awards do, Johnson joked that after Brexit he feared being politically strangled like Michael Heseltine's Alsatian – a nod to a then-current news story – and was delighted to have been granted a reprieve at the Foreign Office. May, rising later that evening to give her own speech, delivered a stinging punchline: 'Boris, the dog was put down . . . when its master decided it wasn't needed any more.'[23]

Johnson was never a natural second fiddle. 'He always felt that he was the man of destiny. He does have this Churchillian perception of himself,' said Lidington, who served as May's de facto deputy prime minister.[24] Will Walden, one of Johnson's longest-serving advisers, echoed the sentiment:

> Boris is not a number two. The truth is she put him there to isolate him and keep an eye on him and it didn't work. It was never going to work, because he couldn't abide being a number two. As mayor he'd been king over the water, answerable to no one. As foreign secretary he was answerable to a prime minister he didn't get. You're either in charge or you're not: that is Boris's mantra. Nothing in between.[25]

★

It was policy that brought the issue to a head. The 2017 election result had been disastrous for Theresa May's Brexit approach. The attempt to smooth the passage of a deal by securing more Tory MPs had boomeranged, leaving her with fewer than beforehand. There were less tangible impacts too: specifically, a loss of political authority. While May enjoyed a 20-point Tory poll lead, a Cabinet deeply split over Brexit was muzzled in its attempts to shape policy. With May wounded and her heavy-handed co-chiefs banished, ministers were emboldened to push their case. Her weakened position complicated the negotiations with Brussels. It also left her beholden to the Tory backbench. The prime minister had told her MPs explicitly, 'I will continue to serve as long as you want me' at a Commons gathering after the election, thereby securing a reprieve.[26] It was a promise that would be turned into a weapon by May's critics when they moved in for the kill.

What emerged in the following year was a softer Brexit than the one she had articulated in that post-referendum Tory conference speech in autumn 2016. The degree to which this was driven by circumstance or design was still years later debated by senior Tories. Some believe that May would have always pivoted to a less hard Brexit after the election, a big win giving her political space to manoeuvre. Others blame the change on those who were now around her. Out went Nick Timothy, a Leaver whose fingerprints were all over the initial strategy, and into the chief of staff role came Gavin Barwell, a Remain-voting former Tory MP. Olly Robbins, the life-long mandarin, secured the upper hand over David Davis, the Eurosceptic Brexit secretary, in negotiations with the EU. A warring Cabinet and recalcitrance from the EU played their parts too.

It would all come to a head in the summer of 2018. By this time it had been established that an agreement would first be struck on the terms of the UK's exit from the bloc, to be followed later by a wider trade deal addressing the relationship with the EU going forward. Theresa May's proposal would become known as the 'Chequers Plan'. The Cabinet was summoned to the prime minister's grace-and-favour country house, Chequers, on 6 July 2018 to endorse the approach. At the deal's core was an attempt to solve the fiendish Northern Ireland conundrum: how to keep the land border with the Republic of Ireland open while delivering Brexit. May proposed that the entire UK remain in the single market for goods and, in effect, in the customs union too. Only by staying close economically could trade barriers either between Northern Ireland and the Republic of Ireland or between Northern Ireland and Great Britain be avoided, May's team believed. But, to some Brexiteers, such an arrangement was unacceptable. Under these conditions, the UK would still be a rule-taker from Brussels, having to adopt its regulations, despite having left the EU. Free movement of people would be gone, but the European Court of Justice (ECJ) would still have a role in legal disputes. May had once promised to take the UK out of the single market, out of the customs union and out of the oversight of the ECJ before the election. No longer.

The gathering was an ambush dressed up as a debate. The aim was to secure the Cabinet's consent. Johnson blew hot and cold. At one point, in the open Cabinet discussion, the foreign secretary said that selling the exit plan in public would be like 'polishing a turd'. But that evening, at the more informal dinner, Boris raised a toast to the deal. Seizing on the lack of immediate resignations, Downing Street claimed a win. 'Today in detailed discussions the Cabinet has agreed our collective position for the future of our negotiations with the EU,' read the first line in a Theresa May statement issued that day.[27] This unity, so publicly fanfared, would prove illusory.

Throughout his political career Boris Johnson had rarely been first to jump. Over Brexit, the half-a-dozen Cabinet ministers, including Michael Gove, who declared for Leave did so before Johnson picked a side. And over the Chequers Plan, it was David Davis who made the first move. 'Boris, I'm going to turn in my resignation to the prime minister tonight,' Davis told Johnson on the telephone. It was Sunday morning, thirty-six hours after the Chequers discussions. 'Do you have to? If you resign, I'll have to resign!' replied Johnson, according to Davis. He countered: 'You've got to make your own decision. It's entirely up to you, but I'm re-signing.' To the Brexit secretary, Boris sounded 'upset' and 'unhappy'.[28] The political risk was clear. Recent Tory history showed that when a sitting prime minister was forced out the successor was usually a great office-of-state holder. May had been home secretary, John Major and Harold Macmillan were chancellors right before stepping up, Alec Douglas-Home had been foreign secretary when picked. Walking out of the Cabinet meant the uncertain obscurity of the backbenches. But staying too had its risks. Johnson would no longer be the hard-Brexit champion, outflanked by Davis, who was touted in the press at the time as a possible May replacement.

As with his decision to back Brexit, Tory colleagues take different views of Johnson's core motivation in choosing to follow Davis out of the door. Those then around the foreign secretary do not doubt that he was deeply disillusioned with May's plan. Lee Cain, Johnson's special adviser, got a call as his boss was driving away from Chequers. 'Total disaster, everyone capitulated, the deal's terrible, I don't know what I'm going to do,' was the message that made it through via the patchy Buckinghamshire signal. 'You're going to walk?' Cain asked. 'It's difficult to see how I can stay,' Johnson replied, before agreeing to mull it over that weekend.[29] A Downing Street attempt to bounce him and Philip Hammond, still chancellor despite his clashes with May, into writing a joint comment piece backing the deal poured fuel on the fire. Jacob Rees-Mogg, a prominent Brexiteer Tory MP, talked to Johnson too:

> Boris makes his mind up in a discursive way but he ends up where he always wanted to be. So he definitely thought through all his options over that weekend. Did he really want to resign? How was it all going to work out? And came to the conclusion that he was going to.[30]

Others take a dimmer view. Michael Gove thought he would not have walked without Davis: 'I think that it was a wrench for Boris to resign. Also, Boris, I think, would always want to maintain his options. So if he could be the leader of the internal opposition, that's better than being the leader of the external opposition.'[31] Julian Smith, Theresa May's chief whip by then, also thought 'probably not': 'He wasn't being particularly brave at that point, he was being quite risk-averse.'[32] Gavin Barwell, May's chief of staff, said: 'Definitely not, no way.'[33] He pointed to the phone call Johnson made to May calling it quits. The conversation went round and round in circles, before the prime minister said: 'Look, are you resigning or are you not resigning?' From what Barwell, who was with May at the time, could hear of their talk, 'She almost pushed him to say the words.'[34]

David Frost, a Johnson adviser who would go on to head up his

Brexit negotiations and be elevated to the House of Lords in September 2020, had a more nuanced take that perhaps gets closer to the truth. He thought Davis's decision affected the timing but not the outcome. 'The sequencing might have happened differently and the moment might have been different, but to me it was always obvious from the beginning of 2018 that he was going to have to go. It just wasn't going to work,' said Frost.[35] Other allies say Johnson thought much more deeply about Brexit policy throughout his time in office than the sceptics accept.

The harshest interpretation of Johnson's motives came from an MP who went on to serve in a top-five Cabinet job under him, someone without an obvious side in the Brexit battle. 'The reason for Boris's existence in politics is because he wants to be leader,' the figure explained.

> There's nothing wrong with that. There are plenty of ambitious politicians out there that want to be prime minister. But, for him, there were few no-go areas in trying to achieve that ambition. Not many restraining factors, if any at all . . . There's no doubt in my mind that Boris resigned because he felt that if he didn't, maybe David Davis would become the new leader and wear the crown.[36]

On 9 July 2018, three days after the Chequers summit and one day after Davis had quit, Johnson was out.

Knowing what comes next, it is easy to forget how isolated Boris Johnson was in those early months on the outside. Not everyone followed him out of the Cabinet. Prominent Brexiteers like Michael Gove, Penny Mordaunt, Chris Grayling and Andrea Leadsom stayed in. Johnson had given up the Foreign Office, initially getting precious little in return. With the Cabinet job went the perks – the paid-for overseas travel, the chauffeur-driven car, the use of the foreign secretary's country house of Chevening. The ministerial pay bump too was gone. Instead, Boris was handed a poky 'punishment' office in Parliament's Portcullis House, an aide recalled: 'Like terrible university dorms.'[37] It was the Whip's Office, May's enforcers, who picked the rooms.

Being a lowly backbencher meant fewer staff too: no civil servants ready to action demands, no taxpayers picking up the tab for many advisers. Lee Cain, who met Johnson during the Vote Leave campaign and became his adviser after the 2017 election, was one of the few who stayed with him. He saw his job as that of cheerleader-in-chief, keeping up his boss's spirits. 'This is it, this is going to be my career over,' Johnson would complain.[38] Hours would be spent chatting about politics and life. Reporter friends urged Cain to look for work elsewhere: 'Get another job, this guy's finished.'[39]

Compounding his blues was Johnson's lack of MP allies. He had spent the best part of the last decade away from Parliament in London's City Hall. Also, for all his outward affability, Johnson is not a great socialiser. He is not a big drinker. Allies often say he would rather stay home with a book than go out to a party – a nuance lost in the 'partygate' scandal that would later engulf his premiership, where the most raucous behaviour was that of others. Eddie Lister, Johnson's chief of staff as London mayor who played a similar role in the early Downing Street years, said:

> One of his weaknesses then, and actually it was a weakness that stayed with him right the way to the bitter end, was he's not and never has been a very clubbable man. He doesn't spend his hours in the bar at the Commons, or the tea room, he doesn't do that. He's got no real friends amongst the MPs.[40]

Another ally said: 'Boris needs love reciprocated, that's the point. There was no reciprocation just after he resigned.'[41] David Frost, who stayed in touch with Johnson, estimated: 'He was down for two or three months.'[42] Family complications compounded his woes. Leaving the Foreign Office meant moving his family out of the formal residence at Carlton Gardens, bringing to a head marital tensions over his relationship with Carrie Symonds. A split from second wife Marina Wheeler followed.

There were hardcore MP supporters who threw in their lot with Johnson early on. In private, however, he could be scathing about the calibre of some of them. They were political offcuts – 'The Munsters', as Johnson would joke, in reference to the TV show featuring Frankenstein and other misshapen ghouls. He even hummed the *Addams Family* theme tune when discussing them, according to two sources: 'Duddle-der-der, click-click, duddle-der-der, click-click.'[43] At times the humour was darker. 'I've cornered the market in sex pests,' he joked once, according to one source.[44] Two leadership campaign figures, who did not hear the specific remark, provide contextual evidence – one said it was like the type of random, scattergun jokes Johnson cracked; the other made an almost identical comment unprompted, suggesting such humour was not uncommon among the group.[45] Johnson's office denied the claims.[46]

The manifestation of Johnson's lack of political clout came when he would trudge through the glasshouse-like central atrium of Portcullis House, where MPs, aides, journalists and lobbyists gather to drink coffee and gossip. The space acts as a test chamber for raw political power. Cabinet ministers rush through with aides in tow, young staffers surreptitiously snapping photographs and journalists hotfooting it to try to catch a word. When Johnson walked by, no one approached, according to multiple allies. 'It was tumbleweed,' said one.[47]

One press aide recalled watching in alarm as their boss dropped back down the newspaper pages.

At first I'm putting stories out and it's front pages, top of the *Today* programme in the morning, top of the BBC. Then, after a couple of months, he starts to not be on the front page. His *Telegraph* column every week was front-page news and then suddenly it's page five. That's when he was getting worried. 'I'm starting to become less relevant.' You then have to say more robust things to get the coverage. It's a very dangerous place. People forget that.[48]

In one House of Commons debate at this time, Boris Johnson rose to speak from the backbenches. A familiar Brexit anecdote followed, of EU red tape and Brussels overreach. A Tory MP in the chamber was spotted quietly shaking his head. Michael Gove, briefly part of the 'Dream Team' leadership ticket with Johnson, was watching. He would tell others the image that jumped into his mind was that of King Lear – a realm lost, muttering into the wind.[49]

What changed the dynamic was the European Research Group. The ERG, as it is universally known, was established in 1993 but had fallen into obscurity until it was relaunched after the 2016 EU referendum. It would become the vehicle that Tory Brexiteers used to obliterate Theresa May's deal. For the ERG, the primary goal was a hard Brexit. For Johnson, it was securing the premiership. The two spheres would never fully overlap, but there was enough crossover for much mutual benefit to be derived.

The driving force behind the ERG, in its revived form, was Steve Baker. In the chronicles of Brexit there are many Cabinet ministers better known but much less consequential than Baker. Bespectacled, with a mild manner and a thatch of black hair, Baker appeared an unlikely revolutionary. The MP for Wycombe's penchant for skydiving and motorbike-riding hinted at a daring streak. It was his skill at mounting a parliamentary rebellion, however, that scared successive occupants of Downing Street. David Cameron had caved in over various EU referendum process demands pushed by Baker which helped the Leave campaign. May brought him into the fold as a minister after the 2017 election, favouring having a troublemaker in the tent pointing out, but Baker had walked with Davis and Johnson over the Chequers Plan. When he relaunched the ERG in 2016, it had a steering group drawn from across the party's European wings, the hope being to play a constructive role in policy-making. Now, with MPs reverting to their Brexit corners after May's authority was crushed in 2017, it adopted a more singular focus: destroy Chequers.

Baker, a former Royal Air Force engineer, had read up for the fight. There was Sun Tzu's *The Art of War*, an ancient Chinese military treatise which he had read in the past. It was two other books, though, that most shaped his plotting. One was *How to Lose Friends and Alienate People* by the journalist Toby Young – a guide, of sorts, for how you do and do not keep people on board. The other was *The 33 Strategies of War*, by Robert Greene. 'Every chapter is vividly illustrated with repeated examples from history of when this particular strategy has worked,' Baker explained in an interview.[50] The chapter titles give a sense of the inspiration they provided: 'Envelop the Enemy: The Annihilation Strategy'; 'Transform your War into a Crusade: Moral Strategies'; 'Know How to End Things: The Exit Strategy'. Westminster is rife with military lingo. Baker understood why:

Politics is an absolute struggle to get one's will over somebody else's and it is not going to be nice. When it's outright conflict over what's going to be done and what's going to happen it is war minus the shooting and it should be treated as such. A lack of resolve is the main reason why people fail. They refuse to accept once they're in a fight that they're in a fight.[51]

That was a mistake the Eurosceptics were not likely to make.

Baker did not act alone, however. Two innovations strengthened the cause. One was 'The Buddies'. A key advantage Downing Street has in heading off a rebellion is its whips, a group of MPs loyal to the prime minister whose primary job is to ensure the boss's will is enforced. The main focus is votes: making sure enough MPs will back their government in the division lobbies and knowing which carrots and sticks to deploy to get them to do so if they are wavering. Rarely do rebels have their own structured, dedicated whipping operation. But the ERG's Buddies was exactly that. Mark Francois, the ERG deputy chairman who would only reveal the system's existence years later in his book *Spartan Victory*, was Chief Buddy. There were a dozen Buddies in total, Eurosceptic Tories who would sound out colleagues about whether they would vote down May's Brexit deal and then report back to Francois. Their identities were kept hidden even from other senior ERG figures.[52] The intel would be plugged into a spreadsheet kept by Baker and that informed his strategies.

The second innovation was separate from the ERG: the 'Chuck Chequers' campaign. Run by old hands from Lynton Crosby's past ventures and funded by Brexiteer donors, this would take the argument to the public. 'It was a brilliant campaign,' said David Canzini, a veteran Tory strategist involved who would be by Johnson's side at many critical political moments.[53] Facebook groups were used to organise rallies outside Downing Street. Protests were arranged too in Cabinet ministers' constituencies, building on and encouraging Tory members' frustrations with the prime minister's approach.

The ground was gradually beginning to shift. But to depose any Tory leader, you need more than subtly changing contours – you need a weapon. It would take the form of a letter.

★

BLUE MURDER

Sir Graham Brady had one of the best views in Westminster. From his corner office on the fourth floor of Portcullis House, he could look over the very heart of Britain's political life. To the left were the Houses of Parliament and the eleventh-century Westminster Hall, where Charles I was sentenced to be beheaded. Straight ahead was Parliament Square, the culminating point for countless public protests, and beyond was Westminster Abbey, where new monarchs were crowned; the Supreme Court, the ultimate arbiter of British law, could be glimpsed through trees, the Union Jack usually flying outside. And to the right, traffic turned into the road that leads to Number 10. The room itself, too, represented a uniquely British centre of power. For it was there that Sir Graham, the broad-smiled and broad-shouldered chairman of the 1922 Committee, kept the no-confidence letters. Behind a cupboard or inside a drawer – he never revealed where exactly – was the safe that housed the missives, under lock and key and away from prying eyes.

To understand Tory politics in this period, and the decapitation of successive prime ministers, it is essential to understand the 1922 Committee. As William Hague said, the Conservative Party is 'an absolute monarchy, moderated by regicide'. Tory MPs may be the judge and jury but the chairman of the 1922 is the executioner. Trials take the form of confidence votes, triggered if just 15 per cent of Conservative MPs – fewer than one in seven – submit a letter of no confidence in their leader. Officially a majority of Tory MPs need to vote 'no confidence' to oust the leader, though in reality a proportion well short of that can prove fatal. There is a marked difference here with the Labour Party, which does not formally have a 'no confidence' mechanism. For Labour MPs to oust a leader, 20 per cent must sign a piece of paper openly endorsing a different candidate. So not only is the bar higher and rebels have to rally around a single potential successor but they must also declare their betrayal to the world. The Tories maintain a veil of secrecy – letters can be submitted anonymously. Latter-day Brutuses need never wield the knife in public.

Cartoons on Sir Graham's walls capturing the end points of political careers in lurid colour suggested comfort with his Grim Reaper role. One showed a ghoulish Sir Graham dressed in black tails leading a coffin containing the body of Theresa May and carried by Boris Johnson, Michael Gove and Dominic Raab. Another had the 1922's chairman leering over an ailing Liz Truss as Cabinet ministers dissected limbs and peeled back skin. A man squeamish about politics as blood sport this was not.

When Sir Graham took over the role – akin to head Tory backbencher – after the 2010 election, he resisted attempts at influence from the party leadership. David Cameron tried to give government ministers – that is, those reliant on his patronage for jobs – a vote over picking the chairman of the 1922. The move, dubbed by Sir Graham an attempt to 'nationalise' the committee under government control, was thwarted. Similarly, at points Cameron allies made not-so-subtle attempts to sound Sir Graham out about the number of no-confidence letters he had received. Sir Graham learned to adopt a Sphinx-like smile when asked such questions after an exchange with one reporter early in his tenure. 'Of course I haven't got any letters,' he said at first. A week later, asked the same question again, he said, 'You know I don't talk about that.' The difference in responses, suggesting a change, was pounced upon by the journalist. Sir Graham realised a straight bat was needed every time. 'It was an important lesson that the only thing you can do is say nothing,' Sir Graham said in an interview. 'And that includes, obviously and possibly even most importantly, saying nothing to party leaders because that would, in one way or the other, influence the outcome.'[54] Much to the frustration of Westminster bubble-dwellers, he would stay true to his word.

The Tories' letters system has its peculiarities. For one, there is no requirement to tell the truth. At times, a Tory MP has declared that they have submitted a letter whereas, in fact, none has been handed in. Only Sir Graham would know, giving the MP in question a wry smile if their paths crossed. Why the tactic would be deployed was less clear. Perhaps it was an attempt to control when the threshold was hit, creating public space for others to submit letters but holding back their own to retain a degree of influence over the point at which a vote was triggered.

Another peculiarity is that letters can be withdrawn. There was one point, under Theresa May, when a Tory MP handed Sir Graham their letter as they passed outside the Commons Library, saying it was time for her to go. Unbeknown to the rebel MP at that moment the 15 per cent mark triggering a vote had thereby been hit. Sir Graham, back in his office, sat working out how to inform Number 10, mind whirring. There then came a knock at the door. A different MP wanted to withdraw their letter, saying it was not the right time. May was granted a reprieve – though, as it would turn out, only for a short while. Another letter would come within hours, forcing the vote.

Indeed, under Sir Graham a 'letter' did not even have to be a physical letter. All that mattered was that the identity of the sender could be verified. Sir Graham had learned this lesson from his predecessor, Michael Spicer, who once received a slew of no-confidence letters written in different hands on headed paper from the Tory-favoured members' establishment the Carlton Club. On investigation, many were bogus, with some of the signatures apparently forged. Sir Graham allowed MPs to email in their no-confidence submissions, meaning that a parliamentary recess provided no protection for teetering leaders. In some cases, even text messages were deemed acceptable – each one printed and placed in the safe. The impact of the mechanism cannot be overstated. Cameron lived in fear of the 15 per cent threshold. 'Never for a minute' could he forget the 'vital statistic', Cameron admitted in his memoirs, adding: 'Not once during eleven years as Conservative leader did I feel secure for any length of time.'[55] The threshold was never breached during his tenure. May would have no such luck.

It was the combination of these three elements – Boris's angling for the top job, the ERG's determination to kill the existing Brexit deal and the use of no-confidence letters – that would eventually do for Theresa May.

By late 2018, scenting the shift in mood, Johnson got his mojo back. A chief weapon in his arsenal would prove to be his weekly *Daily Telegraph* column. Aside from the financial benefits to its author – he was pocketing £275,000 a year for the work – it would set the political weather.[56] As the rebellion against Chequers gathered momentum, Johnson positioned himself as the Brexiteer king across the water, leaning in via print whenever he wanted. Each Sunday as the afternoon faded a call would be held with Johnson and leading Eurosceptics. One who regularly took part dubbed it the 'Five Families' call after the heads of the five mafia groups in the mobster classic *The Godfather*.[57] Ostensibly the conversation was designed to serve as a check-in on the forthcoming week's activities, but often it would morph into trying to shape Johnson's Monday *Telegraph* article. 'The whole of the political world would wait and see what he'd write,' said a source often on the calls.[58] Inside Downing Street one senior figure acknowledged the reality: Boris had in effect become the leader of the opposition.[59]

It was Jeremy Corbyn who held that title officially. He was safe at the top of the Labour Party after exceeding expectations in the 2017 general election. In the two years that followed Labour was either a few points above or below the Conservatives in the opinion poll averages, but never did it surge far ahead and stay there.[60] The party's own deep divisions on Brexit – around 95 per cent of Labour MPs had campaigned to Remain in the EU in 2016, yet a sizable chunk of their support base passionately wanted out – complicated their approach to May's deal, helping explain why Boris was more feared by Downing Street. As the months passed and May's deal hit the skids, Remainer moderates on the Labour backbenches would start to revolt. Some would even break away to join Tory and Lib Dem malcontents in forming a new political party, the Independent Group, later known as Change UK, in February 2019. But it would not prove another SDP moment, momentum soon fading before wipeout followed at the ballot box at the end of the year. Throughout this period Team Corbyn would also be dogged by claims that they were not tough enough on antisemitism in the party, a roiling controversy that the leadership never fully got under control.

At points Johnson's manoeuvring was deliberately provocative. Returning to his favoured role of Tory conference darling, he and his team secretly booked the biggest venue apart from the main auditorium at the autumn 2018 gathering, though not under Johnson's name. When Number 10 found out, word spread that they were considering blocking the event. 'Great! If they pull it, we can make this massive thing of "Boris silenced at conference" and we'll book somewhere just outside,' one Johnson aide remembered thinking.[61] In the end the event went ahead, giving rise to mayhem when Johnson walked through the main conference hall beforehand. The aide recalled: 'I've been to football matches where it's getting a bit fruity and there's a crush. It was worse than that. Literally, people getting banged everywhere, trampled on. It was absolute chaos.'[62] It was a reminder that even backbench Boris was a blockbuster with the base.

When winter came the situation grew serious for May. For months the volume of the chuntering about the Chequers Plan had been rising. On 15 November 2018, the prime minister revealed her Withdrawal Agreement, essentially the legislative manifestation of the Chequers deal. It led to another resignation – that of Dominic Raab, David Davis's replacement as Brexit secretary. More critically, it made the ERG act. Steve Baker liked to quote Bismarck: 'With a gentleman I am always a gentleman and a half, and when I have to do with a pirate, I try to be a pirate and a half.'[63] It was time for the skull and crossbones to be unfurled. The ERG agreed to call publicly for no-confidence letters to be submitted: that is, for the prime minister to go. It fell to Jacob Rees-Mogg, who had stepped into the ERG chairmanship during Baker's brief ministerial stint, to announce the position at an impromptu press conference.

As a gamble it initially backfired. Days turned to weeks without the threshold of forty-eight Tory MP letters needed to trigger a vote being reached. Far from brutish pirates or Machiavellian plotters, the ERG was portrayed in newspapers as Dad's Army, the blundering wannabe military heroes of the BBC sitcom classic. Then, on 11 December, the threshold was hit. Sir Graham Brady broke the news to May. She was 'very professional, very businesslike, quite calm'.[64] The prime minister has a degree of control over timings, the 1922's rules only suggesting that a vote be held with reasonable speed. Downing Street plumped for the utmost rapidity, wanting it done and dusted in twenty-four hours. Even May's critics nod to the effectiveness of her whips that day, 12 December 2018. When Sir Graham rose in Parliament's ornate Committee Room 14 to announce the result – 200 confidence votes to 117 no confidence – the victory went to May. Loyalists leapt to their feet to applaud. But shrewder observers could see it was a Pyrrhic victory. More than one in three Conservative MPs had revealed that they wanted their leader gone. 'Her premiership never really recovered from it,' said one Eurosceptic critic.[65]

She battled on. The full narrative of how over the next six months Theresa May strained every sinew to force a Brexit deal through the Commons, and how other groupings jumped on the chaos to try to deliver their own desired outcome, would fill a whole book in itself. On the smallest of margins hung vastly differing potential futures for the UK–EU relationship. Some critical moments stick out. Forced to get the approval of MPs through a 'meaningful vote' on her Brexit approach, thanks to a nifty bit of parliamentary manoeuvring from pro-EU Tories, May would at first receive the political equivalent of two fingers. The ERG's Buddies system whipped up internal opposition. Baker, who said he had a Brexiteer source in Jeremy Corbyn's office, co-ordinated with Labour.[66] The result, on 15 January 2019, was disastrous for the prime minister. In total, 432 MPs voted against May's Withdrawal Agreement, to just 202 in favour. It was the largest recorded defeat of the government in House of Commons history, stretching back to the 1200s. 'It was a humiliating defeat. I would argue that's when the parliamentary party decided that the prime minister couldn't survive,' said Canzini.[67]

But still she battled on. There would be an attempt at a new route through the so-called 'Malthouse compromise', named after then-housing minister Kit Malthouse, who headed up a Tory-wide attempt at a solution. May rejected as undeliverable the proposal that eventually emerged, which was to abandon the existing Northern Ireland 'backstop' that kept the UK in the customs union. There would also be talks with Labour. Jeremy Corbyn made a show of being open to compromise but John McDonnell, his politically astute shadow chancellor, explained the challenges to May's chief of staff, Gavin Barwell. 'The problem we've got is we can do this deal with you but we just don't think she's going to be there for very long,' he said, in Barwell's retelling, with McDonnell noting that a significant chunk of Labour MPs wanted a second referendum, not Brexit delivered. Barwell likewise thought that Tory MPs could not stomach a deal with Corbyn: 'I never really thought that was going to work.'[68] There was even allegedly discussion among some Cabinet ministers about a second referendum. One claimed to have walked in on Philip Hammond discussing a second vote with other like-minded frontbenchers in the chancellor's office. 'It was on a flowchart,' the minister claimed: a second referendum on the terms of the Brexit negotiation and what would happen if there was a no.[69] A second pro-Brexit Cabinet minister believed Hammond and others wanted another vote.[70] Theresa May, however, multiple aides attested, never countenanced a second referendum.[71]

To this day, the prime minister's team still shiver when they think about that time. 'I nearly killed myself trying to get this deal through,' said Julian Smith, May's chief whip. 'I lost my hair to it.'[72] He later bemoaned how the debate on both sides had become radicalised. Even Brexiteers echo this sentiment, one likening the ERG to 'the Taliban', driven by fundamentalism.[73] The biggest 'what if' moment came with the third meaningful vote. The second, on 12 March, had been lost by 391 votes to 242 – another hammering. For the third, on 29 March, May played her final card. She announced to the 1922 Committee that she would resign as prime minister if her deal was passed. By then, Cabinet collective responsibility was fraying. Some ministers had ignored the government position in Brexit votes, triggering shouting matches around the Cabinet table. This was May's end game and it worked on some. Johnson, the path now clear to Number 10 and fearing for the state of the party he hoped to inherit, folded and voted for the deal. So too did Jacob Rees-Mogg and Dominic Raab. Some Eurosceptics saw Brexit itself as now at risk. Even Steve Baker wobbled, but then held firm. A hardcore group of just twenty-eight ERG Tory MPs were left. They would dub themselves 'the Spartans', after the small band of Spartan warriors who held the pass from the Persians against the odds at the Battle of Thermopylae.

Downing Street went down to the wire working on three particular groups, trying everything to persuade more ERGers to fold, lock down the DUP and get a handful of Eurosceptic Labour MPs on board. The cohorts were interrelated. The DUP would only join if the ERG was on side; the Labour waverers would only risk their careers with a rebellion if victory was assured. 'We came very close,' said Gavin Barwell.[74] But not close enough. The final result was 344 votes against the deal and 286 for. If just thirty MPs had switched from noes to ayes the agreement would have passed. The twenty-eight Spartans plus two would have been sufficient.

If Theresa May's deal had been passed and implemented, Britain would have been in a much closer relationship with the European Union than what eventually followed, effectively in the customs union and the single market for goods. This poses uncomfortable questions for Remainers. What if those who poured their campaigning into getting a second referendum had focused instead on a soft Brexit? What if the Labour Party had made that its sole goal? What would eventually replace the proposed deal was a much harder Brexit than was ever on offer from May.

And yet still she stumbled on. But the blows from fellow Tories kept coming and soon proved unsurvivable. Unusually in the history of Tory politics, it was not the Cabinet that called time on May. The grassroots played their part. The National Conservative Convention, the most senior body of the party's volunteer wing, was preparing to pass a motion of no confidence in the leader. That would not have been binding on the party but it would have carried deadly symbolism: an explicit rejection from the base. It never was adopted as events took over, but Number 10 knew it was coming. The killer blow came from the 1922 Committee. 'I will continue to serve as long as you want me,' May had told them. And now, they no longer did.

The 1922's rules stated that a leader who survived a no-confidence vote could not face another for a year. But, in true Conservative Party style, no rule is unchangeable if political reality dictates otherwise. The executive held a vote on changing the rules, though the result was kept secret even from the voters. It fell to Sir Graham Brady, the Tory executioner, to do the deed. He went to Downing Street, the result sealed in an envelope. Name your date or we break the seal, Sir Graham told May. Normally the prime minister was coolness personified, but on this occasion she showed a flash of frustration. 'I'll give you my date, Graham,' said May, according to one source familiar with events. 'But before you leave this building today, you've got to tell me if you're going to be a candidate or not.'[75] It was a swipe at Sir Graham, who was indeed mulling over a run for the leadership himself – one he would eventually launch, with little success. May had now accepted the reality. She had lost her MPs. Her time was up.

On 24 May 2019, Theresa May announced her resignation. 'I have done my best' to deliver Brexit, she told the cameras from a podium outside the front door of Number 10, a low sun casting shadows along Downing Street. 'I have done everything I can to convince MPs to back that deal. Sadly, I have not been able to do so.' At the end there was emotion, May's voice breaking as she said it was an honour to have served 'the country I love'. And then it was done. To this day the envelope remains unopened.

When the moment came Boris Johnson was ready. A concerted tilt at securing the leadership had been noticeable behind the scenes since the start of 2019. Back when Johnson resigned as foreign secretary, Jacob Rees-Mogg hosted him for lunch and pledged fealty. 'I said to him he's got to be the leader and that I will support him,' Rees-Mogg recalled of the one-to-one chat at his family home in Somerset.[76]

The campaign for the top job began in earnest in January 2019, when MPs returned after a Christmas break spent contemplating Theresa May's paper victory in the no-confidence vote. Rounds of dinners would be hosted at Rees-Mogg's lavish eighteenth-century townhouse round the corner from Parliament, with Johnson the star attraction. Drinks would be held upstairs among oil paintings and plush sofas, before three courses were served in the dining room below. Chitchat would happen over starters, before more focused discussion on policy and Johnson followed over mains and dessert. The events were held explicitly 'to persuade people that Boris was the right answer', Rees-Mogg said.[77] Johnson, often not drinking himself, would listen as much as talk. The visitors' book, seen by this author, captures the frequency of the gatherings, with MPs in attendance scribbling down their names. There were ten people each on 21, 28 and 29 January, nine on 30 January, eight on 4 February, seven on 25 February and eight on 8 March. Sixty-two guests in total, with some duplications. Johnson would be at the house so often that when the doorbell rang Rees-Mogg's son Alfred, then three, would ask: 'Is that Boris?'[78]

Come the leadership race proper, Johnson would have the use of another tool for securing votes: the Grant Shapps spreadsheet. This document has taken on mythical status in Westminster after so many rounds of Tory leadership purges, much to the frustration of other mini-Machiavellis who see themselves as the real players. Shapps, frozen out of the ministerial ranks by Theresa May and Nick Timothy, began the exercise out of curiosity. A lover of Robert Caro's masterful biography of US President Lyndon B. Johnson, a five-volume epic that captures the raw realities of political power, Shapps wondered what the modern equivalent would be to LBJ's vote-counting method when he was leader of the US Senate.

LBJ had a piece of paper with 'yeas' and 'nays' tallied next to each senator's name only when absolute certainty was reached. Shapps had a spreadsheet and a more statistical approach. Rather than assigning each MP a binary yes or no, he would give them a rating: 1 would represent 100 per cent certainty of voting for a measure; 0 would be the opposite. But MPs could be anything in between: 0.5 if they were deemed to be 50-50, 0.9 if they were very likely to vote your way but not guaranteed to do so. By adding up the individual scores, Shapps found he could predict vote results with surprising accuracy. 'You don't need to know to get the accurate number precisely who will vote for a measure, LBJ-style,' Shapps explained in an interview. 'You just need to know on average who's going to vote for it, because averages will give you the correct answer.'[79]

He used the system for all three meaningful votes, word spreading about its predictive ability. Boris would sidle up to Shapps in the corridor as crunch divisions loomed to ask what the spreadsheet said. Over time, the document would fill with layers upon layers of information. When the author viewed it in early 2023 there were dozens and dozens of columns of intel on each MP: past voting records, whom they backed and when in leadership rounds, quotes or notes from whipping conversations. Links to other documents led to deeper dives into an individual's pet grievances or policy hopes. It was more detailed and dense than anything the Tory whips possessed. In Conservative leadership contests it would prove gold dust.

In the battle for May's premiership, Shapps and Gavin Williamson had been on opposite sides. After her disastrous conference speech in October 2017, May's voice failing and letters falling off the back-drop behind her, Shapps had led a push to topple the leader. Williamson, then chief whip and sensing political danger, ordered a council of war straight after the address. A venue in Manchester where no Lobby hack would stumble across them was picked: a café in the old Kendals department store. There Williamson and two senior whips, Julian Smith and Chris Pincher, devised a plan to secure May.[80] Shapps was outed as a plotter to the press and the sparks of early rebellion fizzled out. But once May was gone in May 2019, Williamson and Shapps came together to get Johnson elected, the former twisting arms and the latter updating his spreadsheet. It proved a potent combination.

Ever since William Hague reformed the system, Conservative Party leadership races have had two stages. The first involves Tory MPs. Candidates who reach the MP support threshold to enter the race are then whittled down by colleagues, one eliminated in each voting round until only two are left standing. The second stage sees party members deciding between the two. The system underscores the way in which the Tory Party is built for power. In the Labour Party, any candidate who hits the support threshold goes forward to the wider, second-stage vote, meaning MPs have less control since lots of hopefuls can get through. It can give the Tories speed too. In 2016, the replacement for David Cameron was in Downing Street before Labour had even announced the full process for the leadership contest challenging Jeremy Corbyn at the same time. It also gives potency. When Tory MPs want a leader gone, they are toast, thanks to the low threshold and anonymity of the no-confidence system. Not so with Labour. In 2016, 80 per cent of Labour MPs voted for Corbyn to go in a manufactured no-confidence vote. Many of them believed he would never win power. Corbyn refused to go and was re-elected by members when the point was forced. In the end, there would be no general election win under Corbyn.

Boris Johnson was always going to be difficult to defeat in the summer 2019 contest owing to the circumstances. For one thing, delivering Brexit was the defining issue. Putting another Remainer in charge would run counter to grassroots sentiment and the instincts of many Tory MPs. The party also needed an election winner. Nigel Farage, ever with a nose for political opportunity, had got behind the launch of the Brexit Party in January 2019, championing a 'clean break' from Brussels. In May it had triumphed in the UK's European parliamentary election, obtaining 31 per cent of the vote, unprecedented for a party that was only a few months old. The Conservatives came fifth, behind the Greens, with a humiliating 9 per cent of the vote. A repeat disaster at a general election loomed. Johnson had the strongest Brexit credentials: he had led the Vote Leave campaign and had rejected Theresa May's deal early on. He also had ballot-box pedigree: two London mayoral victories plus the referendum win.

Michael Gove was one rival, but he had stayed inside May's Cabinet, drawing animosity from the ERG as a result. 'Boris had the best-organised campaign,' Gove said in an interview. 'He and his team had been organising for long enough. People simply believed he had the best chance of saving their seats.'[81] Dominic Raab had eventually walked out over May's Chequers plan, but some colleagues questioned whether he had the pizzazz to win a national election. Sajid Javid was another contender but he knew the odds were stacked against him. 'There's no way I win unless Boris falls under a bus,' he recalled thinking.[82] Jeremy Hunt was a big beast in the race, but he had the handicap of having flirted with a second referendum in the 2016 leadership contest.

Rory Stewart was another hoping to carry the torch for the moderates. He took the fight to Johnson, believing that his rival's promise that the UK would leave the EU by 31 October 2019 was undeliverable, but found pinning him down on Brexit 'infuriating'. 'You simply couldn't get any sense out of him,' Stewart recounted.

> He'd say, 'Rory, I'm not in favour of a no-deal Brexit, why do you keep saying I'm in favour of a no-deal Brexit?' And I'd say, 'What are you in favour of?' And he'd go, 'Well, the Brady amendment [named after a plan floated by Sir Graham Brady], the Malthouse compromise.' I would say, 'Boris, those are all totally different things. Which one of these are you in favour of?' 'Oh, come on, Rory. Show a bit of optimism.'

Stewart likened it to asking a friend if they wanted to drive eight hours to a great location or half an hour to a less good one and being told, 'Let's just get to the better place quicker.'[83]

The ERG executive wanted to stick together to maximise their vote. In the end they opted for Johnson, not out of adoration but after making careful calculations and fully assessing the risks. A senior ERG figure, said: 'We talked at length with each other about Boris and whether he could be trusted to deliver on Brexit . . . Our main concern was that he might implode, that he might be unreliable.'[84] Steve Baker put it more bluntly:

> Boris has never been a man of strong principle and resolute commit-
> ment to ideals and a course of action. He's always been somebody
> constantly angling for his own advancement. He was necessary, we
> needed him to get out of the constitutional crisis we were in. But
> we always knew when we made him prime minister that we were
> playing with fire.[85]

By the first round of MP voting, the writing was already on the wall. Johnson got 114 votes, nearly triple the haul of forty-three of Jeremy Hunt in second place. Yet there were still deals to be done. Conservative MPs like to joke that they are the most devious electorate in the world. Johnson's team wanted to leave nothing to chance. Dominic Raab dropped out and endorsed him, a Brexit big name swinging in behind Boris. What was said between them before Raab's backing was announced is not known, but after victory he would be appointed foreign secretary. When Sajid Javid got knocked out, Johnson was on the phone straightaway seeking another endorsement. No explicit offer was made – leadership candidates always publicly deny deals being done – but a lure was dropped. Javid was 'top of the list' of two or three names being considered for chancellor, Johnson said.[86] The hint was enough. Javid backed Boris and ended up being installed in the Treasury.

There was one final bit of politicking to ease the path. A summer Gove–Johnson slogathon, reliving the psychodrama of the post-referendum betrayal, could do untold damage, Boris's team judged. Moreover, Brexit-backing Gove was better placed than Remain-voting Hunt to pull off a shock victory at the members stage. And so, ahead of the final voting round, Gavin Williamson, effectively Johnson's chief whip, acted with the explicit blessing of Johnson. Hearing from Patrick McLoughlin, Jeremy Hunt's campaign chairman, what their level of support was, Williamson used the cover of proxy votes – each MP could cast ballots for a number of other colleagues – to lend backing to Hunt.[87] The ploy helped him pip Gove into the final two, seventy-seven votes to seventy-five. Boris had the Remainer opponent he desired in the head-to-head. From that point on, Number 10 was his.

There was another force that shaped the Boris project, one hidden from almost everyone involved in the campaign until Johnson's first day in Downing Street, 24 July 2019. Dominic Cummings was not a Johnsonite by nature. It was Michael Gove whom he had worked for in government. Boris and Dom had proved a lethal combination during the EU referendum, Boris the frontman deploying Cummings's take-no-prisoners Vote Leave strategy, but they had gone their separate ways afterwards. As Johnson wrung his hands over Theresa May's Brexit approach, however, the lines of communication had been reopened. When he was foreign secretary, Cummings would sometimes join the gatherings in Carlton Gardens to mull things over, part of the Boris Brexit 'brains trust'.[88] When Johnson quit the Cabinet a three-way WhatsApp group was set up between himself, Cummings and Oliver Lewis, another Vote Leaver, known by the nickname of Sonic owing to his love of the 1990s animated hedgehog. Once or twice a week the group thread would light up with messages, or Johnson would call for advice, according to Lewis.[89] The trio shared a common goal: to see the Brexit they had sold to the nation finally delivered.

Cummings was not visibly present during the 2019 leadership campaign. Johnson went so far as to insist that Dom would not be involved in any government of his, according to Steve Baker.[90] Johnson's office denied the claim.[91] Initially, leaving Cummings on the outside may have been the intention. But as minds turned to the details of office during the plodding summer campaign against Hunt, a coronation in all but name, Johnson grew nervous about the transition. Aides recall one amateurish meeting at campaign

HQ, the townhouse of soon-to-be-MP Andrew Griffith, where senior civil servants were taken through the current plan by the initial Johnson transition team. It was a 'total fucking clown car', as one present put it.[92] Afterwards Lee Cain warned Johnson he was 'not going to last until Christmas' with the present operation.[93] They discussed Cummings coming in instead.

At the same time, Johnson was suspicious of what Whitehall would do once he took over. Eddie Lister, one of his most trusted political confidants, arranged a peace dinner with Sir Mark Sedwill, the Cabinet secretary, and Helen MacNamara, head of the government's propriety and ethics team, at the private members' club Alfreds near London's Berkeley Square. 'These aren't your enemies,' he implored Johnson.[94] The meal seemed to help, but suspicions remained. 'He decided he needed his Rottweiler because he felt the civil service was going to get him,' said Lister.[95] Later Johnson pulled Sir Mark to one side in a transition session and told him that Cummings was coming in, appearing to try to gauge the reaction.

'Faustian pact' is too hyperbolic a characterisation of the deal that brought Cummings into Number 10, but not by much. Certainly, both sides went in with their eyes wide open. Despite everything that would follow, there was mutual admiration between Johnson and Cummings, grounded in their Vote Leave experience. 'Dom was the behind-the-scenes guy, the campaign director organising the troops and deciding on strategy,' one figure, who worked with both on the referendum and in Downing Street said of the 2016 campaign.

> Boris was the rock-star lead singer, the big focal point who could just draw attention and set narratives better than anybody. Those two combined, it was a very formidable partnership. Boris respected Dom's intellect and drive and ability to get things done. At that stage, Dom, although I think he had reservations about Boris's focus, had a good experience of working with him on the referendum.[96]

There was an awareness, too, of the potential flaws in the relationship. Johnson would come to resent how Cummings would dominate his Downing Street operation. 'You've got to be careful with Dominic,' Johnson once told Cain. 'He's like one of those creatures that flies in, lands on its host, burrows itself inside, lays its eggs, and then flies away and waits for them to hatch.' Cain, taken aback, followed the train of thought: 'A parasite?' 'Oh, I didn't say that,' stuttered Johnson.[97] Cummings, sensing his future boss's flakiness, only agreed to join on his own terms, literally. A list of specific agreements – his 'terrorist demands', as one person said Cummings called it – was drawn up. Only when Johnson agreed in writing would he join.[98] Those in the inner circle never saw the actual words but believed they knew the gist: total control for Cummings over staffing, including all special advisers across Whitehall; a gung-ho approach to securing Brexit; a heightened focus on science, a favourite Cummings policy area. For days Johnson would give verbal promises, only to be rebuffed. A yes was needed in writing. Eventually, Johnson relented, sending a brief email signing off on the terms. Dom was now on board.

A final member of the original Brexit squad would also find himself back on the inside. Michael Gove was hated by a sizable portion of Boris's most loyal allies, the 2016 leadership race stab in the back never forgotten. But not by Johnson, a more forgiving man than some might assume, according to friends.[99] The true nature of the Johnson–Gove relationship confounded many Tory colleagues. Throughout his premiership Boris could switch from chuckling with Gove like old pals one day to muttering about treachery another, according to one aide.[100] By offering him a seat at the top table – Gove was put in charge of Brexit preparations as head of the Cabinet Office, his formal title being chancellor of the Duchy of Lancaster – Johnson extended an olive branch. But why? One loyal Cabinet minister recounted Johnson talking through the move during the leadership race: 'He thought that Gove had the intellectual ability to do it and if he gave him a really difficult job it would be done well. That would be to the benefit of the overall government and it would, perhaps, re-establish their relationship.'[101] One Johnson adviser said the plan was to give Gove 'a position of influence, but not power'.[102]

Gove himself got a tip-off the night before the offer was made when Cummings texted him: 'Looking forward to working together.'[103] He had not endorsed a candidate after he was knocked out of the leadership contest, though he privately voted for Johnson and publicly praised his skills. Years earlier, when Johnson was foreign secretary, Gove had sent him a private note. In it, Gove stood by his decision to abandon ship in 2016 but insisted that Boris's place in history was assured – an apparent attempt at atonement. When offering the Cabinet job there was no mention of the 2016 betrayal from Johnson, according to Gove. Just warm words and the big reveal. Asked why he thought Boris brought him back into the fold, Gove said it was about Brexit: 'He wanted to get the Vote Leave team back together. I think his view was, "It's do or die, I need all the resources I can possibly muster."'[104]

It really was do or die. Boris Johnson was in office, the office he had spent so much of his life dreaming of reaching, but not really in power. He had inherited a nonexistent Tory Commons majority from Theresa May, but the situation was worse now. May had largely sat out the referendum campaign, finding herself charged with delivering the outcome when the political status quo collapsed. Boris was the one who had brought it all down on their heads in the first place, a hate figure to the Remain wing of his party.

Dominic Cummings liked to say there were 'two Borises', according to Oliver Lewis, a friend for whom Cummings served as best man at his wedding. 'There's normal Boris and there's Boris with his back against a wall.'[105] That second Boris would be seen on the campaign trail, showing discipline when his political aspirations hung in the balance. He could 'push the boat out' and be 'revolutionary'.[106] Now finally prime minister, but locked in the fight of his political life, it was back-against-the-wall Boris that came to the fore.

One date mattered most: 31 October 2019, more or less a hundred days after his first in Number 10. Johnson had campaigned on Brexiting on that date as scheduled. The problem: he had a handover agreement he did not believe in, an intransigent Brussels refusing to reopen talks and a House of Commons in revolt. The solution? Turning up the volume on no deal.

The strategy was at its core dreamed up by the old Vote Leave gang – Johnson, Cummings, Lewis, Gove and Cain – plus David Frost, an Oxford University contemporary of Boris's who advised him at the Foreign Office, and with the ERG cheering on from the sidelines. Johnson would pick a Cabinet of allies to back up his approach, a deliberate attempt to draw a line under the warfare of May's final frontbench. The primary objective was never to leave the European Union without a deal, those in the decision-making circle consistently said years later, rejecting speculation to the contrary.[107] But equally, there was a genuine willingness to leave without an agreement if nothing changed. Frost believed that no deal would have been better than Theresa May's deal and thought Johnson agreed.[108] Cabinet ministers believe the prime minister flirted with a clean break. But the preference, ultimately, was for a new deal, according to Frost and Lewis, the chief Brexit negotiator and his deputy.[109]

The message was Brexit, boom or bust, and it had two audiences. Brussels had to believe Boris was willing to walk away, in a way it never did with David Cameron or Theresa May, to get EU leaders to budge and restart talks. And, given the need to see off the Brexit Party whenever the election came, the public had to believe that Johnson was busting a gut to deliver the exit they had voted for three years earlier.

Some of the work was done internally. Two Cabinet committees were set up, 'XO' and 'XS', standing for Brexit Operations and Brexit Strategy. Such Whitehall shake-ups normally only set Westminster boffins' hearts racing, but process is the key to wielding power in politics. Cummings and Lewis had realised months earlier that in Britain's ill-defined constitution the authority of the Cabinet is one of the few crystal-clear certainties. Cabinet committees, made up of relevant senior ministers meeting on specific issues, could deliver change fast. XO, headed up by Gove, was critical there. It met daily, with preparations for no deal its focus. During each session orders for the civil service were typed up on the big screen, and the send button on the diktats was hit at the end. The whir of activity communicated a clear message – one way or the other, the UK was getting out.

The biggest controversy would come in the Commons. After the summer the Tory tensions ignited when Parliament returned. The spark was a bill proposed by Labour MP Hilary Benn that would effectively take no deal off the table, binding the government to extend the Brexit deadline into the following year if agreement was not reached by 19 October – in other words, Johnson would miss his leadership campaign promise to deliver Brexit by 31 October.

An attempt to ease the bill's passage was vehemently opposed by Downing Street but, defying orders, twenty-one Conservative MPs voted for it. Johnson then went for the nuclear option. All twenty-one were stripped of the whip, and thereby expelled from the parliamentary party. Some of the biggest Tory names were on the list, including two former chancellors, Philip Hammond – who had held the post just a few months earlier – and Ken Clarke. Seven others were former Cabinet ministers. One, Sir Nicholas Soames, was the grandson of the most famous Tory prime minister in history, Winston Churchill. The move had real bite, since it meant the MPs could not stand as Tories at the next election, risking the end of their parliamentary careers. For many, that was exactly what would happen.

The next day, Johnson, wobbling, pleaded with Cummings and Cain to let him restore the whip to some of the MPs. They resisted; he relented – though later some would get the whip back.[110] More drama followed the vote. Jo Johnson, the prime minister's brother, soon quit the Cabinet. The Remain-voting younger Johnson had only taken up the post of business minister six weeks before but announced he was standing down at the election, citing 'unresolvable tension' between family loyalty and the national interest. Amber Rudd, one of the few Europhiles left around the Cabinet table, followed him out of the door.

More controversy came as the prime minister pulled the lever marked 'prorogation'. Bringing the parliamentary session to a close was a deliberate attempt to limit MPs' time for further Brexit-thwarting mischief as the clock advanced towards 31 October. The manoeuvre would also be declared unlawful, the Supreme Court ruling against the government when a case reached the judges. It did show to the country, though, how hard Johnson was pushing for the Brexit bill, as Number 10 insiders knew. The so-called Benn Bill eventually passed, tying Johnson's hands on seeking a deadline extension. Still Johnson would not relent. On 2 October, he told the Tory conference that Brexit would happen at the end of the month 'come what may'.[III] Like Theresa May before him, Boris had boxed himself in – but on his own terms.

In the end, Brussels blinked. Talks were reopened, despite the previous vehement insistence of EU leaders and Tory critics that changes to May's deal were never going to happen. October saw intense negotiations. An ally was found in Irish taoiseach Leo Varadkar, a joint statement being issued with Johnson saying 'a pathway' to a deal was visible after a meeting on 10 October. Changes emerged. The much-maligned Northern Ireland 'backstop' which effectively kept the UK in the customs union was ditched. Gone too was the political promise to align closely with the EU, leaving the UK fully out of the single market and free to pick its own rules and regulations. A Northern Ireland fudge of sorts remained, the 'Protocol', to keep the land border on the island of Ireland open, but critically the province's politicians had the legal authority to leave the agreement if desired.

May's and Johnson's teams to this day disagree on quite how different their deals were. Boris's Brexit negotiators see fundamental changes: taking the UK out of the single market and customs union, while giving the Northern Ireland Assembly at Stormont the legal ability to reject its trade arrangement with the EU. May's supporters note the consistencies: the end of free movement, the paying of a multibillion-pound debt. The 31 October deadline was in the end pushed back to 31 January 2020, a legal requirement under the Benn Act. But Boris had his own Withdrawal Agreement, as he had promised – a personal triumph. In addition, the ERG had been kept on side. The deal provisionally passed a vote in the Commons, achieving what May had not been able to do. When progress stalled as rebellions mounted once again, Johnson reached for the ace up his sleeve.

An early general election had been on the cards from day one of the Johnson premiership. The very morning Boris walked up Downing Street for the first time as prime minister, Dominic Cummings sat down with Isaac Levido in a Patisserie Valerie in Marylebone. Levido had been on the front line of past Tory ballot battles, wearing the medals of 2015 and bearing the scars of 2017. A disciple of Lynton Crosby, Levido had not only the same Aussie accent and dry wit, but also the same clarity of vision when it came to electoral strategy. The pair did not know each other – Levido was among the Johnson allies who had no idea a day earlier that Dom was going into government – but Cummings had an offer to make him. 'Look, I've heard a lot about you,' Cummings said. 'Everyone whose opinion I respect says you're great. We might have to run an election campaign. I want you to run it.'[112] Levido said yes, on two conditions. First, he had to be in sole charge of the campaign (another echo of Crosby, who demanded the same in 2015). And, second, he wanted reassurance that Number 10 really would go all out for a Brexit deal. Reassurances given, he signed up.

As Prime Minister Johnson twisted arms in Westminster, Levido pressed voters in focus groups for insights about how to approach the likely upcoming electoral contest. Straightaway it was clear that Boris was viewed differently from Theresa May. He was seen as a 'crash or crash-through guy', willing to 'break things' to get what he wanted.[113] He split opinion, no question, but the perception of stasis under May was gone, replaced by something more dynamic.[114] As the weeks passed, the 'pivot' was identified: the critical framing of the debate to maximise the chance of people voting Tory. It was captured in a three-word phrase: 'Get Brexit Done.' Its simplicity was deceptive. The message was not just 'Brexit', appealing solely to Leave voters. That would be too narrow. It was a wider plea, one for it all to be over – all the political wrangling, all the uncertainty. For life to move on. Seen through that prism, it diminished the appeal of the other parties. For those who wanted to 'Get Brexit Done', the Liberal Democrats were not an option: they wanted to stay in the EU. Neither was Labour, which was proposing a second referendum – thanks in no small part to Sir Keir Starmer, who championed the position as shadow Brexit secretary. And nor was the Brexit Party, Nigel Farage's band of merry insurgents. They were not going to win the election, so could never themselves 'Get Brexit Done'. For anyone who just wanted the issue settled, including previous soft Remainers, the Tories offered the clearest route to bringing down the curtain.

Triggering the election held complications. The Fixed-term Parliaments Act was still in place, meaning a snap vote could only happen if two-thirds of MPs backed one. Johnson challenged Labour MPs to put their money where their mouths were and agree to an election. At first, Jeremy Corbyn said no and colleagues held the line. Take a no-deal Brexit off the table, he insisted. Johnson refused. The Liberal Democrats folded first; Labour followed. On 6 November 2019, Johnson announced a general election for 12 December, less than a fortnight before Christmas.

High on the list of Tory objectives was avoiding the missteps of 2017. The austerity backlash channelled by Corbyn last time was headed off with tangible, round-number spending promises: twenty thousand more police officers; fifty thousand more nurses; forty new hospitals. The focus was kept relentlessly on Brexit, amplified by Johnson's Vote Leave-style stunts like bulldozing a wall with 'Get Brexit Done'-branded machinery. Two further years of Brexit wrangling helped the Tory campaign in 2019, with deeper frustrations there to be tapped, making Labour's fudged position a bigger problem than in 2017. Splits in CCHQ were minimised, with Cummings largely sticking to his word to let Levido call the shots. A super-cautious approach to new manifesto promises was adopted.

There were still a few hairy moments. One misstep came at the very beginning when Jacob Rees-Mogg, now in Johnson's Cabinet, suggested in a radio interview that Grenfell Tower fire victims had not shown 'common sense' when they followed orders to stay put in the burning building rather than fleeing. A furious Levido 'put him in the freezer', with Rees-Mogg instructed to stay in his constituency and do no more national media.[115]

Another came over the manifesto, though unlike in 2017 not from the grassroots but the top. The text had been worked up by the policy boffins, with Johnson feeding in at a top level, when it was about to go to the printers. Ever the hack when it came to deadlines, Boris had still not read all of the programme he was promising to drive through as the moment to hit the send button approached. He called Lynton Crosby, still a trusted sounding board. 'Mate, I'm not going to have time to read this, can you look at it for me?' the prime minister asked.[116] Crosby's lukewarm response to the proposals sent Johnson into a panic, as described by two well-placed sources. Boris pushed for last-minute changes. In the end, only his foreword was significantly reworked. A senior Tory campaign figure insisted that, between the Crosby call and the printing, the prime minister did, in the end, read the whole manifesto.[117]

A third curveball came in the form of Donald Trump. The campaign had been ticking along as planned, with no dramatic changes in the polling and the Tories in the lead. But the US president was flying into London for a Nato gathering just a week before the election. Trump liked to call Johnson 'Britain Trump', perhaps on account of their similarities in hair styling, disregard for political norms and populist instincts. But in the UK a Trump endorsement was toxic. And so followed an extraordinary scene. Team Boris concluded that the purported leader of the free world could not be trusted with his tongue. Trump was due to give an interview to Piers Morgan, the tabloid editor turned broadcaster who already had a track record of getting the US president to cause mayhem during UK visits with unscripted remarks. Levido worked Rupert Murdoch contacts, reaching out to Rebekah Brooks, the CEO of News UK, seeking help to get the interview cancelled. Johnson went one further. A call with Trump himself was used to secure a cancellation. 'Please, Donald, don't. It would be unhelpful,' Johnson said, according to a summary given by one source involved in the efforts.[118] 'Please don't go on Piers Morgan.' A second source confirmed the core message of the call.[119] The pleading worked. Trump dropped out. The prime minister had muzzled the Don. Later, at Murdoch's Christmas party in London after the election, Morgan expressed his frustration at losing the interview to a senior member of the Johnson team, according to one present.[120] But it was too late by then.

Even with a comfortable lead in the polls, there was still time and energy for a little political chicanery. One example involved Nigel Farage. Back channels, one passing through Lynton Crosby, were opened up with the Brexit Party leader.[121] The pitch was simple: if you want to deliver Brexit, best get out of the Tories' way. The jeopardy was real. Farage had made taking Britain out of the EU his life's calling. What an irony it would be if, having come so close, he accidentally helped get a party into power that was seeking to overturn the result. Why not stand down Brexit candidates in

Conservative seats? Farage bargained at first, according to a senior Tory campaign source, making a free run in five or ten seats his price for the deal.[122] The demand was resisted. Farage agreed anyway, seeing Brexit as the greater win. Farage still thinks it was the right call, though he acknowledged he faced a backlash as a result: 'I think it was the hardest decision I ever had to take. Probably the decision that caused me more unpopularity in my own party than anything I'd ever done before. I still get abuse for it every day.'[123]

Another wheeze saw a lack of candour. In selling his new version of Brexit to the electorate, Johnson was less willing to admit the reality of the deal he had struck – that a customs border had effectively been erected across the UK in the Irish Sea, splitting Great Britain and Northern Ireland. His Northern Ireland Protocol kept the wider UK out of the customs union, but goods would now have to be checked before arriving in the province from the mainland in case they then were moved over the open border into the Republic of Ireland, and thus the EU. Sajid Javid, who as chancellor oversaw HMRC, the UK's tax, payments and customs authority, knew this to be the case, having seen the paperwork. He thought Johnson was aware of the fact too, the two ministers having sat in meetings where civil servants made it explicit. Javid cautioned Johnson against publicly claiming that there would be no customs border down the Irish Sea during the campaign, according to a Treasury source. The prime minister ignored him. Time and time again the public were told there would be no checks. 'He just kept saying it,' the source added.[124] Johnson's office denied the claims.

Looking back, Jeremy Corbyn, the Labour leader, said that Johnson's relentless focus on delivering Brexit helped explain why in 2019 he failed to replicate the unexpected success of the 2017 election campaign. 'Johnson refusing to engage in debate and just saying, "We'll get Brexit done," was part of it,' said Corbyn in an interview with the author, before citing other reasons. 'Also the fact that I was trying to unite the party with the [second referendum] policy that we ended up getting. Obviously, it didn't entirely work, otherwise we would have won the election. I also think the personality destruction of me between '17 and '19 was a factor.'[125]

★

203

Yet the race also shone a light on some of the prime minister's most envied political assets – qualities easy for rivals and colleagues to turn their noses up at but much harder to replicate. Johnson was a campaigning phenomenon, a communicator unrivalled on the Tory benches: able to stick to a message while avoiding parroting a line, and all the while connecting with voters. This author has seen first-hand how on the stump passers-by will break into grins, declare 'Boris!' – invariably using his first name – and chortle under their breath, 'Oh what's he saying now?' Whether loved or loathed, he was rarely ignored. Few other Conservatives in this period, if any, could boast the same.

Levido, who has been a political consultant on three continents, with stints in Canberra and Washington, DC as well as the UK, summed it up:

> The guy is a force of nature. He is the most talented campaigner and communicator that I've ever worked with by a long way. Lynton has got a line about Boris being a multigrain politician in a white bread world – he's got all these facets to him that enable him to fit into varying situations. He has an authenticity about him which people can just sense. His opponents go mad about it. They just cannot understand . . . If he walked in the door now and you were meeting him for the first time, I'd expect you would turn around afterwards and tell me that was exactly what you thought he'd be like. That is a big part of his appeal.[126]

It was an appeal that would deliver on voting day.

Following the fist-pumping in Downing Street there were nerves. Would the exit poll prove true? They need not have worried. One after the other, pillars of past Labour electoral successes in the Midlands and North crumbled. Workington, the Cumbrian seat that had returned a Labour MP in every election bar one for a century, turned blue. Bolsover, home of the socialist stalwart and former mining union leader Dennis Skinner, was flipped, ending a forty-nine-year parliamentary career. Sedgefield, Tony Blair's old seat, was now Tory-held. 'Things can only get better!' belted out disbelieving staffers in CCHQ.[127] Boris Johnson's electoral strategists had never liked the phrase 'Red Wall', the media's epithet for Labour strongholds in those regions. But whatever it was called, the citadel was being stormed. The opportunity that had been available to Theresa May in 2017, peeling off Labour's working-class Leave voters with a purist Brexit pitch, had been seized with both hands by Johnson. Come the final count, the Conservatives had 365 seats, up forty-eight from May's total. Labour, under Jeremy Corbyn, had dropped sixty to 202 seats, worse than in 1983 and Michael Foot's 'longest suicide note in history' manifesto. It was Labour's lowest seat total in a general election since 1935. Most important was the House of Commons majority: eighty. Better than anything David Cameron had achieved. The best since Maggie in 1987. It meant power – real, tangible, undiluted political power, to be used however Johnson desired.

Amid the celebrations in Thatcher's old study that night, there was a moment's pause for two key players present. Dominic Cummings had always known there were two Borises. Shoved up against the wall, Johnson had fought tooth and nail. From the uncertainty of backbench loneliness, via the toppling of May, to seeing off pretenders for the leadership, facing down Commons critics, forcing Brussels to budge and now securing the approval of the electorate, Johnson had somehow made it through. He had battled and he had won. But now the wall was gone, replaced by an open road ahead. 'He doesn't really need us now,' Cummings told Lee Cain that night, sensing what was to come. 'It wouldn't surprise me if we don't last six months.'[128] It would be longer than that, but not much. For the analysis, at its heart, was right. Johnson had thrown off the shackles, emerging unconstrained and untouchable. But he would discover that freedom was a double-edged sword.

7

Squandered Opportunities

B EFORE BORIS JOHNSON was a stack of note cards and a pen. The task: Write down what you believe. Johnson was alone, on the orders of his team.[1] It was the 2019 Conservative Party leadership contest and the candidates were packing in one-to-one meetings with Tory MPs to persuade them of their worth. Johnson's aides had detected concern about the lack of specificity from their boss when pressed for his stance on issues beyond Brexit. What was his education policy? Did he want tougher sentences for criminals? What balance would be struck on spending and taxes? How should the NHS be reformed? It was time for Boris to commit pen to paper.

That the exercise was even needed said something of Johnson's chameleon ideology. At university, he had toned down the Tory brand after his defeat in the race to be Oxford Union president and ran again by aligning himself with the Social Democratic Party. He won. As mayor of Labour-voting London, Johnson projected a liberal vision, advocating an amnesty for all illegal migrants and championing gay marriage. As chief Brexiteer, he threw in his lot with the Tory Right, warning of uncontrollable immigration from the European Union – possibly even Turkey, a Muslim-majority nation which was hoping to join – without departure. Then backbench Boris took carefully selected policy pot shots designed to create maximum effect. To critics, the clearest thread running through Johnson's stances was saying what was needed to advance his career. Now, though, he needed a vision.

The cards were scribbled on and completed, but never made public. As Johnson romped to victory in the Tory contest that summer, and later with the national electorate that winter, a platform had emerged. Ending austerity was at its heart, though with few details on how it would be funded. There was an eco-friendliness, a toughness on crime, a shiny 'levelling-up' mantra which blurred when people looked for specifics. With a vast new House of Commons majority of eighty, there were so many possibilities. Three dozen Tory MPs could vote to defeat a government measure and still it would pass. It was more than just breathing room. Boris had the numbers to refashion the country in his own image. Yet, ultimately, the ambition would not be realised.

Why? Interviews with Downing Street advisers, senior civil servants, personal aides and long-standing friends, plus his own Cabinet ministers – twenty of whom gave insights to the author – offer clues to an explanation. Circumstance no doubt played its part, a once-in-a-century pandemic rocking the Johnson government. Delivering Brexit, the defining achievement of his premiership, dominated the early months. But these factors alone do not explain an opportunity not maximised.

The prime minister's own whims and weaknesses were factors. Johnson's lack of a deep-rooted personal ideology, combined with an instinct to delay decisions when faced with conflict and a susceptibility to switch positions on issues not key to his political survival, slowed Whitehall. His lack of interest in the boring bits of the job – from churning through the ministerial red boxes to engaging with the mechanics of Parliament or driving agreed changes through to delivery – was problematic. His 'have cake and eat it' economics, avoiding trade-offs in search of a fabled land of ever-higher spending and Tory-beloved tax cuts, presented a contradiction that was never resolved. And then there was a Number 10 operation at times at war with itself, reflecting a boss who would chafe at restraints and was known to declare: 'I'm my own chief of staff.'[2]

Only two prime ministers in the preceding half-century had enjoyed a bigger Commons majority than Boris: Tony Blair and Margaret Thatcher. And yet, beyond Brexit, he would not transform the nation as they had. There would be no 'Johnsonism'. The election triumph, with the possibilities it presented, had sent him into rapture. Yet the paradise would never be reached.

★

One event scars the landscape of the Boris Johnson premiership like an asteroid crater, a bolt from the blue that did untold damage to the country and his plans: Covid-19.

It arrived right after the final delivery of Brexit. Swept back into Downing Street by the electorate, Johnson demanded the all-out pursuit of the UK's exit from the EU to continue throughout December 2019. A final deal was struck with Brussels on Christmas Eve, then voted through the Commons with overwhelming support on 30 December. At 11 p.m. on 31 January 2020, Brexit was achieved. It would be line one of Johnson's legacy, representing a totemic change in the UK's relationship with the world. In six months in power he had delivered what Theresa May had failed to in three years. At a Number 10 gathering to mark the moment, the prime minister struck a miniature gong in celebration, only to see it collapse to the floor – a metaphor to delight his critics. He picked it up and kept on gonging.[3]

That same day, lower down the headlines, another news story had broken. The UK's first two cases of coronavirus had been confirmed.[4] A fifty-year-old Chinese woman had flown from Wuhan province to visit her twenty-three-year-old son, who was studying at the University of York, only for both of them to develop a fever.[5] In medical journals they would become known as 'Patient A' and 'Patient B'. Covid-19 had reached the UK.

It is impossible to capture what it felt like to be at the centre of power that February and March as the scale of the approaching storm began to dawn on its occupants. The sense of dread, of realisation, of normal life collapsing that was rippling across the country was also hitting Number 10. 'Fuck, I'm in a disaster film,' Cleo Watson, a Number 10 special adviser, recalled saying to herself. 'I now cannot watch these films like *The Day after Tomorrow* and *Contagion* without thinking, "God, that weird panic is how it really feels."'[6] Insiders struggled to pinpoint the 'oh shit' moment, but seeing the virus ravaging Italy's health system was a turning point. Boris Johnson would point in shock at TV screens showing Lombardy medical centres buckling, saying with alarm, 'The Italian NHS is really fucking good. I've been to that hospital.'[7]

Measures no politician ever expects to consider were discussed and implemented. Whose life should be prioritised in the event of medical resources becoming scarce? The removal of basic liberties: seeing a relative; travelling overseas; leaving your home. At one point, meeting a friend outside would be outlawed unless you were exercising. Leaders across the globe were fumbling through the same scenario, battling a disease they did not understand using a handbook that was out of date. One set of plans, never made public, is a reminder of just how unnerving those early weeks were inside Whitehall. With the projected death toll soaring, a stark question was asked: Where to store the bodies? A new stream of Cabinet Office work, dubbed 'surplus death management' by one person, was established.[8] The answer: in temporary mortuaries to keep the bodies cold until burial. In an interview, Eddie Lister, then Downing Street chief of staff, revealed a plan to create three such mortuaries in London public parks.[9] Thousands of those killed by Covid could have been stored in them. One was to be out east, in the Lee Valley. A second would be central. Hyde Park has long been named in contingency plans for emergencies but its Royal Park status led to concerns about its appropriateness as a venue. A third park mortuary was to be in the south. 'It was basically going to be tents with big refrigerating units stuffed inside them,' Lister said.[10] As the death projections fell with the introduction of mitigation measures, the project was dropped.

On 23 March 2020, a nationwide lockdown was announced. Boris Johnson, a UK flag at his side, delivered the news in an emergency televised address. 'From this evening I must give the British people a very simple instruction – you must stay at home,' he said, in surely the single most surreal sentence uttered by a prime minister since the Tories took office in 2010.[11] There would be two more lockdowns: one in November 2020, as the virus surged again after a summer of opening up; and then another just before Christmas 2020. Pressure for a fourth, ahead of Christmas 2021 in response to the emergence of the Omicron variant, was ultimately resisted. More than 225,000 people would die with Covid-19 in the UK by the summer of 2023.[12] The number of officially recorded cases would exceed 22 million.[13] The UK economy suffered its sharpest contraction in three hundred years. In total the Government's Covid interventions cost between £310 billion and £410 billion, the equivalent of about £4,600 to £6,100 per person in the UK.[14] The enormity of the figures is head-spinning.

Weighing the merit of each pandemic decision by ministers would become the subject of a lengthy public inquiry. The endlessly shifting facts, and the twists and turns in policy, make reaching simple conclusions on how Covid was handled fiendishly hard. Some broad realities of the approach, though, did emerge in interviews.[15] In the Cabinet, Michael Gove, the chancellor of the Duchy of Lancaster, and Matt Hancock, the health secretary, tended to be the most vociferous advocates for lockdown. The Treasury, then headed by Rishi Sunak, was a consistent voice of caution. Johnson by instinct was resistant to lockdowns but became convinced – swiftly, the first time; less so thereafter – that the science gave him no other choice.

Allies insist that the prime minister got the 'big calls' right; a conclusion sure to be countered by critics and scrutinised by posterity.[16] There were major missteps, releasing elderly hospital patients into care homes without first giving them Covid tests being one. The money poured into Test and Trace was eye-watering. Whether the right balance was struck between curbing virus spread and avoiding the knock-on damage of lockdowns is still fiercely debated.

In two areas, though, there is widespread praise for Johnson. The early decision to invest in vaccine development and procurement earns him one big tick. 'I think forever he should have the credit because he did drive that and it was the right decision,' said Lister.[17] Nadhim Zahawi, appointed to a newly created ministerial position for vaccine delivery, said the same, recalling how for a long period the pair would hold 11 p.m. calls to run through the numbers.[18] Another, less tangible, was his ability as a communicator, Boris's great political strength. The quality of rhetoric deployed on the campaign trail is easily waved away; much less so the ability to rally the nation at a time of crisis and convince a mass of people to follow rules and sign up for newly created vaccines. 'He was a brilliant leader for that vaccine campaign,' said Henry Cook, a Number 10 special adviser focused on Covid policy. 'Bringing a national spirit behind that campaign was a wonderful thing. There were cathedrals full of people getting their jabs.'[19] The UK had one of the highest vaccine uptakes in the Western world. In a deadly pandemic, communication matters.

The pandemic grabbed the attention of the Johnson government just as thoughts were turning to using its newfound Commons majority. 'It just sucked all the energy out of government,' said Gove, who was tasked with co-ordinating much of the Whitehall Covid work.[20] 'It blew out our legislative programme,' said Jacob Rees-Mogg, then Commons leader.[21] Baroness Evans, the Tory leader in the House of Lords, said: 'There was this sucking of all resource, brainpower, manpower and focus, meaning that very little else was done.'[22] From spring 2020 to spring 2021, countering Covid was the most pressing policy issue for Downing Street, and it continued to be so for much of the year after that. Baroness Evans estimated that only around a quarter of the number of normal domestic bills, aside from those about Covid, passed through Parliament during the height of the pandemic. She also said legislation that came later could be threadbare: 'After Covid you then had bills coming through where, frankly, the policy work simply hadn't been done.'[23] Planning reforms, designed to bring about a major loosening of rules to kick-start more house-building but abandoned after a grassroots backlash, were singled out. For Priti Patel, who was Johnson's home secretary and stayed loyal to him, Covid invalidates any straight comparisons that might be made with predecessors. 'The pandemic really changed ways of working. You can't compare that to the way previous prime ministers ran their government, because it dominated so much of Boris's tenure,' said Patel.[24] She has a point.

There was another obvious impact from Covid. It almost killed Boris Johnson. He tested positive for the virus on 2 March 2020 and at first kept working in isolation. His ministerial red box would be left outside his Downing Street flat door, with the odd conversation being conducted through the wood. But as the days went by, those on video calls with him could tell things were getting worse. David Frost, his Brexit negotiator, remembered Johnson looking 'grey', 'tired', 'run-down' and 'exhausted'. 'This looks bad,' he thought to himself.[25] Eddie Lister remembered hearing his boss 'coughing and spluttering' before he muttered, 'God, this is awful,' the remark sticking out as Boris rarely complained about illness.[26] Priti Patel recalled a Zoom call where the prime minister was 'gasping for air', sounding as though a 'big weight' was lying on his chest. She was 'very upset' and also furious with senior civil servants for not doing more to prevent his getting into such a condition.[27] Unlike in America or Australia, the UK's political leader is not assigned a personal physician. Nor is there a chef. According to one friend who dubbed the lack of support for the prime minister 'a joke', Johnson was at points reliant on takeaways left on his doormat while he was battling a deadly disease.[28]

In the end a doctor was summoned. With Johnson's breathing under strain, he was taken to St Thomas' Hospital, located across the Thames from Parliament, on Sunday, 5 April. Then, just a day later, Johnson was moved into intensive care. Cabinet ministers still remember the group call from Sir Mark Sedwill, the Cabinet secretary, revealing the news. There was 'silence' as 'the shock of it all' sank in.[29] Dominic Raab, who as first secretary of state as well as foreign secretary was minister number two, stepped in as acting leader. It would be three weeks before Johnson returned to Downing Street. At the time it was already clear that Covid hit the elderly and seriously overweight worst. Johnson, while not firmly in either camp, was fifty-five and on the larger side. He was also about to become a father again, with his fiancée, Carrie Symonds, expecting their first child in a few weeks. As word spread, one Downing Street figure wondered: 'Is he going to make it through the night?'[30] When one of Johnson's longest-serving advisers was told the news he burst into tears. 'I was devastated. I literally bawled and bawled,' said the source, remembering contemplating the prospect of his friend's death. 'I just sat and drank a bottle of gin to myself that night.'[31]

The concern was well founded. In intensive care, the oxygen level in Johnson's blood kept dropping. He was given 'litres and litres' of oxygen to force it back up.[32] Then came the most serious decision: whether to put the prime minister on a ventilator. It would have involved placing a tube down his windpipe and the lungs being worked externally, a procedure that normally sees the patient kept unconscious. It was a '50–50' call, Johnson said later.[33]

Lister revealed how far preparations went for the transfer of political authority.[34] He recounted that Martin Reynolds, Johnson's principal private secretary, prepared a letter for Buckingham Palace, ready to be sent if Johnson were put on a ventilator or worse. 'There was a formal letter drafted to the Queen, for the Queen to sign, because she would have to transfer power to Dominic Raab. Boris might have been incapacitated or indeed died,' said Lister.[35] In the end, the letter was not needed. As well as the macabre, there was the comic. At one point a 'big parcel' of experimental Covid drugs arrived courtesy of Donald Trump, the US president, intended for Boris. It was 'duly handed over' to Chris Whitty, the chief medical officer for England, not to be seen again.[36]

Johnson would pull through, recovering sufficiently in time to be present for the birth of his new son, Wilfred. He does not doubt how serious the situation became, saying since: 'I owe my life to our doctors and nurses.'[37]

For all of Covid's undoubted impact on Boris Johnson's government, it alone does not explain why the potential offered by his large parliamentary majority slipped through his fingers. One of the most senior mandarins who served Johnson addressed the point:

> He didn't really have a programme. I think that was, in a sense, almost concealed by Covid . . . I'm not sure that you could really make the case that there would have then been a big push on Levelling Up or his other big ideas because he didn't really have a programme for implementing them.

To understand that reality, it is necessary to take a dive into the idiosyncrasies of Boris Johnson's character and approach to the job, as attested to by those who witnessed events first-hand. For there are more depths, shades and nuances to each prime minister's being than is projected to the public via TV cameras and the caricatures offered by reporters' pens.

Johnson's leadership strengths are pointed to with consistency by those who worked for him. He has a formidable intellect and the ability to cut through briefing papers to focus on the core points when required. 'Super-bright,' as an ally put it.[38] The confidence in his own abilities drew comparisons with David Cameron, both honed by Eton and Oxford. He is 'absolutely brilliant with people', putting a smile on faces in interactions, often by using self-deprecating humour.[39] One senior figure on his first London mayoral campaign even claimed that a facial recognition specialist had concluded that Boris inherently had more engaging features than his rival, Ken Livingstone.[40] There is no loftier-than-thou condescension with Johnson, a virtue not shared by all who reach the summit of British politics. One senior aide recalled how as mayor he would go down to the main café in City Hall for his lunchtime soup, sitting and chatting with whoever was around.[41] A younger member of the Downing Street team recalled pleasure at the way he would ask for all opinions in a room.[42] Nor are tales voiced of bullying, another point not true of all top Tories. Ministers and advisers, even those who have soured on Johnson, stress that they enjoyed working with him.

In some ways, the private Johnson was just like his public persona. The same smile would play at the corner of the mouth, hooded eyes looking for a way to elicit laughter from the room. 'He is what he is,' said one of his Cabinet ministers.[43] Jacob Rees-Mogg said Johnson was 'just as amusing and ebullient, unpinnable-down' as he appeared.[44] He recounted how Boris once waved around kippers at a 2019 Tory leadership event to make a point about Brexit, then turned up at his house later that evening, headed to the kitchen and proceeded to cook them. 'Nobody else' in politics would do that, Rees-Mogg concluded.

But others who got close to Johnson saw sides of his personal character that were hidden from the camera lens. One common remark was that Boris is shyer than people think. 'He's an extroverted introvert. He doesn't have many close friends, certainly in politics,' said one senior Downing Street adviser.[45] Another: 'He's actually quite shy and diffident in a way. Rarely is he totally relaxed, only I think when he's alone reading a book or writing.'[46] That second adviser recalled that once, having accompanied Carrie on a trip, Johnson appeared unsure how to say thank you when prompted to do so, unsettled by a newish professional colleague in a private setting.[47] A third adviser called him 'much more of a loner' than the public perception.[48] There was no Boris 'gang' akin to the Cameroons. Johnson, during a dinner with Michael Gove many years in the past at Scott's restaurant in London's Mayfair, is said to have expressed envy at the tight political friendship between David Cameron and George Osborne.[49] If he was looking for one with Gove, it would not be found.

Johnson's comfort zone was in his head. He was an avid reader, and not just of books about the classical world, as the stereotype suggested. As foreign secretary he would stock up on publications about trip destinations. Both in the Foreign Office and in Downing Street, Johnson was a napper, according to two advisers. 'He would read *The Spectator* and lie on his sofa in the office and have forty winks,' said one source.[50] Aides who accidentally walked in on him at such moments would be greeted by their boss jolting awake and a rustling of pages. His go-to newspapers were the *Daily Telegraph* and the *Financial Times*, frustration building if the former carried negative coverage of his premiership, fearing the impact on the Tory base.

Johnson, unlike May, liked to spend weekends at Chequers, the prime ministerial country house. There he would paint, a pastime shared with the former leader he most studied and at times aped, Winston Churchill. Johnson continued to write, despite the pressures of the top ministerial jobs he occupied, usually early in the mornings. Another aide picked out two differences from his public image: 'He is a lot swearier and a bit more short-tempered at times.'[51] There would be outbursts of exasperation – though not directed at colleagues – and sentences littered with the f-word.

Johnson rarely listened to music when being driven in the company of aides, but was known to quote from two favourite films. One was *Jaws*. With knowing provocation, Boris once named as his political hero the town's 'squint-eyed, chain-smoking' mayor, Larry Vaughn, who keeps the beach open only to see its inhabitants mauled to death by the eponymous shark. 'There was one laudable thing about him, and that was his refusal to give way to hysteria,' Johnson wrote in 2003. 'I loved his rationality. Of course, it turned out that he was wrong . . . But the fact remains that he was heroically right in principle.'[52] The second film was *Dodgeball*, the 2004 sports comedy.

When in tight political spots Johnson would repeat the 'five Ds' advice given to players: 'Dodge, duck, dip, dive and dodge.'[53] Both choices were telling.

When it came to the serious work of governing there were notable differences from his predecessors – some mere curiosities, others with more problematic consequences.

Theresa May liked her weekly Cabinet meetings to run long. Three hours was not uncommon. Indeed, they would drag on to such a degree that some bored ministers started taking sweepstakes. They would bet on which colleague would drone on the longest. Greg Clark, the business secretary, once unwittingly set the record, talking for twenty-six minutes on a topic that was not even in his brief, according to one of the renegade ministers.[54] 'A couple of us would literally make a point of going, "No, I've got nothing to add," just to win the bet on who spoke shortest,' the source added.[55] But with Johnson, as with David Cameron, Cabinet meetings would often last just an hour. 'Snappy,' said one minister; another said that 'he didn't want to dawdle'.[56] Many saw it as a positive; less hot air than at May's meandering gatherings.

A less flattering difference concerned the red box. Each evening, the prime minister, in common with other Cabinet ministers, is handed a red box full of papers relating to pressing decisions that need sign-off. It is expected that those papers will be read that night or early the following morning. Final calls are required to keep Whitehall functioning, a critical cog in the machinery of government. Some items are urgent, others more administrative. Cameron liked to tackle the contents of his box early in the morning. Theresa May was methodical, spending hours late at night on hers. Johnson was less regimented than his predecessor, according to multiple Number 10 aides who witnessed both leaders up close. Less systematic would be a kind way of putting it; too often indifferent a harsher one.

'People would get frustrated that he wasn't doing the box,' said one senior adviser. 'Some days he just didn't bother. But he would do it in the end. It's just Boris, doing it on his own time.'[57] Another said: 'There's no way that Boris had the same consistency of taking the box up to the flat every night, doing two hours of it and the box arriving [back] the next day. Often we submitted papers again and again.'[58] One ally stressed that the difference with the approaches of his predecessors should not be exaggerated. But delays did mean that at times decisions had to be forced. Martin Reynolds, Johnson's top private office civil servant, would sometimes have to WhatsApp summaries of the issues in need of urgent decisions.[59] Verbal approvals could be sought. Word even spread that one special adviser had figured out a sure-fire way to grab Boris's attention – start submissions with an eye-catching quote, in the manner of an Oxbridge essay.[60]

The way Johnson approached meetings could also undercut the push for speedy decisions. Here a consistent picture emerges from the accounts of many Cabinet ministers. Civil servants would produce a carefully itemised discussion plan, only for Johnson to ignore the script and roam where he pleased. 'He hates somebody steering a meeting,' said one minister. 'He wanted to have a wider discussion but that means he can go off on a tangent and you have to fight incredibly hard to keep him on track.'[61] Another said that 'you'd be lucky' if 25 per cent of the time in a meeting was spent on the issue at hand.[62] Johnson would zoom in on areas of curiosity or out to big-picture debates. Friendly ministers framed this habit as the prime minister following his nose, honing in on political dangers. Others called it a lack of necessary focus. 'The sensible ones of us learned that you needed to get your headline in early,' said a Cabinet minister, going big with the key demand at the start to ensure approval was secured by the end.[63]

His lack of interest in Parliament, while not uncommon for prime ministers, could be problematic too. Johnson had a massive majority in the Commons, but not in the second chamber, which also needed to vote through any new laws. Not all peers cast ballots in each division but if they did the Tories would be hundreds of votes short of a majority – a reality that necessitated compromise. 'Can't you just bosh this on? Can't you just get this done?' an exasperated Johnson would ask Baroness Evans as legislation stalled in the Lords. 'No, that's not how it works. I'd love to bosh it on, but I can't,' she would reply.[64] In the Commons, Johnson's 'eyes glazed over' if someone mentioned standing orders, the rules that govern how MPs conduct business.[65] These were not big issues, but reflected how he was not a master of process.

It was often said that Johnson is not a 'details' person. That is too simplistic, according to those interviewed. When he needed to, on an issue of pressing importance or personal political risk, Boris would dive into details. On the specifics of Covid spread, or the intricacies of the Brexit deal during talks, or Russian incursions in Ukraine, Johnson would consume information. He had the brain for it. He could surprise Cabinet ministers by drilling into unexpected details in meetings. 'Nobody can go into a room and assume that you can bluff with Boris,' said Michael Gove.[66] At times, though, other ministers left meetings frustrated by his lack of focus.[67] The real problem was that Johnson engaged only when he wanted or was forced to by circumstance. 'Where he was perhaps less good was on the boring bits of the administration,' said Eddie Lister, his chief of staff in City Hall and a senior figure in the early Number 10 months. 'He can do it when he wants to do it and when he sees it's necessary, but it's not where he wants to be.'[68]

Johnson's team stood by his record of delivery at the time and continued to do so. Approached for comment on the specific, varied pieces of reporting by the author in this book, a spokesperson for Johnson issued a blanket denial. There was also a lengthy defence of what he achieved in office:

Boris Johnson's government got Brexit done, delivered the fastest [Covid] vaccine rollout in Europe and restored Britain to global leadership on a range of issues from investment to the environment. Johnson drove forward his vision: to reduce economic inequality and tackle regional disparities by uniting and levelling up the whole country. His government understood that talent is equally spread but opportunity is not. His government believed in delivering on the people's priorities, with 20,000 more police, 50,000 more nurses and building 40 new hospitals. On this basis, Boris Johnson won the largest [Tory] electoral majority since 1987 – an 80-seat majority that remains unrivalled in modern Conservative history. When Johnson left office, the government was a handful of points behind in the polls.[69]

Not everyone painted such a rosy picture, however. A firm friend of Johnson, someone who in public would be considered one of his most prominent and staunchest allies, reached a bleaker conclusion:

> He's a columnist, right? Columnists are used to writing their column, forgetting it and moving on to the next one. And you can't as a national leader operate in that way. You have to follow through, you have to focus on process, you have to have a plan and stick to it. You can't jump all over the place . . . He never made a transition from being someone who could entertain and attract attention and emotionally connect to the hard work of being prime minister. He was ill-disciplined.[70]

*

Perhaps the most consequential of Boris Johnson's idiosyncrasies when governing was his manner of making decisions. Its harshest characterisation is 'The Trolley'. Johnson once conjured the image, joking about how he was 'veering all over the place like a shopping trolley' before picking a side in the EU referendum. But it was Dominic Cummings, once outside power, who turned it into a moniker, suggesting it was Boris's defining characteristic. Some Cabinet ministers and advisers argued that Cummings's view was too critical, but only by shades. The reality warrants examining.

First, there was the way Johnson played out arguments when trying to make up his mind. This habit was captured in the two Brexit articles that he drafted for the *Telegraph*, one for Remain and one for Leave, before that referendum. 'My experience of Boris in a room was he thrived on the back-and-forth. He liked to argue both sides and really work through something to come to a decision,' said Brandon Lewis, his Northern Ireland secretary.[71] Sometimes Johnson would seem to have convinced himself of one position, only to switch mid-meeting, starting to spell out the opposite view. There is nothing inherently wrong with such an approach. It even has its own philosophy tag: Hegelian dialectic. Argue the thesis, articulate the antithesis, arrive at a synthesis. But Whitehall demands clear answers and sometimes that back-and-forth could drag on for months.

Johnson also liked to make decisions late. In the deadline-driven world of journalism he had developed a reputation for filing just under the wire. It was the same in government, as one Number 10 adviser explained:

> One of Boris's techniques is where the system leans towards taking decisions early, he will try to leave it as long as possible because it will remove options. A: the problem may resolve. And B: by leaving it longer other options will drop away. That reduces the risk of the decision being the wrong one.[72]

Political calculation was a factor. A lack of deeply ingrained policy convictions may have complicated things further.

Layered on top is an instinctive aversion to conflict, another feature of his premiership mentioned by many insiders. 'He doesn't like confrontation,' said one long-term friend, 'So to get through a difficult moment he'll say whatever you want to hear and then five minutes later he'll say whatever somebody else wants to hear.'[73] Another ally said: 'He'd prefer not to have conflict. He will have conflict if necessary, but he'd prefer not to.'[74] Prevarication could prove the easier path.

Defences are mounted by allies to the charge of vacillating. Priti Patel insisted she 'never experienced' Johnson swiftly changing position, saying that if it happened with others round the Cabinet table that was because they were 'weak ministers'.[75] Jacob Rees-Mogg said: 'I think people misunderstand Boris. They think because you finish a meeting without him saying no, that he means yes. He's much more deliberative: he goes away, thinks about it and makes up his mind. Then you discover that he didn't agree with you in the first place.'[76] Others still close to Johnson, though, accept the criticism. David Frost, his long-term adviser, said: 'I think his big problem as PM was that he wasn't clear enough on what he thought himself about problems. Sometimes no decision was really final. If somebody could get to him later you'd have a chance of changing it.'[77] This led to scrambles for influence. Sometimes Cabinet ministers would text Johnson in a frantic lobbying effort during group video calls, hoping to sway his thinking in real time. Others used WhatsApp to get round the usual channels. Securing face time was seen as a third route to influence, leading to tussles about who would be last with Boris before a decision was taken. In Johnsonland, a yes was not guaranteed to stay a yes; a no need not be the end of the debate.

This approach – inverting arguments while mulling things over; pushing decisions down the line; a reluctance to say no to Cabinet ministers; a susceptibility to reverse stances on smaller matters – could have negative consequences. The proof of this is in the pudding of successive policy changes.

The anti-obesity strategy was one, as recounted by a senior health department source. After his Covid scare, Johnson had gone on a health drive that stretched into policy-making. A ban on junk food adverts on TV before 9 p.m. was adopted; so too a ban on buy-one-get-one-free deals for food and drink high in fat, salt or sugar, so-called HFSS products. When Sajid Javid became health secretary in June 2021 he asked to pause the legislation, seeing it as non-Tory interventionism. 'No, we're not going to pause it, we're going to plough on,' said the prime minister. Javid kept checking, Johnson kept standing firm, right up to the point where he folded. 'Can we drop them?' Johnson asked in early 2022, just weeks before the new rules kicked in. At the time he needed red meat to see off the growing Tory revolt over his leadership. The measures were dropped, but not without damage being done. 'You've made businesses spend all this money in preparing for something,' said the source. 'Just give them certainty. Either bloody do it or don't.'[78]

Other shifts were more rapid. A senior education department figure still remembers the battle over the Covid 'catch-up' fund, a financial boost for schools to help children make up for the learning lost during the lockdowns. 'On Friday, it was going to be a £10 billion package. By the Monday, it had become a £1.4 billion package,' said an education source.[79] A second government source close to discussions confirmed the story.[80] Amid Treasury pressure before the announcement it shrank to a seventh of its original value in a single weekend.

There are plenty of examples of Cabinet ministers believing the boss was with them, only then to discover otherwise. Theresa Villiers, the environment secretary, thought Johnson was on her side in a tussle with Liz Truss, the international trade secretary, over a new agreement with Australia. 'Of course we must look after our farmers,' Johnson would say, indicating support for Villiers's push for protections for British agriculture. So she was surprised when he then aligned himself with Truss.[81] David Frost had a similar story on post-Brexit border checks, believing Johnson also wanted a looser approach. Again, the prime minister's support was indicated rather than established as definitive: 'Yes, yes, you go ahead with that.' Then Johnson sided with the Treasury, rejecting the more hands-off arrangement.[82]

Sometimes it was the lack of a decision that would do the damage. Baroness Evans, whose Cabinet job was to keep legislation flowing through the Lords, would become exasperated when a dispute between two ministers was not settled, so holding up a bill.

> What happened too often was Boris just wouldn't arbitrate between them. He would say, 'No, those two have to come to a decision.' It was like: 'Yes, but literally we're now six months into an argument. We can't do anything, we are stuck. If you won't arbitrate, then, to be honest, you've decided we're not doing this because we can't.'[83]

That happened over plans for 'lifelong learning' loans to help people to continue their education throughout life. It was announced by Johnson in September 2020.[84] Only in February 2023, two prime ministers later, was the measure put into legislation.[85]

Prioritisation could also be an issue. Johnson would at times latch onto pet projects. He loved the idea of what he called 'Judge Dredd' justice, named after the futuristic cop in the Sylvester Stallone 1990s blockbuster, according to one source.[86] Pursuing measures to use technology to reduce court backlogs in the wake of Covid may have been eye-catching, but implementing them was much trickier. Schooled in stories of the great builders of ancient Greece and Rome, Johnson had a penchant for infrastructure projects. Such was his enthusiasm for creating a transport link between Scotland and Northern Ireland that a technical feasibility study was commissioned, at which point hope smashed into reality. It was estimated that a tunnel under the Irish Sea would cost £209 billion. A bridge would be £335 billion, equivalent to around a third of all annual government spending.[87] One Cabinet minister distilled the problem: 'If he wasn't required to have a single-minded focus, then things could drift.'[88] An anecdote that circulated among Number 10 staffers spoke to the same point. Early on Dominic Cummings told Johnson: 'If you don't prioritise then you won't succeed.' The prime minister is said to have replied: 'Dom, I have priorities. I've got hundreds of them.'[89] Apocryphal or not, the tale still gets retold.

These nuances and flaws of Johnson policy-making are nowhere more clearly seen than in that most consequential of areas: the running of the economy.

A line from Johnson's days as London mayor continued to attach itself to his tenure in Downing Street: 'My policy on cake is pro having it and pro eating it.' It did so for good reason. Johnson had an aversion to trade-offs. He loved to be loved. On financial matters, this would manifest itself in his instincts on spending and taxation. In short, his theory was: spending good, tax bad. Giving the thumbs up to extra investment – more hospitals, more nurses, more policemen, as he had promised on the 2019 campaign trail – was an easy route to applause. For a Tory, so too was declaring a love of tax cuts: the people, not the state, knowing best how to spend their money, as the argument went. But getting both – living by cakeism – was easier said than done, since it would mean huge extra borrowing. Under Boris, spending would shoot up to its highest rate in fifty years. But so too would the tax burden, being sent to its highest point in almost seventy years.

The Covid pandemic undeniably drove this change. Pouring something close to £400 billion of taxpayers' money into propping up the economy – at one point, nine million people were having up to 80 per cent of their wages paid for by the government through its furlough scheme – had an impact on the country's finances that will take many years to repair. Spending soared, taxation soared, borrowing soared. But again, Covid could be a mask to conceal how Johnson was likely to have approached things without a pandemic.

The proof point for that comes in the form of his first chancellor, a man who would be gone from the Treasury before the first Covid lockdown was implemented: Sajid Javid.

The tensions were there from the beginning. Javid, picked to head up the Treasury after backing Johnson in the Tory leadership race, had a background in finance. He had spent almost two decades in banking, rising to the board of Deutsche Bank. As the first fiscal event of the Johnson–Javid era approached, the Budget scheduled for late 2019, points of difference emerged. Downing Street wanted to use the moment to signal the end of austerity, to fulfil a promise made by Johnson to the Tory tribe that summer. Javid pointed out that if taxes were not going to fund the spending increases, then a lot of borrowing would be needed to plug the gap. The Office of Budget Responsibility (OBR), an independent forecasting body created by George Osborne in 2010 to end what he saw as Gordon Brown's Treasury cooking the books, would reveal as much in its official analysis. And so, according to three sources, Johnson and his top adviser, Dominic Cummings, came up with an eye-catching suggestion: why not just not do an OBR forecast? The idea was voiced by the prime minister himself in one of the last meetings to discuss the package. 'Can't we just not bother with the OBR?' Johnson asked Javid, according to one person in the meeting.[90] Another who was present – a Downing Street figure supportive of Johnson – confirmed the account.[91] A third source, a senior figure in the Treasury, summed up the broad thrust of Number 10 demands: 'Why do we need to go to the OBR? Why can't we just ignore them?'[92] The request was rejected point blank by Javid at the meeting. The law anyway required two OBR forecasts a year. In the end, the general election was triggered and the Budget was delayed. Johnson's office denied the claim, despite multiple sources giving first-hand accounts, as part of a blanket rejection of reporting points put forward for comment by the author.[93] It would be for Johnson's successor, Liz Truss, to find out how the markets reacted when huge new borrowing was announced with no OBR oversight.

But the December 2019 election only created another front in the battle over taxation and spending. Number 10 wanted to get rid of the Tory fiscal rules. Naming explicit targets for reducing debt had been a hallmark of the Osborne–Cameron economic strategy, creating a hard dividing line with Labour over rebuilding the country's finances after the 2007–8 financial crash. Javid thought ditching the rules would be an 'absolute disaster', according to a senior Treasury source, and set about trying to convince Johnson.[94] He sent the prime minister a one-page note via WhatsApp explaining the need for fiscal rules and then talked him through it in the Downing Street garden over the weekend, taking advantage of the access granted to him by the fact that they both lived in flats on site. A short summary, a direct message to the prime minister's phone, a face-to-face meeting to hammer home the point: these were as direct a route to getting the nod in Johnson's court as could be found. Boris acquiesced. The fiscal rules made it into the manifesto: not borrowing to fund day-to-day spending; getting debt lower by the end of the Parliament; an agreement to reassess matters if debt interest rates soared. Later, word reached the Treasury that Cummings was 'really pissed off'.[95]

After the election win, with Johnson enhanced and Dominic Cummings emboldened, the strains grew worse. One clash came over High Speed 2 (HS2), the new train line connecting London with cities in the North. Cummings and his allies saw the project, with its endlessly soaring budget, as a money pit and wanted it killed off. The Treasury was told that Number 10 wanted to pull the plug and was requesting alternatives to be worked up. But on further investigation it was found that Johnson was actually four-square behind HS2. Javid blamed Cummings. In the end the chancellor took an unprecedented step, telling his office to disregard orders from Number 10 unless they came directly from the prime minister or the head of his private office, Martin Reynolds.[96] This meant Javid often checking directly with Johnson on any points of uncertainty, cutting out Dom.

The in-fighting would lead to Cummings and Lee Cain hatching a plot to oust Javid. They explicitly urged Johnson to remove his chancellor, according to two sources in their own camp.[97] When the prime minister demurred, a scheme was devised to bring about the same end by different means. Why not just get rid of Javid's special advisers and replace them with a 'joint economic unit' shared between Number 10 and Number 11? It was not just a blatant land grab, given that Downing Street would pick the advisers, but a deliberate ploy to oust Javid: a 'big trap', as one source who was involved put it.[98] Cummings and Cain laid out their idea to Johnson. He signed it off. Cain mentioned that Javid might quit. 'Resign, over some spads?!' exclaimed Boris. To this day those involved are unsure whether Johnson, known to be capable of playing dumb when it suited him, was only feigning ignorance of what was likely to follow. Leaving Boris, Cain turned to Cummings: 'Saj will definitely quit, right?' 'Yes, hopefully,' came the response.[99]

The pair's calculations proved right. Summoned on reshuffle day, 13 February 2020, Javid was informed about the joint economic policy idea by the prime minister. It meant sacking all six of his special advisers. Javid, in an interview with the author, recalled what happened next:

> I said, 'Look, in the end, Cummings has put you up to this, he's running rings around you, you can't see it. He's not going to be content until he burns the house down.' Boris said, 'No, you've got it wrong, this is nothing to do with Cummings.' I said, 'It so obviously is, why even pretend? You've got to choose now, it's me or him.' He said, 'Don't put me in that position, I'm not going to choose when I need both of you.' So I said, 'Fine, you've made your decision and you can keep him because I'm out of here.' And I walked out.[100]

Cakeism saw Johnson lose a chancellor in under seven months. Not even Theresa May, trading constant blows with Philip Hammond, had managed that.

A senior Treasury figure summed matters up:

> Boris didn't want to accept the trade-offs. He wanted to say both that he was going to cut taxes and be spending more . . . He wants to be both a small-state Conservative but also a big fat socialist. He loves spending money, increasing the size of the state and thinks the Conservative bit is low taxes, but doesn't accept that if you're going to spend lots of money and be a Conservative then there's a big gap in the middle.

The contradictions in Johnson's economic approach had tested relations between Number 10 and Number 11 to destruction. It was not the only occasion this would happen, as Javid's successor – Rishi Sunak – would find out.

It is more than just the identity of the person who wears the crown that determines how a reign will unfold. Courtiers influence the course of events too. During Johnson's three years on the political throne there would be three different inner circles. That is more than Theresa May, who in a premiership of the same length had two: the Nick and Fi court and the rescue team that followed; more, too, than David Cameron, who largely kept the same core team throughout his six years in office.

There was, however, one constant during the Johnson tenure: Carrie Symonds, or Carrie Johnson as she became halfway through their time in Downing Street. The marriages of prime ministers have always been of interest to a public eager for insights into their leaders' real lives. Understandably, those in power have usually wanted to defend their privacy. As a consequence, assessing how one half of a couple shapes the thinking and decision-making of the other is as difficult in the political sphere as it is in normal life – though, given the impact of those decisions on the country, the exercise is not wholly without merit.

Carrie would be dragged into the press spotlight more than her predecessors, Philip May and Samantha Cameron. Two realities help explain why. For one, she was already a creature of Westminster. Carrie had been a special adviser to Sajid Javid, when he was communities secretary, and John Whittingdale, then culture secretary, with responsibility for dealing with the media. Later she became the Conservative Party's head of communications. Reporters, including this author, found her sharp, engaging and savvy in navigating the cut-throat world of politics – just what her jobs demanded. Given this background, questions about her influence were inevitable. Second, there were the specifics of their pairing. Carrie is twenty-three years younger than Boris. The relationship emerged as the marriage to Johnson's second wife, Marina Wheeler, collapsed. The result was more tabloid intrigue than the Mays or Camerons ever faced.

Tensions emerged between the old guard of Johnson advisers and Carrie during the 2019 summer Tory leadership campaign and spilled over into Downing Street. Self-interest on the part of the former camp, suspicious of the appearance of a new point of influence, may have been a driver. Whatever the cause, the rift was real. Two claims were made by multiple figures engaged in the leadership campaign. One was put forward by four different people: that Carrie would sometimes send text messages from Boris's phone. One source said that one campaign figure was dubbed the 'text whisperer' for their apparent ability to tell whether the author was Johnson or Carrie.[101] 'It was just the tone. Boris is quite chatty in his messages, Carrie was blunt,' they added. Examples given included demands for comments to be issued rebutting press stories. A second source was also convinced that Carrie messaged from Johnson's phone.[102] A third campaign figure said: 'You could always tell, because she used block capitals. He didn't use block capitals. She used words that he didn't use. You know, Boris has a very particular use of language and it's very easy to see if he has written or somebody else has written it.'[103] A fourth person said the habit was seen during their time in Downing Street: 'You could tell when she was texting on his phone. His normal messages are like anyone's mum or dad texting . . . completely sporadic punctuation and the minimal amount of texting required. Just like a question mark or something like that. Whereas hers were properly punctuated, quite long messages.'[104] Ultimately the sources could not, of course, prove who authored the messages. A spokesperson for Carrie Johnson categorically rejected the claims: 'It really is totally untrue that Carrie ever texted campaign members or Number 10 staff from Boris's phone. 100% rubbish.' The spokesperson added that Boris Johnson 'would never have let anyone else access his phone and nor would Carrie have ever wanted to message anyone from it.'[105]

The second set of claims concern how those running the campaign handled Carrie on the trail. Again, they were made by multiple sources. They describe steps taken to keep her away from Boris after she was deemed a distraction. One campaign source explained:

> It was finding things for her to do. We'd say, 'Oh, well, Carrie, we've got this event with some donors. Can you pop off to that?' And while she was, in theory, getting ready for that, we'd whiz Boris out to some remote part of the country, to get him meeting members, getting his daily picture, and get her out of his hair. And then, about said event [to Carrie]: 'Oh, they've just cancelled.'[106]

Another campaign source said: 'Once they put her in a taxi to go to an event and there were roadworks in one part of London, so they got the driver to go through the roadworks purposefully so she'd be late.'[107]

In Downing Street, Carrie would face a constant barrage of claims about her behind-the-scenes influence. Many insiders expressed sympathy with her: a woman in her early thirties, living under the intense scrutiny of Number 10, while also almost losing her partner to Covid, getting married and giving birth twice – to Wilfred in April 2020 and Romy in December 2021. Allies saw, not without some justification, misogyny in the claims of her Lady Macbeth-like string-pulling. On policy, her environmental background – she had roles with the Aspinall Foundation animal charity and the sea conservation charity Oceana – led some to join the dots with Johnson's policies such as banning the import and sale of foie gras and fur. But the picture is complicated by Johnson's other eco allies, such as his father Stanley Johnson and friend Zac Goldsmith. The zeal with which Boris embraced making Britain a net zero carbon emitter by 2050 suggested a depth of personal belief that exceeded the possible influence of any single outside source.

Suspicions that Carrie offered her thoughts on personnel, however, are widely acknowledged by Downing Street figures across all factions. One senior Number 10 adviser said that '100 per cent' Carrie urged Johnson to get rid of Brandon Lewis as Northern Ireland secretary in the February 2020 reshuffle.[108] Lewis had headed up CCHQ when Carrie had her expenses looked into. Nothing was made public about the inquiries and there is no suggestion of wrongdoing. Lewis would stay on after senior advisers pushed back. Another Number 10 figure said the return of Carrie's old boss John Whittingdale to the frontbench was thanks to her. 'Oh Christ, I've been up half the night having to find a home for John Whittingdale,' the source recalled being told by someone involved in the reshuffle.[109] A third source who told Johnson they would only join Number 10 if a senior figure linked to Carrie was removed was warned that this would cause problems.[110] At times the prime minister did little to dispel the idea of his partner's influence. On occasion he would 'grimace' and 'literally point' upwards to the flat he lived in with Carrie, indicating the topic of discussion would not wash.[111]

Allies of Carrie have consistently rebutted such claims. They have noted that, of course, all couples discuss details of their professional lives, but that snippets of conversations have been 'weaponised' by Carrie's enemies to suggest a false narrative of her political influence. A spokesperson for Carrie Johnson said she had 'no view whatsoever' about Brandon Lewis as Northern Ireland secretary and 'never discussed' it with her husband, though accepted she had talked up John Whittingdale's credentials.[112]

The real fireworks, however, would follow a breakdown in relations with another court figure. Dominic Cummings, speaking before two parliamentary committees after his exit from Number 10, would sum up the extent of his personal power. The Westminster bubble 'underestimated the influence that I had between July and December 2019', said the architect of the all-or-nothing Brexit strategy pursued in the early months of Johnson's premiership. But 'they massively exaggerated the influence that I had after the election'.[113] The triumph at the ballot box had meant that Johnson no longer had his back against the wall. Out went the necessity for Dom, just as he had predicted on results night.

The popular portrayal of Cummings the maverick, wild-eyed and brooding, does him a disservice, according to many who worked with him. One longtime colleague said: 'There's an intensity. He doesn't suffer fools and if he thinks you're a fool then you'll probably feel like a fool. But it's not a brash, loud, bullying approach. He's a much more understated character.'[114] Cabinet ministers offered compliments. David Frost, also in the Brexit trenches for those first six months, did not see eye to eye on everything but was a 'big admirer', acknowledging his 'strategic ability'.[115] Baroness Evans valued the 'absolute clarity' he offered when he was pressed for guidance.[116] To one senior press aide, he was 'collegiate' and could 'see round corners'.[117] Johnson too understood his talents. One friend said that Boris had a 'very high opinion' of Cummings's ability to 'drive through' change.[118] Another said he called Dom a 'once-in-a-generation' political strategist.[119] But that was before relations soured.

The Johnson–Cummings partnership had been a 'marriage of convenience', the pair being united initially by their determination to deliver Brexit.[120] That bond dissolved with the 2019 election win, which secured the EU exit. 'Both were big characters, both thought they were responsible for victory, both thought they were the king. Unfortunately, that led to the schism,' said one who watched the disintegration from the inside.[121] The idea of Cummings being the power behind the throne would come to grate on Johnson. Once the prime minister was driven past a protest outside Downing Street where vast fake puppets portrayed Dom as the master pulling Boris's strings. 'It was seared onto his brain,' said a source in the car.[122]

It was said that Johnson thrived when he was pointed at a target and the same observation was made about Cummings. Matthew Elliott, the Vote Leave founder who picked him as his campaign manager, noted:

> If you are running the SAS and you want an elite unit to take a tricky position under fire, he's the guy to go to because he will bring together a small team, storm the enemy position and go balls out to deliver in a brilliant and exceptional way. But if you're looking for someone to lead a wide-ranging programme of policy change, requiring tact and cajoling to achieve the objectives, he's less suited to that sort of task, because it's not his natural modus operandi.[123]

With Brexit secured, the war had been won. What to do with the peace would split the Vote Leave generals. Cummings would later claim casually in a BBC interview that he discussed ousting Johnson within days of the 2019 election victory. However hyperbolic this may have been – there is no evidence that anything beyond loose grumbling took place, nor indeed was there any realistic path to achieving such an outcome – it did speak to his disillusionment, even in the immediate glow of triumph.[124]

The Covid pandemic, and specifically the Barnard Castle saga, would lay the gunpowder for the explosion to come. Cummings was a lockdown proponent and has since been scathing of the resistance Johnson offered at various points to government measures. In May 2020, though, controversy struck when the *Mirror* and *Guardian* newspapers revealed that Cummings had travelled more than 200 miles from London to his home town of Durham during lockdown. Cummings's wife had Covid and the couple feared for their son if they both became ill, so decided to take him to stay with relatives. As the backlash escalated that weekend Cummings explained the full story to Johnson and communications chief Lee Cain in the Downing Street flat. Backing was given. 'Commissar, don't you worry. Full support for Dominic Cummings, right behind him,' the prime minister told Cain.[125]

But that Sunday, Johnson got a roasting over the saga at a Covid press conference. The next day, he decided Cummings should face the press. And so the Downing Street garden briefing was set up. In the hours beforehand, it was Dom who was fussed over by the Number 10 operation. One pro-Cummings adviser recalled seeing the prime minister looking on: 'He was standing in the doorway of his office while we were all crowding round Dom at his computer, helping him draft his statement. He just looked a bit lost and a bit jealous.'[126] Cummings's turn before the cameras, when he explained that he had driven to Barnard Castle from the Durham house to test his eyesight – a claim widely ridiculed in the media – would dominate the next day's papers. Johnson, credited by friends with an underappreciated trait of loyalty to staff, stuck by his man. But in doing so, he spent 'a hell of a lot of political capital'.[127]

Come the autumn of 2020, with Covid cases rising again and renewed discussion of lockdowns, tensions were now detectable to colleagues. Cummings would 'go very, very quiet or almost withdraw', missing meetings that he would usually attend.[128] At other points he would become 'vocally grumpy'.[129] One aide recalled a meeting where he declared, 'Do you know what, I'm not wasting my time with this crap,' and walked out.[130]

The spark that ignited the final explosion seemed trivial. Cummings and Cain, operating as a duo since entering Downing Street, wanted to televise a daily briefing for political reporters. Partly there was a desire by so doing to open up the closed shop of the 'Lobby', as the grouping of Westminster correspondents is known, given that such briefings were never on camera. The Covid press conferences had also proved an effective communication tool. The search for a telegenic spokesperson to present the briefings, which saw candidates undergo practice sessions, with video footage then being shown to focus groups, led to Cummings and Cain favouring a BBC reporter.

But Carrie wanted Allegra Stratton for the job, a former *Guardian* and BBC *Newsnight* veteran turned comms chief for Rishi Sunak at the Treasury.

The three Cs – Cummings, Cain and Carrie – had been clashing for months, competing for Johnson's ear. The flashpoint came when Boris sided with Carrie. Cain made clear he would quit in protest. Cummings followed him out of the door. Their final meeting with the prime minister was surprisingly jovial.[131] Aware that the end had been reached, the trio shared stories of their past joint achievements – Vote Leave, Johnson's ascent to the leadership, the 2019 routing of Corbyn. An aide outside heard laughter.[132] As the trip down memory lane ended, Johnson delivered a message. 'Just one thing, though. Carrie says you guys are briefing against her. It's all very terrible,' the prime minister said, according to a source familiar with what happened.[133] The pair protested, claiming in turn that Johnson's other half had been briefing against them. Cummings eventually shot back: 'Boris, if I start briefing against you, you will fucking know about it. Be assured of that.'[134] As much would prove true.

Brutal anonymous knifings would appear in that weekend's newspapers. Carrie would be dubbed 'Princess Nut Nut'. Relations would never be repaired. In November 2020 – almost six months later than he had predicted after the election night exit poll – Cummings passed through the Downing Street front door, a cardboard box in his hands, as the photographers clicked. By the following spring he would be in open warfare with the prime minister. A Substack blog would be created and wielded like a rocket launcher aimed at Johnson's premiership. Boris's most influential adviser would become his nemesis.

Johnson had re-established Vote Leave in Downing Street at the start of his premiership, determined to deliver Brexit. Now the clash meant the court of Cummings and Cain had fallen, and other figures would soon be frozen out too. Oliver Lewis, who had helped negotiate the EU deal with David Frost, and Cleo Watson, a friend of Dom's who had been brought into the centre, would soon be gone. There would be two more 'inner circles'. The next one would be characterised by some as allies of Carrie and Michael Gove. Dan Rosenfield, a long-term Treasury civil servant turned business adviser, would be brought in as chief of staff at the start of 2021 in an attempt to draw a line under the political warring. The two Henrys, Newman and Cook, both former Gove special advisers, would be elevated to more senior roles. A third court would emerge in early 2022, one of arch-loyalists parachuted in as regicide loomed. The point is not the intricacies of each grouping and how neatly the simplistic labels fit them, rather the fact of the endless overhauls. It speaks to Johnson's apparent aversion to being controlled.

The fallout from Cummings's departure, one longtime aide to Boris admitted, was a 'tragedy'.[135] The centre would become less antagonistic but less political too. Worse, one of the most effective Tory operators of the last twenty years was now outside the tent, pissing in.

Boris Johnson had standout qualities as a frontline politician. He could connect with voters like no other Tory in his generation. He could capture an argument with vividness, humour and optimism, maximising votes in the process. His intellectual confidence and determination when put on the spot guided his path. Covid exploded on his watch, dominating much of his premiership. 'Why did this have to happen to me?' he would mutter to a friend later, cursing his bad luck.[136] But to say that it was just the pandemic that caused him to squander the opportunities of a huge election win requires wilful blindness to his faults. For there were personal failings and frailties to Johnson the governor that cannot be explained away in this manner. Indecisiveness slowed the Whitehall machine. Amenability left Cabinet ministers thinking they could change his calls. Limited interest in the dull bits of the job reduced efficiency. Pursuing the milk-and-honey world of soaring spending and plummeting taxes was always illusory. Nor can a prime minister be blameless if Number 10 descends into civil war during their occupancy. Beyond delivering Brexit, was there ever a Johnsonian transformative vision for Britain equal to the moment? 'It was an eighty-seat majority looking for a purpose,' a senior Treasury figure concluded. 'That always amazed me.'[137]

The box of Boris note cards is said still to exist. It sits in the corner of a once-supportive Tory MP's office, long forgotten and gathering dust. An artefact from another age. A reminder of what could have been.

8

Downfall

'FUCK! FUCK!' BORIS Johnson was seething. 'He's trying to fuck me!'[1] The prime minister had just been told that the second most important figure in his government had quit. Rishi Sunak was out – and without giving his boss any warning. No meeting was requested by the chancellor to explain his reasons, as had been the case with Sajid Javid, the departing health secretary, earlier that day, 5 July 2022. There was no conversation over the phone; not even a text. It fell to Declan Lyons, the Number 10 political secretary, to tell his boss a resignation letter was on the way. Johnson was raging. 'Who the fuck does he think he is?'[2] Sunak had been a lowly local government minister when Boris had reached the top as Conservative Party leader back in 2019. It was Johnson who had brought him into the Cabinet, first as chief secretary to the Treasury and then, aged just thirty-nine, as chancellor. And now, three years on, he was going, swiping at Johnson's ethics and economics as he went. 'It was basically a knife in the front,' said a Boris ally who was by his side that day.[3]

The power dynamics between the pair had been shifting Number 11's way for months. During the Covid pandemic and its unprecedented peace-time expenditure to prop up the economy during lockdowns, the pair had worked well together. It was over what came next – how to control spending and meet Tory demands for tax cuts – that tensions emerged. By the start of 2022, with the prime minister facing backbench revolt and Sunak topping potential successor lists, things were deteriorating.[4] As Johnson called in allies to Number 10, Sunak sounded out colleagues for support. That July evening, with Boris facing questions about what he knew – and when – regarding his deputy chief whip Chris Pincher's inappropriate behaviour, things came to a head. Javid and Sunak have always insisted that they reached their decisions independently.[5] The chancellor had the letter already written when Javid tweeted his out at 6.02 p.m.[6] Blindsided by the move, Sunak's team rushed to reveal their own news – that was the reason, they argue, that Johnson was left in the dark. It dropped on Twitter at 6.11 p.m. – just nine minutes after Javid's announcement.[7] The letter had no date, another indication that it was released in haste.

The act would cast a long shadow over the Conservative Party. 'Boris betrayer' would be the tag stapled onto Sunak, with consequences in the leadership race that would follow. A year on, Johnson allies would still be pointing the finger of blame his way when explaining Boris's downfall. But the narrative ignores the wider reality. The reason Boris Johnson lost his premiership was not Rishi Sunak. It was not Sunak who had allowed a culture of Covid law-breaking to develop in Downing Street, with some 126 fines being issued to eighty-three people over at least eight different events.[8] It was not Sunak who rolled out blanket public denials that would be proved palpably false.

And yet it had been Sunak, with Javid, who triggered the end. Their resignations were akin to knocking out two base points in a house of cards, the structure collapsing inwards with a whoosh. Within twenty-four hours, following dozens more ministerial departures, Cabinet members gathered to tell Johnson it was all over. Nadhim Zahawi, the new Chancellor, warned just a day into the job that the situation was unsurvivable.[9] Brandon Lewis, the Northern Ireland secretary, said it was 'over'.[10] Transport secretary Grant Shapps, master of the fabled spreadsheet, said the numbers did not add up.[11] Über-loyalists, like home secretary Priti Patel, echoed these points.[12] Even those not there managed to deliver the message – business secretary Kwasi Kwarteng spoke to Johnson down the line from outside a Toby Carvery in Teesside; Thérèse Coffey was in hospital but still made her views clear.[13] Earlier that day Boris had alluded to a distant relative who had holed up in a room with a shotgun during a planning dispute, and vowed to do something similar now.[14] But the executioners had smashed down the door, too many to overcome.

Boris's downfall was exceptional, a head-scratching collapse not easily explained by a single factor. He had won the biggest Tory majority since Margaret Thatcher in 1987. Then, just like Maggie, he lost the support of colleagues so drastically that he was ousted before having the chance to defend it at an election. The morning after the Cabinet had uttered its truths – just over thirty-six hours on from the Sunak–Javid resignations – Johnson addressed the nation. David Cameron's voice had cracked as he quit the morning after Brexit. Theresa May too had wobbled. But from Boris, there were no tears. Just an acceptance of the end: 'Them's the breaks.'[15]

Nine months. That is how long it took to turn Boris Johnson from top dog into mincemeat. October 2021 to July 2022. To capture the slide properly, the starting point has to be understood. Johnson was all powerful at the Conservative Party annual conference of autumn 2021. Just over two years into his tenure, the prime minister should have been experiencing what is commonly dubbed the 'mid-term blues'. Johnson was approaching halfway through his expected first full term, the Tories themselves past the eleven-year mark in Downing Street. The government and the country had been buffeted by a deadly pandemic. Even in the week before the conference a fuel crisis had hit Britain, queues of vehicles snaking out of petrol stations as Covid impacted supply chains. And yet, under Johnson, the Conservatives were still riding high.

A polling average on the final day of the conference, 6 October 2021, put the Tories on 40 per cent and Labour on 34 per cent – a 6-point lead.[16] Some of that may have been down to the glow of the successful Covid vaccine roll-out which had seen the UK streak ahead of its European rivals on jabs earlier in the year. But it spoke, too, of the struggles of Sir Keir Starmer, Jeremy Corbyn's centrist successor as Labour leader, in going beyond just detoxifying the party brand and breaking through with the wider electorate.

In a conference turn replete with trademark gags, Johnson took aim at seemingly the only man standing between him and another election victory. Sir Keir was 'captain hindsight', changing positions with the public mood. Or the 'human weathervane', pointing which-ever way the wind blew on Covid policy. Or 'a seriously rattled bus conductor pushed this way and that by a Corbynista mob of Sellotape-spectacled sans-culottes'. Colleagues too were put in the spotlight.

Michael Gove's recent throwing of shapes on an Aberdeen dancefloor, captured on camera, saw him dubbed 'Jon Bon Govey'. Critics of the new Australia–UK–US defence pact (known as Aukus) were given a dismissive wave of the hand as the 'raucus squaukus from the anti-Aukus caucus'.[17] Johnson, urged on by the party faithful, was in his element.

Another reality has to be acknowledged to understand what followed: Boris Johnson was a hired gun.

David Cameron's Tory leadership, for good or ill, was a political project. He would have the best part of five years between taking up the post in 2005 and his first general election in 2010; time to reshape the party, build a policy platform, promote like-minded allies and get loyalty in return. Cameron would last eleven years. By contrast, there was no Johnson 'project'. Boris was a 'break glass in emergency' candidate, a battering ram the party reached for in its hour of need. 'Boris was a classic decision by the Conservative Party,' explained David Canzini, the long-time Tory adviser who helped Johnson win the leadership in 2019. 'The Conservative Party likes winning elections. It looks around and says, "Who's going to win us elections?" And if you are the person about whom they think, "We will be in power for a while with you," then you are selected.'[18]

But the reverse is also true. And between October 2021 and July 2022 the polls would flip. Labour drew level in November, then pulled ahead in December – a lead that would be retained. On 7 July, the day of Johnson's resignation speech, Labour was on 41 per cent in average polls and the Conservatives on 31 per cent. A 4-point lead had become a 10-point deficit.[19] The switch would be underscored by a succession of thumping by-election defeats, suggesting that the polling was correct. What is the point of Boris Johnson if he cannot win elections? That was the question Tory MPs were left asking themselves. That dynamic underpinned everything that occurred. What drove the change, though, was fatal missteps.

The slide began with Owen Paterson. Boris Johnson was not especially close to Paterson, who became a Conservative MP four years before the prime minister, rose to environment secretary under

David Cameron and was then sent packing to the backbenches in 2014. The episode that came to a head in October 2021 involved Paterson's paid work as a consultant for two companies – the clinical diagnostics firm Randox and Lynn's Country Foods – and the question of lobbying. An investigation by Kathryn Stone, then the independent parliamentary commissioner for standards, concluded that Paterson had breached rules on paid advocacy. A thirty-day suspension was proposed.[20] That number mattered – a suspension of ten days and above, if voted through by the House of Commons, would allow a recall petition to be lodged against an MP to trigger a by-election. The rule had bite, as Johnson himself would come to learn. It meant that Paterson was facing the end of his parliamentary career.

Why did Johnson move to protect Paterson despite the evidence? Certainly he was advised to by some. Jacob Rees-Mogg, the Commons leader, and Mark Spencer, the chief whip, were fighting Paterson's corner. 'I was very much part of that . . . I am, to a degree, responsible,' Rees-Mogg would later say.[21] Other prominent Tories were pushing Paterson's case, such as former party leader Sir Iain Duncan Smith. The prime minister's presence at a dinner with ex-*Telegraph* colleagues at the Garrick Club, including the paper's former editor Lord Moore who had penned a supportive column about Paterson, has been cited as another factor. The tragedy that struck Paterson, his wife Rose killing herself during the period when he was being investigated, certainly engendered deep sympathy from colleagues who asked: 'Has this man not suffered enough?' Then there was the question of whether Johnson, only just back from the Cop26 UN climate change conference in Glasgow, had actually read the jarring details of the case.

Whatever the reason, Johnson signed off a clumsy rescue mission. Tory MPs were whipped to park the thirty-day suspension by voting instead to create a new cross-party committee to look at the standards process. Should there not be a right to challenge rulings? The decision on Paterson would wait while such issues were debated, no doubt at length, by the new committee. The move was transparent – an attempt to save a colleague under the cloak of improving processes. Johnson's own past frustrations with Stone – he had been hauled over the coals for a donor-financed Christmas holiday in Mustique, though eventually cleared – may have shaped thinking. The move on 3 November succeeded but with widespread Tory hand-wringing – thirteen Conservative MPs voted against it and almost one hundred more abstained. The victory was Pyrrhic. Labour, the Liberal Democrats and the SNP vowed to boycott the committee, immediately exploiting the plan's glaring flaw. The next day Downing Street backtracked. Paterson then announced he would quit politics anyway. The row led to wider scrutiny of MPs' second jobs which dominated the headlines for days more, throwing the spotlight onto well-paid Tories. In the end, when the by-election for Paterson's safe North Shropshire seat took place in December, the Conservatives would lose – the first time in 115 years the constituency was not Tory-held.[22]

The Paterson case acted like a microcosm for how Johnson blunders would play out during that nine-month slide: a public position set out with insufficient prior weighing of the facts; a belief Tory MPs could be bludgeoned into supporting their leader; an approach to ethics that allies might charitably dub relaxed and that critics saw as unconscionable; and with a final raising of two fingers by the electorate. The loop would repeat itself again and again, each time doing more political damage.

'Partygate.' The term is heavy with political baggage. It was the defining scandal of the Boris Johnson premiership, the one that did more than any other to drain its lifeblood. The word owes much to Fleet Street's love of a simple epithet to tag controversies. The '-gate' suffix has been attached to political sagas in Westminster and Washington ever since Richard Nixon's downfall. Indeed it is so overused that *Politico* once published a piece headlined '46 Political Scandals That Were "Worse than Watergate"' to make the point.[23] The 'party' bit too needs some unpacking. 'Partying in Downing Street' became the common distillation of what happened, but it contains a spectrum of shades.

So thoroughly investigated are the events in question, first by Sue Gray, at the time the second permanent secretary at the Cabinet Office, and then by the Metropolitan Police, that the facts can be recounted with some confidence. Sixteen events in total were scrutinised.[24] The earliest occurred on 15 May 2020, just a few months into the Covid-19 pandemic. The latest was on 16 April 2021, mid-way through the 'roadmap' out of nationwide lockdown in the pandemic's second year. The principal question was simple: did the gatherings break lockdown rules? The specificity of that – whether laws or just non-binding advice were breached – would become part of the debate. The Met ended up investigating a dozen of the original sixteen gatherings in what was called 'Operation Hillman'. Fines were then issued for events on eight dates. There was no breakdown given by Scotland Yard of how many people were fined for each event. What can be said for certain is that at least one person at each gathering was concluded to have broken Covid laws.

It is worth listing the eight. In chronological order they were:

1. A 'bring your own booze' Number 10 garden event on 20 May 2020.
2. A Number 10 private secretary's leaving do in the Cabinet Office on 18 June 2020, for which the then government head of ethics, Helen MacNamara, was fined.
3. An afternoon get-together for Boris Johnson's birthday in the Cabinet Room on 19 June 2020, for which the prime minister, his wife, Carrie Johnson, and Rishi Sunak were all fined.
4. A farewell event in Number 10 for special adviser Lee Cain on 13 November 2020. (This, rather than the Downing Street flat gathering on the same evening when Abba music was allegedly played, is believed to have triggered the punishment. When multiple events took place on a particular date, the Met did not specify which led to a fine.)
5. At least one of the three events – a Cabinet Office leaving do, a Cabinet Office Christmas quiz, a Downing Street leaving do – on 17 December 2020.
6. The Christmas 'wine and cheese' party on 18 December 2020 which was joked about in leaked footage of a recorded Downing Street practice press conference.
7. Farewell events for two Number 10 private secretaries on 14 January 2021.

8. At least one of two leaving parties for James Slack, Number 10
   director of communications, and a photographer on 16 April 2021,
   the night before Prince Philip's funeral.

The degree of Boris Johnson's involvement on each occasion
should also be recorded. He was not at all the events that led to
fines. When he did attend, his presence was often brief – 'ten or
fifteen minutes, perhaps a maximum of twenty-five', as he formally
testified to the Commons Privileges Committee after the Met had
completed its work.[25] At some the prime minister raised a glass of
alcohol – photographs show as much.[26] But the worst excesses
revealed did not involve Johnson. No reporting has suggested he
stayed up drinking late into the night, like some of his advisers.
Indeed, despite his bon vivant public image, he rarely drank much.
At arguably the most raucous event – the two farewell parties the
night before Prince Philip's funeral, which carried on into the early
hours despite the official period of national mourning – Johnson
was not even in London, but at his countryside retreat of Chequers.
The prime minister's defence was always that attending leaving events
and saying a few words fell within the boundaries of what constituted
work for him. Given the Met's decision to fine Johnson only once
– over the early afternoon birthday gathering, seemingly one of the
tamer events but undeniably social in nature – it can be assumed
that his 'there for work' argument was largely accepted.

But that does not absolve Johnson of blame. Far from it.

The details of Sue Gray's final report, released in May 2022 after
the Met had issued its fines and concluded its investigation, revealed
in stark detail how socialising – not working – had taken place.[27]
At one event, the Number 10 official's farewell celebration on
18 June 2020, pizza was ordered, Prosecco bottles were popped and
a karaoke machine was set up. 'There was excessive alcohol consump-
tion by some individuals,' ran Gray's deadpan prose. 'One individual
was sick. There was a minor altercation between two other individuals.' The right verb to describe this, undeniably, was 'partying'.

A similar picture was painted of the press office Christmas event
on 18 December 2020. The 'Wine & Cheese Evening' included

Secret Santa gifts and special 'awards' being handed out. 'Some members of staff drank excessively,' concluded Gray. 'The event was crowded and noisy.' One person accidentally set off a panic alarm. 'A cleaner who attended the room the next morning noted that there had been red wine spilled on one wall and on a number of boxes of photocopier paper,' Gray noted. Again, this was, according to any common understanding of the word, a party. Likewise the two farewell events the night before Prince Philip's funeral. 'Wine was available and music was played from a laptop on top of a printer. A number of those present drank excessively,' wrote Gray.[28] At one point people played on the child's swing in the Number 10 garden, damaging it. The security system revealed just how late the revelry went on for some: two attendees left, one at 3.11 a.m., the other at 4.20 a.m.

These events happened on Boris Johnson's watch. They took place in the building where he lived. Some involved his most senior advisers. He may not have been at all the events and at others his attendance may have been brief. But at those where he was present – ones that led to fines – there is no known indication that he urged the gatherings to be broken up. Photographs showed him near open bottles of alcohol with people close together. The prime minister's defence has always been that he did not think that the events broke the rules. There is evidence to back up this claim. Why would the official Number 10 photographer be allowed to capture proceedings if they were deemed at the time to be illegal? Why would someone have briefed *The Times* that Johnson had enjoyed a cake at a birthday gathering for which he would eventually be fined?[29] No doubt it was true too that Number 10 staff, working long hours alongside each other in a cramped Georgian townhouse and battling the pandemic as necessity dictated, thought that an evening drink would add little extra risk of Covid spread.

But surely – the argument went – the prime minister *should* have known? These were his rules. They were the single most thought-through and loudly communicated policy of the day. During that period Johnson often stared into a TV camera urging the country to abide by them. Would such scenes have played out under Theresa May, who never swore and gave up crisps for Lent? Or Gordon

Brown, who obsessively worried about what the press would write next? Who knows. But they happened on Johnson's watch. This was his Number 10, his advisers, his laws. It was his responsibility to set the working culture.

Secondly, there was what happened when the facts began to emerge. This was in late 2021, long after the events had taken place. The first story, revealed by the *Mirror*'s Pippa Crerar, appeared on 30 November 2021 and pointed to two gatherings that seemed to have broken Covid rules, including the Christmas 2020 press office do.[30] As is the way with big Westminster scandals, once momentum began to build other media outlets piled in, *ITV News* revealed footage showing a Number 10 spinner joking about denials that the Christmas event broke Covid rules – triggering Johnson to launch an internal inquiry that became the Gray investigation – and an email from the prime minister's top private office mandarin inviting staff to a 'bring your own booze!' garden event.[31] Other papers broke fresh ground, with the *Daily Telegraph* revealing the partying before Prince Philip's funeral complete with a suitcase full of wine.[32] The stance of Number 10 for weeks was categorical: deny, deny, deny.

How that line of defence – that no rules were broken – came to be constructed is clearer thanks to the Commons Privileges Committee, which investigated whether Johnson deliberately misled MPs. In his written evidence Johnson pointed to reassurances he had been given about specific events by senior press office figures. But the basis for his blanket denial was less detailed. Indeed Simon Case, the Cabinet secretary, replied 'no' in a questionnaire when asked if he had ever reassured Johnson that rules were followed at all times in Number 10.[33] Martin Reynolds, the head of Johnson's private office, even said he 'questioned whether it was realistic to argue that all the guidance had been followed at all times' before one Prime Minister's Questions in early December 2021.[34] Nonetheless, Johnson went on to issue a complete denial in the Commons: 'The guidance was followed and the rules were followed at all times.'[35] Variations of this line would continue through late 2021 into early 2022, until the Gray inquiry and Met police investigation led to the cessation of direct Number 10 comments about the events.

What Johnson said proved to be wrong. He had denied that guidance and rules were broken. The Met concluded that that was incorrect in relation to no fewer than 126 incidents.[36] Why had the prime minister been so absolute in his denials? The spinners involved – some of whom were at the events – must shoulder some of the blame. 'We fucked up,' one conceded after Johnson's fall.[37] Was there fault too with the prime minister? Whatever inquiries may have been made before the blanket denial was first issued, they were far too shallow. Dismissing damaging claims point blank was a strategy Johnson had adopted before: for example, over a row about the financing of a Downing Street flat refurbishment that ended up with an Electoral Commission fine for the Tories over incorrect donation declarations. 'Dodge, duck, dip, dive and dodge' was the mantra Boris Johnson liked to repeat from one of his favourite films.[38] Perhaps 'Discover, declare and defuse' would have been a wiser approach. Not least because the strategy adopted infuriated Cabinet ministers – including Sajid Javid – who were sent out to deny wrongdoing, only then to have their claims quickly proved false. The denials were voiced, again and again, by Johnson. Whether deliberately or not, they misled the public about what had happened.

Partygate did untold damage to the Johnson premiership. From the first news story in November 2021, through the escalation and appointment of Sue Gray in December, further claims and the launch of the Met's investigation in January 2022, the announcement of Johnson's fine in April, and the Met wrapping things up and Gray's final report in May, it dogged his administration, sapping support from voters and Tory MPs.

Whatever his protests, on those two points – allowing the partygate culture to develop in the first place, and being so categoric, so explicit with denials that crumbled on inspection – the buck stops, ultimately, with Boris.

In order to oust a Conservative Party leader outside a major election defeat, a chunk of Tory MPs must act. Such actions might take the form of a public denunciation, or a private letter to the 1922 Committee, or a tick in a no-confidence ballot. What did for Theresa

May was the Brexiteers, with an organised and motivated faction dead set against her deal – the European Research Group – blending with Boris Johnson's supporters as he emerged as the most obvious deliverer of a harder Brexit. For Boris, there was no single grouping that led the backbench rebellion. It was a more complicated assemblage of disillusioned colleagues coming to believe that the prime minister had served his function.

Separating out the different subsections of the parliamentary party does, however, help understand what happened. One was the 2019-ers, the group of new Tory MPs swept into power under Johnson. It was huge – 109 in total, close to a third of all the party's MPs. Theoretically they should have been Johnsonites, owing their seats to his knock-out election victory. Yet the picture was complicated. First, some had never expected to win their seats in 2019. One person bemoaned being handed a no-hope constituency, only to find themselves an MP after voting day.[39] A CCHQ source recalled having to wake one candidate in the middle of the night with news of victory after they had gone to bed certain of defeat.[40] Many also had slim majorities and so were skittish when the Tory poll figure dropped. It meant that MPs who did not necessarily have deep ties to the party hierarchy were elected. The pandemic also played its part. Instead of spending their first two years under the thumb of the Tory whips, the newbies were largely away from Parliament, working remotely during lockdowns.

A Number 10 adviser helping Johnson see off the Tory revolt explained the issue:

> The 2019 cohort who came in who should have been the Boris phalanx weren't in Parliament for very long before they all fucked off. That's why the 2019 group has been such a problem and were pretty feral. The party was never given a chance to fold them up and say, 'Here's your job, here's what you do and by the way you wouldn't be here without him.'[41]

Come early 2022 some of the 2019-ers were flipping on Johnson. In the new year some of the malcontents met in the office of Tory MP Alicia Kearns, whose constituency included Melton Mowbray. The gathering was leaked to the chief whip, Mark Spencer, who quickly dubbed it the 'pork pie plot' and tipped off reporters to flush out the rebels. It worked at the time.

There was a wider problem, however – it was not just newbies. There were Tory Remainers, some in London seats, who loathed Johnson for bringing about Brexit. There were moderates alarmed by what they saw as Johnson's cavalier approach to ethics and morals. There were Tory traditionalists who grew disillusioned by the promises of tax cuts forever just over the horizon as the tax burden soared towards a seventy-year high. And there were even ardent Eurosceptics: Steve Baker, who ushered his ERG grouping behind Boris in 2019, would eventually call for his head.

The breadth of discontent can be seen in those early calls for Johnson to go, beginning at the start of 2022 and snowballing from there. 12 January: William Wragg, a Brexiteer in his early thirties, cites partygate and says he is 'frankly worn out of defending what is invariably indefensible'. 13 January: Caroline Nokes, a long-time Johnson critic, dubs him a 'liability' and urges him to go 'now'. 15 January: Tim Loughton, the clubbable Commons Home Affairs Committee chairman who first became an MP in 1997, calls on Johnson to 'stand down'. 19 January: one-time party leadership hopeful and former Johnson Brexit ally David Davis quotes the famous jibe thrown at Neville Chamberlain, telling the prime minister in the Commons to 'in the name of God, go'. 31 January: Andrew Mitchell, a Tory moderate first elected in 1987, publicly withdraws his support. 4 February: Sir Nick Gibb, the mild-mannered and widely respected former schools minister, says 'to restore trust, we need to change the prime minister'. On the same day Aaron Bell, one of Johnson's 'Red Wall' destroyers as 2019-elected MP for Newcastle-under-Lyme, asks 'does the Prime Minister think I'm a fool' for following Covid rules at his grandmother's funeral. Downing Street tried to dismiss the growing list of names as the 'usual suspects'.[42] But Wragg, Nokes, Loughton, Davis, Mitchell, Gibb, Bell – no politico would suggest they are all part of the same Tory tribe. For Johnson, the fires were breaking out all across his backbench.

It was the darkest of developments overseas that would temporarily stabilise Johnson's premiership at home. Britain awoke on 24 February to footage of Russian tanks rolling over the Ukrainian border and missiles exploding across Kyiv: the full-scale invasion so long feared but only days earlier still doubted by some had arrived. War had broken out in Europe again. Johnson had few rivals as an orator in Parliament and he would deploy his rhetoric to stand four square with the Ukrainian people and condemn Vladimir Putin, the Russian president, in the months ahead. There would be more than words too. The UK, under Johnson's leadership, would be at the forefront of the push to sanction Putin's Russia and then ramp up the provision of weapons and other military support for Kyiv. Given what some saw as Russia's deliberate testing of the West's resolve, such forthrightness was not guaranteed. The war shaped the mood in Britain. Some rebels announced that they had withdrawn confidence letters. One 1922 Committee executive said the threshold for a vote had almost been hit before the invasion, but then the letter total dropped.[43] Politicos would roll their eyes whenever tricky news for Johnson would be swiftly followed by a call with Volodymyr Zelensky. But the warmth and gratitude Zelensky showed towards Johnson suggested the Ukrainian president knew the value of that support.

The reprieve, however, was temporary. Johnson was about to attend the finale of the Platinum Jubilee celebrations for Queen Elizabeth II on 5 June 2022 when he got a phone call from Sir Graham Brady, the shop steward of Tory backbenchers. The no-confidence vote threshold had been reached. Johnson sat watching the entertainment that evening outside Buckingham Palace, wife Carrie by his side and Labour rival Sir Keir Starmer a few seats away, knowing the following day could be his last as prime minister.

Ceremonial duties done, a council of war was called in the Downing Street flat. Steve Barclay, his chief of staff, Chris Heaton-Harris, the chief whip, Nigel Adams, a Cabinet Office minister and long-term Johnson loyalist, Guto Harri, the Downing Street communications director, and Ross Kempsell, a senior political figure at Tory Party headquarters were all there. Lynton Crosby advised from afar. No alcohol was served, just tea and water – in keeping with the sober mood. A battle plan was drawn up.

Ministers would be urged to go public with their support the next morning: twenty-one of thirty would do so within three hours of the conclusion of the Cabinet meeting. All Tory MPs were issued with a one-page note talking up Johnson, 'the Conservative Party's most proven and thoroughly tested election winner', and warning that 'a blue-on-blue civil war will be vicious and tear the party apart'.[44] Grant Shapps's spreadsheet of past Tory MP voting habits was again utilised. The prediction it generated would be one vote out in the end. Some 148 Tory MPs voted no confidence, with 211 Tory MPs voting confidence. The rebels were short of the 180 votes needed to force Johnson out, but it was still a damningly high number. The prime minister rushed onto TV to dub the result 'convincing' and 'decisive'.[45] It was anything but – 41 per cent of his own MPs were now on record as wanting him gone.

The other factor that eroded Johnson's standing was a succession of by-election defeats. He was once the 'Carlsberg candidate', reaching parts of the electorate no other Tory could, but losses called into question his Midas touch. In May 2021 it was the by-election victory in Hartlepool, Labour-held since 1974, that had seemingly cemented his political dominance. So when the dynamic flipped it created vulnerability. Chesham and Amersham the following month had been a warning shot, the Liberal Democrats seeing their vote share jump 30 percentage points to allow them to seize the previously safe Tory seat in a shock triumph. The loss of Owen Paterson's true blue seat of North Shropshire in December 2021 was bad too – though the circumstances helped Number 10 to play down the magnitude of the defeat.[46] The local elections on 5 May 2022 re-inforced the picture, the Tories winning just 24 per cent of seats available while Labour took 52 per cent.[47] Then there was a double blow on 23 June, when two Tory constituencies were being contested after sleaze scandals. Wakefield (Tory majority: 3,358) was available because Imran Ahmad Khan resigned after being found guilty of sexually assaulting a teenage boy. Tiverton and Honiton (Tory majority: 24,239) was free after Neil Parish quit having admitted watching pornography twice in Parliament. Both seats were lost, Wakefield to Labour and Tiverton and Honiton to the Liberal Democrats. Here was a sign that in 'Red Wall' former Labour heartlands and also in 'Blue Wall' Tory shires the BoJo magic was not working. It set the mood for what followed in July.

★

Boris Johnson and Rishi Sunak were not always rivals. Quite the reverse. For much of his premiership Johnson saw their relationship as one of 'mentor' and 'mentee', according to one Boris aide.[48] Another said that he grew to view Sunak as his natural successor.[49] In meetings with senior journalists the prime minister would gush at his chancellor's brilliance. It was Sunak's obvious financial expertise that saw him handed the keys to the Treasury when Sajid Javid quit on 13 February 2020.[50] He was thrown straight into an economic challenge of mind-spinning proportion: the biggest drop in national output for three centuries as the first country-wide lockdown to stop the spread of Covid-19 was announced six weeks later. During the countless internal debates about pandemic policy that followed, the pair were often of similar mind, Sunak being one of the firmest lockdown sceptics around the Cabinet table and Johnson being instinctively cautious about such measures too – though surging poll ratings for 'dishy Rishi' as he poured in cash to protect jobs was noted in Number 10.

It was not at the height of Covid but during its aftermath that the Sunak–Johnson tensions really escalated. As the crisis eased with the mass roll-out of vaccines in early to mid-2021, the focus turned to how to manage the post-pandemic economy. Johnson with his populist instinct was a big spender, having vowed to end austerity and seeing pound signs as the easy way out of many political binds. Sunak had a firmer ideological commitment to traditional low-spend, low-debt and ideally low-tax Tory economics, seeing fiscal prudence as the way forward. 'He was quite alarmed by how much the state had grown during the pandemic,' said one by Sunak's side then.

> It was obviously necessary but the spending pressures had grown massively during Covid and with the furlough scheme. It was hard to pare back because the country got addicted to it. He always wanted to get back to a form of state where you don't need to tax as much and the private sector does more of the heavy lifting.[51]

But Johnson had other ideas. There would be an early, telling clash. After his triumph in the Tory leadership election in July 2019, Johnson had told the nation from the steps of Downing Street that he had a 'clear plan' to fix the long-term social care crisis.[52] That

Mutual admiration, mutual suspicion. The curious case of Michael Gove's and Boris Johnson's relationship is a thread that runs through the long Tory years in Downing Street.

VIPs only. Lee Cain, long-time spinner and operator for Boris Johnson, at the back of the Conservative campaign battle bus during the December 2019 election.

Front-page material. Boris Johnson and Carrie Symonds, as she then was, the morning after the Tories won their biggest Commons majority since Margaret Thatcher.

With the help of Sir Chris Whitty (left) and Sir Patrick Vallance,
Boris Johnson attempted to steer the country through a once-in-a-century
pandemic as Covid-19 ended normality.

Partygate was the defining scandal of the Johnson premiership, sapping support
from voters and colleagues. One spinner involved in the denials that proved
untrue admitted: 'We fucked up.'

Dominic Cummings. Out with a bang and a box of secrets.

Battling the elements with a beanie and Dilyn the dog, May 2021.

A Pyrrhic victory in ornate surroundings, as 1922 chairman Graham Brady announces Boris Johnson has survived a confidence vote in June 2022. Boris would resign within six weeks.

Third time lucky? Sir Keir Starmer took Labour to opinion-poll highs never seen under Ed Miliband or Jeremy Corbyn in the bid to finally turf out the Tories.

Rishi Sunak secretly moved to quit Boris Johnson's Cabinet three months earlier than he eventually did in July 2022, penning a resignation statement he was talked out of submitting.

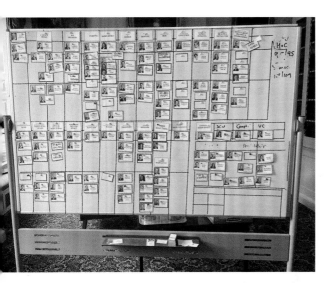

ever-before seen: the Cabinet reshuffle
niteboard in Margaret Thatcher's old
idy in Downing Street, on the night
pris Johnson scrambled to keep his
vernment alive, 6 July 2022.

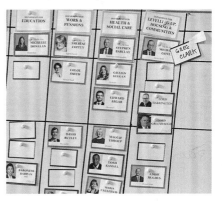

The chaos up close: a Post-It
replacement for Michael Gove
after Johnson sacked him;
hollowed-out departments with
white cards in spaces created by
resigning ministers.

Boris Johnson's
original resignation
speech compared
Tory rebels to family
members trying to
force a relative into the
Swiss euthanasia clinic
Dignitas; the line
was scrubbed.

They were fellow free-market tax-slashers and close political friends,
but Kwasi Kwarteng now thinks Liz Truss did not have the right temperament
to be prime minister.

Day one: Can Liz Truss outlast this lettuce?

As Liz Truss wobbled, the *Daily Star* set up a live webcam to see which
would last longer: the prime minister or a lettuce. Only one was still
standing come the end.

David Cameron,
11 May 2010.

Theresa May,
13 July 2016.

Boris Johnson,
24 July 2019.

Liz Truss,
6 September 2022.

Rishi Sunak,
25 October 2022.

A sodden Rishi Sunak. According to his aides, the prime minister made the final call to launch his 2024 general election campaign outside despite the threat of rain.

Three world leaders ... and one ex-leader. David Cameron standing in for Rishi Sunak at a D-Day commemoration event in France, with Emmanuel Macron, Olaf Scholz and Joe Biden, backfired spectacularly on the Tories and forced a speedy apology.

Changing of the guard as a jubilant Sir Keir Starmer and his wife Victor sweep up Downing Street the morning after the July 2024 general election, bringing to an end fourteen years and fifty-five days of Conservative rule.

was not accurate, according to multiple government insiders – no detailed proposal had been worked up.[53] Two years on, still nothing had been unveiled. And so Johnson, Sunak and Sajid Javid, back in the Cabinet as health secretary after Matt Hancock's departure following an affair, negotiated the details. Javid had been here before. When he was chancellor in early 2020, Number 10 had asked him to crunch the numbers on possible tax rises – including a new mansion tax on property wealth and equalisation of capital gains tax rates – to fund the package.[54] Javid saw both tax hikes as foolhardy. He would be gone before the stand-off was resolved.

This time the prime minister was determined to deliver his social care vow. He wanted a version of Sir Andrew Dilnot's original 'cap and floor' proposal, the one adopted in principle by David Cameron and then replaced by the infamous 2017 Theresa May manifesto policy. The 'cap' on lifetime care costs for an individual would be set at £86,000. The 'floor' of someone's total assets – below which the state would start helping to pay for care – was to become £100,000. The problem? Both Sunak and Javid thought it a bad policy. Sunak considered it 'crap' because the change would not stop people having to sell their homes to fund care.[55] Javid was nervous about a big expansion of the state. The pair were 'at one' in opposition, but Johnson '100 per cent' wanted the policy, according to a source who sat in on the talks.[56]

Sunak also made clear that the new permanent spending stream could not be covered by borrowing, given the mountain of Covid-era debt, so the money would have to come from cuts elsewhere or raised taxes. Since Johnson would not countenance the former, it left only the latter. The Treasury proposed raising National Insurance by 1.25 percentage points – a breach of the Tory manifesto, which promised no National Insurance, VAT or income tax rate increases – to pay for the move. Johnson said yes. 'I think Rishi was hoping that Boris would say, "I'm not going to raise tax," but he went for it,' said a source familiar with the discussions.[57] It would be repackaged as a new tax – the 'Health and Social Care Levy' – to mask the manifesto breach, with little success. The tax rise, announced in September 2021, infuriated some Tory MPs and became a running sore in the party, pain that Liz Truss would successfully tap into by vowing to reverse it in her Tory leadership bid. Its origins resulted in Sunak and Johnson blaming each other – the prime minister for demanding the spending; the chancellor for insisting a tax rise not borrowing had to fund it. Sunak, who hung a photograph of Thatcherite tax-slasher Nigel Lawson on his Treasury office wall, was now hiking rates despite the pandemic easing.

When did Rishi Sunak start thinking about the Tory leadership? And when did he start acting on that thought? Perhaps it is an unfair question. As Boris Johnson liked to remind aides when things got turbulent, almost every Tory MP always has half an eye on becoming prime minister.[58] He spoke from personal experience. Westminster was a place of personal ambitions and outsized egos, something Johnson could be forgiving about, according to allies.[59] But over that nine-month descent, there are an array of facts – some of which can be made public here for the first time – that speak to actions taking place behind the scenes earlier than is commonly acknowledged.

One such indicator came in late autumn 2021, after the social care move and the Owen Paterson saga that saw the Tory poll lead evaporate. A special adviser to Brandon Lewis overheard the chancellor's inner team in a Westminster pub discussing the shape of a Sunak premiership. 'They were literally plotting out who they thought should be in various positions in the Cabinet,' said a source familiar with the incident.[60] Idle chitchat, perhaps. Another came later that year, on 23 December, with the registration of a website domain name: ReadyForRishi.com.[61] It was the slogan that the Sunak campaign would adopt come the Tory leadership race the following July. By that point the site was redirecting visitors to the official campaign website, ready4rishi.com. More than a year on Sunak allies were making only a half-hearted attempt to suggest the registration had not been done by someone in his orbit. There is no explanation – if the purchase was made by a random outsider – as to how they had correctly guessed Sunak's campaign slogan.

During the festive period of December 2021–January 2022 Johnson saw off pressure to declare a new nationwide lockdown as the Omicron variant of Covid surged. By then he was already reeling from the partygate revelations of the preceding weeks. In February, Johnson swept out a host of senior Number 10 figures, some involved in the partygate denials, and in their place brought in ultra-loyalists including Guto Harri, his old spin doctor from London City Hall, and David Canzini, a Tory veteran who helped with his 2019 leadership bid. Lynton Crosby, Johnson's most trusted political sage, also played a much more involved role – though still from the outside. It was during that winter that the prime minister let slip his worries about Sunak as a potential leadership rival. 'Just promise me one thing,' Boris pleaded with Crosby, who was back in Australia, during one of their many calls preparing for the new year reset. 'You won't help Rishi.' 'Why would I help him?' replied Crosby. 'Oh well, you know . . .' the prime minister tailed off.[62] His suspicions of a Downing Street neighbour considering what next were not without foundation.

Sunak insiders admit that at the start of 2022 – seven months before Johnson eventually fell – they knew things were 'looking bad for Boris' and were thinking about being ready if things moved. Around then some Cabinet ministers felt they were being sounded out by Sunak with an eye to potential support. Lewis, the Northern Ireland secretary, was invited to breakfast with Sunak in late 2021 and again in early 2022. During one of their conversations Sunak remarked that Lewis would make a good home secretary, according to one well-placed source.[63] It would be later in the year, around June, that Priti Patel was urged by Sunak allies to meet him, another approach interpreted as a sounding-out for support.[64] Both were ministers loyal to Johnson, meaning recollections may have been coloured by what followed, but the claims circulate nonetheless.

Some approaches were much more explicit. In February, after the publication of Sue Gray's initial findings about partygate, Sunak talked to ministers and parliamentary private secretaries under him in the Treasury asking outright for their backing. 'Boris Johnson isn't going to carry on for ever. There will be a contest at some point. Will you support me if I decide to run?' Sunak said, or words to that effect, according to one who was approached.[65] All but two of the MPs connected to the department would end up endorsing Sunak. Whispers of Rishi backers on manoeuvres also reached

Number 10. A senior Downing Street adviser heard two reports around April of Oliver Dowden, the Conservative Party chairman and a close political friend of Sunak, going 'slightly off topic' during dinners and 'building the case for Rishi'.[66] The source dismissed the speculation, believing Dowden loyal – something that they later deemed a miscalculation.

Were other leadership contenders also eyeing up a run? No doubt. Kwasi Kwarteng was caught by the chief whip sounding out a Cabinet colleague on behalf of Liz Truss.[67] Penny Mordaunt and Nadhim Zahawi were also said to be sounding out MPs. Team Sunak had been right, too, to judge that Johnson was on the brink of falling in February, given how close the number of no-confidence letters is believed to have come to the vote threshold before the Russian invasion of Ukraine at the end of that month.

The public nature of Sunak's willingness to hold the prime minister at arm's length, though, was different from that of other future leadership rivals. It was underscored on 12 January, when Johnson confirmed that he had attended the 'bring your own booze' Downing Street garden party and apologised in the House of Commons, prompting a first flurry of Tory MP resignation calls. Amid a feverish atmosphere in Westminster, Cabinet ministers went public with messages of support for the prime minister. Loyalists were effusive in their praise of Johnson and quick to offer it. As the hours ticked by, the number of silent ministers dwindled. With newspaper first-edition deadlines approaching, Liz Truss, the foreign secretary, and Sunak had still not uttered a single word in public. Truss would eventually declare, 'I stand behind the Prime Minister 100 per cent' – a formulation of total backing she would repeat for the next six months, perhaps aware of the Boris-loving membership base.[68] Sunak, however, was more equivocal: 'The PM was right to apologise and I support his request for patience while Sue Gray carries out her enquiry.'[69] So his support was conditional, tied to the Gray report whose outcome was unknown. The chancellor's team, ever eager not to 'fall for the media circus', noted that on that day Sunak had been in the Devon town of Ilfracombe.[70] But patchy signal alone does not explain an eight-hour silence.

A second public holding of the nose came a few weeks later over Johnson's swipe at Sir Keir Starmer about Jimmy Savile. The Labour leader had been the director of public prosecutions when it was decided not to bring a case against the former BBC presenter. Savile was later revealed to have been a predatory sex offender. During a heated Commons debate over partygate, Johnson declared in passing that Sir Keir in his DPP role had 'spent most of his time prosecuting journalists and failing to prosecute Jimmy Savile'.[71] The off-topic jibe was deemed a low blow by Johnson critics. At a press conference days later Rishi Sunak distanced himself from the remark when he was asked about it, saying, 'Being honest I wouldn't have said it.'[72]

Questions offering Cabinet ministers a chance to criticise the prime minister directly are often asked, and almost always dodged. But not this time. Simon Clarke, number two at the Treasury as chief secretary but loyal to Johnson, was soon texting the prime minister. 'This is going to come to a head,' Clarke warned, fearing Sunak could jump. He had seen first-hand how dismissive the Treasury team had become towards Johnson. 'The dynamic was incredibly uneasy,' said Clarke. 'The ministerial meetings would be characterised by Rishi expressing deep scepticism about Number 10. It was very much us and them, like "we're the grown-ups over here".'[73] The prime minister would not hide his frustrations about Sunak's Savile slap-down when speaking to ministers. Johnson deployed the c-word about his Downing Street neighbour.[74] It would not be the only time. Guto Harri, Boris's chief spinner, would later claim that Johnson wanted to send Sunak a video declaring the word after he quit as chancellor.[75] Johnson's team would issue a blanket denial of the general account Harri gave in his podcast making the claim.

Boris Johnson was prone to believing political conspiracies. Many friends and former advisers attest as much.[76] One wild and unsubstantiated rumour he voiced to others was that Rishi Sunak's father-in-law, the Indian billionaire Narayana Murthy, had Dominic Cummings on a retainer. There is no suggestion it was accurate. Yet 'Boris believed it to be true,' the senior Johnson Cabinet minister who relayed the story said.[77] Despite the total absence of proof, the idea of great forces thwarting his progress – money, a Tory rival and a former adviser turned nemesis all wrapped up together – somehow appealed. No doubt Cummings by 2022 wanted his former boss gone. His Twitter profile declared as much: 'Regime change.' Publicly Cummings would release damning claims about Johnson in his Substack blog posts, soon jumped on by the media. The idea that something similar was happening in private is not fanciful. But seeing a Cummings puppet master behind every negative story was incorrect. Partygate stories emerged because there were provable facts of rule-breaking that reporters across newspapers and broadcasters could stand up. The narrative pushed by Johnson allies of an 'orchestrated' ouster is too convenient – it absolves him, and them, of any responsibility.

There are, however, three stories grounded in fact that are worth retelling when it comes to the question of Sunak's allies and their role in Johnson's fall.

One involved a man known to almost nobody outside Westminster: Dougie Smith. The Scot was a constant feature behind the scenes in the long Tory run in government since 2010, though precisely what he did remained a mystery to most. For years only one photograph, three decades old, could be found of him online. Smith, variously described in press cuttings as a political fixer and a modern-day Machiavelli, had a Number 10 pass that allowed him to come and go from the centre of power as he pleased. Smith was married to Munira Mirza, the head of Johnson's policy unit in Downing Street who had played a similar role during his London mayoralty. Boris grew to rely on Smith to fix political problems, according to Number 10 insiders.[78] But Smith was also close to Sunak. The Tory adviser played a key role overseeing the party's general election candidates list – the make-or-break moment for wannabe MPs, since only those on the list can apply for selection from local associations. Smith had helped Sunak get selected as Richmond's candidate in the 2015 election. A Sunak ally said Smith had been 'continually supportive', was 'definitely a friend' and that the pair were 'close'.[79] Which makes what followed so intriguing.

On 3 February 2022, Mirza left her role in Downing Street. Her resignation letter criticised Johnson's Savile jibe at Sir Keir Starmer:

'There was no fair or reasonable basis for that assertion.' That part of the story played out in public. What has not been reported before was a call that Johnson then got from Mirza's husband, Dougie Smith. Six Johnson inner circle figures have described it to the author, most saying it happened on the evening of Mirza's resignation. Smith warned Johnson he was at risk of being forced from office. The phrase attributed to Smith is variously quoted as 'they're going to get you' or 'we're going to get you'.[80] Given that only Johnson and Smith are likely to have been on the call, and that the remarks are in wider circulation because Boris described the conversation to others, it is difficult to prove categorically what was said. Was the tone one of warning or threat? What is certainly true is that Johnson has since concluded it was the latter – that is, part of an organised plot against him – and told others as much. Smith would find himself sidelined under Liz Truss, Johnson's successor. But when Sunak took over, he was back in the fold, once again with a Number 10 pass and the freedom to roam in Downing Street.

The second incident came on 12 April 2022, the day both Johnson and Sunak were fined for breaking Covid laws over the prime minister's brief birthday gathering in the Cabinet Office. Johnson was at Chequers when the news broke. Allies rejected their first thought of getting him driven back to Number 10 because there was a broadcast helicopter hovering overhead – they did not want an 'OJ' moment, with Boris's car being tracked as it sped along – so went to join him there instead.[81] That afternoon things got worse. Rishi Sunak was on the brink of resigning. Those at Chequers recalled a fraught Johnson, one saying it was 'very clear' that Rishi might walk.[82] A Sunak insider confirmed that this was correct, explaining: 'He believes a lot in upholding rules.'[83] Such a development would have been disastrous for Johnson – if the chancellor was quitting over the fine, then why wasn't the prime minister?

In the end, Sunak took the eye-catching move of actually drafting a full resignation statement.[84] The words were shared with Lord Hague, the former Tory leader and a *Times* columnist who had preceded Sunak as MP for Richmond. Soon, with more people at the company also having separately found out about the draft resignation statement, whispers of the dramatic move were spreading among senior figures at Rupert Murdoch's newspaper. Boris Johnson even told others that Murdoch intervened to urge Sunak not to quit, saying the media tycoon had personally told him as much. The story is still passed on by Johnson's allies. However, a Sunak source said Rishi did not get a direct call or text from Murdoch. A spokesperson for News UK, Murdoch's British publishing company, declined to comment, while a Johnson spokesperson said he did not recognise the account. At the end of the day, Sunak was warned off quitting, some of those consulted fearing that naivety was being shown given that inadvertently toppling Boris could damn his leadership hopes. He backed down, but a hint of the wobble was found on the next day's *Times* front page. Rishi had come closer than the public ever knew to quitting Johnson's Cabinet – and likely bringing down the prime minister – three months earlier than he did.

The final story involves Oliver Dowden. 'Olive', as he is known in Tory circles, has been another constant feature of the party's Downing Street run since 2010.[85] He rose to be David Cameron's deputy chief of staff in Number 10 before becoming an MP in 2015. Dowden's political skills were widely acknowledged, leading to him helping brief a succession of Tory leaders for Prime Minister's Questions, the trickiest Commons clash of the week. Dowden was also a friend of Sunak. In the 2019 leadership race, Sunak, Dowden and Robert Jenrick had co-written an article endorsing Johnson for the leadership – a move viewed as a key staging post in the race, given that the three MPs represented a younger Tory generation. All three, in turn, were handed Cabinet jobs when Johnson won. But Dowden had slipped down the pecking order, moved from culture secretary to Conservative Party chairman in September 2021 – theoretically a senior role but one with no direct impact on government policy. The demotion smarted, multiple Johnson and Sunak allies have said.[86] On the morning after the double by-election loss – Wakefield, plus Tiverton and Honiton – on 24 June 2022, Johnson was in Rwanda for a G20 summit and had just been for a swim in his hotel when Dowden called. He was quitting the Cabinet. 'Somebody has to carry the can, somebody has to take responsibility for the bad results in the local elections,' Dowden told Johnson.[87] The prime minister felt as though his party chairman was reading from a script.[88] Dowden quickly hung up and Johnson sounded the alarm. A Cabinet ring-round confirmed that no one else was walking, but it was another blow. Within a fortnight, Boris would be forced out. Did Dowden quit to help ease Sunak's path? He has vehemently denied as much and Sunak allies insisted there was no 'coordination'.[89] But Johnson thought otherwise even then. 'Rishi will be next,' Jake Berry, a Tory MP loyal to Johnson, recalled telling the prime minister. 'One hundred per cent. They're working together on it,' came the response, according to Berry.[90] Dowden would even- tually become Sunak's deputy prime minister.

Three Ps toppled Boris, some of his Cabinet ministers would later conclude. Paterson marked the start of the slide. Partygate did the most damage.

But the one that would prove the final straw arrived in June 2022. Chris Pincher had only been brought back into the Whip's Office because of Boris Johnson's woes. Loyal MPs had rallied to the prime minister's side when things were wobbling at the start of the year and launched their own set-up to secure the support of colleagues. It was dubbed 'Operation Save Big Dog' in one media report, a tag always denied by those at its centre, but which soon became the press's favoured name for the outfit.[91] It worked in tandem with the efforts of the official whips, though some Number 10 insiders say it was much less influential than its chattiest Tory MP members liked to make out. Pincher was at its heart and was rewarded in a reshuffle that followed with the role of deputy chief whip.

There was already chatter about Pincher. He had resigned once from the Whip's Office over an allegation made by Alex Story, an Olympic rower turned Tory candidate. Story claimed that when the pair were alone Pincher had massaged his neck and talked about his future in Tory politics, then changed into a bathrobe 'like a pound shop Harvey Weinstein'.[92] Pincher referred himself for investigation and was later cleared by the Conservative Party of breaking its code of conduct. He also issued an apology. It would be a fresh allegation that sped up Johnson's fall.

On 29 June 2022, Pincher joined scores of other Tory MPs for drinks at the Carlton Club, an almost two-centuries old establishment whose members sign a pledge to uphold Tory values. There Pincher, fuelled with alcohol, was alleged to have groped two men. In one account, detailed in Sebastian Payne's book *The Fall of Boris Johnson*, an inebriated Pincher was seen grabbing someone's left buttock and groin after buying a round of drinks.[93] When the claims leaked via the *Sun* the next day there was an immediate uproar. Pincher quit as deputy whip, admitting in his letter: 'I drank far too much' and 'I've embarrassed myself'.[94]

But at first he remained a Tory MP, angering critics. He would lose the Tory whip as the backlash swelled. Over the days that followed, Downing Street spinners declared that the prime minister had not been aware of any past allegation about Pincher. It later emerged that Johnson had been alerted to a claim when he was foreign secretary. The revelation was made with maximum political effect by the department's former permanent secretary Lord McDonald live on BBC Radio 4's *Today* programme. Dominic Cummings poured fuel on the fire by claiming that Johnson had once dubbed the MP 'Pincher by name, Pincher by nature'.[95] Pincher himself had denied wrongdoing over the claims. A parliamentary investigation would later conclude his behaviour had been 'deeply inappropriate' and recommend an eight-week suspension.[96]

The political fallout was brutal. The incident combined the elements that had long been infuriating Tory MPs: Johnson's record on telling the truth; his stance on matters of ethics; and his willingness to have ministers go out to bat for him publicly, only for the facts to change afterwards. It would prove too much. After Lord McDonald's revelation, Sajid Javid and Rishi Sunak penned their letters of resignation. The end was nigh.

'Fuck! Fuck!' After the outburst when Rishi Sunak resigned, there was composure. Boris Johnson, the great performer, had a knack of putting on a show when in the tightest of political spots. And so when he walked into a room in Parliament for a chat with a few dozen Tory MP loyalists, news of the double resignation having just spread, there were jokes. 'You may have noticed that I've lost a chancellor,' Johnson said, breaking the ice. 'That might please some of you who are into having their taxes cut.'[97] Soon, though, it was back to Number 10 and crisis stations. First things first: a Sunak replacement was needed before the markets opened the next day. Three names were floated.[98] Liz Truss was one, but the on-going fighting in Ukraine meant a change at the top of the Foreign Office was tricky. Steve Barclay, Johnson's chief of staff, was interviewed for the role too, but was eventually sent to replace Sajid Javid at the health department. So it was that Nadhim Zahawi got the chancellorship, with Michelle Donelan taking his education brief. Johnson let his frustration about Sunak out again with Zahawi. 'I've been wanting to get rid of him for a while. I wish I'd done it sooner,' he told Zahawi. 'I trusted this guy so much.'[99] The prime minister was blaming himself — as he often did in such circumstances — for having dropped the ball.

By the end of Tuesday, 5 July 2022, things seemed to have stabilised. No other Cabinet ministers had bolted for the door. 'When you go hunting, you've got to kill with your shot,' Johnson's allies said triumphantly.[100] It was a woefully premature victory declaration.

Wednesday, 6 July, would prove one of the most dramatic days in recent Westminster history. A drip-drip-drip of ministerial resignations would bring Boris to his knees. Hard truths from the Cabinet would deliver the killer blow.

The day began with Michael Gove asking to see Johnson either before or after Prime Minister's Questions. He was slotted into the diary early, close to 10 a.m., with the message he wished to deliver unclear to everyone but the communities secretary himself. The night before Gove had watched a double bill at the Royal Opera House: *Cavalleria Rusticana*, a tale of death and revenge, followed by *Pagliacci*, about the fall of a clown. Alone with Johnson in his Number 10 office, Gove — who for years had meandered between advocate and undercutter of Boris — now returned to the latter role. 'I knew at that stage that there were going to be many more resignations, including people who were very close to him at one point,' Gove recounted. 'And I explained to him that I thought that his position was going to be untenable later on. He was very measured and perfectly reasonable.'[101]

Johnson said: 'If there are resignations, we can fill those posts.' Gove replied: 'We won't be able to form a government, there won't be enough people.' When Johnson referred again to his shotgun-toting relative, Gove countered: 'You'd be better off if you took your fate in your own hands.' But it was a no from the prime minister. 'Mikey, thank you very much, you always deliver the bullet with such gentle manners,' he said.[102] It was, it appears, a civil conversation – not that all of Johnson's allies reacted that way. Gove then sat in on PMQs prep as usual, chipping in with suggestions for the man he had just told to quit, much to the disgust of one loyalist who joined. Nigel Adams said: 'I walked in and I walked out. I don't think I would have been able to hold my peace. I just thought: "This is fucking extraordinary."'[103]

PMQs, for all its faults, can be a brilliant exposer of parliamentary mood. On this occasion the sombre faces and near-silence on the Tory benches were a bad omen. Throughout the day the realisation that it was over for Boris would strike different people at different times. Soon after PMQs, Number 10 adviser David Canzini and new health secretary Steve Barclay were sitting in a Commons office together. 'We're done, it's over,' said Canzini, a view apparently shared by his fellow Tory.[104] But there were still prime ministerial duties to be carried out. For two hours that afternoon, with the nation's leadership hanging in the balance, Johnson answered minutely detailed policy questions during his appearance in front of the Commons Liaison Committee. All the while phones were pinging to register more and more resignations – that day the ten-minister mark was passed, then twenty, then thirty. As a snapshot of the British parliamentary system – a prime minister at centre stage furrowing his brow over the specifics of fertiliser imports and whether UK airlines cancel too many flights while his colleagues kill off his career in the wings – the scene takes some beating.[105]

By now, Cabinet ministers had begun to gather at Number 10. Nadhim Zahawi, alarmed by the scramble for the exit, had texted Dominic Raab, the deputy prime minister, and Chris Heaton-Harris, the chief whip, suggesting a Downing Street gathering. In a first-floor dining room in Number 10 the trio spoke bluntly. 'Mate, it's over, right?' Zahawi asked Heaton-Harris, according to one source familiar with the events. 'I mean, we can't form a government. This is moving so fast.'[106] Heaton-Harris was said to have agreed with the assessment. More Cabinet ministers would filter in and out over the course of the next few hours: Priti Patel, the home secretary;

Grant Shapps, the transport secretary; Simon Hart, the Wales secretary; Brandon Lewis, the Northern Ireland secretary; Kit Malthouse, the policing minister who had been Johnson's deputy mayor. Some of the first arrivals suggested that they should see Johnson en masse when he returned from the Liaison Committee. But – in an apparent attempt at a last-gasp defence of the prime minister's position – the MPs were told to go in one by one, boosting the chance of persuading some. And so, for the first time since the final days of Margaret Thatcher, a procession of Cabinet ministers went to see the sitting prime minister and call time on their tenure.

Zahawi was one of the first up, given his seniority in Cabinet. 'What do you think?' asked Johnson, an opening gambit used with others too. 'Boss, you know I will do everything in my power to get this economic plan together,' Zahawi began, picking up on the tax-cutting package they had discussed the night before and which was being prepared for the following week. 'But that's not what I'm here for. I think the herd is stampeding . . . You can see what's happening and I'm heartbroken. I can't bear to see this happen to you. They're going to drag your carcass out of this place.'[107] Zahawi agreed not to resign and returned to the Treasury. It was only when Number 10 briefed that there would be a joint chancellor–PM speech announcing the new plan the next day – something never agreed – that he grew angry. A Zahawi letter urging Johnson to go would eventually come the following morning.[108]

Priti Patel delivered a similar message in her one-to-one meeting with Johnson. 'I just think this is it now. And for all the wrongs, and there are too many wrongs here, this is an untenable situation,' Patel told the prime minister.[109] Dominic Raab, the deputy prime minister who stayed loyal, did not pull punches: 'You realise by now it's gone? Tell me what you want me to do, but it's gone.'[110] Grant Shapps, whose spreadsheet had helped Johnson claim the leadership and then win the confidence vote, was just as downbeat. 'I've got the data. Unfortunately, it's over,' Shapps told Johnson. 'But really, resign? Why don't we just really show them?' the prime minister tried to counter. 'I'd love if that were possible, it's not,' said Shapps. 'Since I've been here today, another twenty ministers have resigned. Boris, it's over.' With some, the prime minister attempted to make urgent concessions. Kwasi Kwarteng, speaking to him down the line from Teesside and being urged to name his price by Johnson, said he wanted the corporation tax rise scrapped. Johnson said yes – a huge reversal of fiscal policy agreed on the hoof. Putting down the phone, Kwarteng did not celebrate. 'If he can drop that pledge that easily, he's going to say anything and do anything,' Kwarteng told a Treasury colleague. 'This is not a way to run a country.'[111]

There were other visitors. Sir Graham Brady, the 1922 Committee chairman, had attempted to avoid the cameras by looping up Whitehall and reaching Number 10 by the less well-known entrance to the Cabinet Office but had been spotted by the press photographers. As he finally escaped them, a couple watching on from the Clarence pub joked about the attention the MP was getting – then added: 'But he's got to go.'[112] Sir Graham said the same to Johnson.

Michael Gove would not get another bite of the cherry. News of his private utterances to the prime minister had leaked – Gove's team insisted not via them. Johnson had been grinding his teeth all day at the pre-PMQs ambush, according to advisers, who were infuriated by what was seen as another Gove betrayal.[113] Around 8 p.m., Johnson phoned his communities secretary: 'Michael, I'm afraid I'm going to have to ask you to stand down.' Gove, taken aback, countered: 'I see, but you should stand down, Boris.' 'No, no, no,' said Johnson. 'I'm afraid you're standing down, Mikey.'[114] The call was brief, terser than the early morning meeting. Guto Harri, Johnson's comms chief, gleefully briefed that the 'snake' Gove had been driven out of town. Nadine Dorries, loyal to the last, was also around all evening trying to lift the spirits.

A hard core still remained. Nigel Adams, Tory advisers Ross Kempsell and Charlotte Owens, the former *Daily Telegraph* editor Will Lewis – a long-time Johnson confidant – and Heaton-Harris, the chief whip, were hunkered down in the Thatcher study. It was the very same first-floor room where Johnson double-punched the air in 2019 on emulating Maggie's mammoth majority, only now those present were trying to keep a government afloat. The traditional reshuffle whiteboard was wheeled out. The board is never shown in public but a photograph of it taken that night can be revealed in these pages.[115] It captures the chaos. Cutout faces of politicians, green rim for MPs and red rim for Lords, are pinned to the board, which is divided into departments. The Education department is almost entirely hollowed out by resignations, with just two politicians remaining. On a Post-it the scribbled name of Greg Clark is stuck over Michael Gove, indicating the hastily arranged replacement after the latter's surprise sacking. John Redwood, an ardent Tory tax-cutter, is slotted into a Treasury spot – an eye-catching move that never came to pass. One Cabinet minister – Simon Hart – is left discarded in the tray below the board after he handed in a resignation letter to be published if Johnson was not gone by the morning. The letter would not be needed.

Others there attest to the hectic scenes. At one point, a name was put forward for a ministerial post, only for someone to point out that the individual in question was no longer in Parliament. Cabinet members were shocked by some of the people that appeared on the board, aware of scandals lurking from previous roles.[116] One was so unsuitable it was 'just mental'.[117] At points ministers still pinned up had actually already resigned. 'Deck chairs and *Titanic*,' summed up a Tory veteran who saw the board.[118] Madder ideas were being floated. One Johnson loyalist was said to have proposed – with no sign of making a joke – locking the Number 10 front door to stop more Cabinet ministers arriving to give Johnson their views.[119] Someone even suggested getting Ukrainian President Volodymyr Zelensky, busy fighting a war, to issue a message of support.[120] At one point, such was the scale of resignations, Simon Case, the Cabinet secretary, was asked what the minimum number of ministers was for the government to function. Case suggested in reality around seventy to one hundred, but strictly speaking, according to the rules, just one – the prime minister.[121]

That evening, publicly, Johnson was bullish. Bang on print deadline, newspapers were briefed, improbably, that he would fight on. 'There will be no lectern moment tonight,' a senior Downing Street spinner told hacks. But privately, the prime minister was softening. In his hour of need, he turned to a man whose political judgement he had always trusted. Very late on Wednesday night he got through to Lynton Crosby over in Australia. Downing Street insiders wanted him to fight on, Johnson explained. 'Can you win?' asked Crosby.

'No,' conceded Johnson, finally saying out loud what his Cabinet had concluded. 'I think it's over,' he continued. 'I think I will stand down. I don't want to be the one who's destroyed the Conservative Party.' Crosby did not try to change his mind: 'Look, based on everything I can see from here it looks like the right decision. In which case you need to work to have a clear view about what your legacy is and communicate it.'[122] Carrie, too, urged her husband to accept the same reality, according to one Boris friend.[123] Finally, there was acceptance. And in the morning, there would be a farewell.

The first written confirmation that Boris Johnson's premiership was over arrived in the form of an email at 7.23 a.m. on Thursday, 7 July 2022. Sent from Johnson to just a handful of trusted advisers and allies, it had no subject line. But there it was: the first draft of his resignation speech. It would be watered down before delivery but the original – shared with this author – was raw. The opening read:

> In any of the battles of our lives there comes a time when you have to understand that you are beat. And I am afraid that moment has come for me today. In the last 48 hours, I have been struck by how many colleagues have asked me to resign with dignity, as though they represented some euthanasia clinic. And I have replied that dignity is a grossly overrated commodity and that I prefer to fight to the end. But this is about far more than my so-called career. It is about our country, our future. And I cannot ask good friends and colleagues to superglue Humpty together again, when they are frankly hesitant or not supportive. So I want to say to the millions of people who voted for us in 2019, many voting Conservative for the first time, thank you for that incredible mandate, the biggest Conservative majority since 1987.[124]

There was also a swipe at social media's role in the proceedings: 'There is still a part of me that thinks if only we could have turned off Twitter and sent the MPs off to the beach we could've sorted this out and gone on to crush Labour in the next election.'[125] It was close: the House of Commons would break up for its summer recess fourteen days later. But not close enough.

The references to the Swiss assisted-dying clinic Dignitas, Humpty Dumpty and Twitter would be scrubbed by the time shortly after noon when the prime minister stepped out of the black Number 10 door, throngs of cheering MPs and aides lining Downing Street, to deliver the words. He would borrow Nadhim Zahawi's metaphor from the night before in the final version. 'Of course it is painful not to be able to see through so many ideas and projects myself. But as we've seen at Westminster, the herd is powerful,' Johnson said. 'And when the herd moves, it moves.'[126] This was a swipe at animalistic Tory MPs. There was an acknowledgement there too, though, of realpolitik. Boris, so long the leader of the pack, had been trampled by his own.

Boris Johnson was one of the most consequential British political figures of his generation. He led the Brexit campaign, won the public's backing and then delivered that change in office, reshaping the country's entire economic and diplomatic strategy in a single swoop. He held the levers of power when a deadly pandemic struck and rushed to Kyiv's support when Russia invaded, returning Europe to war. But he had been toppled after a slew of unforced errors.

One former Conservative Party leader, among just a few politicians to have seen the pressures of that job from the inside, said historians would 'struggle' to comprehend Johnson's fall from the biggest Tory Commons majority in thirty-two years to his ouster. 'He kept making exactly the same mistake, which was getting himself into a terrible position by not telling the truth, getting other people to go out and say the same thing, and then the house of cards collapsing,' the former leader said. 'If you ask the question "Why is Boris Johnson not still prime minister?" the only answer I can come up with is that there were these personal failings. I mean, how do you go from having an eighty-seat majority to going in three years?!'[127] How indeed.

9

Forty-Nine Days

LIZ TRUSS WAS in tears in the Cabinet Room.[1] Before her was Kwasi Kwarteng, the chancellor she was sacking. How quickly everything had turned. Just six weeks earlier the pair had been mapping out her premiership in the late summer sun, high on the inevitability of triumph in the Conservative leadership race. Three weeks before to the day Truss had sat grinning by Kwarteng's side as he outlined a tax-slashing 'mini'-Budget that delivered on more than a decade of joint dreaming. But what had followed – a tanking pound, soaring interest rates, a Bank of England intervention to save pension funds, a Tory revolt – had brought Truss to this point. Now, on Friday, 14 October 2022, there were dire warnings of mayhem when markets opened on Monday unless she went further. Her £45 billion package of tax cuts had to be shredded, senior civil servants said, with inevitable consequences for the man who announced them.[2] The prime minister felt she had no choice but to sack one of her best friends in politics.[3]

Almost to the last Kwarteng was disbelieving that such a fate awaited. He had been hauled back from an International Monetary Fund (IMF) summit in Washington, DC, a gathering Truss had pleaded with him not to attend as the lights began to flash red that week. The day before he had waved away speculation, responding, 'Absolutely, 100 per cent,' when asked in an interview whether he would be still be chancellor in a month's time.[4] The same response came in private when a senior Treasury aide passed on rumours that a sacking was coming and urged him to pre-empt the move with a resignation.[5] Even as he touched down back in London, the chancellor did not expect dismissal.[6] Then, minutes away from Number 10 in his ministerial car, he saw a tweet from *The Times*'s political editor Steven Swinford revealing that he was 'being sacked'.[7]

'I thought it was mad, I thought it was completely insane,' said Kwarteng in an interview.[8] The chancellor knew things were bad, the markets turbulent and a wing of the parliamentary party sharpening knives. He believed there was still a 'fifty-fifty' chance of the Truss administration making it to the new year.[9] And if that could be achieved, who knew? But one surefire way to bring everything tumbling down was sacking your right-hand man and junking the policies that had won you the Tory leadership. For twenty fraught minutes, sitting around the coffin-shaped Cabinet table, Kwarteng tried to persuade Truss that killing off his Cabinet career would also sound the death knell for her.

'They're going to come after you now,' warned Kwarteng. 'They're coming after me already,' replied the prime minister. 'They're going to ask you: If you've sacked him for doing what you campaigned on, why are you still there?' the chancellor warned.[10] Reporters would do just that hours later in a painful press conference, without drawing a clear answer. Kwarteng asked who his replacement would be. The answer: Jeremy Hunt. 'Hunt?! He's going to reverse everything!' exclaimed Kwarteng.[11] (Hunt, a Tory centrist, would be no less surprised himself by the news of his selection. Early that morning, on holiday in Brussels, he would get a text from Truss on her new number asking him to call. Hunt would ignore the message, assuming it was a hoax.[12]) Kwarteng's pleas fell on deaf ears. The decision had been made. Before leaving the Cabinet Room, that epicentre of British political power, the now ex-chancellor made a prediction: 'You've got three weeks.'[13] He would be wrong, but not by much. Truss would announce her resignation six days later.

What explains the meltdown that was the Liz Truss premiership? At forty-nine days, it was the shortest tenure of any prime minister since the position had been established three centuries earlier. Just seven weeks. There are longer summer internships. The second shortest premiership, that of George Canning, lasted twice as many days and only finished because he died. Near the end, as events spiralled out of control, the *Daily Star* newspaper set up a webcam trained on a photograph of Truss and a wilting lettuce with stuck-on googly eyes to see which would last longest. The lettuce won.

For so much of her Cabinet career Truss had appeared a pragmatist.

Keeping a seat at the top table from David Cameron's 'hug a hoodie' Conservatism, through Theresa May's sober and serious striving, to Boris Johnson's 'out with a bang' hard Brexit had required political malleability. But that cloaked an essential truth: Liz Truss was an ideologue. She had a core set of convictions – perhaps more deeply felt than those of any of her three predecessors – centred on low taxes, pared-back regulation and the state getting out of the way. Once she was in the top job, the constraints were gone. Egged on by fellow 'true believers', the mini-Budget grew and grew, remaining 'mini' in name only. Then it collided with reality. In the eagerness to bring about her long-held vision for the economy, Truss went too far, too fast. The irony was that the implosion that followed put the promised land she so longed for even further out of reach.

It was only by the slimmest of margins that Liz Truss had reached Number 10 in the first place. When Boris Johnson resigned, she was on the other side of the world. The then foreign secretary had ummed and ahhed about whether to attend the G20 summit in Bali with Johnson teetering amid ministerial resignations. Even at a refuelling stopover in Dubai, Truss was still debating turning the plane around. A clear message from a senior civil servant that she would have to quit the Cabinet to do so, since the minister's attendance was required, helped clear minds.[14] Truss did attend, but just hours after arriving Johnson went. 'It was nuts. I watched Boris resign on TV in my hotel room,' recalled Truss in an interview.[15] Now with the head of the government's departure official, she hurried back to join the successor race.

Truss had long thought about a leadership run. Her aides knew she wanted the top job, though it often went unspoken.[16] Elevation to the Foreign Office in September 2021 gave her the great office of state platform that has so often provided a stepping stone to Number 10. From early 2022 her team knew that, given Boris's woes, they had to be ready. The usual MP engagements that any Cabinet minister carries out – part policy soundings, part keeping the troops on side, part building connections for future career progression – were turned up: 'fizz with Liz', as some of the drinks dos were dubbed by the media. Yet, in terms of the spectrum of leadership manoeuvrings going on at the time, many insiders insist she remained near the 'back Boris' end of things. 'She was fiercely loyal to Boris,' said one Truss adviser.[17] Another aide felt she was 'slightly holding herself back'.[18] Ranil Jayawardena, a key MP backer, recalled being rebuffed when he urged her to do more to win over colleagues: 'She was pretty resolute that she wasn't willing to do anything.'[19] Adam Jones, then Truss's press adviser in the Foreign Office, summed it up: 'It would be wrong to say we weren't thinking about a possible leadership bid at some point, but Liz was always explicit that she would never do anything to destabilise Boris.'[20] In public, Truss adopted a '100 per cent' support position for Boris, having half an eye on the pro-Johnson membership that would pick the next leader. If 100 per cent was an exaggeration, any sober assessment of loyalty to the incumbent prime minister would have put a higher figure on hers than that of Rishi Sunak.

Once back on terra firma, Truss joined the scramble for colleague support. There were just thirteen days between Johnson's resignation on 7 July 2022 and the final ballot selecting which two candidates' names would go forward to the party members for the deciding vote. The usual arm-twisting and carrot-dangling played out as Tory MPs whittled down the list of contenders. Some did not raise enough support to make the first vote: Sajid Javid, Grant Shapps and Rehman Chishti. Others were knocked out early: Jeremy Hunt first, followed by Nadhim Zahawi, Suella Braverman and Tom Tugendhat. Deals were done to secure the support of those who quit. Braverman was explicitly promised the home secretary role by Truss if she endorsed her quickly, according to two Truss campaign sources.[21] Braverman did so and would get the job. Tugendhat was considered for the Foreign Office, but he hesitated on a public declaration.[22] Eventually he would become security minister, a more junior role.

The problem throughout was that Truss was not in the top two. Rishi Sunak had stormed into an early lead, which he kept. But it was Penny Mordaunt, the former defence secretary whose fluid speaking style and Navy backstory chimed with the base, who occupied second spot. For rounds one, two, three and four, Truss was in third. Eviction loomed. The departure of Kemi Badenoch – Team Truss suspected her candidacy was backed by Michael Gove as a way of splitting the Right and helping Sunak get a clear run, though that was never proved – set up a final ballot of Sunak, Mordaunt and Truss. The result was announced on 20 July. Sunak had won votes from 137 Tory MPs. Truss got 113, leapfrogging Mordaunt on 105. She had done it, but only just. If five Truss backers had voted for Mordaunt instead, it would have been the latter in the final two and, judging by the grassroots hostility to Sunak that would emerge, possibly also in Number 10. On such margins hang the fates of nations.

For the second leg, the contest with Sunak alone, Truss strengthened her operation. Mark Fullbrook, an experienced political operator, was drafted in as campaign manager. Fullbrook had been the 'F' in Lynton Crosby and Mark Textor's company 'CTF' before going his own way. He had also headed up Boris Johnson's 2019 leadership triumph. There had been less success during the current campaign, Fullbrook hitching his wagon first to Zahawi, then to Mordaunt. But when the call came through from Truss, Fullbrook expressed his interest in the role – even though pursuing it meant cutting short a holiday in Lebanon with his wife.[23] Meeting later at the townhouse just off Westminster's Smith Square that was acting as her campaign HQ, Fullbrook had a 'frank and open' chat with Truss, as he did with all his candidates, asking about any skeletons she might have in her closet.[24] The foreign secretary gave reassurances before removing Fullbrook's phone from the room and admitting one: 'I think the Russians have hacked my phone.'[25] The extraordinary alleged targeting, which would later come out publicly, was already known to those who needed to know. Fullbrook said yes to the job.

The stark difference in the positions of the two potential prime ministers was clear from the start, especially on the economy. At the heart of her pitch Truss had put reversing two tax rises that Rishi Sunak had announced as chancellor – a 1.25 percentage point increase in National Insurance and a jump in corporation tax from 19 to 25 per cent. This matched what she genuinely believed. It also exploited a Sunak weakness. Alongside Johnson, he had set the UK's tax burden on its trajectory to its highest point since the 1940s.

Truss's allies dubbed Sunak the 'socialist' chancellor. Meanwhile Sunak preached fiscal prudence. It would be morally irresponsible to pay for such tax cuts with debt piled on future generations, his argument went. It would also be economically foolish. The biggest threat was not stuttering growth but out-of-control inflation. Slashing tax would encourage spending just as prices were rocketing up, whilst Truss's plan to pay for it all with borrowing would leave the UK more exposed to rising interest rates.

Weeks later, Sunak supporters would repeat the lines with 'told you so' smiles as Truss's theories were tested on the open market. The problem is that, in politics, you only get to enact your policies if you win enough votes. The skill is fusing your beliefs and ideal approach with what the electorate wants. In this, Sunak, still in only his seventh year as an MP, was trumped by Truss, who was running for Tory council seats when her rival was still a teenager. 'The campaign was very straightforward,' said Fullbrook in an interview. 'The fundamental difference between the Rishi campaign and the Liz campaign was that they fought the wrong war.'[26] Team Sunak appeared to be pitching for the electorate at large, not the 'selectorate' that would determine the race: 170,000 paid-up Conservative Party members. Evidence that the 'no tax cuts yet' message was misfiring came in a switch of position from Sunak on the last day of July. He announced a 4p cut in the basic rate of income tax. The small print showed it did not strictly undercut his position: the reductions were way off, coming in between 2024 and 2029. But the fact that Sunak felt the need to sell a major tax cut, after weeks of decrying rivals for doing just that, was telling. From that point Fullbrook knew they would win.[27]

What was more hidden from view was the dislike, at times bordering on contempt, in which the two candidates held each other. As much can be revealed via the testimonies of multiple members of the Truss and Sunak inner circles. As Cabinet colleagues, the pair had tussled over policy. Truss was one of only three ministers, alongside Jacob Rees-Mogg and Lord Frost, to oppose openly the National Insurance rise to fund social care reforms during the Cabinet discussion in September 2021, earning a rebuke in the room from Sunak. Another friction point was the question of sanctions on Russia after its full-scale invasion of Ukraine in February 2022. Truss saw Sunak, defender of the UK economy as chancellor, as an obstacle to tough action. According to two sources, the foreign secretary was pushing for action so firmly that she offered to have a secure phone driven from London to Sunak's constituency home in Yorkshire one weekend to obtain a speedy decision from him.[28] One aide recalled Truss being so frustrated with the chancellor's refusal to go further in punishing Vladimir Putin that she once jokingly dubbed him 'Russi Sunak'.[29] In turn, Sunak expressed frustration at Truss opposing Treasury plans to pay for extra military support for Ukraine out of the overseas development aid budget. A Truss aide recalled overhearing the chancellor pushing back forcefully down the line, apparently angered at press briefings about the rift, as they were being driven in a ministerial car.[30] Near the end of the Johnson years Sunak told one of his most supportive ministers that he would never serve in a Truss Cabinet if she won.[31] A Truss adviser summed the situation up: 'They had no relationship. They clashed a lot.'[32]

Those confrontations had been grounded in policy differences, albeit heightened by a lack of personal connection and laced with a growing sense of leadership rivalry. Once Johnson fell and the contest to succeed him erupted the real bitterness followed, at least from the Truss camp. Sunak's allies were blamed for spreading malicious rumours about her private life. Truss's biographers Harry Cole and James Heale reported that two ministers and four MPs backing Sunak briefed journalists with unverified gossip, including claims of an affair with an aide – claims dismissed as outright smears by her allies.[33] There was cold fury at the groundless slurs from the top of the Truss team. Other barbs grated. Sunak's mocking question in an ITV-screened leadership debate during the initial stage of the contest – 'Liz, in your past you've been both a Liberal Democrat and a Remainer. I was just wondering which one you regretted most?' – angered Truss's team.[34] Though she too would not hold back, responding to the jibe by citing Sunak's public-school education and more widely portraying her opponent as a Boris-betraying Lefty in Tory clothing.

Before that TV debate, while getting their make-up done the

pair had sat next to each other for ten minutes, no more than a metre apart, and barely exchanged a word. 'I can see the make-up ladies and the hairdresser just wanting the ground to swallow them up,' recalled one person there.[35] By the time of the head-to-head stage of the contest, when the remaining two candidates had to do a dozen leadership hustings in front of party members across the UK, relations had deteriorated further. Truss would wait in her room rather than at the edge of the stage when up after Sunak to avoid seeing him.[36] She would also refuse to listen to his performances, turning off TVs when he was on and instead asking to be briefed by aides.[37] Even at the final hustings event at Wembley Arena, Truss tried to get out of a joint photo with Sunak and complained about being bounced into it afterwards.[38] A senior Truss campaign figure spoke of the bruising nature of the contest: 'It was brutal, really brutal. I think it poisoned the well. I thought it was much nastier than the Hunt–Boris race [for the leadership in 2019].'[39]

By results day, 5 September 2022, Truss's victory was close to a certainty. Every poll of Tory members had put her streets ahead. Members of Sunak's campaign who would have been heading into senior government roles if he won had already booked overseas holidays. The two candidates were told the result together backstage in the Queen Elizabeth II Centre a few minutes before the announcement. Truss had won 57 per cent of the vote, comfortably beating Sunak on 43 per cent, though by a smaller margin than early polls had suggested.[40] There was a 'very brief' well done from Sunak, according to one person there.[41] In the auditorium when the news was broken, amid cheers and applause, Truss did not even acknowledge Sunak as she strode to the stage triumphant. It did not matter now. She was victorious.

As with all prime ministers, clues about the real Liz Truss can be found in her life away from the cameras. Truss was a lover of karaoke. Aides disagree on whether Oasis's 'Champagne Supernova' or Pulp's 'Common People' was her favourite karaoke tune, though it was the latter that got press aides worried given the 'Tory toffs' stereotype.[42] One flight back from a G20 summit in Rwanda saw the then foreign secretary order that a mic be hooked up to the plane's sound system so songs could be belted out.[43] Truss liked a drink, usually white wine. She had a particular favourite brand of Sauvignon Blanc.[44] She would share a bottle with aides over dinner, or on the way back from an overseas trip, or at an ambassador's residence during visits – always after work. She was a reader. Advisers recalled her thumbing a biography of the US President Ronald Reagan: a telling choice given that 'Reaganomics' – cutting tax, supply-side reforms and an ease with rising deficits – was an economic lodestar for her.[45] A former Soviet Union agricultural minister's musings on the economy and future-facing works by the science journalist Matt Ridley also made her reading list.[46]

Truss had 'a very dry, contrarian sense of humour'.[47] In small meetings with trusted aides – her favoured format for chewing the fat – there could be blunt, 'say the unsayable' jokes to prompt a chuckle. 'She liked to use humour to liven things up, especially if it kept officials on their toes. She had a remarkable ability to talk about topics normally only to suddenly say something eye-wateringly provocative or mischievous,' said Asa Bennett, her chief speech-writer.[48] On the other hand, some who worked with Truss at times found her socially awkward. Two close aides said she lacked 'emotional intelligence', showing a disconnect in conversation.[49] 'Not a natural manager of people,' added one.[50]

She was family-oriented. Her husband, the accountant Hugh O'Leary, was another long-time Tory who, like Truss, had stood to be a councillor in the late 1990s. Their daughters, Frances and Liberty, would be Facetimed by their mother during trips abroad and introduced to aides.[51] When this author interviewed Truss during the Tory leadership race, both teenagers were in campaign HQ. To keep them busy one had been tasked with auditing all her mother's past departments. (The Department for Environment, Food and Rural Affairs came out on top because it had brilliant tea ladies.)[52] Allies who saw Truss away from Westminster would note how normal and grounded her home life appeared. 'She doesn't have a wide social circle. She lives and breathes politics and her family,' said Adam Jones, her communications chief at successive government departments.[53]

Born to a university mathematics lecturer father and a mother who was a nurse and a teacher, conviction politics appeared to be in the family's blood. Both her parents were 'to the left of Labour', with her mother a committed member of the Campaign for Nuclear Disarmament (CND).[54] Truss, who spent much of her childhood in Paisley, just west of Glasgow, recalled attending Scottish CND marches, chanting along with 'Maggie, Maggie, Maggie – oot, oot, oot'.[55] Strictly she was not the first prime minister ever to have attended a comprehensive school – that claim by Truss at Tory conference was disproved by some media outlets – but at most only a handful of others had.[56] Truss favoured shopping at Tesco, often reached first for the *Daily Express* and was thrifty when it came to home refurbishments, according to aides – not habits that characterise, say, David Cameron's Notting Hill set. Her intellect got her to Oxford – another PPE-er, like Cameron and Sunak, going to Merton College – where she would become president of the university's Liberal Democrats group. That early party allegiance was held against her during the Tory leadership race. A kinder interpretation of her political evolution would be of an instinctive liberal working out which party fitted her convictions best.

Once elected to Parliament in 2010, representing South West Norfolk, Truss was a quick riser up the ministerial ladder. She was given her first proper government job, the childcare brief, in 2012 and became Cameron's environment secretary in 2014, kick-starting an eight-year unbroken run in Cabinet that would end only when she quit as prime minister. Justice secretary would come next, her career dented when she failed to defend the judiciary properly when Theresa May's Downing Street railed against judges who ruled that Parliament had to approve the formal triggering of Brexit. According to one aide Truss still cursed going against her instincts years later.[57] A stint as chief secretary to the Treasury – an adviser said that the chancellorship was for a long time her dream job – was followed by the trade brief under Boris Johnson, before she reached the Foreign Office.[58] The rise saw her ride the Brexit divide that had split her party. Truss was a reluctant Remainer. David Cameron in his biography admitted surprise that she voted to stay in the European Union. Jason Stein, a long-time Truss adviser, said by way of explanation that 'the things that really bother Liz –

regulation, taxes, house-building, childcare -- none of them are to do with Europe.'⁵⁹ She also feared it would dominate Westminster's bandwidth for a decade to come. Even so, morphing publicly from an 'Osbornite Remainer to Johnsonite Brexiteer' was some political feat.⁶⁰

During her rise up the Westminster ladder two realities emerged that are key to understanding what came next. One was the bond she formed with a like-minded fellow 2010 newbie. Kwasi Kwarteng was an economic historian by training, having secured a PhD from Cambridge University with a study of the late seventeenth-century currency crisis – a useful grounding given what happened once he reached the Treasury. A year after their election, Kwarteng persuaded Truss to contribute to *After the Coalition: A Conservative Agenda for Britain*, a book co-written with three other new Tory MPs. Another, *Britannia Unchained: Global Lessons for Growth and Prosperity*, would follow, as did a body to push their twenty-first-century Thatcherism: the Free Enterprise Group.

Truss and Kwarteng were not identical in their outlook. She was more libertarian – her younger daughter's name, Liberty, was a clue in that regard – while he considered himself more of an orthodox Conservative. But the overlap was sizable. Kwarteng explained:

> We genuinely believed the tax burden was too high, we genuinely thought that we needed to incentivise growth. I loved the fact that she kept saying that profit wasn't a dirty word, I think that was really refreshing. And I think there was a frustration with 'splitting the difference', that kind of centrism where you're both social democracy parties and you're both putting up taxes and you're kind of hugging the centre. She wanted – rightly, I think – to strike out in a different direction.⁶¹

In an interview Truss distilled her political outlook in a similar manner: 'I've always been a low-tax Conservative. I mean, that's my DNA . . . I'm sceptical of government, fundamentally, and that is why I joined the Conservative Party in the first place. I believe in people being able to run their own lives.'⁶² When the time came to turn ideals into actions, the pair would largely be seeing things from the same point of view.

A second trait would also emerge in Truss's eight years in the Cabinet, one largely hidden from view but nonetheless critical. It would be dubbed the 'Spinal Tap' approach, a phrase coined by her speech-writer Asa Bennett. Truss always wanted to 'turn it up to eleven and, only if necessary, turn it down again', said Bennett – just like the band in the 1984 comedy mockumentary who delighted in the fact that their amps went one higher than the traditional ten.[63] Fellow Cabinet ministers had other words for it: a 'manic intensity', an 'energy' for change, a determination to go as big and bold as possible.[64] Dominic Cummings, a special adviser in the Department of Education when Truss was a minister there, coined a more derogatory term for her – 'the human hand grenade', liable to explode at a moment's notice. Multiple aides who saw her approach first-hand offered generalised scenarios for how things typically played out in her departments. Civil servants would say fifty things could be done. Truss would say she wanted a hundred and fifty. Civil servants and aides would then have panicked conversations. Eventually they would offer one hundred or seventy-five things. Truss would then settle for one of those options, having succeeded in bouncing officials to go higher. It would be similar in negotiations with Cabinet colleagues. 'She always turned things up to the max and beyond, then she'd get whittled down,' said one adviser who was by Truss's side for years.[65] The approach could work well during Whitehall bargaining for a politician with convictions but without the final say. The issue came when she got the top job. For when the prime minister says turn it up to eleven, there is no one above them to say no.

In retrospect, where things began to go wrong was at Chevening. Set in 3,000 acres of lush fields and woodland in the Kent countryside, the seventeenth-century country house has been the preserve of foreign secretaries seeking a getaway for decades. Its lake, maze and walled gardens offer a chance to breathe away from the stuffy corridors of Westminster. The Grade I listed mansion's rooms – all 115 of them, including fifteen bedrooms – provide a backdrop of splendour to evening entertainments. And it was here, in the second half of August 2022, that Liz Truss holed up. The race for the Conservative Party leadership was still officially ongoing, but her campaign chiefs were confident of victory. Planning for power, not spending every minute canvassing members, was the focus now. It was time to prepare the transition.

There was a heady atmosphere. Truss was on the cusp of obtaining the premiership, secured with an undiluted message of low-tax Tory economics and cheered on by an adoring grassroots base: Outside the sun was beaming, the late-summer heatwave scorching the turf. On the first of Chevening's three floors, Truss would sit with varying groups of aides and would-be Cabinet ministers, windows wide open with the gardens glimpsed beyond, engaged in blue-sky thinking. 'There was a very giddy sense that Thatcher is back,' recalled Simon Clarke, one of Truss's MP champions soon to be handed a plum Cabinet job, who sat in on many of the discussions. 'It really was a sense of untrammelled opportunity,' he added, not least in regard to the economic policy package they were assembling.

> There was a very intense sense that Liz's instinct was that we go now, we go strong. She once joked to me that basically we do what's needed, then we go into a bunker for six months while it all shakes down and we send you out on TV to defend it. It was going to be a big, powerful moment.[66]

Truss had already begun to map out the shape of her Cabinet. Allies with a similar outlook would be placed in key economic posts: Kwarteng as chancellor, Clarke as communities secretary, Jacob Rees-Mogg as business secretary, Chris Philp as chief secretary to the Treasury. Her closest political friend, fellow East Anglian MP Thérèse Coffey – the pair were known as 'Liz and Tiz' inside the campaign – would become deputy prime minister and health secretary. Leadership also-rans would be rewarded with Cabinet spots: Mordaunt, Badenoch, Tugendhat, Braverman, Zahawi. But for the runner-up, Sunak, there would be no olive branch of a job offer, breaking with a precedent set by Boris Johnson, Theresa May and David Cameron. Truss told friends that his 'nihilistic' campaigning approach ruled him out of her Cabinet.[67]

It was not just Sunak – almost all of his big backers were denied ministerial positions. Out went Grant Shapps and Dominic Raab, as well as Michael Gove – Tory heavy-hitters with a feel for realpolitik.

The choice not to tie in Rishi-ites was deliberate. One senior Truss campaign figure said that she 'couldn't trust them' and would later express no regret over the call.[68] Certainly loyalty is a valuable asset in Cabinet. Theresa May found how difficult it was to deliver Brexit with a split top team. But, with the last two party leaders having been killed off by colleagues, it was also a risk. Mark Fullbrook, who would become Truss's chief of staff in Downing Street, now sees a misstep. 'The answer is, in hindsight, yes,' he said when asked if more Sunak allies should have been brought in.[69] Instead, already bruised by their defeat, they were now locked out of government, egos dented and with all the time in the world to plot.

But it is in policy, not personnel, that Chevening's significance lies. The seeds of the mini-Budget spectacular were planted there. Truss had two immediate challenges. One was how to help families with soaring energy costs after Russia's full-scale invasion of Ukraine. During the campaign she had warned against 'handouts' but privately, encouraged by Kwarteng, she had accepted the need to intervene.[70] As was the Truss way, she wanted the package to be big – a one-time move that would hold until the general election in two years' time – rather than have a steady drip of announcements. What would eventually be revealed in the first days of the Truss premiership was one of the biggest single fiscal moves in recent British politics. Households would have their average annual energy bills frozen at £2,500 for two years. It was a blank cheque: every penny by which the real cost rose above that amount would be paid by the Treasury. Business too would be protected. The Treasury later suggested the package could cost £60 billion for the first six months alone.[71] A final total of £100 billion-plus looked likely, or possibly as high as £150 billion on some estimates. On this occasion, political pragmatism had won the day over small-state ideology.

The second challenge was implementing the big tax cuts she had promised during the leadership campaign: reversing the National Insurance rise and cancelling the corporation tax hike. A third, removing green levies from energy bills, would go into the cost-freeze package. Truss wanted to unveil the tax cuts formally early in her tenure, partly to project momentum, partly because the National Insurance rise was already biting. Moreover, she believed that the sooner a major fiscal injection was made into the economy, the better the chances of avoiding recession and bringing about the growth that held the Tories' best hope of re-election. But that was not all. Truss wanted to go further still, encouraging new tax-shredding proposals. And so it was that the fatal mission creep began.

Simon Clarke, a believer to this day in the Truss low-tax vision, captured the dynamic:

> Things just started to overheat. Much as I love her, there can be no doubt that was absolutely at Liz's express instruction. There was no challenge brooked to the fact that the fiscal event needed to be as significant as it could possibly be and that opposition to that was profoundly unwelcome, And that is where, I think, Kwasi fell into the trap . . . He wanted expressly to be an enabling chancellor.[72]

One extra announcement would come to define the mini-Budget: the abolition of the 45p income tax rate. The so-called 'additional rate' had been a political trap laid for the Tories by Gordon Brown. It had not existed throughout New Labour's thirteen years in office but, with the end of the party's period in power appearing nigh, Brown timed the tax rise to take effect just before the 2010 election. If the Tories won and wanted to reverse it, they would have to take the political pain of cutting tax for the wealthiest during an economic recovery. George Osborne as chancellor tried to scrap the additional rate – then at 50 per cent – in 2012, but, amid Liberal Democrat coalition pressure, could only get it down to 45 per cent. So when getting rid of the tax band was floated there were nodding heads at Chevening, with the idea eventually included in a summary document drafted by Chris Philp, who would become chief secretary to the Treasury. For the principle, at least, there was near-universal support from the Truss brains trust.

That was not the last of it. It can be revealed that even bolder tax cuts were considered for the mini-Budget. One dwarfed the additional rate proposal: knocking out not just the 45 per cent top income tax band but also the 40 per cent middle band, leaving a single income tax rate of 20 per cent for everyone who reached the threshold. It was dubbed going 'full Estonia' by the ministers in the loop, since it echoed the Baltic nation's taxation system. The idea came from Rees-Mogg, the proposal detailed in a six hundred-word memo sent to Truss and seen by this author. One part read:

> The opportunity for a flat tax on income should be explored. Hungary and Romania have flat taxes of 16%, Lithuania and Georgia have 20% (less developed countries such as Mongolia and Kazakhstan also use them). Estonia has a flat tax of 20% (although changes in 2018 created exemptions bands, so strictly speaking this is now a partial flat tax). Research suggests the Baltic States' adoption of these in 1994–5 helped their rapid growth. We should aim for a 20% flat tax for income tax, corporation tax and capital gains tax (without changing National Insurance).[73]

The move would have cost around £41 billion, according to Rees-Mogg's estimates based on public Treasury numbers, and would have been funded by the abolition of tax reliefs on pension schemes and National Insurance contributions. It would have been the biggest shake-up of income tax in at least forty-four years and might have even exceeded Nigel Lawson's Tory-loved 1988 Budget which got rid of the 60 per cent upper rate. The proposal was, however, dismissed firmly by Kwarteng. Another blue-sky idea, scrapping inheritance tax in its entirety, was also proposed by Rees-Mogg. That was much cheaper, but again Kwarteng said no. Other proposals, though, got a receptive audience. Why not cut stamp duty, given that rising interest rates were hurting property prices? How about knocking off VAT on shopping for overseas visitors to help retailers in a flagging economy? And could the 1p basic income tax rate cut not be brought forward? Individually, each policy would be music to traditional Tory ears. Each too may have had its merits. Collectively, they swelled an already bulging tax-cutting package to bursting point.

Two other consequential decisions would be taken at Chevening. One: to avoid asking the Office for Budget Responsibility (OBR) to run the numbers on the mini-Budget. And two: to hold back announcements on spending cuts until later in the year. There was a rationale for both in the eyes of Truss and her inner circle. Assessments by the OBR, the government's official, independent forecaster created by Osborne in 2010 to provide more impartial economic figures, were only formally required twice a year. Already in 2022 there had been a flurry of fiscal moves as Johnson and Sunak wrestled soaring inflation and stuttering growth, not all of them assessed by the OBR. Nor had all the emergency injections of Covid cash – much bigger in total financially than Truss's tax cuts – been given the once-over before their announcement, such was the speed of lockdown decisions. Indeed, there was always going to be another fiscal statement in late 2022. That would reveal the Truss–Kwarteng plan for spending restraint – existing departmental budgets were to be kept, meaning inflation would take a huge bite out of them – and detail supply-side reforms, such as looser planning rules to boost house-building and a major push on broadband rollout. The OBR could run the numbers then, when everything was known.

There had been a big push from some that August to include spending restraint in the first set of announcements. Kwarteng, Clarke and Philp all made the case. An internal document pulled together by Philp that month explicitly made the point. 'Reasonable targeted reductions in the size of the state and public spending will support tax reductions and increase the productive capacity and growth of the economy', read part of one line. Another declared: 'We also need to maintain the confidence of the bond markets in our fiscal plans or we will find ourselves paying higher interest rates on new gilt issues.'[74] The truth of that statement would become clear all too soon. Philp, looking back, said in an interview:

> If the measures in the mini-Budget to reduce tax and deregulate had been accompanied by credible plans to restrain public spending and a clear fiscal framework then the financial markets would have been much more likely to accept it. That's why, at the time, I advocated internally to include credible and specific measures to restrain spending and a fiscal framework.[75]

The stance towards the official forecaster was shaped additionally by hostility. Truss had railed against the 'Treasury orthodoxy', and by extension the OBR, on the campaign trail. She thought that its forecasts underestimated the impact of tax cuts on improving growth and were almost always proved wrong in the end. The OBR's five-year prediction for the economy and government finances was seen as excessively constraining, boxing ministers into policy decisions with numbers that may well never come to pass. Kwarteng was of the same mind. So the incoming prime minister made a call before the summer was over: spending restraint and the OBR could wait. Let the tax cuts rain down, unfiltered.

It was pouring as Liz Truss approached Downing Street for the first time as prime minister. As she was being driven towards her new home in a ministerial car, having touched down in London after 'kissing hands' with the Queen at her Scottish estate of Balmoral, the heavens opened.[76] The podium placed outside Number 10 for her maiden speech as the country's leader, a series of wooden blocks spiralling like a precarious Jenga tower, was covered with a black bin bag to protect the microphone. Aides scanned radar forecasts to see if the rain would relent for a moment. It did, eventually, but as omens go it was a gift for the parliamentary sketch writers. 'As strong as the storm may be, I know that the British people are stronger,' Truss would declare in the speech. 'I am confident that together we can ride out the storm.'[77]

That same day, 6 September 2022, the firings began. With the new Cabinet appointed, it fell to Kwasi Kwarteng to deliver the most eye-catching dismissal. Arriving at the Treasury moments after being appointed chancellor, he was greeted, as is the custom, by the department's permanent secretary, Sir Tom Scholar. The pair shook hands and posed for a photograph. 'Don't publish the photographs,' Kwarteng muttered to Cameron Brown, his media-facing special adviser, as they headed into the building, entourage in tow. 'Why?' his aide asked. 'We're going to do it,' said his boss. 'What, now?!' 'Yes, we're going to do it now.'[78] Reaching the chancellor's office, Kwarteng asked Sir Tom for a word alone. There the blow was delivered: after a discussion with the prime minister, it had been decided that Sir Tom was surplus to requirements. He was being sacked, in practically Kwarteng's first act in the job. A Treasury career, including six years as the department's top official and five more as number two, was over. Sir Tom was 'totally outraged', Kwarteng recalled.[79] There was some resistance. 'This is what we want,' said the new chancellor.[80] And the deed was done – though not immediately announced. Sitting straight afterwards in a meeting with Kwarteng and other senior Treasury officials, Sir Tom was 'dead-eyed' and 'stony-faced', according to one person there, 'like he'd been hit by a bus'.[81] The ghosts of chancellors past would attend his farewell do: George Osborne, Philip Hammond, Sajid Javid as well as Labour's Alistair Darling. It would be hosted in the Bank of England by its governor Andrew Bailey. Here, personified, was the economic establishment Truss vilified. 'You could literally see the plotting taking place,' a former Treasury minister was told by one person there.[82]

The sacking was a joint decision. Truss saw Sir Tom as one of the architects of the 'Brownite' economic orthodoxy that had been established under New Labour and was not challenged hard enough by Cameron and Osborne. She too, according to multiple aides and colleagues, had bristled at Sir Tom while chief secretary to the Treasury, when she felt sidelined. One Cabinet colleague maintained that Truss 'deeply disliked' Sir Tom and had felt 'very thwarted' in the role.[83] An aide with her then said, 'No one at the Treasury had the time of day for her.'[84] She even once got a Budget summary smuggled out of the building to know what was about to be announced because the Treasury, under Hammond, had locked her out of discussions.[85] Kwarteng too wanted a change: 'This was someone who was part of Cameron's Brexit renegotiation team. My view was that it was best to move him on quickly.'[86]

As with much of the Truss premiership, it was not that the individual move was inherently wrong. Sir Tom had been in post since 2016. A Cabinet minister can have a say in the senior team: Tories often look at the US system and wish they had more power to hire and fire senior officials. Truss, after all, had projected her desire to take on 'Treasury orthodoxy' and won a mandate to do so. It was, rather, the manner of the sacking, combined with the wider questioning of economic norms, that really raised eyebrows. 'I thought it was gratuitous,' said one Truss Cabinet minister, seeing it as further evidence of the new prime minister's 'ultra-high-octane approach'.[87] Kwarteng has wondered if the move was too brutally done but played down its significance: 'Given what we did, him being there wouldn't have made much difference.'[88]

When posterity considers the Liz Truss tenure, its most memorable moment may well be one totally unlinked to her premiership: the death of Queen Elizabeth II. It was from the House of Commons that the wider world first got wind that something was wrong, notes being passed on the frontbenches as Truss presented her energy bill guarantee. That day, 8 September 2022, was Truss's third in the job. The news that the monarch had died, ending a seventy-year reign, was announced on the BBC at 6.30 p.m. For the nation, a period of official mourning and reflection followed. For the prime minister, plans were put on ice. Truss, never the most natural orator, had to become communicator-in-chief, channelling the country's mood and capturing the moment of history. A funeral had to be staged: the plans had already been prepared, but it was still the biggest operation in the Metropolitan Police's history as scores of world leaders and dignitaries descended on London. Usual government business was paused for the eleven days between the announcement and the funeral.

The ceremonies were nonpartisan. There were, though, political impacts for a premiership that was just getting going. Members of the Truss inner circle identify two. One had to do with the energy intervention. It was not just eye-wateringly expensive but, according to opinion polls, overwhelmingly popular.[89] No surprise, really, when a government announces that the entire population will be protected from exorbitant energy bills for two years. The idiosyncrasies of timing, however, meant the move was lost on much of the public. A story sure to dominate that night's TV headlines and the next day's newspapers slid down the bulletins when news of the monarch's death broke. 'Liz got no credit for the energy package,' one senior Number 10 figure noted.[90] Secondly, the funeral pushed back the tax-cuts announcement, which had been pencilled in for week two, to week three. That gave time for the package to swell further, the extra week allowing for more changes and more temptation to up the ante. 'It probably led to her downfall because she had more time to think about it and put more things in,' a Truss Cabinet minister who has worked on tax policy would later remark.[91]

Journalists commonly misunderstand the development of a Budget, Treasury insiders often argue.[92] It is less a single, neatly shaped package, and more a process revolving around a spreadsheet – dubbed the 'scorecard' – where a huge list of policies are either switched on or off, the overall cost totted up at the bottom. One morning a policy can be in, out in the afternoon, and by the evening back in again. Final lock-in comes late. Officially the Truss and Kwarteng intervention was dubbed 'The Growth Plan'. It soon acquired the nickname 'mini-Budget' from reporters trying to explain to readers what was coming.

From mid-August to mid-September the circle informed of what was coming shrank markedly. At first MP supporters could chip in with thoughts at Chevening. Then the group narrowed to only incoming Cabinet ministers with economic briefs. Then each senior minister began focusing on their own areas – Simon Clarke on planning reforms, Jacob Rees-Mogg on the energy intervention – losing sight of the overall package. Senior advisers who voiced scepticism in the group chats got icy stares from their boss and soon found themselves on the outside. Two recalled a conversation at Chevening where skipping the OBR assessment was floated. 'That's mental,' said one – or words to that effect.[93] 'That's the one thing that really gives us credibility,' said another.[94] Truss asked for other opinions. From then on, the pair felt they were 'totally sidelined'.[95] Some insiders saw a division in Team Truss between 'true believers' and 'pragmatists', with those in the latter camp frozen out of discussions.[96] By the end of August, all the core elements that would be announced were there, but it was not yet clear which were fixed and which were only potential. Come September and the entry into government, it would be just Truss, Kwarteng and a handful of others – especially in the Treasury – who were in the loop.

There has been much focus on whether each individual element of the mini-Budget came first from Truss or Kwarteng. That, though, distracts from the central dynamic that explains the overall package. Both politicians signed it off, both believed in its measures. What transformed the announcements from the mere fulfilment of core campaign promises into a bolder shredding of tax was a new prime minister determined to go big and a like-minded chancellor happy to go along with her. Kwarteng was already on record talking about the importance of Number 11 backing Number 10 after the Johnson–Sunak clashes. 'They were too close,' one Truss Cabinet minister later concluded. 'They were drinking the same Kool-Aid.'[97]

Kwarteng, looking back, could see errors. 'We were committed to delivering the things she did on the campaign trail and then everything got ramped up. I think that was a mistake,' he said. 'Liz's obsession was that she only had two years [before the next election], which is actually quite a long time. She was obsessed that she'd do everything now . . . It was high-risk.' Kwarteng's biggest regret was not announcing spending restraints alongside tax cuts to show it was not all just to be paid for with more debt. 'I can't stress enough – I wish I had the paper trail – but there was spending restraint in that package as well,' he said. 'If I could do the mini-Budget again, I would have announced it later [in the year] and I would have had spending in there.'[98]

Truss expressed fewer regrets. She saw the mini-Budget as not just the manifestation of the approach she was elected to deliver but a chance to push back on the New Labour-era economic orthodoxy which she believed was wrong for Britain. Truss explained her thinking in an interview:

> Over the last two decades we have not done enough supply-side reform to grow the British economy – like deregulating planning to get more houses built, axing unnecessary red tape for business, especially after Brexit – and cutting taxes. This left us in a very difficult economic situation. I was trying to defibrillate the patient at a very late stage in the day. And you could say, 'Well, maybe I shouldn't have done that, maybe I should have watered stuff down.' But you can't campaign in a leadership election as an insurgent and then go into Number 10 and not follow through. It was a difficult set of policies to enact with stiff opposition, but I believed the alternative of doing nothing was worse.[99]

Around 8 p.m. the night before the mini-Budget, Kwarteng completed one last read-through of his speech in the wood-panelled Number 11 dining room before aides and smiled. 'We're just about to undo twenty years of social democratic malaise,' he said, according to one there. 'This is going to excite everyone.' The source added: 'He was happy.'[100]

★

'We promised to prioritise growth,' thundered Kwasi Kwarteng. 'We promised a new approach for a new era. We promised, Mr Speaker, to release the enormous potential of this country.' His voice was hoarse as he bellowed over the hear, hears of gleeful Tory colleagues. 'Our Growth Plan has delivered all those promises and more. And I commend it to the House.'[101] Amid cheers from the green benches behind him there came a pat on the arm from the prime minister, who was sitting by the chancellor's side. It had taken just twenty-five minutes to deliver one of the most eye-catching UK fiscal statements in the twenty-first century. The biggest tax cuts since 1972 had been announced, worth an annual £45 billion. So many rabbits had been pulled from hats it was hard to keep count. The fine print revealed the sting – £72 billion in extra borrowing in the next half-year alone to fund the tax bonfire and energy price cap.[102] The argument had been put with naked boldness. 'For too long in this country, we have indulged in a fight over redistribution,' the chancellor had said. 'Now, we need to focus on growth, not just how we tax and spend.'[103]

The two costliest tax cuts were the ones that had been well advertised in advance. Scrapping the corporation tax hike would cost £19 billion a year come 2026, while reversing the National Insurance rise would end up at £15 billion, according to Treasury estimates. Together this pair of campaign promises made up more than two-thirds of the total tax cut – far and away the most significant measures. It was not in terms of raw cost but of surprise factor that the extra sweeteners had their impact. VAT-free shopping for visitors (£2 billion), raising the stamp duty threshold (£1.6 billion), freezing alcohol duties for a year (£600 million) and bringing forward the 1p cut in basic income tax (set actually to make money come 2026) were individually not that costly. Nor was the biggest reveal: abolishing the 45p additional income tax rate (£2 billion), a move announced with a flourish by Kwarteng near the end of the speech.[104] But all together they significantly exceeded expectations.

'Jesus Christ!' a Tory MP was heard exclaiming in the Chamber as the abolition of the 45p rate was announced.[105] Figures closer to the centre of power felt the same shock. Many senior government ministers had been in the dark, the 45p cut not mentioned in

Kwarteng's pre-Budget Cabinet address – though such briefings are usually kept vague to avoid market-sensitive leaks. Mark Fullbrook, Truss's chief of staff, did not know the 45p move was coming.[106] Nor did Jamie Hope, her director of policy, or Iain Carter, her director of political strategy.[107] Adam Jones, the political director of communications whose job it was to spin the news, was only updated late in the process.[108] Senior Number 10 folk had sought out versions of the final mini-Budget document before the speech, only to be told their name was not on Truss's approved list.[109] Some caught wind of early snippets. Jason Stein, one of Truss's closest political advisers, found details of the stamp duty cut left on a printer and was taken aback that it had been included.[110] Another measure, the lifting of the bankers' bonus cap, set alarm bells ringing with the comms team when it leaked a few days early.[111] When the official document did drop, Hope and Carter were amazed by how much had made it in. 'That's going to piss people off, that's going to piss people off,' Hope said at the time, picking out surprises.[112] Others beyond Westminster had their noses put out of joint too. David Cameron texted his friend and former chancellor George Osborne during the mini-Budget speech to make clear his fury as Kwarteng suggested that none of his Tory predecessors had pursued a plan for growth.[113]

The eager nods from Tory MPs were matched by right-leaning newspapers, which had long championed many of the moves. 'At last! A true Tory Budget,' cheered the *Daily Mail*'s front page. 'Kwarteng gambles on biggest tax cuts in half a century,' declared the *Daily Telegraph*. 'We've got the "courage to bet big" on Britain,' splashed the *Daily Express*.[114] Business bodies too tripped over themselves to give two thumbs up. Glowing comments from executives at the Confederation of British Industry, UK Hospitality, the British Chambers of Commerce, the Federation of Small Businesses and the Scottish Chambers of Commerce, to name but a few, were circulated in a press release by the Treasury.[115] So the Tory media influencers and corporate movers and shakers had given double ticks. A third source of reaction, though, had not been given as much consideration: the markets.

What was it that led traders to take fright? It is a question that still loops around the heads of the mini-Budget's authors. There had been no panic when the government spent around £400 billion to prop up the economy during the Covid pandemic, paid for by debt. Nor had major tremors been felt when Truss revealed her energy bill guarantee, cost estimated at north of £100 billion. Was it the extra tax cuts? They went further and faster than had been predicted, no doubt. The 45p tax cut also showed a willingness to take political risks, given Labour's inevitable framing of it as handouts for the wealthy during a cost-of-living crisis. Was it the new mountain of debt? By effectively placing a 'come back later' sign by the void marked spending cuts and supply-side reforms, Kwarteng and Truss had underscored their comfort with piling up borrowing for unfunded tax cuts despite rising interest rates. Or was it the OBR's absence? Think tanks filled the silence, the Institute for Fiscal Studies predicting that the Tory promise to bring down debt over five years would be missed, as investors cast a wary eye over the new leadership which had chosen to act without the familiar framework of official independent forecasts. Sir Tom Scholar's sacking added to the sense – an accurate one – of the economic status quo being under fire. Whatever combination of the above factors caused the reaction, the markets were definitely spooked.

Chris Philp, number two in the Treasury, jumped the gun when he tweeted early on Friday: 'Great to see sterling strengthening on the back of the new UK Growth Plan.'[116] In a list of ill-fated victory declarations in recent Westminster history, this would take some beating. Later that day, as the announcements sank in, the pound slid to a thirty-seven-year low against the US dollar. Worse was to follow. On Sunday, Kwarteng casually remarked that there was 'more to come' on tax cuts during an interview on BBC One's *Sunday with Laura Kuenssberg*.[117] Number 10 and Number 11 press aides had talked before the interview about the need not to lean in on tax cuts.[118] Kwarteng, an academic and financier by training, was never the most disciplined media performer, often making the mistake of trying to answer the question asked. 'You are given a script. Your job is to read it out on TV and not answer the question and engage,' a Treasury insider would later moan.[119] Kwarteng played down its impact, saying the measures not his words were most significant, but admitted: 'Looking back it was probably a mistake.'[120] The implication was that the mini-Budget was just the start. Nadhim Zahawi, Kwarteng's predecessor as chancellor, who had advised waiting until the new year before unveiling tax cuts, was watching the interview on TV. When the remark dropped he turned to his wife: 'Just wait for the markets to open on Monday.'[121]

On that day, as Zahawi had foreseen, the pound plummeted again. Now the red lights were flashing in the Treasury. 'It was chaotic,' recalled one who watched it all unfold from inside the building.

> Everybody had the pound sterling on their laptops and we were refreshing it every two seconds. We were getting updates from Treasury officials and the Bank of England. Number 10 was freaking out and saying: 'We need to engage with the City, we need to meet people, do roundtables, pick up the phone, fucking travel there if you need to.' We were doing all of it.[122]

At one point Cameron Brown, a Treasury special adviser, told Kwarteng only half in jest that he would have to resign as chancellor if the pound hit parity with the US dollar – that is, £1 being worth $1. The chuckle in response carried a hint of recognition.[123] That Monday the pound crashed to $1.0327, the lowest rate recorded since the currency began to be calculated using decimal points in 1971. It was dangerously close to parity.

But there was another problem. As the pound sank, the interest rates on long-term government bonds – known as gilts – began to soar. The metric can act like a live confidence tracker in the government's economic competence. If there are doubts, investors will demand higher interest payments in return for agreeing ten-, twenty- or thirty-year loans. That week, the interest rates (the technical term was 'yields') rocketed. Movements that usually played out across a year were condensed into a day or two. Deutsche Bank would later find that UK borrowing costs for ten-year bonds rose more after the mini-Budget than in any other five-day period in almost half a century.[124] Bank of England analysis, moreover, showed it to be a UK-specific phenomenon. A graph tracking UK, US and euro thirty-year gilts showed only the first soaring up in the days after Kwarteng's speech, with the other two rising only a fraction of that in Britain.[125]

The changes mattered: the bond market fed into the mortgage market. Banks began pulling mortgage offers, crushing the dreams of scores of would-be new homeowners overnight. When deals returned, they were markedly more expensive. In mid-September, the interest rate on two-year and five-year mortgages was 4.5 per cent, according to analysis by Reuters. By mid-October, they were near 6.5 per cent.[126] Yes, they had been ticking up for months, but the leap right after the mini-Budget was there in black and white. Labour would dub the difference the 'moron premium'. Truss and Kwarteng had attached a Tory rosette to interest rate rises.

The sudden movements also exposed a bomb hidden under the UK financial system. So-called 'liability-driven investments', or LDIs, were even more complicated than gilts and yields. Basically, these involved holding government bonds as collateral for borrowing to purchase more bonds. Pensions funds, it emerged, were doing so to a degree never fully appreciated. When the value of bonds dropped that week, so did the value of the collateral that pension funds were holding. A 'doom loop' emerged, bonds being sold off, which drove their value down, which triggered more sales. So catastrophic was the development that suddenly UK pension funds – including at least one household name – were locked in a cash-flow crisis. On the Wednesday after the mini-Budget the Bank of England announced that it was stepping in, setting aside £65 billion to buy bonds. 'Financial stability' was at risk, the official statement made clear.[127] The Bank was cleaning up Downing Street's mess.

To this day there is righteous anger from Team Truss that no one had flagged the LDI issue. They argue, fairly, that it is for the Bank of England and Treasury officials, not ministers, to detect such problems. Yet no warning is known to have been voiced.[128] Bank figures would later note that they flagged concerns about LDI use back in 2018, but had stress-tested scenarios much less severe than what followed the mini-Budget. Everyone, it appears, was blindsided. Such nuances, though, have a habit of being missed in the cut and thrust of politics. Soon, Fleet Street had a name for the package that had sent the markets spinning: the Kamikwasi Budget. Cruder hacks had a one-word term: Trussterfuck.

★

Imagine spending a quarter of a century climbing the greasy pole to get to the pinnacle, only for your grip to start slipping. Imagine that happening in full view of every person you have ever met: friends and relatives and colleagues and rivals. Politics is a brutal pastime, but even so Liz Truss endured a unique form of personal torment in the weeks after the mini-Budget as her world began to fold in on itself.

The 2022 Conservative Party conference was meant to be a coming-out celebration for the new leader before an adoring membership. Now it had morphed into an opportunity to galvanise waverers and reset the narrative. Early prep meetings for the gathering in Birmingham at the start of October had seen Truss talk about 'a bolder Britain that we can believe in'. The feel was to be 'modern yet traditional'. It was all about 'getting Britain moving' and 'build, build, build'. The tone changed in the days immediately after the Growth Plan announcement, but the prime minister was still upbeat. 'What's the worst that can happen? Britain will still be able to raise money,' Truss told aides. She believed that Labour had been 'wrong-footed' by the tax cuts, unsure how to respond. Truss wanted to project a message of a 'new era' having dawned.[129]

But by the end of the week, stronger emotions were on display. They could be seen at a gathering on Thursday, 29 September to discuss Truss's conference speech. That morning the prime minister had broken her public silence on the financial fallout from the mini-Budget. Spinners had kept Truss away from the cameras that week, knowing privately that she did not accept there was any link between her measures and the tumbling pound.[130] But with accusations of her hiding from scrutiny mounting, they agreed to go ahead with a round of BBC local radio chats, a regular pre-conference feature for prime ministers. It turned into a media machine-gunning. In interview after interview, regional radio hosts fired questions about the market turmoil. Truss's prevarications and long pauses were leapt on, dominating the morning headlines.

In the conference prep session that followed there was defiance. It was here that the blast against the 'Anti-Growth Coalition' which Truss would deliver from the podium in Birmingham took form. It emanated from the prime minister like a visceral roar against the economic and media establishment panning her mini-Budget. A contemporaneous note passed to this author captures the unfiltered, swearier original version of that section, spoken by Truss in full flow. 'From broadcast to podcast they peddle the same old answers,' the prime minister began, knocking the words around with advisers. 'It's always more taxes, more regulation, more interference, more meddling.'

Warming to her theme, and with an eye partly on the state-funded BBC, she went further. Truss, interrupted occasionally by cheering aides, let rip:

> They don't understand aspiration, they don't understand initiative, they don't understand that when people feel that the government's taking all their money they just don't want to go into work, they don't want to set up a business. They don't understand. They don't understand what's paying their fucking left-wing journalism wages.

To whoops of support she continued:

> They don't fucking understand it. They do not understand who's paying their fucking wages. Do you know who's paying their wages? It's plumbers in Dartford that are paying their wages. It's people who actually make things in this country who are paying their wages. You know, the ceramics workers in Stoke-on-Trent, the bridge-builders. These are the people paying their wages. They don't understand who's paying their fucking wages. The IMF, the Labour Party, the Treasury officials, the BBC. Have they ever seen a tax rise they don't like?!

The last line triggered a peal of laughter from the prime minister. 'Have they ever been outside North London?' she added. 'And now, thanks to Zoom, they never need to leave!'[131] This was Truss unchained. A version of the lines, only a little pared back, would be used in her real conference speech.

It was not just defiance on display in the prep session, though. There was raw emotion too. As Truss read out a passage about the hardship she had seen in her upbringing in Paisley – empty food shelves and workless adults turning to drink – she began to well up. Truss's childhood had not been one of public-school comforts and the trappings of wealth, unlike that of so many of her predecessors. She had fought tooth and nail to climb to Number 10, a dream achieved that was now turning nightmarish. Speaking the words appeared to bring it all back.

When the conference eventually arrived on 2 October there would be open revolt. An unappreciated reality of the Truss premiership is that she was only the second Tory leader since the new election rules came in during the late 1990s not to win the MP round of the contest. David Cameron, Theresa May and Boris Johnson were all ultimately the first pick of their colleagues as well as of party members. Only the short-lived Iain Duncan Smith was not (Michael Howard had been selected unopposed). It was Rishi Sunak, not Truss, who had come out top among Tory MPs. It was Sunak allies, too, who went public with their discontent after the mini-Budget.

Mel Stride, who had led the MP stage campaign for Sunak, used his position as chairman of the Commons Treasury Select Committee to sound the alarm over the lack of OBR oversight. Julian Smith, a former chief whip in Sunak's corner, publicly castigated the 'huge tax cut for the very rich' on Twitter, calling it 'wrong'.[132] Grant Shapps, sacked from the Cabinet despite the advice to the contrary of some Team Truss figures, showed off his rebels spreadsheet on a folding smartphone to journalists at the conference. Michael Gove had publicly backed Kemi Badenoch, not Sunak, but was suspected by the prime minister of being in cahoots with the former chancellor. A week before the Birmingham gathering there had been an attempt to neutralise him with the offer of the ambassadorship to Israel, which would have meant him quitting as an MP.[133] During the chat with Truss when the role was floated Gove declined but pledged loyalty, according to her camp. Then, on Tory conference day one, Gove eviscerated her economic plan live in a BBC studio with Truss sitting just a few metres away, calling the mini-Budget 'a display of the wrong values' and the vast unfunded tax cuts 'not Conservative'.[134]

The accusations that Team Sunak had neither accepted her victory nor stopped campaigning is voiced consistently by the figures at the very top of the Truss project. A senior Downing Street figure bemoaned 'Rishi's campaign continuing after the contest'.[135] A government whip trying to keep party discipline, said: 'After we won, they didn't give up. It felt like they were determined that she was not going to have the chance.'[136] Jake Berry, the Conservative Party chairman, spoke of 'disloyalty and the organised nature of resistance' in those weeks.[137] Simon Clarke concluded: 'They never stopped.'[138] But one senior Number 10 adviser, in the trenches for years by Truss's side, captured a wider truth: 'She made it so easy for her enemies. This is the point. She gave them all the ammunition.'[139]

It was the 45p tax cut that would become the rallying point for Tory rebels. The politics of it – as Gordon Brown had known when he first laid the trap of the additional rate in 2010 – was tricky: an unambiguous financial boost for the wealthiest Britons. When prominent Tories joined Labour in condemning the move the danger of parliamentary defeat ramped up. Truss had inherited Johnson's sizable Commons majority but it was not insurmountable: fewer than forty Tory MPs switching sides and voting with the opposing parties would be enough to force defeat on the government. On Saturday and much of Sunday, the defences were manned. 'The lady's not for turning,' the media were briefed, harking back to Maggie, and the message duly headed onto the front pages. She was not for turning . . . until she was. Come Sunday evening, Truss was wobbling. Sir Graham Brady, the 1992 Committee chairman, and Damian Green, head of the liberal Tory 'One Nation' faction, had spelled out the scale of rebellion. By around 6 p.m., a reversal was close to being signed off. There was a break for obligatory conference appearances, then the prime minister and her inner circle regathered in her suite on the twenty-fourth floor of the Birmingham Hyatt. Amid the detritus of a Mexican takeaway of tacos and dips, the decision was taken. Get rid.

Kwasi Kwarteng was hauled in from a dinner with senior journalists at the *Sun* – the paper's political editor, Harry Cole, would break the story online after midnight, spidey senses set tingling by the chancellor's hasty exit – and he quickly agreed. 'My view was if it kept the party in a good place we should ditch it,' Kwarteng said.[140] He had in mind George Osborne's Omnishambles blunder and Philip Hammond's Budget reversals. 'People do U-turns,' he added.[141] It was survivable. Others wonder to this day if the line could have been held. Simon Clarke favoured that approach, daring moderates to vote down a new prime minister's first fiscal statement. 'My perception is that wing of the party will always blink, always, so force them to blink,' said Clarke.[142] But it was Truss and Kwarteng who blinked. Just twenty-six days into her premiership, Truss's first major U-turn had been signed off.

The Tory conference broke up after the prime minister's address on Wednesday, 5 October. Kwasi Kwarteng would be sacked on Friday, 14 October. This was the moment that Liz Truss, accepting the need to junk much of her mini-Budget, sealed the coffin lid on her premiership. But what forced her hand? For the first time, the dire private warnings that caused the prime minister to change course can be detailed.

There was an episode before those warnings emerged, however, that caused alarm in the Treasury. It happened in early October and involved Truss's attempts to secure Britain's long-term energy supply. What happened has been described by five sources directly involved.[143] The prime minister favoured striking a deal with the Norwegian state-owned energy company Equinor. The idea was a twenty-year mega-deal to import tens of billions of cubic metres of gas. It would mean that the UK had the security of a legally promised gas supply – an important issue, as the fallout from Russia's invasion of Ukraine had highlighted. The problem? It came at an exorbitant cost and substantial financial risk, given the uncertainty regarding future price fluctuations.

The deal was being negotiated by Madelaine McTernan, director general of the government's Energy Supply Taskforce in the business department, but Truss was the key supporter. The package would cost around £130 billion and proposed, according to three senior Treasury sources, that the UK would buy gas at 180p per therm.[144] (A source in the business department insisted the exact price was still being negotiated.) The problem was that the gas price was set to fall. Internal government estimates suggested that an eye-watering £30 billion loss would be incurred, a number that would have to be made public later that year. Kwasi Kwarteng challenged Truss over the figure, which came from the calculated 'net present value' of the deal, in a Number 10 meeting. 'I know what NPV means,' Truss is said to have responded dryly.[145] The agreement was just days away from being struck when the Treasury said no. 'We basically put our foot down and refused to go along with it,' said a senior Treasury source.[146] A Truss ally insisted she decided not to go ahead.[147]

The theoretical argument for the deal, one not without merit, was the long-term energy security it brought the UK. Furthermore, the net present value could change if prices rose. But some involved believed the saga showed that Truss had not learnt any lessons from the mini-Budget, her instinct for going to the max still alive and kicking. 'Equinor were licking their lips,' said a senior Treasury source. 'That is when I realised she had completely lost the plot.'[148] Another dubbed it 'mad'.[149] Six months on, gas would be trading at below 90p per therm, so half the proposed price. It would have meant a loss in value of even more than the £30 billion first estimated.

The mood after Tory conference was already bleak due to the 45p reversal. It darkened over the following weekend. Downing Street had always planned to prepare a proper fiscal statement in the autumn. This had been clung to like a life raft in the choppy waters after the mini-Budget. It would be the point when spending would be curtailed, when all the supply-side reforms would be published, when it would be proved that the government had a plan for bringing down debt. It was the moment, too, when the OBR would reveal its public forecast.

By the end of conference week, the OBR had given the Treasury its first private estimates. The Conservative Party, which prided itself on sound economic management, had long adopted 'fiscal rules' to show its prudence. At the time the rules promised that debt would be falling within five years of any given date – a claim the Treasury always wanted backed up in the OBR five-year forecast, changing policies if necessary to hit the target. After the bonfire of taxes and huge energy bill guarantee, Number 11 knew that would be tricky to achieve this time round. Officials had discussed what total savings were needed. Worst-case scenario, they concluded: £40–50 billion.[150] Then the OBR's first estimate dropped: £72 billion. It was way higher than expected. That amount had to be saved in tax increases or spending cuts within five years to satisfy the fiscal rules. Breaking them, given the new leadership's credibility with the markets was already paper thin, was deemed unconscionable. The gap had to be filled.

At Chequers that weekend, the prime minister, the chancellor and their inner circles talked through options. Perhaps tax thresholds could be frozen for the full five years? Or the windfall tax on oil and gas giants extended? They were not palatable options for the pair of tax-cutters, but the ideas were on the table.[151] Not discussed at length during that weekend, according to one there, was reversing more elements of what had already been announced.[152] But that would change in the coming week.

By Wednesday, there was a feeling among economic officials inside the government that Truss and Kwarteng were not grasping the seriousness of the situation. The new fiscal event, dubbed the 'Medium-Term Fiscal Plan', had been shunted forward from mid-November to 31 October, speed prioritised over the inevitable 'Halloween horror show' headlines. But another date, earlier and even more significant, now loomed: the moment the Bank of England would end its intervention and stop buying up bonds. That was just a few days away now, on Monday, 17 October. This amounted to removing the stabilisers from the markets, which would then be free to reveal what they really thought about the current UK leadership. Did the prime minister and chancellor realise how hard it would be to hit the £72 billion figure? And did they know what traders were planning to unleash on Monday? Some on the inside believed not, a conclusion drawn from the fact that Kwarteng, despite the uncertainty, decided to travel to the IMF summit in Washington, DC rather than lead preparations from London.[153] Truss had explicitly urged him not to go. Kwarteng, thinking that cancelling the engagement would itself trigger alarm bells, went anyway.

The jitters were now spreading. Shabbir Merali and Adam Memon, two special advisers focused on economics – Merali in Number 10 and Memon in Number 11 – were growing increasingly nervous about how the markets would react on Monday. They got permission to sound out industry leaders and spent Wednesday afternoon in the Number 11 boardroom talking back to back to half a dozen managing director-level executives at investment banks and asset management companies. The message they heard was consistent and horrifying. The end of October was too long to wait for any announcements. Traders would make their moves on Monday. Either unpick the tax cuts Truss had placed at the centre of her premiership by the end of the week or risk 'financial crisis'. They knew what that term theoretically entailed: a plunging pound, interest rates soaring, banks struggling to stay afloat, with further dire consequences to follow. It was a dark road.

'When people talk about "financial crisis" that is something you read in history books,' said one involved. 'When you hear serious players say, "Come Monday morning, you might be heading into one," it puts everything in a very tight focus. We did not have long to act. We had about forty-eight hours. The situation felt pretty dire.'[154] Merali and Memon stayed in Downing Street until close to 11 p.m. writing a two-page note for the prime minister. It had three sections. The first summarised what they had heard, underscoring that the markets were betting against Britain. The second explained the wider context: how securing economic growth, Truss's defining goal in office, was only possible with financial stability. And the third laid out the bluntest of conclusions. To fill the £72 billion OBR black hole, an axe had to be taken to the mini-Budget. Scrapping the corporation tax rise, the costliest tax cut, had to be reversed. That meant Truss would have to oversee a rise from 19 per cent to 25 per cent – the very Rishi Sunak-authored policy she had railed against all summer. Small tax reversals would be needed too, the note said: getting rid of VAT-free shopping for foreigners and raising taxes on dividends. The National Insurance cut could stay: it was so strongly associated with Truss and no one wanted to reopen that Tory Pandora's box, given how it had split the party when announced by Boris Johnson. But a line had now been crossed. Shredding mini-Budget measures was on the table. Yet still Truss was refusing to concede.

On Thursday, 13 October, the note was discussed at an early morning gathering of senior Number 10 political staff. The memo's writers wanted it to become an official recommendation. Printouts were soon travelling round the building, the circle of knowledge about what was feared to be around the corner widening. As is the way in Westminster, the dark mood led to gallows humour. 'We're going to be like Venezuela,' joked a political aide, according to one insider.[155] Alongside concerns over a newly plunging pound – possibly going below the psychologically significant dollar parity mark – one anxiety stuck out most starkly: that the government would not be able to fund its debts. If round after round of bonds were issued but not purchased, it was game over. Truss had waved away that possibility just a fortnight earlier. Now it was a probability.

James Bowler, incoming as Sir Tom Scholar's replacement as the Treasury's permanent secretary, was summoned to tell Truss to her face how challenging the situation was. One senior Number 10 figure said he was 'marched in at gunpoint', another said he was 'wheeled in'.[156] It was highly unusual for the Treasury's top mandarin to brief a prime minister without the chancellor also being present – a point Bowler made in his opening remarks. Once launched, however, he did not hold back. One source in the room summed up his message:

> He just made crystal clear that there were a lot of very intelligent, very wealthy people who don't do politics, who look at numbers only, who were absolutely prepared to smash Britain to pieces on the markets. They were betting against us and they were going to win. We'd lost the confidence of the markets and we were in a very weak position. And the whole thing needed to be junked.[157]

A second source in the room said Bowler's tone was more constructive, running through options for how the £72 billion figure could be saved, but confirmed that the overall message was downbeat.[158] It was not just Bowler. Senior Treasury officials reached out to Nadhim Zahawi, the former chancellor who now headed up Truss's Cabinet Office, fearing that the prime minister was failing to accept how bad things were and urging him to voice concern. A meeting between the pair was scheduled but later cancelled.[159] Chris Philp, the chief secretary to the Treasury who was resisting big changes to the mini-Budget, felt he was being cut out of the loop as Number 11 mandarins pushed for reversals. He wanted to put forward an alternative savings plan but was urged not to by senior Treasury officials. In the end he WhatsApped his proposals direct to Truss, but by now the pressure was building.[160]

The warnings, in the end, came from the very top of Whitehall. Simon Case, the Cabinet secretary, saw Truss that day. He also put his official advice in writing. The letter warned that the government would struggle to fund its debt on Monday unless Truss reversed the corporation tax cut, according to two sources who saw its contents.[161] It made clear a 'major financial crisis' was about to rock Britain without urgent action.[162] Case is also understood to have communicated the concerns of Andrew Bailey, the Bank of England governor – Truss and Bailey did not speak directly to one another. The message was loud and clear. Britain's most senior civil servant and central banker were now joining the chorus of concern. Earlier on Thursday the prime minister had been resisting calls for dramatic reversals. Then the mood changed, confidence ebbing away with each catastrophic warning. She was being told there would be a 'major market meltdown without a U-turn, with the UK struggling 'full stop' to raise funds.[163] Eventually Truss agreed to act. She would later tell others it was a case of 'once bitten, twice shy', given how the mini-Budget had played out.[164]

If the policies had to go, so too did the man who unveiled them. And so, that evening, Kwarteng was summoned back to London for political execution.

By now the end was inevitable. Out went Kwarteng and in, once he eventually called Truss, came Jeremy Hunt. Nadhim Zahawi had also briefly been considered for the chancellorship before Hunt was picked.[165] Before markets opened on Monday almost every tax cut in the mini-Budget except reversing the National Insurance rise and the cut in stamp duty to support the property market had been torched. The two-year energy guarantee was also slashed to a little over six months. Truss – who had given a stilted eight-minute press conference defending the changes which did little to calm nerves – was still in office but no longer in power. What finally tipped her over the edge was the obscurest of issues: a Labour Party attempt to seize control of the House of Commons order paper, which dictates what is debated and is usually determined by the government, for a vote about fracking. The scenes in Parliament that followed, according to some there, were the wildest witnessed in the long Tory run since 2010.

Labour can claim credit for spotting the bruise on which to apply the punch. Tory MPs had been elected in 2019 on a manifesto that promised to ban fracking unless the science proved categorically that it was safe. Truss, however, had reversed the position, a statement being issued shortly after she took office lifting the moratorium on shale gas extraction. With the prime minister's authority depleted and some Tories boxed in by their constituents' opposition to fracking, the opposition now put the issue to the test.

As soon as Labour's gambit dropped, late on Tuesday 18 October – the day after Hunt's statement reversing the mini-Budget – the Conservative whips judged it had to be treated seriously. Wendy Morton, Yorkshire born and bred and with a distinctive ginger bob, had been made chief whip after helping lead the MP stage of Truss's leadership campaign, though only after former party leader Iain Duncan Smith had rebuffed soundings-out for the Cabinet post.[166] Craig Whittaker, the no-nonsense Tory MP for Calder Valley, was deputy chief whip. The pair saw the danger: if the Labour move passed, it meant that the opposition could decide what MPs debated and voted on – a humiliating position for Downing Street. It was, in effect, a vote of confidence in the government, the pair concluded, since losing control of the order paper given Truss's current instability was not an option. How widely Number 10 was aware of that call is unclear, but both Morton and Whittaker were categorical in interviews that the decision was signed off by Downing Street.[167] The lack of evidence of protest from Number 10 for much of Wednesday, 19 October – the day of the vote – lends the account credence.

At 10.42 a.m. Tory MPs' phones pinged with a text sent to every one of them from Whittaker. 'The second debate is the main event today and is a 100% hard 3 line whip!' read part of the message, seen by this author. 'This is not a motion on fracking. **This is a confidence motion in the Government**. We cannot, under any circumstances, let the Labour Party take control of the order paper and put through their own legislation and whatever other bits of legislation they desire.'[168] The bold lettering was his, contained in the original text. There was no room left for doubt. A confidence vote, however, has implications. Britain is a parliamentary democracy. The government's legitimacy comes from its ability to win votes in the Commons. If a confidence vote is lost, convention dictates that the government resigns or triggers a general election since it has proved it cannot continue.

That day, heavy with the sense of Truss's time running out, had been hectic in Downing Street. The prime minister had lost a home secretary, with Suella Braverman resigning after immigration policy papers were leaked to a Tory MP and issuing a parting shot about the importance of accepting responsibility for one's actions. There had been Prime Minister's Questions to prepare for and endure, featuring a gutsy performance by Truss that won Tory plaudits given the dire backdrop. But as the minutes ticked down to the vote, expected around 7 p.m., Downing Street got nervous. If the whips were calling this a confidence vote, were they 100 per cent certain they would win? With less than an hour to go, senior Downing Street political figures put Morton on speakerphone and asked the question. She did not give a categorical assurance that the vote would be won, according to three Number 10 insiders on the call – though Morton disputes this.[169] Alarm bells were now sounding. Was the government just minutes away from collapse? Morton was urged to cancel the declaration that this was a confidence vote. She did not rule it out but was reluctant to do so. At which point, Number 10 took matters into its own hands.

Graham Stuart, the grey-haired and broad-smiled energy minister, was on the Commons frontbench and about to get to his feet to close the debate when the message arrived. Two parliamentary private secretaries – Tory MP 'departmental bag-carriers' sat on the bench behind – urged him to check his phone. 'Hi Graham, It's Iain Carter from Number 10 here. The whips should be arranging an intervention. It's essential that you say from the Despatch Box that this is not a confidence vote in the government in your closing,' read the message.[170] Carter was Truss's director of political strategy. The time was 6.47 p.m., just minutes before the vote. Stuart checked with the PPSs – they had similar messages from Number 10. The orders were categorical, despite what some Truss allies would later claim. 'Ok. I'll say it at the beginning,' Stuart texted back. 'Thank you,' replied Carter.[171] Blame should not be pinned on the message-bearers, however; those higher up the chain were involved too. Thérèse

Coffey, the deputy prime minister, was involved in discussions. She pointed out that positions could be changed from the Despatch Box, urging Number 10 figures to check with the whips if they were certain of victory.[172] There was a logic to it: by making it explicit before the vote that it was not an issue of confidence, defeat would not as a matter of course result in the government's ouster. And so Stuart tried to slip the phrase in unnoticed: 'Quite clearly, this is not a confidence vote.'[173] Looking back, he said: 'I was ordered to light the touch paper so I did.'[174]

As soon as the words were out the chaos began. Ed Miliband, Labour's shadow energy secretary, gleefully started slapping his hand at the Despatch Box demanding an intervention so that he could twist the knife. Tory Cabinet ministers on the frontbench were startled. Nadhim Zahawi thought to himself: 'Have we checked this with the PM? This is insane.'[175] Confusion reigned among Tory backbenchers too. Those who opposed fracking and wanted to vote with Labour had been told all day that they would be stripped of the Tory whip – in other words, expelled from the parliamentary party – if they did so. Given that it was now not a confidence matter, could they vote with Labour without incurring that punishment? 'That is a matter for party managers,' Stuart responded when questioned by one Tory MP in the Chamber.[176] 'What?!' came the mounted response. Then in walked the most senior party manager, Morton, with a face like thunder. The chief whip had not signed off the late change. She believed they were about to win the vote – as would be proved correct, with the Labour move rejected by more than ninety votes. But Number 10 had pulled the rug from under her feet. 'I just couldn't believe what I heard from the Despatch Box and so I felt completely undermined,' said Morton.[177] At 6.59 p.m., just as the division bells were ringing, the chief whip fired off two texts to Liz Truss: 'I resign.' And then: 'With immediate effect.'[178]

As MPs marched towards the voting lobbies there was mass confusion. 'It was complete carnage,' said one of the whips.[179] 'Chaos,' said Jacob Rees-Mogg, who as business secretary held the fracking brief.[180] Anti-fracking Tory MPs were desperately trying to work out if they would lose the whip if they voted for the measure. One was so emotional they appeared on the brink of tears, according to multiple witnesses.[181] Rees-Mogg and Coffey were urging them to vote with the government. Joyful Labour MPs heckled from the sidelines as their foes' attempts at party discipline descended into farce. An accusation that some Tories were manhandled through the No Lobby was later rejected by an investigation carried out on behalf of Commons Speaker Sir Lindsay Hoyle, but the report still captured the disorder: 'It is undoubtedly the case that it was very intense in the lobby – voices were raised; some Members were clearly stressed and intemperate.'[182] Complicating the matter – the Cabinet minister in charge of party discipline had just quit. 'Don't ask me, I'm not chief whip anymore,' Morton would tell any MP who asked.[183] The news sent one Rishi Sunak supporter into celebrations, the MP rushing around with hands raised, saying, 'The chief whip's resigned!' Craig Whittaker, the deputy chief whip, also at the end of his tether, now quit too. 'I am fucking furious and I don't give a fuck anymore,' he erupted in front of MPs.[184] The comment leaked immediately: a clip of a German reporter speaking her native tongue before uttering the sweary sentence in English soon went viral.[185] The world was laughing.

The chief whip is meant to be the prime minister's iron fist and enforcer of decisions. That night, the roles were reversed. It was Liz Truss, in full view of colleagues, who chased after Morton, pleading with her to stay in post. The vote won, Morton and Whittaker agreed to meet Truss in her parliamentary office. A 'shouting match' ensued, according to one there.[186] The prime minister insisted that she had not known about the decision to deny it was a confidence vote. Whittaker questioned whether that was true.[187] Truss pleaded for them to stay. Their price was a public statement which made clear that blame for the evening's reputationally damaging events lay squarely with Number 10. The stand-off continued. Downing Street, fearing the worst, lined up Greg Hands as the new chief whip.[188] The prime minister was then urged by Morton and Whittaker to see the entire Whip's Office, where she thanked them for their hard work.[189] The country's leader was having to prostrate herself before MPs whose role was meant to be to support her. Meanwhile Labour MPs popped Champagne bottles in the Strangers' Bar. A government that could not even competently tell its MPs how to vote was a goner. It would not be until 1.33 a.m. that a full Number 10 statement confirming that Morton and Whittaker were staying on was issued to the press.[190] By then, it was over.

Liz Truss had considered resigning the weekend after sacking Kwasi Kwarteng. At Chequers she had gone for a walk around the gardens with her husband, Hugh. Three Downing Street advisers also there – Mark Fullbrook, chief of staff, Ruth Porter, deputy chief of staff, and long-term ally Jason Stein – had done likewise in a different direction. Meeting back near the house, they talked it through. Some advisers felt the game was up.[191] Hugh urged Truss to go. She decided to fight on. But the night of the fracking vote, a few days later, she accepted her fate. There would be no hanging on by the fingernails, Boris Johnson style. No intervention by Sir Graham Brady, sealed envelope in hand. There was just a statement on the morning of 20 October 2022, the Jenga podium wheeled into Downing Street one last time, to lower the curtain. Truss did her best to summarise her achievements. The speech lasted ninety seconds.

It had all unravelled so quickly. That rainy opening address was on 6 September 2022. She left office, once a successor had been picked, on 25 October 2022. David Cameron had spent 2,253 days as prime minister, Theresa May 1,106 and Boris Johnson 1,139. Truss was forty-nine and out. The August heat of Chevening, heavy with optimism, felt like a lifetime ago. Events in the last week had spiralled at an alarming rate, a surreal vortex captured in the wedding plans of Adam Jones, Truss's top spinner for years. He had left Number 10 to get married on Thursday, 14 October. At his rehearsal service on the Friday news broke of Kwarteng's sacking – something not being discussed when he left. During the wedding that weekend, as Truss wobbled, his phone was confiscated by friends to prevent distraction. He was honeymooning in Mauritius when Number 10 pals called the following Thursday to say Truss was about to resign – meaning he had no job. Rather than watch her speech, Jones went cycling with his new wife. Half a year on he still had not seen it.[192]

Truss was a conviction politician – a type all too rare in Westminster. But in politics convictions have to be matched with pragmatism.

There can be no doubt that the mini-Budget was a Truss Budget. It was based on her campaign promises, it was formed from her deep-held belief that the economic orthodoxy needed smashing, it ballooned under her urging to go further, faster, bigger in scale and bolder in ambition. It is easy to pick at specifics and ask: 'What if?' Had she consulted the OBR, or not scrapped the 45p rate, or announced spending restraints with the tax cuts, or not sacked Sir Tom Scholar, would things have been different? That is like asking, when a child has been sick after eating a vast ice cream sundae, whether it was the sprinkles or the flake that tipped the balance. It was the whole lot. At some point, the parents have to accept responsibility.

Kwasi Kwarteng has thought a lot about how things played out. His friendship with Truss, strained by office, has not been destroyed. But with the passage of time has come clarity about how unripped his old ally was for the job. 'I love her dearly, she's a great person, very sincere and honest,' said Kwarteng. 'But if it hadn't been the mini-Budget, she would have blown up on something else. I just don't think her temperament was right. She was just not wired to be a prime minister.'[193]

10

Comeback Kid

Rishi Sunak and Boris Johnson were alone together, two dozen floors up. The sky outside Millbank Tower was black, the evening obscuring the views along the Thames. This was Boris territory, the suite of offices a few minutes' walk south of Parliament where he had set up shop since being booted out of Downing Street. Even so, it was his rival who had the upper hand. In the scramble for Tory support that had broken out after Liz Truss resigned, leaving the premiership up for grabs for the second time in 2022, Sunak had breezed past the hundred MP-mark needed to qualify for the first vote. Johnson was struggling, but was still a comfortable second. And so a meeting had been brokered to see if a deal could be done.

Both men had reasons to be bitter. They had not seen each other since Sunak resigned as Johnson's chancellor without a word of warning, triggering a blizzard of expletives from the prime minister. Boris still saw the betrayal as the reason for his ouster. In the leadership race that followed he had broken with convention by voting for a successor, backing Liz Truss via a proxy ballot cast by ally MP Nigel Adams.[1] Sunak, too, was smarting. A politician who prizes being right, he had always taken a dim view of Truss and her 'big bang' economics of debt-fuelled tax cuts. And yet it was Liz, not Rishi, whom the party members had chosen as Johnson's allies threw rocks at Sunak from the sidelines. That the financial backlash he had warned of came to pass was little compensation.

The room where they met was sparse. The walls were a blanket of white, no photographs or patterns adding character. The carpet was dull, with just a rectangular table and swivel office chairs for company. Arranging the meeting on Saturday, 22 October 2022, two days after Truss had quit, had been fraught. It was the Johnson camp that was pushing, Team Sunak resistant at first, before relenting. The topic of discussion was simple: Which of them should lead Britain? Yet it was also remarkable: the governance of the country had effectively come down to a rhetorical arm wrestle.

The conversation lasted around an hour. The door was shut, with just a handful of aides outside. At times there were 'raised voices', indicating 'robust discussion', according to one who was present.[2] The full details of what was said remained with Johnson and Sunak, who swore not to brief the contents of the meeting out. But, via figures in both men's inner circle, the thrust of the conversation can be revealed.

Boris was the one pitching. Some likened his offer to a 'joint' leadership, with Sunak, the details man, driving forward policy and Johnson, the salesman, touting it to voters. Others said it was more akin to a chief executive and chairman arrangement. Whatever the spin, the core proposition was clear: I'll go back to being prime minister and you go back to being chancellor.[3]

Johnson kept pushing the mandate argument: that it was he who had won the 2019 election. To keep the party united and the support base appeased, it was best to return to how things had been before. Rishi resisted, according to allies. One summarised his argument:

> I'm just not going to do that, it didn't work before. I left because I didn't agree with how you were handling the economy, I didn't agree with how you were handling all of the partygate stuff. And we can't just breeze over the fact that we fundamentally disagreed on how much we could borrow.[4]

When the door finally opened, advisers looked for the white smoke. 'Don't worry, folks,' said Johnson. 'Rishi's just agreed to be my chancellor.' There was the nervous laughter of uncertainty. Sunak chuckled too, then patted Johnson on the shoulder: 'See you at the debates.'[5] If Johnson had hoped his rival would blink, he had miscalculated. A day later Boris would drop out of the race, accepting that he could not unite the parliamentary party. The day after that, Sunak became the Conservative Party leader, and thus prime minister.

It was a stunning political comeback for Rishi Sunak. Defeat and despair in September; victory and vindication in October. Aged forty-two, he had made it to Number 10 just seven years after becoming an MP – a blisteringly fast ascent. There had not been a younger prime minister since Lord Liverpool in 1812. And yet, taking the edge off the excitement was an unrelentingly gloomy in-tray: soaring inflation and interest rates, forecasts of recession, a war in Europe. Plus a Tory Party fighting with itself and more than 20 percentage points behind Labour. There was also a deadline: within a little over two years Sunak would have to call a general election, whatever the polls were saying. The most almighty patch-up job would be needed to avoid defeat. The clock was ticking.

Of all the Conservative Party shape-shifting that had taken place between leaders during its run in power since 2010, the move from Liz Truss to Rishi Sunak was perhaps the starkest. For a few weeks the public had been told the best way to secure Britain's economic future was a dramatic reduction in tax to kick-start growth. Those opposed were talking down the UK, scaremongering or lacking in boldness. And then, turning on a dime, the top of the party was now preaching the opposite message. Only by jacking up taxes and battening down the hatches could the country get through the travails of rocketing prices and interest rates. In September, debt equalled good, a useful pot of money that could be dipped into to deliver what was needed. In October, debt equalled bad, a dangerous temptation that if reached for would cripple future generations. Within the space of a single season the party had redefined its economic strategy twice. Believers in the internal Tory trigger system would argue that it had worked, the party acting quickly and decisively to remove Truss when it found that her experiment had misfired. But the public were still entitled to be confused. What exactly do you stand for? And if the last lot were wrong, perhaps you will be too? The opinion polls suggested that after a dozen years it would be much harder to find public support for yet more reinvention.

Losing to Liz Truss had taken it out of Rishi Sunak. The summer 2022 leadership campaign had been gruelling, stretching almost two months from Boris Johnson's resignation announcement on 7 July to Truss being declared the victor on 5 September. In the final weeks, as Sunak continued to travel the country pushing his message of fiscal prudence at hustings, tiredness had set in. An aide recalled him looking despondent when being briefed for one of his last newspaper interviews.[6] But throughout August, as opinion polls showed a huge Truss lead with party members, Sunak had persisted. He had doubled down on his economic message, being even 'more robust' in his argument against unfunded tax cuts.[7] Yet when it came, defeat still stung.

'We were all pretty exhausted,' said Dominic Raab, the deputy prime minister under Johnson and Sunak who had been the latter's most senior MP supporter in the contest. 'He had run a hell of a campaign, he'd put his heart and soul into it. Physically it was very draining.'[8] Other figures by Sunak's side at the time echoed the point. 'We were all disappointed, obviously,' said one senior campaign figure. 'I think, genuinely, there was a sense that we believed what we were fighting for and advocating.'[9] The team was pleased that Sunak had appeared to close the gap – early polls had put Truss more than 30 percentage points ahead with members, but in the final result she won by just 15 points. But, for a serial achiever, these were small comforts.

The inner core – Rishi Sunak and his closest advisers – had moved on straightaway. Trussites would later point to Sunak's MP supporters causing trouble after her mini-Budget, and such figures' opinions were on the record. But among those at the centre minds had turned to what was next. As much is underscored in the way Sunak acted with his team. Loyalty was the watchword for the Sunak camp, a message preached from the top – an irony Johnson allies would no doubt counter, given his resignation. There was no month-long holiday after defeat, nor a drifting apart. Instead Sunak organised one-to-one coffees with long-term aides to offer advice and guidance on their future careers. One lasted two hours, another ninety minutes. The focus was on them and their job prospects, not him. 'He was very sweet, he made such an effort,' said one beneficiary, noting how for Sunak 'loyalty cuts both ways'.[10] There was also a weekend away in late September. Close aides were invited up to Sunak's Grade II listed constituency home in the village of Kirby Sigston, North Yorkshire, for countryside walks, pub visits and a dip in his swimming pool, the construction of which had made the headlines. For wider teams, there were thank-you drinks at the five-star Londoner hotel in Leicester Square – one for the Treasury team (he left so quickly there had been no proper goodbye) and another for the campaign team. All were proof of Sunak's instinct for expressing gratitude and paying back support.

Given that Sunak met his wife at Stanford business school in California and the couple owned property there, the idea of a move back across the Atlantic one day was a common topic of speculation in Westminster. But quitting the Commons and heading to America was never considered after defeat, according to allies. 'It's easy to write but it's total rubbish,' said an ally. 'He was going to stay as an MP. He loves Yorkshire.'[11] So keen was Sunak to spend more time in the constituency that he tried to join the Kirby Sigston cricket team, with little success. 'They told me that I shouldn't assume I could make their starting XI, because they'd won their league two years in a row,' Sunak later told *The Spectator* of his discussions with the team's organisers. 'They said I might have to go and play for the next village down.'[12] Having just missed out on becoming prime minister, Sunak was now struggling to get picked for a game of cricket.

He did, however, stay alive to what was happening in Westminster, as Truss's mini-Budget sent the pound tumbling and gave the markets jitters. Memes showing the implosion would pop up on the WhatsApp groups Sunak shared with friends. One just depicted a dumpster on fire. Another had a mocked-up conversation with Volodymyr Zelensky, the Ukrainian president battling a Russian invasion, in which he offered help to the UK, the two countries' recent roles being reversed. A third – said to be Sunak's favourite – spun off the plummeting UK currency exchange rates. It showed the US rapper 50 Cent asking whether he should be rebranded £1. The jokes provided light relief but no joy was taken in seeing the economic warnings of his leadership campaign being vindicated. 'I was sad,' Sunak would tell others later. 'There was no relish in it.'[13]

When the moment came, Rishi Sunak was at TGI Fridays. Liz Truss quit as prime minister on 20 October 2022 while Sunak was in

Teesside on a day out with his two daughters, Krishna and Anoushka. 'We were finishing off lunch and about to head to take them bowling,' Sunak would recall later on TalkTV. 'I had somewhat moved on after everything that happened over the summer. My head wasn't completely in that space, if I'm completely honest. And obviously she resigned and I had to think about what to do.'[14]

The fall from power was not totally unexpected by then: already there had been the backfiring mini-Budget, the Tory conference 45p reversal, Kwasi Kwarteng's sacking and the bonfire of other tax cuts. But even so, the end for Truss, when it came, was rapid. Sunak was not the only member of his old core team away from Westminster that day, the morning after the blunder-filled fracking vote. Nerissa Chesterfield, Sunak's communications chief in the Treasury, was in rural Wales on a break. One former senior adviser was about to start a new job in around a fortnight, another had pretty much agreed terms to do likewise.

Consideration was needed from Sunak about whether to plunge back into another leadership race. Over salads in his parliamentary office earlier that week the former chancellor and Dominic Raab had discussed what should be done if Truss fell. Both were frazzled from the summer campaign, but felt alarm at the worsening economic situation. 'Look, if this comes, you're going to have to step up to the plate and I'll support you,' Raab told Sunak.[15] Discussing the former chancellor's decision to opt back in, Raab said in an interview: 'This was a problem that the Conservative family had to own. I think he had a very strong sense of that duty.'[16] Sunak mulled things over with his real family too. But time was short and the decision was ultimately a quick one. By Thursday evening, the Sunak inner circle had reassembled at the Conrad London St James hotel just a few minutes' walk from Parliament. It was all systems go.

In the summer campaign, Team Sunak had set up what they dubbed a 'many-to-many' whipping system, with two people at its heart. Mel Stride, the clear-sighted Commons Treasury Committee chairman, was effectively chief whip, the operation being run out of his parliamentary office. Rupert Yorke, a long-time Tory special adviser with a sharp political brain who handled lots of MP engagements for Sunak, controlled the spreadsheet.

One ring out in the structure was a group of ultra-loyal Tory MPs, among them two former chief whips, Julian Smith and Mark Harper, two former parliamentary private secretaries to Sunak, Claire Coutinho and Craig Williams, and other supportive MPs such as Huw Merriman. Sir Gavin Williamson, the recently knighted former chief whip, was involved, though not – Sunak allies insist – at the very heart of the campaign. Those MP backers then sounded out colleagues and fed back information. 'What we set out to do was just figure out who knew the person best,' said one involved in the whipping operation. 'It's all about thinking for an MP: Who are his or her friends? Who actually knows him or her? What drives them? If you figure that out, you can work out what they need to succeed as an MP.'[17] It worked for the summer race, Sunak comfortably winning the MP stage only to lose to Truss in the party members' vote. A repeat was now attempted at double speed, with as many MPs as possible encouraged to declare for Sunak in the hope of creating a wave of support that would sweep him into office.

At the start of each Conservative leadership campaign the specific terms of the race get set. The executive of the 1922 Committee, elected from Tory backbenchers, and the Conservative Party board are the two deciding bodies. Given the Truss implosion, picking a successor quickly was deemed the best approach. The 1922 therefore decided that to qualify for the first round of voting a candidate must be nominated by at least one hundred Tory MPs. This meant no-hope candidates would be barred from running, since a maximum of three contenders could achieve that level of support. Boris's allies saw the threshold – five times higher than it had been in the summer race – as a way of keeping Boris off the ballot. But a 1922 executive source said that speed, not thwarting Johnson, was the reason for the higher bar.

There would be controversy, however, with the other body involved in determining the process, the Conservative Party board. It involved Jake Berry, the Conservative chairman, and the question of a membership vote – the second stage of the contest to pick the leader. That second leg presented a sizable political risk for Sunak, who had lost with the members to Truss in the previous campaign.

And so eyebrows were raised when Jeremy Hunt, who endorsed Sunak in the summer race, summoned Berry to the Treasury on the day Truss resigned. In an interview, Berry for the first time revealed his account of what happened. The Treasury's two most senior officials – James Bowler, the permanent secretary, and Cat Little, the second permanent secretary – were said to have laid out why it was essential for financial stability that the chancellor be allowed to carry out his fiscal statement on 31 October as planned. That was just eleven days away. Hunt supposedly echoed the message. To Berry's ears, the request was clear – a membership vote should be dispensed with as it would take too long. Berry said:

> The entire thing was that If you as chairman allowed Conservative Party members to have a vote then the chancellor won't be able to hold this Budget on October 31st and therefore the four horsemen of the apocalypse are going to come over the horizon in terms of the economy and that couldn't be allowed to happen.[18]

A contemporaneous note taken by Berry and seen by this author appears to capture snippets of the conversation. One line has the name 'James' written, an arrow and then the words 'respite until 31st'. Another has Cat's name (though it is misspelled 'Kat'), an arrow and words including 'frank about what faces us'. A third line appears to warn of a Bank of England intervention if the 31 October date was missed. 'If [we] do not do this through fiscal policy on 31st bank will step in', read some of the words, followed by references to 'looking at 100 125 basis points' – apparently estimates of market movements.[19]

According to Berry it was '100 per cent' clear that both the officials and Hunt were pushing for the membership vote to be scrapped. His response to the civil servants could be summed up, he said, as 'none of your fucking business'.[20] A second source familiar with what happened confirmed the broad accuracy of Berry's account of events. Jeremy Hunt's recollection, however, appears to have differed. A source close to Hunt said:

> Jeremy's sole priority was to avoid a collapse in financial markets, which was very close to happening. Jeremy was worried about a protracted membership campaign like in the summer – the markets

needed stable government now. Jake said he could do an entire leadership campaign within a week, Jeremy leaped at the suggestion. Jeremy just did not want the campaign to be lengthy, like the previous summer. He had nothing to do with candidates – he wanted a new prime minister, and a stable administration, to prevent financial collapse.[21]

In the end, the point proved moot. Means for a speedy membership vote were indeed put in place, but would be needed only if two candidates got over the hundred-MP threshold. Boris Johnson had flown back from holiday in the Dominican Republic when the Tory leadership ball had once again come loose from the back of the scrum. Come the evening of Sunday, 23 October 2022, though, twenty-four hours after the Sunak showdown, he was still well short in terms of public declarations of support from MPs. 'I could put my nomination in tomorrow. There is a very good chance that I would be successful in the election with Conservative Party members – and that I could indeed be back in Downing Street on Friday,' Johnson insisted that evening in a statement that carried a sting. 'But in the course of the last days I have sadly come to the conclusion that this would simply not be the right thing to do. You can't govern effectively unless you have a united party in parliament.'[22]

If that sounded like sour grapes, the first claim was not without foundation. The day after the withdrawal, Nigel Adams, the Johnson-backing Tory MP, showed the signed nomination papers that could have been submitted before the deadline to Bob Blackman, the joint secretary of the 1922 Committee, to prove Team Boris had the numbers. Blackman confirmed as much at the time and repeated the same to this author. 'I was able to verify that Johnson had more than enough numbers to enter the contest,' Blackman said in an interview.[23] Some supporters had declined to go public, as the Tory process allowed, presumably as they hoped for ministerial jobs if Sunak won. As Blackman recalled, there were around 110 Tory MP nominations for Johnson – a figure that Adams, who kept the papers, said was broadly accurate.[24]

Boris's withdrawal left one other candidate: Penny Mordaunt, the fluent and forthright former defence secretary who had been pipped to the post in reaching the members' vote by Truss in the summer contest. As the 2 p.m. deadline on Monday, 24 October approached Mordaunt's team claimed that she had reached the ninety MP mark, though the figure was way above public declarations of support. Ultimately, she fell short. Sunak was the only candidate still standing to have the support of over one hundred Tory MPs, so he was the next Conservative leader – and the next prime minister.

There was 'elation' in the Sunak camp when the news came in. 'It was emotional, it was incredible,' said one inner-circle member.[25] He had pulled it off, a Lazarus-like restoration to life. Minutes later Sunak was addressing the 1922 Committee, delivering a simple message: 'Unite or die.' And then, the following day, it was up Downing Street, past a nonchalant Larry the cat, and through the famous Number 10 door. Sunak, at the second time of asking, had reached the pinnacle of British politics.

What type of person was the new prime minister? That was a question many Britons would have been asking after he took office, with Rishi Sunak only having been in the spotlight of frontline politics – courtesy of a Cabinet position – for three and a half years.

As with each of his four predecessors, clues are offered by how time was spent away from the job. Sunak is a fan of 'trash TV', according to those who know him well.[26] *Bridgerton* and *Emily in Paris* are two favoured Netflix box sets.[27] Heart 00s is his radio station of choice, packed with cheesy classics from the first decade of the new millennium.[28] One aide recalled how during a late-night ride back in the ministerial car, security detail in tow, Sunak belted out Britney Spears's '. . . Baby One More Time'. 'He was singing along. He knew all the words,' the source said.[29] Sunak can rap the opening to Vanilla Ice's 'Ice Ice Baby', as he once proved in a *Sunday Times* interview.[30] His love of Jilly Cooper bonkbusters also appears genuine, the prime minister eagerly telling the press pack on one foreign trip that the series with *Riders* in it was his favourite. These are all described as outlets and distractions to take his mind off the intensity of work. 'He just wants to do something that is just total escapism,' said a Downing Street adviser.[31] Anything too close to his profession is vetoed. He waved away the recommendation to start watching the political series *The Diplomat* for that reason.[32]

Sunak's pastime pursuits can have the ring of teenage banality. The Star Wars and James Bond franchises are among his top movies.[33] The Beatles was picked as his favourite band.[34] His penchant for Nando's, the chicken restaurant chain, was such that he kept his own set of their branded sauce bottles in the Treasury. 'He was a medium-hot guy,' said an aide.[35] Chicken club sandwiches were also a favoured lunch order.[36] Despite being slim-built and only 5ft 6in tall, he has a notably sweet tooth. 'He just always has some sort of chocolate bar on the go,' said a Treasury insider.[37] Sunak does not drink alcohol: he was made to down vodka shots on his stag do and hated the taste.[38] His love of Coca-Cola has been broadcast far and wide, not least thanks to a giggling clip featuring two school pupils that went viral in which he confessed to being a 'total Coke addict'.[39] A full-sugar version of the pop drink served as a treat for Sunak on Saturday nights when running the UK economy.[40] Following a meeting in California with the 'leader of the free world', President Joe Biden, the plane home was stocked with bottles of Mexican Coke, known for being especially sickly. As Christmas approached, at the Treasury Sunak was known for singing aloud the brand's festive advertising theme tune: 'Holidays are coming! Holidays are coming!'[41]

But the geek portrayal is not a perfect fit. There is also a strong strain of 'tech bro', honed during his years surrounded by the unicorns of Silicon Valley while studying for his MBA. During flights on foreign trips Sunak will often change into a hoodie, tracksuit bottoms and socks before padding down to the back of the plane for a chat with reporters: a striking change from predecessors who would stay in formal attire. Sunak's Palm Angels black sliders – plastic slip-on footwear – caused such a stir when he was pictured in them as chancellor that they made it onto the front of his Christmas cards. He has a weakness for gizmos. He got into hot water when a £180 'smart' coffee mug that constantly maintains the liquid's temperature was seen in photographs that were released showing his Budget preparations.[42] In Number 10 he was spotted using an 'erasable ink' pen, allowing for corrections.[43] He also has a Peloton bike installed in the Number 10 flat. He has previously named Cody Rigsby as his favourite Peloton instructor, noting – again – the frequency with which Britney Spears is played in classes.[44]

It is in the tech scene that Sunak feels most comfortable, according to one of his fellow former Tory chancellors: 'When he's sitting down with a bunch of corporates, FTSE CEOs, his eyes glaze over. When he sits down with some start-ups and unicorns and Californian types, his eyes light up.'[45]

Cycling is not his only sporting pastime. Sunak runs. He clocked in a 10k at 47 minutes and 41 seconds in May 2023 – a time none of his prime ministerial predecessors is likely to have matched.[46] He genuinely follows football, specifically his hometown club of Southampton. According to one of his aides, he expressed bemusement at Johnson dressing up in an England football shirt despite not liking the sport.[47] Sunak is also a cricket fan. At the Treasury he had a signed England team bat in his office that he would swing about, practising forward defensive shots and cover drives while mulling things over with officials.[48] In the evenings he would sometimes head to nets at the Oval with his cousin.[49] During the working day, when an England test was on, he would keep the BBC's ball-by-ball online coverage up on his computer so that he could track the match's progress. Appearing on the BBC's beloved live commentary programme *Test Match Special* in July 2023 during the Ashes series, Sunak admitted diving into a statistical breakdown of England's 2022 performance to investigate whether 'Bazball' was working.[50] The prime minister, whose grandparents were from cricket-loving India, described past family days out at Hampshire matches, rushing onto the pitch during breaks to throw down a few balls.[51]

Another reflection of his Indian ancestry comes in Sunak's religion. He is the first Hindu prime minister, holding dear the teachings and principles of the religion, according to those who know him well. 'The thing that Hinduism gives to him is about values and what it teaches about how you treat other people, what respect means, what kind of person you are. He is a very values-based person,' said one ally.[52] On becoming chancellor, Sunak placed a small statue of the deity Shri Ganesh on his desk, a symbol of good luck in new endeavours. He left it there for Boris Johnson when, battling Covid-19, the then prime minister was isolated in an area of the Downing Street complex that included the chancellor's study.[53]

The statue would continue to sit on Sunak's desk in Number 10. The prime minister sometimes fasts. He also wears a coloured thread – often red – around his right wrist, another outward indication of his religious faith. While chancellor, Sunak lit candles to mark Diwali and later spoke about how much the act meant. 'It was one of my proudest moments that I was able to do that on the steps of Downing Street,' he was quoted as saying. 'It meant a lot to a lot of people and it's an amazing thing about our country.' About his Hinduism Sunak added: 'It gives me strength, it gives me purpose. It's part of who I am.'[54]

When it comes to his professional life, one feature is universally pointed to by colleagues: Sunak's unrelenting work ethic. 'He feels the weight of the responsibility very strongly. It's a very Indian thing, this idea of public service and duty,' said an ally.[55] Some of his team traced it back to his childhood. Despite the 'richest MP' tag regularly attached to Sunak, that vast wealth came through his marriage to Akshata Murty, whose father, Narayana Murthy, is an Indian billionaire entrepreneur. When he was growing up, the Sunaks were not dripping in money. His mother, Usha, ran a pharmacy, the young Rishi at times helping keep the books. His father, Yashvir, was a GP, staying on the job round the clock to pay to send Sunak to board at Winchester, a public school. 'His dad literally worked seven days a week without a day off, taking every on-call shift that he could, because he wanted to earn money to put away to save for education,' said a Sunak ally. 'He grew up watching his dad do that and, as the eldest of the three children, Rishi was much more attuned to what his parents were doing.'[56] The prime minister cited the positive impact his parents had on their local community as his inspiration for becoming an MP.[57]

In Number 10, as in the Treasury, Sunak prefers working late rather than starting super-early. He is normally at his office by 7.30 or 8 a.m., with meetings frontloaded in the first half of the day where possible so that he can dedicate time to his ministerial red box in the second half, sometimes until 10 p.m.[58] He has a sharp intellect, honed while rising through the educational ranks, invariably as a prefect. Sunak was head boy at his prep school, Stroud School, then head boy at Winchester. He got a first-class degree in, of course, Philosophy, Politics and Economics (PPE) from Oxford University – he was at Lincoln College – before beating fierce competition to a Fulbright scholarship which took him to Stanford. 'Sunak the head boy' became a favourite trope for political cartoonists, the cleaner-than-clean swot image taking hold largely because it rang true. But it also ignores the hours he puts in. 'Rishi is fifth gear, 100 per cent, full energy, committed to his work,' said Dominic Raab, who served as Sunak's deputy prime minister. 'If it hadn't been in politics he would have been like that in business.'[59] A former Treasury colleague said: 'His answer to most things is to work harder.'[60]

This approach brings an intensive thoroughness to his ministerial work. A long-time Treasury insider summed it up:

> Having worked with a lot of chancellors, he was the most interested in running the Treasury like an organisation where he was actually like the CEO. Often what happens is the minister sits above it all and just barks instructions to their private office or advisers and doesn't take a huge amount of interest in how everything all happens. Whereas Rishi took huge interest . . . Maybe it comes from having private-sector experience, so actually understanding that part of your job was genuine leadership, motivation, and setting direction and vision.[61]

Sunak would dive into the mechanics of Covid pandemic schemes like furlough or 'eat out to help out', a drive later much mocked over fears it helped spread the virus.

One result is that others are expected to step up too. Sunak as chancellor had a habit of requesting to talk to junior officials whose speciality he wanted to master. It was a sign of his determination to understand policy in depth and his willingness to listen to young staffers – but it also meant them being contactable at the drop of a hat, even at weekends or in the evening. One Number 10 official who had served multiple prime ministers would describe how on over-seas trips Sunak would read his briefing all the way to the bottom and then demand extra information – like whether the Canadian prime minister Justin Trudeau had daughters – as he prepared for a bilateral meeting.[62] He also developed a habit of keeping annexes from briefing notes in his own coloured plastic folders, so the next time the topic came up he could rapidly check how the numbers had changed. Some in Downing Street believed Sunak had a photographic memory, such was his ability to conjure up specifics from reading materials, though he always denied that that was the case.[63]

One innovation summed up his approach. It became known as the 'three-page briefs' or, during the Treasury years, the 'Rupert briefs', so named because special adviser Rupert Yorke helped with the drafting. Having dived deep into policy specifics, Sunak liked to zoom out and carefully plan the 'big picture' sell. When he was chancellor, every major policy announcement – especially around Budgets – would be distilled into a 'three-page brief'. This would spell out in tight, short paragraphs why the move was needed, what it would do and how criticisms were to be countered. Sunak was often involved himself in refining the arguments; occasionally, the process even led to tweaks in policy. These were not press releases. They were a way for Sunak to stress-test approaches and to work out how to sell them to fellow Tory MPs and the media. It was telling that, during his tenure at the Exchequer, though Budgets would prompt heated debate and grumbling from the Right – not least over tax rises – none unravelled in the days afterwards. There were no repeats of Philip Hammond's accidental manifesto breach when raising National Insurance for the self-employed or George Osborne's 'Omnishambles' blunders that led to U-turns. Indeed, in another indication of his thoroughness, Sunak was the only one of Osborne's successors to call him regularly in order to test out potential policy moves, just as George had done with the old Thatcherite chancellors.[64]

This determined focus meant there could be frustration, often not well hidden, when reporters used press conferences on specific announcements to ask him about other topics. Sunak was not an avid consumer of newspapers. He would sometimes scroll through the front pages and emerging stories when the first editions arrived around 10 p.m. but would not usually read the papers in the morning, an unusual arms-length approach to the press. Instead he would rely on the early briefings from his communications team telling him what he needed to know. The Sunak inner circle would pride itself on not being distracted by the 'media circus'.[65]

It was also manifested in tight control. In the summer 2022 leadership race Sunak was the only contender who would not allow newspaper photographers to take shots for interview pieces, his team instead issuing their own portrait pictures. When he became prime minister, newspaper interviews with Sunak could be limited to just ten minutes – less than half the time usually given by his predecessors – meaning that it was hard for reporters to dive into topics beyond the one chosen by Number 10 for discussion at the outset. Sunak prepared for interviews and press conferences more than outsiders might imagine, according to Number 10 aides.[66] The result was smooth performances, with every counter to a question thought through in advance – though delivered without the linguistic dexterity of Boris Johnson, which led to criticism at times of his robotic repetition of lines.

As with all politicians, press scrutiny could lead to irritation. 'He could sometimes be a bit thin-skinned on the media coverage,' said one colleague from the Treasury days. 'You see that in interviews, he can sometimes get a bit grumpy.'[67] The coverage of his wife's non-domiciled status, reports noting that she paid no UK tax on sizable overseas earnings while he raised rates as chancellor, clearly triggered frustration. Sunak rushed out to claim she was a victim of 'unpleasant smears' when the story first surfaced.[68] Akshata Murty changed her tax status soon afterwards. In the work sphere, it was the editorials of the City of London favourite the *Financial Times*, with its varied advice on policy, that grated on Sunak the most when he was chancellor. A Treasury figure explained:

> He found it frustrating that the *FT* would just write, 'Oh don't put up corporation tax, but also spend more on all these things.' And he was like, 'If you took all the *FT* editorials over a period of time they don't add up to having a coherent fiscal structure.' He would call them out on it.[69]

One other feature of Sunak the boss was the strong bond he built with a tight-knit group of advisers. His core team barely changed between the Treasury and Number 10. Liam Booth-Smith, a thoughtful think-tanker who proved a hit with the Westminster snappers on account of his leather jacket, occupied the chief-of-staff role. Nerissa Chesterfield, who began as a special adviser to Liz Truss and was held in high regard by the press pack, was point person for communications. Rupert Yorke focused on politics, seeing round corners when it came to the parliamentary party. All three first joined Sunak via the 'joint economic unit' between Number 10 and Number 11 created in early 2020 and which had forced Sajid Javid out as chancellor. All three would still be with Prime Minister Sunak. Other Treasury team members made the switch too. Cass Horowitz, son of the author Anthony Horowitz, was a tech whiz who helped build 'Brand Rishi' via social media. Eleanor Shawcross and James Nation were the policy brains he relied on in both Cabinet roles; likewise Douglas McNeill when it came to economics advice. Other senior figures would join them in Number 10, but the Treasury core remained – a testament to the loyalty Sunak instilled.

All these attributes would be on display during Rishi Sunak's testing first month in the job. First, there was a Cabinet to construct. Team Sunak opted against the Liz Truss approach of packing the top table with arch-loyalists, realising the weakness that brought when the party was so deeply divided. 'We observed that Liz hadn't done the best job of forming a government of unity, both in the Cabinet and lower down [the ministerial ranks]. We saw how that arguably didn't help her in office,' said one source involved.[70] Having witnessed the toppling of three Tory leaders in just over three years as colleagues lost faith, Sunak would opt for a Cabinet of all the factions.

Jeremy Hunt was kept on as chancellor. He would probably not have got the role if Sunak had won in the summer: Oliver Dowden and Mel Stride were at the front of the queue for that job, according to one senior campaign figure.[71] But Hunt's ministerial experience, moderate instincts and smooth media performances made him a good fit. Moving a chancellor after the financial upheaval of the Truss premiership was also judged to be unwise. Other key posts were given to big-name backers of Boris Johnson. Ben Wallace, the defence secretary, and James Cleverly, the foreign secretary, both kept their jobs, while Chris Heaton-Harris became Northern Ireland secretary. Likewise Thérèse Coffey, Liz Truss's deputy prime minister and best friend in politics, was made environment secretary. Former Tory leadership hopefuls were also given Cabinet spots: Suella Braverman, Penny Mordaunt, Kemi Badenoch, Tom Tugendhat, Grant Shapps and Michael Gove. 'What we needed to do for the first six months of government was essentially stabilise the economy but also stabilise the party,' explained a Number 10 insider.[72]

The process was not all smooth sailing, however. Sir Gavin Williamson had been rewarded for his campaign help with a Cabinet Office role, loosely defined in public. But soon hostile texts he had sent to Truss's chief whip, Wendy Morton — 'Well let's see how many more times you fuck us all over. There is a price for everything,' read one — became public amid bullying allegations.[73] On 8 November 2022, Sir Gavin resigned. In his letter to the prime minister he said he had apologised to Morton and refuted other claims made against him, saying he wanted to 'clear my name of any wrongdoing'.[74] The prime minister had lost his first Cabinet minister just fourteen days into the job.

The priority for the first month was financial stabilisation. Sunak was often described by Cabinet colleagues as having a stronger ideological belief in traditional Tory economics and values than may be assumed, given the cheery moderate public persona he projected. Later in his premiership Sunak would seek to dilute some net zero measures and turn up the rhetoric in the trans debate in the search for 'wedge' issues to carve off voters from Labour. Circumstances, though, limited his early ability to move. Despite Hunt's warnings about the importance of sticking to the Halloween date for the fiscal statement, it was shunted back to 17 November, giving Sunak time to play a more direct role in its development. And so a bumper set of tax rises was prepared. The big moves had already been announced in the dying days of the Truss premiership: gone were her plans to scrap the corporation tax rise, abolish the 45p additional rate of income tax and bring forward the 1p basic rate cut. The stamp duty reduction would remain, given fears over plummeting property prices, and the reversal of the National

Insurance rise would also go untouched. But this meant that a string of other stealth tax rises were needed. The thresholds above which people started to pay the basic and higher rates of income tax, as well as National Insurance and inheritance tax, were all frozen for another two years, boosting Treasury coffers by dragging more people into the higher bands as their salaries increased. Meanwhile departmental spending budgets remained unchanged, and thus would be hollowed out by rising prices, though state pensions and benefits would increase in line with inflation. In total, it amounted to a £55 billion package of tax rises and spending cuts designed to shore up the country's finances. In the view of the Sunak camp, it was nasty medicine but the treatment demanded by the economic malaise. 'You cannot borrow your way to growth,' Hunt would declare in his Autumn Statement address in the House of Commons, a not-so-subtle dig at forerunners Liz Truss and Kwasi Kwarteng.[75]

Trying to unite a divided party; losing a Cabinet minister; preparing a 'grin and bear it' fiscal statement – if that were not enough for Sunak's first month, he would be awoken one morning with the prospect of Britain being dragged into war. It came on 16 November 2022. The prime minister was asleep in Bali where he was attending the G20 summit when around 4 a.m. there was a banging at his door. Sunak, feeling he had only closed his eyes for a moment, scrambled to put a top on and answer the summons. His foreign policy team broke the news: a missile had hit a Polish village just the other side of the Ukrainian border. The cogs began to spin. Poland was a member of the Nato military alliance and thus was protected by Article 5, which states that an attack on one member state is considered an attack on all. Was Russia responsible? And if so, how would Nato have to respond? The prime minister's planned meeting with Chinese president Xi Jinping was scrapped, a scrambled G7 leaders' gathering instead arranged, with a condemnation issued as defence and intelligence services searched for information. In the end, it was established that the missile had been fired by Ukraine. Russia carried some blame – the missile was only shot to counter an incoming assault – but it was not directly responsible.

The brief crisis added to Sunak's baptism of fire. He would later joke that he did not need to experience every prime ministerial challenge in his first few weeks: 'Save some for the other months!'[76]

At the beginning of 2023, Rishi Sunak's first and last full year in Number 10 before having to call a general election, the prime minister announced his flagship plan for his time in office. It centred on five priorities, which would take up most of his focus and against which he wanted to be judged. The insight that underpinned the strategy was simple enough. The public, after almost thirteen years of Tory rule and the financial turmoil of Liz Truss's leadership, had largely lost faith in the governing party. Pollsters and political advisers were telling Sunak that he would have to earn the right to be listened to again by disillusioned voters. It would be no good just to talk about long-term visions for the country's economy or public services. What punters wanted was the immediate fires to be put out.

And so, before a press pack gathered at the former London 2012 Olympic Park in the first week of the new year, Sunak outlined his priorities.[77] There were five of them, though essentially they concerned just three areas: the economy, the NHS and immigration. The first priority was halving the rate of inflation by the end of 2023. That built on a central plank of Sunak's economic agenda in both leadership races, the argument that inflation was the worst of all economic evils, 'eroding' the pound in your pocket, triggering interest rate rises that impacted mortgages, and fuelling strikes as public-sector workers pushed for price-linked pay rises. The second was to grow the economy. No time frame was put on the pledge but essentially it amounted to avoiding or minimising the forecast UK recession. The third was making sure the national debt was falling. This was a long-term goal – usually defined as government debt as a proportion of GDP coming down within five years – and again reflected his campaign warnings about borrowing. The other priorities broached issues that had long made headlines. Getting NHS waiting lists down was the fourth. The Covid pandemic had sent them shooting up – though the rises had begun before then – and they were still increasing. The fifth was about small boats carrying asylum-seekers across the English Channel, with numbers continually hitting record highs in the preceding years. That push would be distilled down to a 'stop the boats' message in communications, but the promise was much more specific and narrow: simply to pass a law to tackle the crossings.

In an interview with the author in June 2023 for the *Daily Telegraph*, Sunak outlined his thinking. By then the prime minister had faced persistent sniping from Conservative critics who dubbed him a technocrat managing decline rather than a big-vision innovator bold enough to turn around the party's fortunes. Wearing a life jacket aboard a Border Force vessel off the coast of Dover, with the *Telegraph* invited along to discuss progress on his fifth priority, Sunak defended his focus on the five-point programme:

> I think in general people are fed up with politicians talking about things and not actually doing them. I want to be a politician who makes a difference to people's lives, I want us to be a government that is impactful on people's lives, changes people's lives for the better. Those five priorities that I've set out are measurable, they're tangible, they will make a difference to people's lives and that's why it's really important that we deliver them. And I think that's how you earn people's trust. You earn people's trust by doing the things that you say you're going to do. That's really important to me. Now that's not an ideology, but that's just about my approach to leadership and my approach to governing.[78]

The prime minister also offered an insight into his wider vision, on which he said he would focus more after progress had been made on the five priorities. Asked about his personal ideology, Sunak talked about the wide agenda hinted at in his January speech:

> I talked about having an education system that means that our children have the best education system in the world because that's how you spread opportunity and that's as a Conservative what I passionately believe. I talked about how do you create an economy which is dynamic, which is attracting investment, which is rewarding hard work. Those are all things that are important to me. I talked about supporting families because I wouldn't be here if it wasn't for the love and support and sacrifice of my own family and it's important that we recognise that. You've seen what I've done on anti-social behaviour, right? Growing up in communities which are safe is

important to me as a parent, first and foremost. And that's why I've been very tough on tackling anti-social behaviour. There's a new plan that we've outlined that we're implementing. I think that's starting to give you a sense of the things that are important to me.[79]

A supportive member of Sunak's Cabinet dismissed the criticisms more bluntly:

I don't buy that he's some visionless twerp who thinks he's managing a bank. What I think is that he's trying to play to the sentiment that we're fed up with the ongoing soap opera that politics has become. He believes politics is about the acquisition of power to govern wisely in the interest of people. I think he believes in low taxes, he believes in limited government. One of the misunderstandings is to say when he was chancellor he spent all the money. The reason he did was because he was basically working to a Number 10 that had political incontinence.[80]

The problem Sunak faced – the challenge that dogged his whole early premiership – was the woeful conditions that greeted him when he was handed the keys to Number 10. The inflation problem he inherited proved more difficult to tackle than hoped, price hikes being 'stickier' than expected. The resulting repeated increases in interest rates by the Bank of England sent government debt payments jumping up too. Economic forecasts were changed from recession to growth during the early months of the Sunak–Hunt partnership – a great political boost – but the potential impact of rate rises meant they were not fully out of the woods. NHS backlogs continued to lengthen in the first half of 2023, with Sunak instead pointing to improvements in a subsection of the statistics – long ambulance waiting times – to defend his record. In a BBC interview in June 2023 he accepted that overall waiting lists would not start falling until 2024. Small-boat numbers were down in the first five months of 2023 compared to 2022, but whether that would hold for the whole year remained to be seen. The political question was whether it was wise to be endlessly drawing the public's attention to the areas where the government was most struggling. A Downing Street insider waved away the criticism: 'I know there's a lot of people saying, "Oh it's fixing problems for now but what about the long term?" . . . If we didn't set out priorities then everyone would be like, "Well, you're not doing the things that people care about."[81]

The problematic Tory inheritance would trouble Sunak on another front too: integrity. The prime minister has always placed a high value on ethics and morals, according to those who work for him. It was his belief that resigning after incurring a Covid fine was the right thing to do that almost saw him walk out of Boris Johnson's government in April 2022, before he was persuaded otherwise. He had put an explicit reference to such things in his Downing Street steps speech, telling the public: 'This government will have integrity, professionalism and accountability at every level.'[82] The words would be thrown back at him by critics over Cabinet controversies. The incidents that followed could fit into what has been dubbed 'long Boris', headaches passed on from his predecessor that happened to cause political pain on Sunak's watch.

After Sir Gavin's exit there was the departure of Nadhim Zahawi as Conservative Party chairman. Zahawi, another Johnson supporter kept around the Cabinet table, had agreed to pay a penalty and millions of pounds in unpaid tax to HMRC over the historic sale of the YouGov polling firm he had helped found. The prime minister sacked him, saying there had been 'a serious breach of the ministerial code'. A third Cabinet minister, Dominic Raab, found himself in trouble over a succession of bullying claims. He denied wrongdoing, defended his conduct and vowed to resign if an investigation upheld any of the formal complaints. When it did, Raab went, with a swipe at the 'dangerous precedent' that had been set.[83] Suella Braverman too would find herself in the firing line after asking her civil servants to help deal with a speeding fine. Sunak would stand by his home secretary on that occasion. But the incidents – Sir Gavin going in November 2022, Zahawi sacked in January 2023, Raab resigning in April 2023, Braverman avoiding a scare in May 2023 – kept the question of senior Tory conduct in the headlines, making it tricky for Sunak to draw a line and live by his self-proclaimed 'integrity, professionalism and accountability' mantra.

There was another distraction that initially showed no signs of disappearing. Boris Johnson had revealed his hand in that brief,

333

scrambled return from the Dominican Republic in the hope of retaking Number 10 just six weeks after leaving it. He would later tell others he regretted not pushing the race to a membership vote, insisting it would have been 'fun' to take on Sunak in a battle decided by the grassroots.[84] Many Johnson backers believed his plan was never viable – if he won, the parliamentary party would not have had him for long, went the assessment.[85] But it showed that Boris still longed to be back on top in the great game of politics.

In the early months on the backbenches there would be few attempts at troublemaking. Focus turned to the speaking circuit: Johnson able to pick up a quarter of a million pounds for a conference appearance – more than he had made in a year running the country. Interventions, when they came, were on expected topics: a plea for more defence support for Ukraine here, a swipe at rising taxes there. The Conservative Democratic Organisation was formed, a body led by Johnson allies that championed empowering members who had never voted for Sunak. But Boris himself kept the group at arm's length, playing down his involvement to some friends.[86]

Two moments proved critical. One was about Brexit. Johnson, the Vote Leave figurehead, was the Tory most associated with the cause, but Sunak too had been a believer. A year into his parliamentary career, the MP for Richmond – a seat he inherited from former party leader William Hague – went against Downing Street and supported the UK leaving the European Union in the 2016 referendum. Sunak's CV would not necessarily denote him a Brexiteer, more a member of the globe-trotting financial elite that Nigel Farage so often derided as Ukip leader. But the view was sincerely held, according to allies. 'I think in his heart and soul it made sense for someone that had been involved in global businesses and both had heritage in India and professional experience in the US,' said Dominic Raab.[87] Others echoed the idea, wondering if the future-facing Silicon Valley, where innovation and nimbleness led to leaps forward, shaped his views on the concept of rules and regulations decided by a twenty-eight-member bloc. It would be 'free ports' – ultra-low-tax, low-red-tape UK coastal zones designed to drive up post-Brexit enterprise – that became Sunak's most prominent policy push from the backbenches. Others wondered if politics had played a part too. Richmondshire voted Leave by 57 per cent to 43 per cent: higher than the national average. One leading Cameron-era figure suspected that Sunak saw the way the Eurosceptic Tory base was heading, whatever the final referendum result.[88]

Taking over in Number 10 meant inheriting a post-Brexit headache from Johnson via Truss: the Northern Ireland Protocol. The deal, struck by Boris to secure the UK's EU departure, was essentially a fudge: agreeing that customs checks would take place for goods travelling from Great Britain into Northern Ireland in order to keep the latter's land border with the Republic of Ireland open. But, once out of the EU, UK ministers had protested at the implementation of those checks, which were due to be phased in, pushing for renegotiation instead. Johnson had begun legislating to allow the UK unilaterally to renege on parts of the agreement, a move whose legality was up for debate. Sunak was more cautious, parking the proposed new law and intensifying negotiations. In February 2023, after weeks of painstaking talks – Sunak often liaised directly with Ursula von der Leyen, the European Commission president – a deal was eventually struck. The 'Windsor Framework' was seen as a triumph by the Sunak camp, agreeing a set of intricate solutions to knotty problems that had real-world implications for trade in Northern Ireland. At its heart was the 'Stormont Brake', which gave the Northern Ireland Assembly the ability to object to changes to EU laws that applied in the province.

But would hardline Tory Brexiteers back the deal? The group had already forced out Theresa May and developed a reputation for ruthlessly efficient rebellions, but that was in the past now. Sunak's Downing Street had been carefully managing MP relations, backing down during early clashes with Tory rebels about on-shore wind turbines and house-building targets as it tried to smooth over deep divisions. But on the Windsor Framework, it chose to square up to them. On the morning of the vote on 22 March 2023, Johnson, returning to his comfort zone as leader of backbench Brexiteers, went over the top, announcing that he would vote against the proposals. So too did Liz Truss. Other leading Eurosceptics such as Priti Patel did likewise. It was a moment of political danger for Sunak, a calculated and co-ordinated push to build up momentum for a defeat. Yet the putsch failed. In the end, as Johnson jumped out of the trenches sounding the war cry, barely two dozen Tory MPs followed. In the critical vote, 282 Conservative MPs backed Sunak's Brexit plan, while just twenty-one joined Boris in voting against it. 'That was a major moment,' said a senior Downing Street figure.[89] Getting the Democratic Unionist Party to accept the compromise and return to power-sharing at Stormont would continue to be a struggle. But Johnson's Brexit mutiny had been crushed.

The second key moment would prove politically deadly for Johnson. The Commons Privileges Committee investigation into whether he had misled MPs when denying lockdown-breaking in Downing Street had hung over him for more than a year. In June, its brutal conclusions were finally delivered. The seven MPs on the committee – four of whom were Tories, members of Johnson's own party – found that he had deliberately and repeatedly misled his colleagues over partygate. Eventually the committee would recommend a ninety-day Commons suspension for Johnson – way above the ten-day threshold that allowed constituents to trigger a by-election if enough signatures were collected. But before the report was released publicly Johnson shocked Westminster by announcing that he was quitting as an MP. The decision, made after being handed a draft version of the report's scathing conclusions, was announced on 9 June 2023. 'Their purpose from the beginning has been to find me guilty, regardless of the facts,' Johnson fumed about the committee members. 'This is the very definition of a kangaroo court.' And then there was the dramatic reveal: 'It is in no one's interest, however, that the process the committee has launched should continue for a single day further. So I have today written to my Association in Uxbridge and South Ruislip to say that I am stepping down forthwith and triggering an immediate by-election.'[90]

It was a huge moment, for both Johnson and Sunak. For the former, it was the end of his frontline political career. Boris, via the London mayoralty, Foreign Office and the backbenches, had risen to the top of British politics. After Downing Street, a glimmer of hope of a return remained, however dim, as long as he was an MP, since only parliamentarians can become prime minister. But standing down from Uxbridge, a move seemingly designed to avoid the by-election defeat that loomed, ruled that out, at least in the short term. In the vote on the report's conclusions and the punishment of stripping Johnson of his parliamentary pass, just seven Conservative MPs tried to block the move. Boris was isolated and on his way out of Westminster. The departure from Parliament was only 'for now', Johnson had written in his resignation announcement, teasing a return.[91] But it had the ring more of hope than expectation.

For Sunak, the announcement lifted a burden from his shoulders. The Tory rival who had dogged his premiership, the person best placed to seize the party leadership if there was any attempt to oust Sunak before the election, was now off the scene. But there was damage done too. Out with Johnson went two acolytes, Nigel Adams and Nadine Dorries both declaring they would step down as MPs after peerages proposed for them by Boris were blocked by the House of Lords vetting body. This would result in further by-elections being held, with the Conservatives way behind Labour in the opinion polls. One of Sunak's biggest political weaknesses was his absent track record of electoral wins. He had lost to Liz Truss. He had secured the premiership by avoiding the membership. And now his electability was to be tested. A hat-trick of defeats in by-elections on 20 July 2023 was avoided, just – the seats of Adams and the departing David Warburton were lost, but the Tories hung on by 495 votes in Johnson's constituency. Even so, it had been a parting two-fingers from Boris, happy to give his old rival a kick on his way out of the door.

Every prime minister is bound by their circumstances. For Rishi Sunak, though, this was especially true. His early Tory leadership felt akin to an agile swimmer being forced to don an old-fashioned diving suit for a race. However nimble the movements, however wise the course plotted, he was weighed down by the outfit he had been obliged to wear. There were the anchors of the economy: stubborn inflation, soaring interest rates and stuttering growth. For a party whose economic credibility was at the centre of its electability, the numbers were debilitating. There were the energy-sapping Tory divisions. Many Johnsonites and Trussites loathed Sunak, the former for Boris's ouster and the latter for how he opposed Liz's economic agenda. Scores of Tory MPs, more even than the 1997 election when New Labour was dominant, decided not to stand again. And then there was the heavy burden which came from more than a decade in office. When a party has been in power so long, voters have no one else to blame for real-world problems not solved. None of that was inherently insurmountable. With hard kicks and firm arms it is possible for a swimmer to rise up, whatever weight is being carried.

But as the finish line of the next general election approached the shimmering water surface seemed far, far above.

11

Wipeout

IN THE END, when it came, there were tears. Downing Street advisers and officials lined the corridor leading up to the door of Number 10, clapping out their prime minister. Rishi Sunak and his wife Akshata Murty worked their way slowly along the carpet, expressing thanks. There were hugs. There were words of gratitude. And, among some, visible sadness. 'It was an emotional moment,' said one there.[1] 'People were upset and crying,' remarked another.[2] A third said: 'Lots of staff had tears in their eyes . . . he was held in great affection.'[3]

The farewell was for a premiership. But the curtain was closing, too, on something else: a remarkable stretch of one-party dominance. For fourteen years and fifty-five days without break the country had been run by a Conservative prime minister. No more. The streak had been stopped not with a whimper but a bang. Sunak had inherited an economic and political mess when he had been parachuted in after Liz Truss's implosion in late 2022. He had cleaned up the former but, it was now clear, he had failed categorically on the latter. The day before – 4 July 2024 – the electorate had delivered their verdict, the voting equivalent of a raised two fingers. Just 121 Tory MPs had been elected, the party's worst result since the birth of modern British democracy in 1832. The wilderness of opposition beckoned.

Each election defeat has its own distinct feel. In 2016, amid the disbelief, the shock Brexit vote brought raw pain for David Cameron's team, nobody expecting his tenure at the top to end then. In 2017, the loss of the Tory majority landed like a gut punch to Theresa May's entourage who, predicting a landslide win, had convinced her to call the vote.

There was no surprise about the Tory hammering in 2024: 'For several weeks, there was just the impending sense that this was how it was going to end,' one trusted Sunak ally put it.[4] So that morning, 5 July, there was a 'sad playing out of what had become an inevitability'.[5] The mood was 'sombre', funeral.[6] This was not a shock political death, delivered by a middle-of-the-night phone call. It had looked terminal for some time.

In his final few hours in power, Sunak was 'businesslike'.[7] There had been a brief conversation with Simon Case, the Cabinet secretary, and some practising of the last speech he would deliver as prime minister, on the steps of Downing Street. Sunak was exhausted. He was worried about losing his voice. He was tired and 'under the weather', said one by his side that morning.[8] There was also a sense of responsibility. 'He felt a kind of sadness and a regret that he couldn't get more colleagues home.'[9] An all-staff gathering had been held upstairs in Downing Street's Pillared Room, around a hundred aides and officials standing under the chandeliers. 'The election defeat's all mine,' Sunak told the crowd, some now unemployed. 'You guys have done a brilliant job and should be proud of the things that you've helped with.'[10] This is where the tears began, not just from political appointees but civil servants too.

And then came the long walk. Down the Number 10 stairs, past the portraits of each previous prime minister – a reminder that all things come to an end – and along the corridor to that famous black door. The prime minister – the title still holding for a few moments more – kept stopping to show his appreciation. One junior official was urged to keep up their jogging club.[11] A political aide was asked: 'What are we going to do now we're not seeing each other every day?'[12] 'It was a beautiful moment,' said one Sunak adviser looking on. 'You saw the human side of everyone come to the surface.'[13]

A few present had also been there when David Cameron and Nick Clegg swept into power in May 2010, the Tory–Liberal Democrat coalition christened in Downing Street's garden of roses. It was a distant memory now. Many more had only seen the centre of power under Rishi. For Sunak himself, the last of the five Conservative prime ministers, there was acceptance. 'He was calm,' said one of his advisers. 'He was very at peace with it.'[14]

For something like twenty minutes the applause rang out, Sunak and his wife inching towards the exit. So loud was the clapping it could be heard in the street, where the world's media had gathered to witness the Tory finale. And then there was light, the door opening inwards as the pair stepped out into the grey morning. It closed like a full stop. 'It felt like the end of an era,' said a Sunak aide.[15] And it was.

Was defeat unavoidable? It is tricky to construct a campaign scenario which would have kept the Conservatives in power without having to rely on implausible developments in the race. The party was asking for a historic fifth term, stretching their rule to nineteen years, when the political mood of the country tends to change on a shorter cycle. The baggage of a double prime-minister switch in 2022, including a calamitous mini-Budget from Liz Truss that exploded Tory trust on the economy, was there long before election decisions were made. The result suggests a sea-change in voter sentiments not easily countered.

Yet nothing is fated. The exact shape of how the votes landed – in particular how low the Tory seat count dropped, leaving the party only just able to pull together a meaningful opposition – was not inevitable. Decisions carried consequences. And for those left spitting blood at the Tory battering, Team Sunak is to blame for one original sin: calling the election early.

The general election was scheduled for July 2024. It did not have to be held until January 2025. It was Rishi Sunak who chose the date. He and his team decided to forgo six months of Conservative government to gamble on a summer election. They lost. It is a call sure to be long debated inside the party and beyond. And so it is worth laying out the thinking in all its nuances – as told by those directly involved, who were among twenty-five insiders from across the parties who spoke to the author in interviews for this chapter.

Sometimes momentous political decisions can be pinpointed to a single moment. Not so for this one, according to members of Sunak's inner circle. Instead, there was a rolling, morphing discussion, some options were closed down swiftly, others moved from possible to probable before eventually one date – 4 July – was locked in as a certainty.

The backdrop was mounting frustration with the consistency of Labour's lead in the opinion polls. Throughout 2023, Sunak made progress on some of his 'five priorities', with inflation falling and the number of migrants arriving on small-boat crossings down from 2022.[16] Yet early tightening in the polls to spring had hit the buffers when Boris Johnson's partygate saga made headlines again with the parliamentary investigation that would force his resignation. Come the autumn there had been a net zero reset and a party conference speech that saw the prime minister try to embody change, railing against the 'thirty-year political status quo' – a repositioning soon abandoned when he made David Cameron, a predecessor, his foreign secretary.[17] By the start of 2024 Labour was sitting on a poll lead of around 20 percentage points, landslide victory territory. Sunak declared his 'working assumption' was to hold the election 'in the second half of this year', a line he would stick to whenever asked.[18] But, as a senior Tory campaign figure admitted, the position was 'entirely media management' – something to say to endless 'When's the date?' reporter questions.[19] In private, the deciding team was much more open to going early and catching their opponents off guard.

Two gatherings on Sunday nights in Number 10 were key. The location was on the building's first floor, the cast list short. It included: Oliver Dowden, the deputy prime minister whose instincts Sunak had, over the years, come to rely on; Liam Booth-Smith, Sunak's chief of staff who had been with him since his Treasury days; James Forsyth, the school friend who made Sunak his best man and had deep Tory connections as *The Spectator*'s former political editor; and Isaac Levido, the Australian strategist who led the party's winning 2019 campaign and had the same role this time round. Others would shape thinking throughout this period too: Nerissa Chesterfield, Sunak's director of communications; Rupert Yorke, his deputy chief of staff focusing on political matters; Simon Hart, the clubbable chief whip; and, of course, Akshata, the prime minister's wife.

The first Sunday night gathering was on 10 March. The subject at hand: whether or not to call the general election for 2 May, when the country would already be voting in the local elections. Stumbling blocks soon emerged. The economic recovery was always a central plank in the Tory campaign but the country was then, technically, still in a recession. Plus turning local elections into a general, driving up turnout and making voters think nationally, hurt the chances of Tory mayors Andy Street in the West Midlands and Ben Houchen in Tees Valley using their strong local brands to win re-election. A quick consensus was reached that May would not work.

Hence the second Sunday gathering, on 28 April. The question now was whether to call a summer election or wait until the autumn – October or November, as was widely expected in the Westminster bubble. It was here that the path was set for a summer election. The final lock-in came after the local elections, when Houchen's victory offered a glimmer of hope and forecasts pointed to inflation dropping back down to the 2 per cent target set by the Bank of England, allowing the prime minister to declare an economic victory of sorts.

But why? Why forgo the possibility of things improving by firing the starting gun, especially when the Tories were 20 points behind in the polls? Sunak's inner circle put forward three broad reasons.

Firstly, there were plenty of signs that things would get worse on policy, not better. Sunak had promised deportation flights to Rwanda – his flagship immigration policy – would finally take off in July. There were fears inside Number 10 that the courts, knowing Labour would junk the project, could delay the scheme. One Downing Street source claimed: 'It was being made very clear to us by legal professionals that the judges were going to do everything possible, up to and including breaking legal precedent, to stop the flights.'[20] Plus a summer surge of small-boat crossings loomed as the weather improved, possibly further locking in signs that 2024 would break records despite a fall in numbers in 2023. This would undercut Sunak's message of improvement.

Another red light was flashing over prisons. Ministers were being told prison places were about to run out, with officials pushing for urgent early releases. The problem could 'blow up' if they waited until autumn.[21] Some felt 'the system' – aka the civil service – was increasingly resistant. 'It just totally clammed up', said a Number 10 insider, feeling Whitehall's focus turning to the probable Labour government.[22] Then there were issues like strikes. Another round of pay recommendations for teachers, doctors and the like from independent review bodies were about to be submitted, which trade unions would demand were approved. 'We were never going to pay the sort of sums that they wanted, and we would have had a summer beset by industrial action across the entire public sector,' said a member of the Sunak inner circle.[23]

The second reason for not waiting longer was MP management. The Tory parliamentary party, bound together pretty loosely after hurt feelings from the year of three prime ministers, was beginning to come apart at the seams. Two Conservative MPs defected to Labour within a fortnight: Dan Poulter, the former health minister, switching on 27 April over the NHS, and Natalie Elphicke, the Dover MP on the party's Right, flipping on 8 May citing border security. The latter blindsided the Tory whips who had pulled together a list of half a dozen potential defectors that did not include Elphicke. Who else could abandon ship? Reform, ticking up in the polls, was seeking defections too, its leader Richard Tice sounding out disillusioned Tories. Word that a scandal-hit outgoing Conservative had been offered £10,000 to run for Reform reached the Tory whips – a claim denied by a source close to Tice.[24] Added to this was the endless possibility that enough malcontents could submit 1922 Committee letters to trigger a no-confidence vote in Sunak. Simon Hart believed the number of letters was in the low twenties, about halfway to the threshold but still too close for comfort.[25] Then there was the prospect of more Tory scandals. As one senior campaign figure bemoaned: 'There is no strategy that's good enough to withstand rolling fucking sex pests and unending fucking by-elections because of MP behaviour.'[26] Going long meant more time for the Tory Party to further implode.

Thirdly, it was feared that the rosy economic news everyone was expecting later in the year might not come to pass. Tories were anticipating interest rate cuts, but Number 10's top brass had spotted the markets pricing in fewer reductions than earlier in the year.[27] Plus the existence of so many fixed-rate deals meant many families would actually experience a jump in payments when remortgaging after a few years – and so would direct more anger at the party –

even if the rates dropped a little. Hopes of a tax-cutting Budget giveaway in the autumn had also faded, with mega compensation payouts to the victims of the infected blood and Horizon IT scandals further tightening public finances. It all acted to dull the appeal of biding time.

But that was not all. There was a fourth factor. It went largely unsaid in the key meetings, according to those present, but was still detectable. Sunak was feeling a sense of 'fatigue'.[28] It was not, to be clear, a willingness to give up. The idea Sunak wanted to 'end it all', claimed by some, was 'rubbish', said one who knows him well.[29] But it was something subtler: a political leader, relatively new to the scene and accustomed to success, taking flak for month after month after month with little respite. A man who believed hard work could solve most problems seeing no uptick in the polls despite all his efforts. In fact, the opposite: a decline in his own personal approval ratings, the prime minister becoming the butt of jokes where once he had been 'dishy Rishi' the Covid chancellor. He was not dragging the Tory Party up; it was dragging him down.

One who had Sunak's ear called it the 'emotional element' in the decision, a sense of 'the PM just wanting to get this thing on with'. The grind 'took its toll', the source added, summarising Sunak's thinking as: 'What else is going to move the bloody dial? Do we just need to bring this to a head and call an election?'[30] Another Downing Street insider echoed the thought: 'The fucking bombardment we were getting. He was absolutely beaten up. He was knackered.' It was 'not a reason to go early itself' but contributed to the thinking, the source added.[31] A third figure, one central in election-timing discussions, said of Sunak: 'The job had made him a glass-half-empty kind of guy, rather than half-full, because everything had gone against him. He was making a judgement that "everything is probably going to go against me, so sooner was better".'[32]

There was some resistance to the call in the Sunak camp. The central figures did not go 'hammer and tongs' at each other; civility was maintained with everyone understanding there was no perfect date given the political terrain. But there were differences in advice, often reflecting the position in the Westminster ecosystem in which they dwelt. Oliver Dowden was the keenest on going in the summer, multiple sources say.[33] His role at the centre of government made him acutely aware of the policy problems looming, though he is said to have expected the prime minister to 'baulk' and go for autumn.[34] Liam Booth-Smith and James Forsyth, always by Sunak's side and sensitive to his personal outlook, both ended up convinced of the merits of July, acknowledging fears that things could deteriorate if they waited. Isaac Levido, however, offered the most push-back. As campaign manager focusing on the election, not government delivery, he had laid out a 'plan is working' narrative that built towards an autumn vote. By then, interest rates would likely have been cut, the electorate would have had the summer to switch off and – who knew – maybe England could have won the Euros. Levido remained unconvinced of going in spring while acknowledging that others were closer to the policy problems. Ultimately all involved accepted it was Sunak's call.[35] So 4 July it was to be.

The prime minister set in train the general election without telling Cabinet, asking King Charles to dissolve Parliament before informing his ministers on 22 May, the day the public, too, was told. Some disapproved. Grant Shapps, the defence secretary, raised concerns in a pre-meeting of senior Cabinet ministers, telling Sunak: 'I personally think it might have been better to wait.'[36] Esther McVey, dubbed the minister for 'common sense', spoke up in the wider Cabinet meeting: 'I see it differently. I think it is a big mistake.'[37] Chris Heaton-Harris, the Northern Ireland secretary, was less critical but made clear he favoured an autumn election.[38] Others stayed silent despite reservations, one Cabinet minister likening the situation to a friend saying they are getting married tomorrow, asking you to be best man, then saying 'any doubts?'[39]

Perhaps the most damning indictment comes from past Tory election victors. It is understood almost none of the key players in recent Conservative successes would have gone for the summer over the autumn. David Cameron, who returned the Tories to office in 2010, 'would not' have made that decision.[40] Sir Lynton Crosby, who masterminded the Tory majority of 2015, was said to have been against it.[41] George Osborne, who helped call the shots in both those races, favoured going as late as possible so the economic benefits of low inflation and returning growth could be felt.[42] Michael Gove, who was at the top of the Brexit campaign, favoured putting 'more runs on the board', despite his warm words around the Cabinet table.[43] And as for Boris Johnson, deliverer of the 2019 landslide: 'No one in their right mind who understands politics and cares for the party would have gone in July,' said one Boris friend who served in his Downing Street. 'Boris was not consulted and clearly is not stupid.'[44]

And then it was time to go public. As usual, a podium was positioned in front of the door to Number 10 Downing Street. The dark clouds overhead had led the Sunak team to sketch out a back-up plan if the weather did not hold. The prime minister would call the election from the state rooms upstairs which could be used for political announcements – unlike regular government offices – as they were considered part of his residence. But the 'dry launch' plan was left unused.[45] Why? Because the forecasts suggested the weather was brightening, one Number 10 insider said.[46] Another thought launching indoors would lead to 'Sunak is scared of getting his hair wet' headlines.[47] A third said, in the end, the prime minister made the call: 'He felt quite strongly he should crack on and do it.'[48]

The miscalculation was apparent within minutes. As Sunak laid out his pitch to the nation, a protester blared out 'Things Can Only Get Better' by D:Ream. The song – Labour's 1997 election anthem – could be heard clearly on TVs broadcasting the moment. And then the heavens opened. As the prime minister persisted, the shoulder pads of his dark suit jacket became visibly drenched and shiny. As his opponent Sir Keir Starmer would declare later: the man who claims his plan is working could not even find a brolly for the rain. The other side of the door, in the dry, Cabinet ministers watching along felt their hearts sink. One would later sum it all up: 'Number 10 Drowning Street'.[49]

The sodden Sunak announcing his election became the defining image of the campaign. But it was those preceding weeks, when the country's leader and his small team of advisers risked it all on 4 July, that rankled most with the Tories later swept away by the tsunami of public opinion. They see a group too willing to gamble their colleagues' careers, too lacking in political nous.

One Sunak Cabinet minister, red-hot with rage after being voted out, seethed: 'It was a bloody stupid time to call an election. It was utter incompetence . . . You have just given up six to seven months of your premiership! It is always better to have a Conservative government.' The ousted MP had a particular phrase for the prime minister's behaviour: 'punch-drunk'. A leader reeling from blows, his thinking becoming muddled. 'It was a punch-drunkenness. It was a tragic mistake,' the source said. 'How much worse could it really get? It could have gotten better.'[50]

With the election called, focus turned to the short six-week campaign. There would be many twists and turns for those watching closely, both blows landed by the Tories and blunders committed. But stepping back, one moment stands out in significance above all others: the decision by Nigel Farage to return to the political frontline.

It came on Monday, 3 June, at the start of the second full week of campaigning as the deadline loomed for candidates to register. At an 'emergency' press conference in central London, Farage revealed with a gleeful smile that he would be taking over as leader of Reform and running to become the MP for Clacton. 'What I intend to lead is a political revolt,' he declared, adding: 'I've done it before. I'll do it again. I will surprise everybody.'[51]

The threat from Reform UK – the party's official title – to the Conservatives at the election was never of leap-frogging them as a parliamentary force, despite all Farage's claims that they could become the real opposition to a Labour government. The danger was found in the crossover of voters. The higher Reform rose in support, the lower the projected Tory vote share dropped, given the party was largely attracting disillusioned Conservatives. The dynamic risked handing Labour victory in swathes of Tory-held seats.

It was here Farage's impact was felt. 'There are only two rock stars in British politics: Boris Johnson and Nigel Fararge,' a veteran Tory MP once said.[52] With the former long gone from Westminster, the latter had returned to the limelight. There are plenty of voters and commentators horrified by Farage's tub-thumping populism and immigration rhetoric, seeing it as tapping into the electorate's darker instincts. His allies defend his approach as channelling the views of voters whose concerns are overlooked by the London bubble. But even his critics would acknowledge he is a potent political communicator, much more so than Richard Tice, the Reform leader he replaced. Plus, he attracted bucketloads of media coverage.

The evidence is there in the polls. Reform was averaging 11 per cent of the vote two days before Farage returned, squeezed down from 13 per cent in April. Support soared afterwards, hitting 17 per cent, with the odd poll even showing the party above the Conservatives.[53] Reform would finish getting 14 per cent of the vote. 'We needed them down at 10 per cent', a senior Tory campaign source acknowledged. With Tice, it was deemed possible. Not with Farage.

Which leads to two intriguing questions. How close was Farage to not running? And could a deal have been struck to keep him out?

To answer the first, the trail of breadcrumbs must be followed back to the lunch table at the central London branch of Boisdale, the upmarket Scottish steaks and seafood restaurant. There on Tuesday, 23 April, the same week Rishi Sunak's team would huddle to plot a summer election, Nigel Farage and Richard Tice met to discuss the future of Reform. On the bright red walls hung framed paintings and historical trinkets, but on the white-clothed tables there were no bottles of wine associated with the normal Farage lunch. 'It was a very sober do, actually,' Farage claimed to the author. 'It was very restrained.'[54]

It was here that Tice, Reform's leader since shortly after it was renamed from the Brexit Party in early 2021, and Farage, who as the majority owner of the entity was effectively in control, are said to have struck a pact. At least, according to the narrative pushed by senior Reform figures. The terms were said to be that Farage would become leader, Tice would be shunted to chairman and Farage would run to become an MP at the autumn election. Tice and Farage both confirmed the outline of the agreement to the author.[55] A one-page memo capturing its terms exists, it is claimed, though it has not been produced – meaning some doubts must remain.[56]

Plenty of doubt exists about whether Farage would really have run in the autumn, given the US presidential election – featuring his 'friend' Donald Trump – was scheduled for 5 November. One long-time Tory strategist claimed Farage had already signed a contract to be a surrogate for Trump on TV.[57] 'I had signed nothing,' Farage insisted, though added: 'I had offers on the table.'[58] A source high up in the Tory campaign said: 'Clearly it would have been far, far, far, far more likely that he wouldn't have got in in the second half of the year.'[59] Others critical of the summer election echo the point.

Farage's position is clear: he was always going to stand in the autumn. Indeed, it was the July election that almost scuppered the plan, Farage initially announcing he would not be a candidate only to backtrack with that press conference. 'I would have run if it was an autumn election,' Farage told the author. 'I was very unsure when it was a summer one. I'd given up on the idea. And then the first few days, going round the country trying to help people, suddenly I felt this demand to do something. In the end I gave in to that pressure. It was not what I planned at all. It was a very, very last-minute decision.'[60]

The position – if taken as accurate – will be seized on by Number 10 aides as proof that their best chance of knocking Farage out of the race was by going early with the election, not late.

But there was a possibility even before then of sidelining Farage. It came in the tantalising prospect of a deal. Boris Johnson's rout of Jeremy Corbyn's Labour in the 2019 election had been helped by the then Brexit Party leader agreeing not to put up candidates against sitting Tory MPs. Could a similar pact have been struck in 2024? One thing is clear from interviews with key players: there was an openness to the idea at the heart of Downing Street. 'If it helps win, fuck it. We'll have a go,' was the view of one of Sunak's most trusted political lieutenants.[61] Whether it was really on the cards is another question. But more was done to scope out the idea than has been acknowledged publicly.

There were roughly seven months of activity. The first phase, dating between November 2023 and March 2024, involved putting out feelers in Eurosceptic circles, where both pro-Brexit Tory and Reform figures moved, and seeing what came back. By then support for Reform was rising, giving Downing Street an incentive to explore possibilities. People who knew Farage and Tice would ask them: 'Look, this is only going to end up with a left-wing government. What can we do?'[62] The conversations were not always prompted by Number 10 but often found their way back there, sometimes reaching James Forsyth, well-connected in such worlds thanks to his *Spectator* past. A sense soon emerged that while Farage was more open to the idea, Tice was actively hostile. For their part, Farage and Tice did not deny loose entreaties were made but insisted they were rebuffed. 'Zero interest from me,' said Farage. 'After 2019, are you kidding? No interest.'[63] Tice acknowledged 'third- or fourth-party' approaches, adding: 'Anybody who intimated it was put firmly back in their box. It was "over my dead body".'[64]

A second wave of activity, in April and May 2024, revolved around a specific proposal pushed by Dame Andrea Jenkyns, the Brexit-backing, Boris-supporting Tory MP for Morley and Outwood who faced a Reform challenge in her seat. She wanted 'joint ticket' Tory–Reform candidates in the 'Red Wall', those traditionally Labour-voting seats in the North and Midlands that went blue in 2019.[65] Dame Andrea had identified a part of the Conservative Party constitution which would need to be changed, one which ruled out helping rival parties. She had sounded out Farage and Tice about the idea. She had also directly brought it up with Rishi Sunak, first over the phone and then in a face-to-face meeting. The proposal was not immediately rejected by Number 10. The prime minister discussed it with Liam Booth-Smith and agreed to keep an open mind. Craig Williams, Sunak's parliamentary private secretary, talked to Andy Wigmore, one of the self-styled 'Bad Boys of Brexit' around Farage at the 2016 referendum, to discuss further, the last conversation happening just before the July election was called. But, ultimately, the idea did not morph into anything tangible. 'It never really felt real,' said one Number 10 insider involved. 'There was nothing to grasp on to.'[66]

The prime minister and his most trusted aides are not known to have talked to Farage or Tice directly. Figures in both camps insist that never happened. And discussions did not get to the point where Isaac Levido was asked to factor them into plans, as had been the case in 2019. There were two critical differences between 2019 and 2024: this time Brexit, Farage's personal crusade, was not on the line as it had been in 2019, and Sir Keir simply did not engender the same alarm among the Right as Corbyn had.

For sliding-doors moments on Reform, one veteran of Tory campaigns looked beyond the 2024 election cycle to the wider picture. 'I think the biggest, long-term strategic mistake the Conservative Party has made over the last ten years is that someone should have put Farage in the Lords. We would never have had this problem. Whether it was Cameron, whether it was Theresa, whether it was Boris. It was too late then for Rishi to do it.'[67]

Instead, Farage was left on the political battlefield, ready to wage war on the Conservative Party – once again – to devastating effect.

The art of a successful election campaign is about seeing the world as it is and not as you wish it to be. A deep understanding of the electorate is essential: which voters are with you, which are persuadable, where they are found and how to tilt them your way. It requires a big-picture framing, carefully targeted messages and policy appeals, and the political skill to deliver on the trail. The best campaign pitches have a ring of truth. For months, each party had been planning how to play the cards they were dealt. Now the game had begun.

For the Tory campaign, led by the no-nonsense Isaac Levido, who had inherited the same intolerance for bullshit as his mentor Sir Lynton Crosby, the focus was on somehow keeping together the 2019 coalition of voters. In that election, the Tories had won over staunch Labour backers with a pro-Brexit message. Now, Tory research suggested, just 50 per cent of those 2019 voters were still with them. It was the undecideds remaining in the other half – perhaps a further 25 per cent – who were the real targets.

Levido's approach was to try to 'lock in the base' first, then woo the waverers.[68] A policy blitz was designed, manifesto policies announced early: national service, the 'triple lock plus' that vowed never to tax the state pension, a cap on migrant work visas. 'We needed to do bigger and bolder things than you might normally do to animate the campaign, using policy at the start to try and catch attention,' explained one source involved.[69] At the same time the campaign nuts and bolts were slotted into place. The first daily meeting of senior figures was held at 5.40 a.m., in time to shape 6 a.m. news bulletins. Then a wider meeting around 6.30 a.m. A call with Rishi Sunak would be held usually between 7.30 a.m. and 8 a.m., briefing him on movements, with another at the end of the day at about 8 p.m. Familiar motivational tools were deployed. Stuffed animals – koalas, kangaroos or emus – would be handed out as prizes for standout achievements, sometimes five a day. But there were grumbles CCHQ was caught short by its own early election. Around a quarter of Tory candidates were not selected on day one. 'CCHQ was completely unprepared,' moaned a Number 10 adviser.[70]

Labour was not caught on the hop. Morgan McSweeney, campaign lead, an Irishman with red hair who shared his Tory opposite number's disdain for the commentariat, had told Labour HQ at the start of the year to be '100 per cent' ready for a spring election.[71] When 2 May came and went, he had been considering a July holiday and had a few days off in June locked in for weddings but never fully dropped his guard. It was a call from someone who bets on politics the day before Sunak's election announcement, the odds suddenly shortening on a July date, that put McSweeney on alert before Cabinet ministers. The surge in cash would have more ominous implications for the Tories in time. When Sunak was speaking to the public under stormy skies, Labour candidates across the country were opening boxes of campaign literature sent out weeks beforehand and gathering activists for day-one videos.

Morgan's strategy was all about trying to win over persuadable people who had backed the Conservatives in 2019, internally dubbed 'hero voters', plus Scots now wavering on the SNP.[72] A campaign message had to be adopted broad enough to appeal to all groups: Tory Brexiteers in the 'Red Wall', moderate Conservative Remainers in the south, former left-wing Nationalists north of the border. Hence the decision to break with precedent and go with a single-word slogan: 'Change'. McSweeney and Pat McFadden, Sir Tony Blair's softly spoken former political secretary and the MP given the role of national campaign co-ordinator, had batted around longer slogans earlier in the year: 'Change for the ordinary, hard-working people of Britain' and 'Change you can believe in'. But the boldness of the one-word approach stood out. 'I love it!' McSweeney told others.[73] It had the benefit of imprecision: everybody who wanted change, even if desiring contradictory outcomes, could get behind it. The approach was dubbed by outsiders the 'Ming vase' strategy, carrying the precious 20-point poll lead and avoiding rash movements that could lead to a smash. It was undoubtedly a caution-first campaign: no major policy reveals and as few risks as possible.

The smaller parties also had a significant role to play in how the campaign unfolded. The Liberal Democrat strategy was devised by David McCobb, a forty-four-year-old Hull City councillor with a feel for local politics who was the party's director of field campaigns. He concluded that the 2019 election had seen the Lib Dems run a 'proportional-representation campaign in a first-past-the-post system'.[74] In other words, foolishly seeking to maximise votes everywhere rather than focusing on the specific seats that could be won – the real ball game in the UK's electoral system. It was a mistake he would not repeat, with the Tory 'Blue Wall' in the South-West a particular focus.

Sir Ed Davey, the Liberal Democrat leader, would take to another level the party's long-held approach of stunts to force themselves into media coverage, reminding voters they existed. There would be tumbles off paddle boards, gurning down water slides, interviews aboard spinning teacups at the fair and, right before polling day, a bungee jump while hollering: 'Do something you've never done before, vote Liberal Democrat!' Lib Dem campaign folk always insisted the gimmicks were backed up with a serious message: sewage pollution in the case of the paddle boarding. There were meaty policy proposals too, not least on social care. The manifesto had a whole section on care, and Sir Ed's emotional election broadcast in which he described caring for his disabled sixteen-year-old son John was watched by nine million people on TV and online.[75] By the end, Sir Ed's personal poll ratings had soared. 'He was the most popular leader of the four main parties,' a senior Lib Dem said. They saw vindication in the numbers.[76]

Reform, as with the Brexit Party and Ukip before it, had the shots called by Nigel Farage. However, under Richard Tice the party had already been declaring 2024 the 'immigration election'. A manifesto had also been drafted earlier, though Farage would not use the word, saying to many voters 'manifesto equals lie'. The prospectus was packed with red meat for the Tory Right: vast tax cuts, much tighter border controls, promised action on culture-war issues, all funded via unspecified public-spending cuts which somehow would not hurt the frontline. Farage's personal brand and the 'people's army' he claimed followed him were at the core of Reform's campaign. The day after his surprise return, he had been greeted by hundreds of jubilant supporters at Clacton pier, shouting variously, 'I love you, Nige', 'Preach', 'Become prime minister!' and, alarmingly, 'Will you be my toyboy?' In turn he encouraged the crowd: 'Send me to Parliament to be a bloody nuisance.'[77]

For the SNP, under the leadership of John Swinney, only recently air-dropped into the post after Humza Yousaf's resignation, it was a case of clinging on to as many seats as possible. He had been given a political hospital pass with the party wounded by scandal, its decade-long hold on the Scottish electorate finally loosening. The Greens, co-led by Carla Denyer and Adrian Ramsay, were aiming for four seats, up from the one they held. Shifting public sentiments, with concerns over climate change rising, brought cause for electoral optimism.

Knowing the final result, it can be easy to disparage the Conservative campaign as a blanket failure – as some prominent Tories have done. But the picture was more complicated than that. When some of the key battlegrounds that usually shape campaigns are considered, there were clear successes.

One was on policy. The first week was dominated by the Tory policy blitz. A pledged return of national service, unveiled in the papers the first Sunday after the election was called, led the national media debate for days. Yes, the move proved controversial. Grant Shapps, the defence secretary, was only informed of its details the day beforehand and disapproved of the specifics, spending much of the following weeks explaining on doorsteps that not all teenagers would be sent to war.[78] But it had the intended effect: forcing voters to engage with the election and projecting the sense of the party still having new ideas, fourteen years into government. Polls suggested wavering Tory voters gave it a thumbs up. The daily policy announcements got widespread pick-up, helped by front-page coverage from a set of newspapers which still largely leant Right.

Another marker of success were the debates. Tory attempts to bounce Sir Keir Starmer into weekly TV clashes with Sunak, in the hope of changing the contest's dynamics, were rebuffed by Labour. But there were two head-to-head clashes, on ITV on 4 June and on BBC on 26 June. The prime minister held practice sessions in a studio off London's Trafalgar Square. Brett O'Donnell, the US debates expert used by the Leave campaign in 2016 and the Tories in 2019, led the practices. Oliver Dowden, the deputy prime minister, played Sir Keir. He was given script by O'Donnell and would toss in the new Starmerisms: 'country first, party second', 'You've had fourteen years to deal with it.'[79]

In the first debate, the Tory strategy was to leave viewers in no doubt that Labour would raise taxes after the election. Sunak kept deploying the claim – disputed by Labour – that the average working family faced a £2,000 tax rise thanks to a gap in the party's spending plans. Sir Keir delayed in countering the attack. Labour's scramble to call out the 'lie' the following morning underscored how Sir Keir had failed to do so effectively the previous night. One Labour insider said that Sir Keir was more frustrated after that first debate than at any other time during the election race, beating himself up over the performance. The Tory approach was matched with a wider, relentless tax attack that bounced Labour into promising not to raise VAT or capital gains tax on primary residences.

The second debate saw Sunak riff on the idea of 'surrender' to Labour on a variety of policy areas – tax, borders, welfare. His most effective moment came when pinning Sir Keir down on how exactly he would return tens of thousands of asylum-seekers to their countries of origin. 'Are you going to sit down with the Iranian ayatollahs? Are you going to try to do a deal with the Taliban?' the prime minister asked. 'It's completely nonsensical what you are saying.'[80] Snap polls after both debates indicated Sunak and Sir Keir had done equally well; this result was considered a win by the Tories given how far they were behind, though other polls later handed victory to the Labour leader. To some, Sunak's front-footed interrogation came across as rude and out of touch. But senior Tories claim, with some validity, that on pure debate performance Sunak was more effective.

It is these wins that the Tory campaign controllers hold up in their defence. 'The legacy of the campaign is we put Labour under more pressure and scrutiny over six and a half weeks than they had been under for the previous four years,' said a senior Conservative campaign figure.[81] To which critics would cite two blunders – one laid squarely at Team Sunak's feet; the other which came to embody a Tory Party past its sell-by date – that would blow up CCHQ's best-laid plans.

The call came through around 6.15 a.m. Rishi Sunak had only just woken, the sleep still sounding in his voice. On the line were James Forsyth and Isaac Levido, respectively his best friend in politics and the man he had tasked with running his election campaign. They had an urgent request: a categorical apology had to be issued, and quickly.

The reason why lay in the previous forty-eight hours. On 5 June, the prime minister had spent the day in Portsmouth commemorating the eightieth anniversary of D-Day, the moment that turned the Second World War against the Nazis when the Allies landed on the beaches of Normandy. The next day, 6 June, Sunak had gone to those very French beaches for a morning British ceremony, meeting veterans and delivering a speech finishing with 'please join me in giving our heroes the welcome they so deserve.'[82] But afterwards he had returned to the UK – as had King Charles – missing an afternoon international commemoration and giving an ITV election interview once back.

That evening, realisation of the misstep was starting to dawn on the Tory campaign chiefs. ITV confirmed Sunak had done an interview while world leaders paid their respects in France. The *Daily Mirror* front page dropped online: 'PM DITCHES D-DAY'.[83] Come the morning of 7 June, the row was dominating news bulletins as a jarring photograph whipped round on social media showing a trio of world leaders – Joe Biden, Emmanuel Macron and Olaf Scholz –

posing not alongside Sunak but his stand-in, Lord Cameron, the foreign secretary.

Levido and Forsyth were blunt: the prime minister needed to say sorry. 'I thought we were following official advice?' said Sunak, or words to that effect, not yet aware of the full backlash.[84] His aides had decided the political wound must be 'cauterised' before the damage spread.[85] 'OK,' Sunak eventually agreed.[86] The apology was posted on his Twitter account at 7.45 a.m., ending: 'After the conclusion of the British event in Normandy, I returned back to the UK. On reflection, it was a mistake not to stay in France longer – and I apologise.'[87] Complaints from Cabinet ministers flooded in to Levido over such an explicit apology, fearing it elevated the story – which it did for a period.[88] But saying sorry was deemed inevitable, so best make it quick.

How could it have happened? That was the common reaction from horrified Tories watching on. Surely it did not take a political genius to work out that snubbing veterans when the campaign was straining to win back disillusioned older Conservatives was not a good look? 'He left them on the beaches,' read a viral poster showing a suited Sunak running away.[89] Nobody in the Tory bunker defended the decision after the election. 'It was a complete cock-up', said one senior campaign figure.[90] But how it really unfolded offers an explanation, if not an excuse.

Understanding who owned which bits of the prime minister's schedule is key. CCHQ had its hands on the campaign 'grid', each hour of Sunak's time on the trail planned out and weighed for political impact. The D-Day commemorations, however, were official government business, with Number 10 in charge of scheduling. The political operatives in Downing Street who normally filter such approaches through a party prism had, critically, moved across to the Tory headquarters. There was communication between the groups, of course, but scrutinising the timings of movements at the international event had fallen between the cracks. 'It was one of these classic things where everyone thought that everybody else had thought it through,' said a Tory campaign source.[91]

Then there was the morphing nature of that afternoon commemoration. When Sunak's initial plans had been pencilled in weeks earlier, the precise shape and significance of the gathering had not yet emerged. Macron, the French president, was always going to be there but it was not clear if US President Biden or German Chancellor Scholz would attend until just days beforehand. 'It always sounded to me like it was just people hob-nobbing, get your own sandwiches and everyone starts peeling off,' said a senior Tory campaign source, a stance shared by others.[92] Nor was it known a photo of the 'quad' – US, UK, French and German leaders – would happen; another late addition. Even Cameron was surprised when called over by Macron on the day.[93] Schedules for such world-leader gatherings often move around. Macron, for example, would turn up late to the British event in the morning without any repercussions. So there was no crunch meeting to weigh the pros and cons of leaving early. The timings just stayed in the calendar unchallenged.

Though not entirely. There had been warnings. Two, in fact, issued by Lord Cameron's Foreign Office, in the accounts of two sources then near the top of that department. They came in formal advice issued by the Foreign Office to Downing Street. The first came a few weeks before the eightieth anniversary. The second came just days before the event itself, once it became clear that Sir Keir Starmer, the Labour leader, David Lammy, his shadow foreign secretary, and Ukrainian President Volodymyr Zelensky would all be attending. One source told the author: 'There was very clear advice from the department that it would be an important event to go to and there would be significant risks should he not attend.'[94] Another said: 'The issue was the seniority of who was going. We were clear about the risk of public criticism of the PM's non-attendance and the Foreign Office reiterated clear advice that the PM should confirm attendance at the international ceremony.'[95] A senior Downing Street figure confirmed the accuracy of the accounts.[96] In the end a photo captured Sir Keir and Zelensky meeting, exacerbating the political impact of Sunak's absence, just as had been feared by the officials. Cameron and his team had not picked up the phone to Sunak or his circle, a misstep acknowledged. But the formal guidance had been there. 'There is plenty of advice that Number 10 rightly overrules the Foreign Office on,' one of the two sources added. 'It is just this wasn't the one to avoid. Basically it was just a massive fuck-up.'[97]

The criticism crushed Sunak, who never intended disrespect. He had spent time talking to British veterans in Normandy. So had his wife Akshata who, away from the cameras in Downing Street, had done much to push forward veterans' issues. 'He found it very, very hurtful and felt dreadful about it, absolutely dreadful,' said one Sunak ally.[98] Another who saw him the day after the apology during a campaign stop-off at Bishop Auckland said: 'He was head down, walking around. Looking beaten, completely gutted.'[99] The source added it was Sunak's lowest moment of the campaign so far. Then another came along to rival it.

It was ten minutes before the launch of the Tory manifesto when the request came to clear the room. Rishi Sunak and his advisers were huddling backstage at Silverstone, the home of the British Grand Prix, waiting to deliver what they all hoped would be a turning point in the campaign. The manifesto had been designed as a 'genuine prospectus for change', packed with 'big ideas about the future of the country'.[100] Tax cuts were at its heart: a further 2p cut in employee National Insurance and the abolition of NI for the self-employed. Other options had been considered, but a reduction of income tax was deemed too expensive and could draw focus on to Sunak's frozen thresholds – a hefty stealth-tax raid – while inheritance tax went against his requested focus on working taxes. The publication of a document around fifty pages long spelling out proposed changes to the European Convention on Human Rights had been considered too, a gift to the Tory Right which had complained that the treaty limited action to reduce small-boat crossings, but was kept back in the end. The Sunak team was happy with the overall package, believing it bolder than Labour's offerings.

But then came the request, confused allies trooping out of the room so that a message could be delivered to the prime minister's ears only. The unlucky task fell to Alex Wild, the Conservative Party's director of communications. The urgent news: the press had got wind that Craig Williams, Sunak's long-serving parliamentary private secretary, was being investigated by the Gambling Commission for betting on the date of the election. Williams had been by Sunak's side in both the Treasury and Number 10, his finger on the pulse of Tory MPs. He was considered a core part of Team Sunak, a trusted friend. The allegation, in essence, was insider trading: using private knowledge to make money. The prime minister was being told it could become public at any moment.

Sunak showed no sign of the blow when he took to the stage to launch the manifesto that morning, 11 June, just four days after his D-Day apology, though he was a little punchier than usual when responding to media questions. He was not asked about the story, the reason for being briefed so suddenly. Reporters had approached for comment, meaning the revelation could have dropped at any moment. The *Guardian* would actually break the story the next day, reporting that Williams had placed a £100 bet on a July election just three days before Sunak announced the date.[101] The odds were said to have been 5/1, meaning a possible £500 payout. Williams did not publicly dispute details of the report, commenting: 'I put a flutter on the general election some weeks ago. This has resulted in some routine inquiries and I confirm I will fully co-operate with these.'[102] He later apologised for a 'huge error of judgement'.[103]

And so began the Tory betting scandal. The controversy widened from there. It soon emerged that Tony Lee, the Tory director of campaigning, and Laura Saunders, his wife and a candidate in Bristol North West, were also being investigated by the commission for election bets. So too was Nick Mason, the party's chief data officer. A police officer working in Sunak's close-protection team was arrested over an alleged bet on election timing. Then the number of Metropolitan Police officers under investigation over bets rose to seven. The drip-drip of revelations dominated the closing weeks of the campaign, drowning out the Tory campaign messages as the circle of focus widened. Soon it was reported that candidates – at least one Tory and one Labour – had bet on themselves losing their seats. Whether any rules were broken by all those named was not known before the election. Yet voters were free to make up their own minds on how they felt about it.

Sunak felt deeply let down, according to his friends. 'He was pretty angry about the gambling stuff because it was all a betrayal,' said one source, adding it 'just hit the morale of the campaign incredibly hard'.[104] Another referenced the prime minister's previous career: 'Remember his background. Anyone who works in finance themselves, what is the first thing that is knocked into your head on day one? "You must not use insider information." The point is that this was something that was totally alien to him.' Sunak was not a 'shouter' but felt 'disappointed' and 'exasperated', the source added.[105]

So much of the Sunak clean-up operation since taking office had been centred on trying to move on from the sleaze headlines of the late Boris Johnson premiership. He had put restoring 'integrity, professionalism and accountability at every level' in his first speech in Downing Street.[106] Tory strategists knew the 'one rule for them, another for us' narrative – the real political bite in the partygate scandal – was electorally toxic. And now here was that theme of Tory self-interest again, dominating the news just as voters were putting pen to paper on postal ballots.

It is why the betting scandal was a much more damaging misstep than D-Day in the eyes of those who helped lead the Tory election drive. True, Sunak's approval ratings took a hit when he skipped the world-leaders' event, but five days later they had recovered.[107] As hoped, the wound had been cauterised. Not so with the gambling saga which became the running sore that kept on sapping support from the party.

The impact was captured by one senior Tory campaign figure: 'Gambling was far, far, far more damaging because it spoke to a tired, tarnished, game-playing political brand. "These guys are just fucking trying to make money while Rome burns at the last minute."' Many voters were not enamoured with Labour, the source added, but the scandal forced their hand. 'It was just more politics and just Westminster-insider shit . . . They were just like "Right, how do I make this stop?" And there's only one lever to pull.'[108] That lever was a vote to put Labour into power. And pull it they did.

Come the end, the Tories had embraced the prospect of defeat. A pivot mid-campaign had seen the party's communicators ordered to deliberately play up the idea of a Labour mega-win. It was distilled into a soundbite – a 'supermajority' – and outlined in a five-page strategy note written by Isaac Levido along with his team and circulated on 10 June, a copy of which has been seen by the author.[109] Despite many voters liking the policies outlined at the contest's start they did not believe the Tories could win, the note's authors explained, so it was not proving sufficiently motivating. Instead, another device was needed. Part of the memo read:

> The most important thing that the campaign can do is inform and persuade voters that their vote can influence the outcome of the election. However, given that voters believe the outcome is a foregone conclusion, this means reframing the impact of their vote to demonstrate that it can affect an outcome they care about. Counter-intuitively that means leaning into voters' expectations that Labour are on course to win – in order to demonstrate to them that their vote does still matter.[110]

Another part read:

> To do so, the campaign must vocalise that Labour are on course to win a large majority, or 'supermajority'. That such a supermajority presents a grave and lasting risk to issues that voters care about. And that the Conservatives are the only party able to prevent that undesirable outcome . . . This does not mean that the campaign, or the prime minister, should concede defeat and accept that the party is going to lose the election. Rather, it is a tactical communications device to force voters (particularly defectors to Reform, the Lib Dems and undecideds) to consider the consequence of their vote.[111]

It was a final throw of the dice. Voters were warned that Labour could be in power for ten years, then twenty years, then all their lifetimes, in a series of escalatory warnings that tested credulity. It was pinned on the idea that Labour would change the rules to give prisoners and EU citizens the vote – which was not being proposed – as well as sixteen- and seventeen-year-olds. Do not hand Sir Keir Starmer a 'blank cheque' and 'uncontrolled power', Cabinet ministers pleaded. The series of warnings hit new heights the day before the election with a remarkable media round by Mel Stride, the work and pensions secretary, effectively conceding the race by saying polls showed Labour would win the biggest landslide in history. There are signs the messaging worked. Tory campaign data-tracking found 'expected Labour majority' was one of the most damaging and effective messages deployed against their rivals. (That same tracking showed 'have had their time' and 'have behaved badly over the last few years' were the most damaging messages against the Tories – further proof of the betting scandal's impact.)[112] Even so, the self-proclaimed 'natural party of government' publicly arguing that its opponents were about to win big was a stark reminder of how low expectations had fallen.

That Stride was willing to deploy the message so candidly and so often – he did more morning broadcast media rounds than any other Cabinet minister – was itself a reflection of another weakness of the campaign. Tory frontbenchers were declining to come out swinging for Sunak. 'Most of the Cabinet' was avoiding doing national broadcast rounds arguing the Conservative case, one senior Tory campaign source revealed after the election. 'A lot of them were having to be in their seats fighting for re-election and it would not have necessarily done them very well to be on national media every day,' the source said, adding that they were 'incredibly frustrated that we were not getting people out'.[113] Many ministers were said to be curiously unavailable when requests were made. Claire Coutinho, the energy security secretary, Laura Trott, the chief secretary to the Treasury, and Kemi Badenoch, the business secretary, were singled out as figures the campaign leadership wanted to have seen doing more TV and radio interviews.

And then the clock ran out: 4 July had arrived. A day of British election rituals – photos of dogs at polling stations, the absence of electioneering on the news – gave way to a build-up of nerves ahead of the moment of truth: the 10 p.m. exit poll. There was a universal expectation of defeat among Tory campaign figures. 'None of us thought that we would be delivering a speech declaring "delighted that the country has given us a fifth term"',' said one.[114] It was a question of scale. And so there was a morbid sense of relief when the Tory seat prediction flashed up: 131. Polling analyses in the race's final weeks had pointed to sub-100 results, even as low as in the fifties or sixties. The party was still standing, just. 'Immense sadness' for defeated Tories was mixed with relief that the number of MPs was in three figures and greater than the Liberal Democrats, according to one Sunak inner circle figure.[115] Another concluded: 'We managed to basically save the party.'[116] That avoiding extinction was considered good news says it all.

On the final count Labour secured 411 MPs. That was more than triple the Tories in second place with 121 MPs, way down on the 365 elected just five years earlier. The Lib Dems had surged to seventy-two MPs, six times their 2019 haul despite barely increasing their overall vote share – testament to the strategy of focusing on specific seats. 'People hugging each other, screaming, shouting,' said a source in Lib Dem HQ when the exit poll dropped.[117] Reform ended with five MPs, including Nigel Farage who would enter the House of Commons at the eighth time of asking. The party came second in almost a hundred other seats, many seeing Tories ousted as Labour took advantage of Reform eating into the Conservative vote. The SNP slump proved more dramatic than predicted, leaving them with just nine MPs compared with forty-eight in 2019. The Greens had their breakthrough, winning all four target seats.

Labour, it should be noted, did have a low vote share. Indeed at 34 per cent, it was the lowest of any single-party government since the Second World War. That was also only 10 points ahead of the Tories on 24 per cent, when average polls throughout the campaign had suggested a 20-point lead. Team Sunak demanded the pollsters explain how they had got that so wrong. Labour may have won a 'loveless landslide', as some dubbed it, but it was a landslide nonetheless. At a campaign watch party at Tate Modern in London, the vast Turbine Hall bathed in red light, Sir Keir and Morgan McSweeney hugged in delight.[118]

For the Conservatives, it was not obliteration. But it was something just short: the biggest Tory wipeout in modern history. Track election results back to when the shape of today's British democracy began to emerge via the Great Reform Act in 1832, and no worse Conservative result can be found. The 121 seats Sunak's party clung on to was worse than Sir John Major managed in the New Labour rout of 1997: 165. It was worse than when Labour was swept into office in 1945 to build the welfare state: 197. It even sank comfortably below the previous low point: the 156 MPs the Tories got in 1906, when Conservative leader Arthur Balfour lost his seat. The closer the results were inspected, the more jaw-dropping they appeared. Eleven cabinet ministers – roughly a third of Sunak's Cabinet – were booted out. Oxfordshire was said to have had no

Tory MP for the first time since 1777. Perhaps the most telling statistic was linked to the former Conservative prime ministers, those figures who had overseen this fourteen-year run in office. Constituencies held by four of them – David Cameron, Theresa May, two by Boris Johnson and Liz Truss – were lost. Truss's defeat was the moment of the night for those seeking Tory retribution. Only Rishi Sunak's seat stayed blue.

When the black door of Number 10 closed on Rishi Sunak that morning after election night, his premiership was not quite done. Departing words had to be delivered from Downing Street, as tradition dictates. There was no lump in the throat, as there had been with Cameron and May. Sunak did not make jokes, as Johnson had with his 'them's the breaks' resignation address. But there was humility, a note lacking in the final speech of Truss, his immediate predecessor. 'To the country, I would like to say, first and foremost, I am sorry,' the outgoing prime minister said, his wife Akshata a few feet behind him and grasping the rolled-up umbrella that was needed six weeks earlier. 'I have given this job my all. But you have sent a clear signal that the government of the United Kingdom must change and yours is the only judgement that matters.'[119] The words had the ring of sincerity.

Members of Sunak's senior team have wondered, and will keep wondering, whether they could have convinced the public to reach another judgement. There were missteps, they accepted. Most found themselves looking beyond the campaign – 'the die was cast beforehand', said one – back to earlier times. Could a surprise election in spring 2023 have worked? What if Sunak had more decisively broken with Truss and Johnson at the start of his tenure? Some Tories like to find comfort in other alternative universes: ones where Boris was not ousted by his colleagues, or where Truss had offered a more fiscally balanced set of tax cuts, or even where Penny Mordaunt had won the few extra MP votes to beat Truss into the final two of the leadership contest in 2022, possibly becoming prime minister. Perhaps such dreaming will one day give way to a starker realisation: that the forces which delivered the Conservatives their fourteen-year run in government – a mechanism to topple leaders at will; a system built for regicide; the rivalry and egotism it encouraged and fed off – were the very same that brought about its end. An electorate exasperated by Tory in-fighting had delivered a punishment beating at the polls. How quickly the party learns from its bruises may dictate when – if – it will return to office.

As Sunak headed to Buckingham Palace to formally resign and as his advisers headed to the Clarence nearby to drown their sorrows in early-morning pints, Labour was already moving in.[120] At the Cabinet Office adjoining Number 10, where Sunak aides had just handed in their security passes, Sir Keir Starmer's team were picking up their own. There is a brutality in the swiftness of Britain's handover of power, allowing no time for the defeated to lick their wounds in office. And when the victor finally strolled up Downing Street, cheered on by carefully stage-managed crowds of supporters, there was time for one final political cliché. As Sir Keir addressed the nation, the Tory government now confined to the past, the grey clouds gave way to sun. A new dawn had broken, had it not?

Conclusion

O NE WEEKEND IN May 2023 a milestone of sorts was passed. The 4,757 days in which New Labour were in power was overtaken by the Conservatives' run since 2010. Tony Blair and Gordon Brown's tenure had been exceeded by that of David Cameron, Theresa May, Boris Johnson, Liz Truss and Rishi Sunak. It got little fanfare but, in its own way, it was a historic moment. In the century before Sunak took office only one stretch by a single party had lasted longer: the eighteen years of Tory governance under Margaret Thatcher and John Major.

Both of those earlier periods are remembered for considerable reimaginings of the state. Both have been endowed with their own 'isms' by posterity. Thatcherism rolled back the frontiers of government, privatising whole industries, crushing trade union influence and driving down the tax burden. Blairism offered a 'third way', investing in public services while injecting elements of competition and introducing eye-catching innovations: the minimum wage, Bank of England independence, new parliaments in the devolved nations. Many of the changes those prime ministers and their successors brought to pass became so embedded that later governments of different political stripes were unable – or unwilling – to unpick them. Their survival, at least in the medium term, was secured.

Will the same be said of this Conservative era? Certainly some reforms pioneered under Cameron and George Osborne look set to remain. Universal Credit, which merged six major welfare benefits into a single monthly payment – championed by Iain Duncan Smith and not without controversy – was kept by the incoming Sir Keir Starmer government. Free schools, a Michael Gove initiative turbocharging Blair's academies programme which permits groups of people to launch schools and receive state funding for them, similarly looked safe. The independent Office for Budget Responsibility, an Osborne creation, looked set to be strengthened, not scrapped, by Labour. Free childcare provision for toddlers is an expansion of the welfare state that is set to stay – an idea poached from the Liberal Democrats, and an important reminder that for the first five years the Tories shared power.

There were also landmark moves matched elsewhere in the Western world that may prove among the longest-lasting elements of the Tory years: gay marriage, which always appears high up when Cameron lists his achievements; the commitment in law to make the UK a net zero carbon emitter by 2050 – an acknowledgement of the profound threat posed by climate change. Another could arguably be raised defence spending, a reflection of geopolitical tensions ramping up once again. Would these have happened under a Labour rather than a Tory government? Possibly, or even probably. The same could be said of progressive social measures adopted under New Labour, though. Leaders are entitled to the credit as well as the blame for decisions taken on their watch, even if these are part of wider societal changes.

There were promises not delivered. Cameron's pledge to bring down annual net migration to below 100,000 went unfulfilled; the total hit 606,000 in 2022. UK annual house building did not reach the target of 300,000. True, economic conditions – an inheritance of recent recession rather than 1997's soaring growth – imposed strains that New Labour avoided for a decade. Yet there were developments that ran against the Tory stereotype. Under the Conservatives, public spending was ultimately put on a path to a fifty-year high and taxation a seventy-year high. The Covid-19 pandemic which demanded unprecedented financial interventions is a major part of that story, though perhaps not the whole of it.

And all the while, as the party skipped between the ideals and instincts of five different leaders, there was policy zigzagging. Take one example: grammar schools. Cameron kept in place Blair's ban on new grammars. May championed their return, only to back down after election disappointment. Johnson buried the issue, sticking with the ban. Then Truss vowed to overturn it, again . . . only to be toppled and replaced by Sunak, who vowed to keep it, again. Or take fracking for shale gas. May's 2017 election manifesto promised to legislate so that licences could be issued. Johnson's 2019 manifesto replaced this with a 'moratorium'. Truss announced that the fracking ban was over after taking office . . . only to have Sunak do the opposite. These may not have been defining policy positions, but they showed how endless upheaval at the top could undercut delivering on a long-term agenda. Shape-shifting to sustain power was not without its downsides.

There is, of course, one matter of great consequence that will forever be associated with this Tory period. As a single policy move it arguably dwarfs anything in the Thatcher and Blair eras. Its full effects are yet to become clear and it was brought about against the expressed will of the government of the time: Brexit. Hate it or love it, that word sits at the top of any legacy list of the Conservatives' fourteen years in power. Voted for on 23 June 2016 and delivered at 11 p.m. on 31 January 2020, the UK's departure from the European Union transformed the country's economic and foreign policy. When asked why the arcs of reform that trace themselves across 1979–97 and 1997–2010 are not as visible in the period from 2010, some leading British political figures of the last quarter of a century point to the impact of Brexit.

Sir Tony Blair, the Labour prime minister from 1997 to 2007, who gave some written thoughts to the author, made the connection, saying there had been no 'consistent ideology' during the Tories' years in office.

> They [were] divided between the traditional business-oriented Conservative Party and the Brexit-ideology party. But also do not underestimate the huge bandwidth problem they [had after] Brexit. The Cameron government might have been a reforming government, but once the referendum was lost they decided to become the Brexit-delivery party. And that [was] an all-absorbing task.[1]

So too did George Osborne, Conservative chancellor between 2010 and 2016, who said Brexit would 'probably' be what the Tory run in power will be 'remembered for by history':

It killed essentially all public service reform when it happened. So after 2016 there was never another word on education reform, there was never another word on welfare reform and a whole series of other things that the Cameron coalition had been doing: criminal justice reform, prison reform. I mean, all of this died.[2]

Both men, of course, passionately supported remaining in the EU. Brexiteers would firmly counter Osborne's portrayal of the referendum result as stifling all policy innovation. But when seeking to explain the lack of policy follow-through from 2010 to 2024, the totality of focus demanded in Westminster and Whitehall by Brexit is undeniably part of the answer.

How, then, to draw lessons from another feature of this period: the Conservative Party's ability to kill off its leaders, alter its image and retain power? Electorally, it often worked. Cameron's modernisation project and nimble footwork got them back into office; Theresa May's 'time for the grown-ups' sobriety initially chimed with the public, before the botched 2017 election; dethroning May with 'Brexit or bust' Boris Johnson resulted in a huge House of Commons majority. But in the latter years the regicidal instinct proved costly. The toppling of Johnson led to the spectacular implosion of Liz Truss, the Tories' opinion poll ratings plummeting to depths rarely seen before and leaving Rishi Sunak facing an almighty patch-up job that proved too much. Is the party's ruthless pursuit of power, and the structures put in place to enable it, now malfunctioning?

Not so, according to the Conservative leader who came just before this five-Tory-prime-minister streak. 'Well, in a key way, it's been beneficial. We've ended up with the right leader,' said Lord Howard, who headed the Tories between 2003 and 2005, about Sunak becoming prime minister.

As to the process, people say, 'We had three prime ministers in a couple of months and we were the world's laughing stock.' I think you can look at it in an entirely different way. We had two changes of government in a matter of weeks, there were no demonstrations in the streets, not a shot was fired, no one invaded the Palace of Westminster. Our institutions worked as they should work.[3]

For Lord Howard, there is one change that is of interest:

> It isn't a particularly popular thing to say but it's the truth. I think you do have to reduce the role of the [Tory Party] members and increase the role of MPs. Because, as history has proved over the years, if a leader doesn't have the confidence of the MPs, he or she doesn't survive.[4]

In other words: after fourteen years of bloodletting, perhaps more power should be in the hands of Tory MPs to pick their leaders.

And what now for the Conservative Party itself? It has been humbled and humiliated by the electorate, sent packing into opposition. Never before has the party had to rebuild with so few MPs since the shape of modern British democracy emerged almost two centuries ago. Yet the regeneration has begun. The Tories will try to rediscover what they stand for in the 2020s, in the hope of governing for the 2030s. The future is uncertain. No political party has a God-given right to exist. But if there is one common factor running through their fourteen years in government, perhaps it is this: the Conservative lust for power. Underestimate it at your peril.

Acknowledgements

Having never written a book before, I assumed it would be an isolating pursuit. The opposite has proved true. I have been lucky enough to be supported by a remarkable group of individuals whose belief in the project and encouragement have meant so much. Their guidance for a first-time author stumbling through the unknown cannot be underestimated.

Blue Murder would most likely not exist without my agent, Max Edwards. It was his advice to consider looking back at the whole Conservative run from 2010 when another pitch on a subsection of that story petered out. Max's energy and drive are infectious, his ability to match an author's interests with what an audience might want to read inspired. I am so pleased our paths crossed at just the right time.

I will be forever indebted to Joe Zigmond, associate publisher at John Murray, for taking a punt on the book. There is no small amount of risk in gambling that a newspaper hack can apply the approach involved in daily reporting to a much longer form. Joe's perceptive suggestions have no doubt shortened the odds. There are countless ways he has improved what I filed – tweaks to structure, turning up elements overlooked, challenging assumptions. He got the idea from day one and has honed it brilliantly since then. As the project's top dog, it is thanks to Joe that the book has reached the shelves.

So many other figures at John Murray, and the wider team at Hachette UK, have my sincere gratitude. I could not have wished for a more engaging and dedicated publisher. It is a thrill to be printed by a publishing house whose origins can be traced back to the early days of Fleet Street. There are too many at the company who have helped to name, but I will give it a go.

Caroline Westmore dedicated weeks of her life, including many late evenings, to making sure the book hit its tight schedule. This makes the good grace she invariably showed whenever I missed a deadline or pleaded for extra time all the more appreciated. Robert Shore was given the burden of having to wade through my copy line by line. That he did so with such thoroughness, sparing my blushes more times than is worth admitting and adding incisive comments, brought immeasurable benefit. Likewise Howard Davies's razor-sharp proofreading kept me in line whenever I slipped into slang. Kirsty Howarth's legal advice was invaluable as we navigated the nuanced Westminster world of on- and off-the-record comments and claims. Alice Herbert's experience as we aimed to land the book with the best splash possible was a great boost. So too were Alice Graham's skills and keen eye at maximising promotion. Juliet Brightmore picked out the images that captured fourteen years of political upheaval with aplomb and good humour. Amanda Jones as production manager made sure everything got off on time while juggling a huge number of different balls at once. Zoe Ross must take all the credit for the book's forensic index. And sincere thanks to Jocasta Hamilton for all the guidance and backing on the project throughout.

A deep thank you must also be given to the *Daily Telegraph*. Chris Evans, the editor, Robert Winnett, the deputy editor, and Ben Clissitt, the managing editor, signed off the project and have been supportive throughout, for which I am most grateful. It is because the *Telegraph* trusted me to report from Holyrood, Westminster and Washington that I have managed to carve out a career covering politics. My *Telegraph* Lobby colleagues too deserve a shout-out. Daniel Martin, the deputy political editor, never once grumbled when picking up the slack while I was off writing. And the entire team (almost) never complained about me banging on about the book: Christopher Hope, Camilla Turner, Tony Diver, Jack Maidment, Nick Gutteridge, Dominic Penna, Amy Gibbons, Edward Malnick, Will Hazell and Charles Hymas. You could not dream of better colleagues to be in the trenches with on the Westminster frontline.

Political reporting is still, to a large degree, a matter of who picks up the phone. If those who have eyes on what is happening never talk to journalists, it is exceptionally hard to tell the public what is really going on. And so I am thankful to everyone who gave up time for an interview. Some stories retold in these pages may not inspire confidence and so it is worth saying explicitly: MPs overwhelmingly are not the greedy, self-interested, unprincipled figures that the harshest caricatures suggest. Most are driven by a sense of public service. Many could be much better paid doing something else. They are also human, just as fallible as the rest. The press and the public rightly hold them to a high standard. But we will all suffer if the pursuit of politics is made so unappealing, and its participants are so vilified, that it puts off tomorrow's would-be MPs.

There are some specific thank yous. Peter Dominiczak and James Kirkup, two predecessors of mine as *Telegraph* political editors, took the time to read some of the chapters and gave thoughtful feedback that was acted upon. The brilliant Morten Morland allowed his cartoons to be used for the book jacket. Fiammetta Rocco's advice helped me along the path of book-writing. Mats Persson kindly looked over some of the distillation of the Brexit narrative. The Institute for Government helped check some historical facts. So many fellow Lobby reporters, and others, gave kind words and their own takes. Further back, Professor Richard Rex and Professor Tony Badger offered wisdom and showed patience to a student historian trying to learn the craft. And thank you to those who provided an escape, like the Queens' College friends who kept me sane, and Meyhem for the light relief.

But above all thank you to my family, who have put up with me talking about the book in practically every conversation for nine months: my parents, Louisa and Tristram, whose love and encouragement underpins everything I have done, and my brothers, Olly and Piers, who know better than anyone how to make me laugh. And, lastly, to my partner, Agnes. The rapid turnaround of the project has impacted her as much as me, and yet she has been there with endless support and understanding every step of the way. Thank you, Agnes.

Credits

Text

Extracts from *For the Record* by David Cameron reprinted by permission of HarperCollins Publishers Ltd © 2019 David Cameron. Extracts from *22 Days in May* by David Laws © David Laws 2010 reproduced by permission of Biteback Publishing. Extracts from *Why the Tories Won* by Tim Ross © Tim Ross 2015 reproduced by permission of Biteback Publishing. Extracts from *5 Days to Power* by Rob Wilson © Rob Wilson 2010 reproduced by permission of Biteback Publishing.

Pictures

AFP via Getty Images: 7 centre right/Ben Stansall, 8 above right/Justin Tallis. Alamy Stock Photo: 3 below/Mark Severn, 5 below left/WENN Rights Ltd, 10 below/Gavin Rodgers. Associated Press/Alamy Stock Photo: 1 below, 2 above, 4 below, 5 centre right, 12 below, 15 below centre. © Charlie Bibby/FT: 2 centre. Bloomberg via Getty Images: 11 above right/Holly Adams. Crown Copyright via Getty Images: 8 centre/Joel Rouse. *Daily Star*/Reach Licensing: 14 below. Getty Images: 10 above and 13 below/Leon Neal, 15 above right/Kate Green/Anadolu Agency. Courtesy of Paul Grover: 8 below left. In Pictures via Getty Images: 9 below left/Richard Baker. ITV via Getty Images: 1 above/Ken McKay. Ludovic Marin/AFP via Getty Images: 16 centre. PA Images/Alamy Stock Photo: 2 below, 4 above, 6 below left and below right, 9 above left and centre, 11 below, 14 above, 16 above. REUTERS: 5 above left/Darren Staples, 6 above/Neil Hall. Shutterstock: 7 above left/Andy Rain/EPA-EFE,

7 above right and below left/Tom Nicholson, 11 above left/Peter MacDiarmid, 15 below left/David Hartley, 15 below right/Anthony Harvey, 16 below/Tolga Akmen/EPA-EFE. *The Sun*, 6 May 2015/News Licensing: 3 above. UK Parliament/Jessica Taylor/Hand-out via REUTERS: 12 above. UK Press via Getty Images: 15 above left/John Phillips.

Notes

Introduction

1. Rishi Sunak was in his twenties – just – when David Cameron became prime minister. Cameron entered Downing Street on 11 May 2010. Sunak turned thirty the day after. At the time Sunak was also spending much of his time in California.
2. Labour MPs voted no confidence in Jeremy Corbyn as Labour leader by 172 to forty on 28 June 2016, after the country backed Brexit in the EU referendum. The vote, however, was not binding. Corbyn, once formally challenged, won the following contest and stayed in post until April 2020.
3. David Cameron, *For the Record* (London: William Collins, 2019), p. 235.

Chapter 1: A Lighter Shade of Blue

1. Eight million people were watching at the start of the first election debate on ITV, according to Attentional, the media analytics company. At its peak, the audience was judged to be 10.3 million.
2. David Cameron, *For the Record* (London: William Collins, 2019), p. 128. Cameron wrote: 'I'd never been so nervous in my life.'
3. Interview, David Cameron, January 2023.
4. Ibid.
5. Cameron, *For the Record*, p. 132.
6. Ibid., p. 128.
7. Ibid., p. 129.
8. Interview, George Osborne, December 2022.
9. Ibid.

10. Cameron, *For the Record*, p. 45.
11. Interview, Osborne.
12. Ibid.
13. Cameron, *For the Record*, p. 2.
14. Interview, Cameron.
15. Interview, Cameron inner circle.
16. Ibid.
17. Interview, Kate Fall, December 2022.
18. Interview, William Hague, December 2022.
19. Cameron, *For the Record*, p. 5.
20. Ibid.
21. Rob Wilson, *5 Days to Power: The Journey to Coalition Britain* (London: Biteback Publishing), p. 80.
22. Ibid.
23. Interview, Cameron inner circle.
24. BBC election night coverage, 6 May 2010.
25. Interview, Fall.
26. Interview, Cameron inner circle.
27. Ibid.
28. Interview, Cameron.
29. The phrase was picked for the title of Peter Mandelson's memoir, *The Third Man: Life at the Heart of New Labour* (London: Harper Press, 2010).
30. Interview, Cameron inner circle.
31. Cameron, *For the Record*, p. 131.
32. David Laws, *22 Days in May: The Birth of the Lib Dem-Conservative Coalition* (London: Biteback Publishing, 2010), p. 23.
33. Wilson, *5 Days to Power*, p. 99.
34. Ibid., p. 98.
35. Interview, David Laws, December 2022.
36. Interviews, Cameron and Clegg inner circles.
37. Interview, Oliver Letwin, October 2022.
38. Cameron, *For the Record*, p. 4.
39. Ibid.
40. Wilson, *5 Days to Power*, p. 86.
41. Interview, Laws.
42. Laws, *22 Days in May*, p. 139.
43. Interview, Laws.
44. Interview, Letwin.
45. Ibid.

46. Ibid.
47. Interview, Laws.
48. Interview, Hague.
49. Wilson, *5 Days to Power*, p. 133.
50. Cameron, *For the Record*, p. 7.
51. Wilson, *5 Days to Power*, p. 28.
52. Ibid., p. 29.
53. Made by Alison Suttie and shared in Laws, *22 Days in May*, p. 52.
54. Laws, *22 Days in May*, p. 54.
55. Made by Alison Suttie and shared in Laws, *22 Days in May*, p. 55.
56. Interview, Alison Suttie, December 2022.
57. Laws, *22 Days in May*, p. 61.
58. Cameron, *For the Record*, p. 6.
59. Speaking in the BBC documentary *Five Days That Changed Britain* (2010).
60. Laws, *22 Days in May*, p. 18.
61. Interview, Danny Alexander, December 2022.
62. Interview, Hague.
63. Quotation from Laws, *22 Days in May*, as it appeared in extracts run by the *Daily Mail*, 20 November 2010. Various slightly different versions have appeared over the years. William Hague confirmed in an interview in December 2022 that he had made a remark along those lines.
64. Dan Bilefsky and Landon Thomas, 'Greece Takes Its Bailout, but Doubts for the Region Persist', *New York Times*, 3 May 2010.
65. Liberal Democrat 2010 election manifesto, p. 1.
66. 'Conservative Liberal Democrat Coalition Negotiations. Agreements reached, 11 May 2010', copy published online by University College London, https://www.ucl.ac.uk/constitution-unit/sites/constitution-unit/files/initial-agreement-11-may-2010.pdf
67. Ibid.
68. Wilson, *5 Days to Power*, p. 171.
69. Mandelson, *The Third Man*.
70. Vince Cable, May 2010; Matthew d'Ancona, 'The "LibiLeaks" Actually Show How Robust This Coalition Is', *Sunday Telegraph*, 26 December 2010.
71. Laws, *22 Days in May*, p. 43.
72. Interview, Alexander.
73. Interview, Laws.
74. Laws, *22 Days in May*, p. 144. Confirmed in interview, Clegg inner circle.

75. Wilson, *5 Days to Power*, p. 195.
76. Cameron, *For the Record*, p. 10.
77. Wilson, *5 Days to Power*, p. 209.
78. Ibid., p. 207.
79. Interview, Chris Grayling, December 2022.
80. Interview, Theresa Villiers, January 2023.
81. Interview, Mark Francois, January 2023.
82. Interview, Grayling.
83. Interview, Francois.
84. Interview, Cameron.
85. Cameron, *For the Record*, p. 11.
86. As told to Gary Gibbon of Channel 4 News, https://www.channel4.com/news/by/gary-gibbon/blogs/an-outline-deal-today-but-no-full-scale-coalition
87. Wilson, *5 Days to Power*, p. 224.
88. Ibid., p. 238.
89. Cameron, *For the Record*, p. 140.

Chapter 2: Brothers in Arms

1. Interview, David Laws, December 2022.
2. Ibid.
3. Ibid.
4. Ibid.
5. Interview, Steve Webb, December 2022.
6. Interview, Norman Baker, December 2022.
7. For a detailed breakdown of the 2015 general election results see 'General Election 2015', House of Commons Library briefing paper, 28 July 2015, https://commonslibrary.parliament.uk/research-briefings/cbp-7186/
8. Interview, George Osborne, December 2022.
9. Danny Alexander became chief secretary to the Treasury when David Laws left the role just weeks after being appointed owing to a row about expenses.
10. Interview, Danny Alexander, December 2022.
11. Interview, David Cameron, January 2023.
12. Ibid.
13. Interview, Alexander.

14. Interview, Osborne.

15. Interview, senior Tory involved in appointing Lynton Crosby to lead Boris Johnson's campaign.

16. Interview, Tory source.

17. Tim Ross, *Why the Tories Won: The Inside Story of the 2015 Election* (London: Biteback Publishing, 2015), p. 22.

18. Ibid.

19. Ibid., p. 302.

20. Ibid., pp. 20–1.

21. Interview, Cameron.

22. Boris Johnson, interview with Channel 4 News, June 2013.

23. Interview, Tory 2015 campaign insider; Tim Ross, *Why the Tories Won*, p. 31.

24. Interview, Tory 2015 campaign insider.

25. Interview, Stephen Gilbert, October 2022.

26. Ibid.

27. Ibid.

28. Interview, Osborne.

29. Widely reported at the time, confirmed in interviews with figures in the room.

30. David Cameron had a net favourability rating of -12 percentage points in Conservative seats (27 per cent favourable, 39 per cent unfavourable) but in Liberal Democrat seats it was just -1 percentage point (33 per cent favourable, 34 per cent unfavourable).

31. Interview, Kate Fall, December 2022.

32. Interview, Cameron inner circle.

33. Interview, Cameron.

34. Interview, Gilbert.

35. Interview, Tory 2015 campaign insider.

36. Interview, Isaac Levido, January 2023.

37. Interview, senior Tory campaign source.

38. Ibid.

39. Interview, Tory special adviser.

40. Interview, Tory 2015 campaign insider.

41. Interview, Nigel Farage, February 2023.

42. David Cameron, interview with LBC radio station, 4 April 2006.

43. Tim Ross, *Why the Tories Won*, p. 15.

44. Interview, Levido.

45. Ross, *Why the Tories Won*, pp. 203–4.

46. Interview, Spencer Livermore, January 2023.
47. Ross, *Why the Tories Won*, p. 187.
48. Interview, senior Labour figure.
49. Interview, Ed Miliband, January 2023.
50. Conversation, newspaper executive, September 2012; conversations, Johnson inner circle, early 2022.
51. Interview, Cameron inner circle.
52. Ed Miliband speech, London, 25 July 2014.
53. David Cameron speech, Manchester, 28 March 2015.
54. Interview, Laws (Laws recalled discussions about seeking to make Clegg chancellor or education secretary); interview, Alexander (Alexander recalled thinking about seeking to make Clegg education secretary or seeking all education ministerial roles).
55. Interview, Laws
56. Interview, Ryan Coetzee, January 2023.
57. Ibid.
58. Ibid.
59. Ibid.
60. Ibid.
61. Interview, Cameron.
62. David Cameron, Scottish independence referendum campaign event, 10 September 2014.
63. Interview, Cameron.
64. Ibid.
65. Interview, Levido.
66. Interview, Lynton Crosby, February 2023.
67. Ross, *Why the Tories Won*, pp. 74–5.
68. Interviews, Tory and Lib Dem Coalition Cabinet ministers.
69. Interview, Andrew Feldman, January 2023.
70. Ross, *Why the Tories Won*, p. 102.
71. Interview, Levido.
72. Interview, Tory 2015 campaign insider.
73. Interview, Grant Shapps, January 2023.
74. Ibid.
75. Interview, Craig Elder, January 2023.
76. Ibid.
77. Ibid.
78. Interview, Levido.
79. Ross, *Why the Tories Won*, pp. 36–7.
80. Interview, Cameron inner circle.

81. Interview, Cameron.
82. Interview, Cameron inner circle.
83. Interview, Feldman.
84. David Cameron, 2015 election campaign event, 27 April 2015.
85. Interview, Cameron.
86. Interview, Elder.
87. Interview, Giles Kenningham, January 2023.
88. Michael Fallon, 'This Unholy Alliance Would Put Britain's Security in Jeopardy', *The Times*, 9 April 2015.
89. Ross, *Why the Tories Won*, p. 45.
90. Ibid., p. 73.
91. Interview, Livermore.
92. Ibid.
93. Interview, Labour 2015 campaign insider.
94. Interview, Vince Cable, December 2022.
95. Interview, Webb.
96. Interview, Baker.
97. Interviews, Clegg inner circle.
98. Interview, Coetzee.
99. Ibid.
100. Interview, Cameron.
101. David Cameron, *For the Record* (London: William Collins, 2019), p. 576.
102. Interview, Osborne.
103. Interview, Fall.
104. Cameron, *For the Record*, pp. 574–5.
105. Ibid., p. 575.
106. Interview, Fall.
107. Interview, Cameron inner circle.
108. Interview, Cameron.
109. Interview, Craig Oliver, January 2023.
110. Interview, Fall.
111. 'General Election 2015', House of Commons Library briefing paper, 28 July 2015, https://commonslibrary.parliament.uk/research-briefings/cbp-7186/. The majority of eleven does not including the Commons Speaker.
112. Interview, Livermore.
113. 'General Election 2015', House of Commons Library briefing paper, 28 July 2015.
114. Ed Miliband speech, London, 8 May 2015.

115. Interview, Coetzee.
116. Ibid.
117. Ross, *Why the Tories Won*, p. 222.
118. Nigel Farage would swiftly reverse his decision, returning as Ukip leader.
119. 'General Election 2015', House of Commons Library briefing paper, 28 July 2015.
120. Cameron, *For the Record*, p. 577.

Chapter 3: Sliding Doors

1. Interview, David Cameron, January 2023.
2. David Cameron, *For the Record* (London: William Collins, 2019), p. 657.
3. Boris Johnson on *Desert Island Discs*, BBC Radio 4, November 2005.
4. Interviews, Johnson inner circle.
5. Cameron, *For the Record*, p. 653.
6. Ibid., p. 654.
7. Interview, Cameron.
8. Cameron, *For the Record*, p. 657.
9. Interview, Will Walden, January 2023.
10. Ibid.
11. Cameron, *For the Record*, p. 657.
12. Interview, Cameron.
13. Interview, Kate Fall, December 2022.
14. Interview, Andrew Feldman, January 2023.
15. Interview, Cameron inner circle.
16. Interview, Craig Oliver, January 2023.
17. *Newsnight*, BBC Two, 4 October 2011.
18. Interview, Cameron inner circle.
19. Interview, Tory source.
20. Interview, Walden.
21. Interview, Cameron inner circle.
22. Cameron, *For the Record*, p. 18.
23. Ibid., p. 68.
24. Interviews, Cameron inner circle.
25. Vernon Bogdanor, *Guardian* interview, 17 February 2009.
26. Interview, Cameron inner circle.
27. *Daily Politics*, BBC Two, 23 April 2012.

28. Barack Obama, *A Promised Land* (London: Viking, 2020).
29. Interview, Ivan Rogers, February 2023.
30. Interview, Fall.
31. Cameron, *For the Record*, p. 42.
32. Ibid.
33. Interview, John Hayes, October 2022.
34. Interview, David Davis, January 2023.
35. Interview, Open Europe insider.
36. Interview, Davis.
37. Interview, Cameron.
38. Interview, George Osborne, December 2022; interview, Jacob Rees-Mogg, February 2023.
39. David Cameron, *Sun*, September 2007.
40. Interview, William Hague, December 2022.
41. Ibid.
42. Interview, Cameron.
43. Interview, Hague.
44. Interview, Cameron.
45. Tim Bale, 'Banging on About Europe: How the Eurosceptics Got Their Referendum', London School of Economics blog, 23 June 2016, https://blogs.lse.ac.uk/brexit/2016/06/23/banging-on-about-europe-how-the-eurosceptics-got-their-referendum/
46. Tim Shipman, *All Out War: The Full Story of How Brexit Sank Britain's Political Class* (London: William Collins, 2016), p. 6.
47. Interview, Rees-Mogg.
48. Interview, David Lidington, February 2023.
49. Cameron, *For the Record*, pp. 331–2.
50. Ibid., p. 332.
51. Shipman, *All Out War*, p. 7.
52. Ibid., p. 10.
53. Ibid., p. 13.
54. Interview, Nigel Farage, February 2023.
55. Shipman, *All Out War*, p. 15.
56. Interview, Mats Persson, January 2023. A Home Office paper in 2003 put the estimate at 5,000 to 13,000 a year. David Cameron mentioned the million figure in his immigration speech in November 2014.
57. Cameron, *For the Record*, p. 338.
58. Ibid., pp. 339–40.
59. Interview, Hague.
60. Interview, Osborne.

61. Cameron, *For the Record*, p. 52.
62. Interview, Osborne.
63. Interview, Michael Gove, February 2022.
64. David Cameron, speech to the Conservative Party conference, October 2006.
65. Interview, Cameron.
66. Interview, Osborne.
67. Interview, Oliver Letwin, October 2022.
68. Interview, Danny Alexander, December 2022.
69. Donald Tusk, in the BBC documentary *Inside Europe: Ten Years of Turmoil*, first broadcast in 2019. Craig Oliver, Cameron's former communications director, called the claim 'completely wrong' when it emerged in January 2019.
70. Interview, Cameron.
71. Interview, Osborne.
72. Shipman, *All Out War*, p. 20.
73. Interview, Ivan Rogers, February 2023.
74. Interview, Cameron.
75. Interview, Gavin Williamson, February 2023.
76. Interview, Iain Duncan Smith, February 2023.
77. Interview, Cameron.
78. Interview, Ivan Rogers, February 2023.
79. Interview, Rees–Mogg.
80. Interview, Lidington.
81. Interview, Cameron.
82. Interview, Tory source.
83. Interview, Osborne.
84. Interview, Cameron.
85. Interview, Osborne.
86. Cameron, *For the Record*, p. 506.
87. Interview, Cameron inner circle.
88. Interview, Cameron inner circle.
89. Interview, Gove.
90. Interviews, Tory sources.
91. Interview, Cameron inner circle.
92. Interview, Tory minister.
93. Interview, Cameron inner circle.
94. Cameron, *For the Record*, p. 650.
95. Interview, Gove.
96. Ibid.

97. Interview, Cameron.
98. Interview, Tory source.
99. Interview, Osborne Treasury insider.
100. Interview, Eddie Lister, January 2023.
101. Interview, Walden.
102. Interview, Lister.
103. Interview, Walden.
104. Interview, Tory source.
105. Ibid.
106. Interview, Cameron.
107. Interview, Hague.
108. Interview, Rogers.
109. Interview, Feldman.
110. Interview, Gove.
111. Interview, Rees-Mogg.
112. Interview, Matthew Elliott, February 2023.
113. Interview, Lister.
114. Interview, Paul Stephenson, February 2023.
115. Interview, Davis.
116. Interview, Theresa Villiers, January 2023.
117. Interview, Tory source.
118. Interview, Farage.
119. Interview, Hague.
120. Cameron, *For the Record*, p. 654.
121. Interview, Tory minister.
122. Interview, Rees-Mogg.
123. Interview, Elliott.
124. Interview, Gove.
125. Interview, Rees-Mogg; interview, Duncan Smith.
126. Interview, Tory source.
127. Interview, Cameron.
128. Interview, senior Vote Leave source.
129. Interview, Elliott.
130. Interview, senior Vote Leave source.
131. Ibid.
132. Ibid.
133. Interview, Tory source.
134. Interview, senior Vote Leave source.
135. Ibid.
136. Ibid.

137. Interview, Oliver.
138. Interview, Elliott.
139. Interview, Gisela Stuart, February 2023.
140. Interview, Oliver.
141. Interview, Seumas Milne, February 2023.
142. Interview, Jeremy Corbyn, July 2023.
143. Interview, Elliott.
144. Interview, Stuart.
145. Interview, Tory source.
146. Cameron, *For the Record*, p. 677.
147. Interview, Cameron inner circle.
148. Interview, Tory source.
149. Interview, Farage. Farage confirmed that the bet had been at least five figures
150. Ibid.
151. Interview, Cameron inner circle.
152. Interview, Fall.
153. Interview, Cameron inner circle.
154. Ibid.
155. Interview, Stuart.
156. Interview, Tory source.
157. Ibid.

Chapter 4: A New Sheriff

1. Interview, Fiona Hill, March 2023.
2. Andrea Leadsom, *Snakes and Ladders: Navigating the Ups and Downs of Politics* (London: Biteback Publishing, 2002), p. 117.
3. Sam Coates and Rachel Sylvester, 'Being a Mother Gives Me Edge on May – Leadsom', *The Times*, 9 July 2016.
4. Interview, Andrea Leadsom, March 2023.
5. Interview, May inner circle.
6. Interview, Leadsom.
7. Leadsom, *Snakes and Ladders*, p. 87.
8. Tim Shipman, *All Out War: The Full Story of How Brexit Sank Britain's Political Class* (London: William Collins, 2016), p. 527.
9. Leadsom, *Snakes and Ladders*, p. 89.
10. Interview, Michael Gove, February 2023.

11. Interview, Tory source.
12. Interview, Tory source.
13. Interviews, Tory sources.
14. Interview, Tory source.
15. Interview, Will Walden, January 2023.
16. Interview, Leadsom.
17. Shipman, *All Out War*, p. 541.
18. Theresa May, Downing Street steps speech, 13 July 2016.
19. Nicholas Watt and Patrick Wintour, 'David Cameron: Our Next Prime Minister?', *Guardian*, 16 July 2008.
20. Interview, May inner circle.
21. Interview, Ben Gummer, March 2023.
22. Interview, David Lidington, March 2023.
23. Interview, May inner circle.
24. Interview, Stephen Parkinson, February 2023.
25. Interview, Katie Perrior, February 2023.
26. Interview, May Cabinet minister.
27. Interview, Gavin Barwell, March 2023.
28. Interview, May inner circle.
29. Ibid.
30. Interview, Parkinson.
31. Interviews, May inner circle.
32. Interview, May inner circle.
33. Ibid.
34. Interview, Parkinson.
35. Interviews, May inner circle.
36. Ibid.
37. Ibid.
38. Interview, Perrior.
39. Interview, Damian Green, March 2023.
40. Interview, May inner circle.
41. 'From Edward Whymper to Agatha Christie: Who Would Be at Theresa May's Dream Dinner Party?', *Daily Telegraph*, 20 May 2017; Theresa May, *Daily Telegraph* interview, 21 May 2017.
42. Interviews, May inner circle.
43. Interview, Ivan Rogers, February 2023.
44. Interview, May senior civil servant.
45. Interview, Parkinson.
46. Interview, Liz Sanderson, March 2023.
47. Interview, Gummer.

48. Interview, May Cabinet minister.
49. Private information.
50. Interview, Perrior.
51. Interview, May inner circle.
52. Interview, Lizzie Loudon, March 2023.
53. Interview, Sanderson.
54. Interview, Barwell.
55. Interview, Hill.
56. Interview, May Cabinet minister.
57. Interview, May inner circle.
58. Interview, Paul Harrison, March 2023.
59. Interview, May Downing Street adviser.
60. Ibid.
61. Gary Gibbon, 'Blond Ambition: Boris Johnson Plans One Last Attempt at Becoming Prime Minister', *i* newspaper, 29 September 2019.
62. Interview, May Cabinet minister.
63. Interview, May inner circle.
64. Interview, May Downing Street adviser.
65. 'Nick Timothy and Fiona Hill: How Civil Servants Lived in Fear of the Terrible Twins at No 10', *The Times*, 17 June 2017; Alasdair Palmer, 'The Prime Minister Ruined by her Gruesome Twosome', *Sunday Times*, 25 June 2017.
66. Katie Perrior, 'Working in No 10, I Was Staggered by the Arrogance of Nick Timothy and Fiona Hill', *The Times*, 10 June 2017.
67. Interview, May Cabinet minister.
68. Ibid.
69. Interview, May Downing Street adviser.
70. Interview, Lidington.
71. Interview, May senior civil servant.
72. Interview, Nick Timothy, March 2023.
73. Interviews, Tory sources.
74. Interview, May Cabinet minister.
75. Alastair Campbell, 'George Osborne: "I've Sat Down and Had a Drink With Theresa May Since All of This"', *GQ*, 27 March 2019.
76. Interview, May inner circle.
77. Ed Caesar, 'George Osborne's Revenge', *Esquire*, 13 September 2017.
78. Theresa May, Downing Street steps speech, 13 July 2016.
79. Interview, Chris Wilkins, March 2023.
80. Interview, Philip Hammond, March 2023.
81. Interview, Wilkins.

82. Theresa May, Conservative Party conference speech, Birmingham, 5 October 2016.
83. Interview, Wilkins.
84. Ben Riley-Smith, 'Theresa May to End Ban on New Grammar Schools', *Daily Telegraph*, 6 August 2016.
85. Interview, May inner circle.
86. Interview, Timothy.
87. Theresa May, speech announcing support for Remain, London, 25 April 2016.
88. Craig Oliver, media interviews for his book *Unleashing Demons*, autumn 2016.
89. Interview, Cameron inner circle.
90. Interview, Timothy.
91. Ibid.
92. Interview, May inner circle.
93. Theresa May, Conservative Party conference speech, Birmingham, 2 October 2016.
94. Interview, Hammond.
95. Interview, David Davis, January 2023.
96. Interview, Rogers.
97. Ibid.
98. Interview, Wilkins.
99. Interview, Hammond.
100. Interview, Timothy.
101. Interview, Tory source.
102. Interview, Hammond.
103. Ibid.
104. Interview, May inner circle.
105. Ibid.
106. Interview, Tory source.
107. Interview, May Treasury insider.
108. Interview, May Cabinet minister.
109. Interview, May inner circle.
110. Interview, Hammond.
111. Interview, Tory source.
112. Interview, Hill.
113. Interview, May inner circle.
114. Interview, Tory source.
115. Interview, May Treasury insider.
116. Interview, Hammond.

117. Interview, May Cabinet minister.
118. Interview, Gummer.
119. Interview, Nick Timothy, December 2022.
120. Ibid.
121. Ibid.

Chapter 5: Mayday

1. Interview, Fiona Hill, March 2023.
2. Interview, Nick Timothy, March 2023.
3. Interview, May inner circle.
4. Ibid
5. Nick Timothy, 'Diary', *The Spectator*, 15 June 2017.
6. Interview, Chris Wilkins, March 2023.
7. Interviews, May inner circle.
8. Interview, Timothy.
9. Interview, Hill.
10. Interview, Tory source.
11. Interview, Wilkins.
12. Interview, Timothy.
13. Ibid.
14. Interview, Hill.
15. George Osborne, *The Andrew Marr Show*, BBC One, 11 June 2017.
16. Interview, Timothy.
17. Ibid.
18. Interview, Hill.
19. Ibid.
20. 'General Elections 2015', House of Commons Library briefing paper, 28 July 2015, https://commonslibrary.parliament.uk/research-briefings/cbp-7186/. The eleven figure does not include the House of Commons Speaker.
21. Interview, Wilkins.
22. Interview, JoJo Penn, March 2023.
23. Interview, Philip Hammond, March 2023.
24. Interview, Hill.
25. Interview, Wilkins.
26. Interviews, May inner circle.
27. Ibid.

28. Interview, Parkinson; interview, Ben Gummer, March 2023.
29. Interview, Tory source.
30. Interview, Timothy.
31. Email, 17 April 2017.
32. Interview, Tory source.
33. 'London & Bury/Bolton Groups Strategic Note – April 2017', C/T Group memo, early April 2017. (C/T Group is the current name for Lynton Crosby and Mark Textor's company. Its name has been through different iterations over the years.)
34. Ibid.
35. 'Strategic Note Lynton Crosby/Mark Textor', C/T Group memo, early April 2017.
36. Interviews, May inner circle.
37. Interview, Wilkins.
38. 'Strategic Note Lynton Crosby/Mark Textor'.
39. Ibid.
40. Conservative Party election manifesto, 18 May 2017.
41. Ibid.
42. Interview, Tory campaign insider.
43. The Conservative Party election manifesto in 2010, when it was trying to win back power after thirteen years of New Labour rule by embodying change, contained far more mentions of the word: 122.
44. Nicholas Watt, 'The Corbyn Earthquake – How Labour Was Shaken to its Foundations', *Guardian*, 15 September 2015.
45. Ibid.
46. Interview, James Schneider, March 2023.
47. Interview, Labour HQ insider.
48. Interview, Seumas Milne, February 2023.
49. 'Narrative Arc', Jeremy Corbyn team document, late April 2017.
50. 'Strategy Paper', Jeremy Corbyn team document, 10 May 2017.
51. Interview, Patrick Heneghan, March 2023.
52. Theresa May, Downing Street speech announcing the election, 18 April 2017.
53. BBC News clip, 18 April 2017.
54. Theresa May, Downing Street speech, 3 May 2017.
55. 'Local Elections 2017', House of Commons Library briefing paper, 8 May 2017, p. 13, https://researchbriefings.files.parliament.uk/documents/CBP-7975/CBP-7975.pdf

56. Interview, Schneider.
57. Ibid.
58. Interview, Jeremy Corbyn, July 2023.
59. Interview, Milne.
60. Conservative Party election manifesto, 18 May 2017.
61. Email, 25 April 2017.
62. 'Policy Assessments 25 and 26 April', document attached to Mark Textor email, 27 April 2017.
63. Ibid.
64. Ibid.
65. Interview, Gummer.
66. Interview, Hill.
67. Interview, Tory source.
68. Interview, Paul Harrison, March 2023.
69. Ibid.
70. Interview, Gummer.
71. Interview, May inner circle.
72. Interview, Timothy.
73. Interviews, Tory sources.
74. Tim Shipman, *Fall Out: A Year of Political Mayhem* (London: William Collins, 2017), p. 300.
75. Interview, May Cabinet minister.
76. Interview, David Davis, January 2023.
77. Interview, May Cabinet minister.
78. Sir Andrew Dilnot, *Today*, BBC Radio 4, 8 May 2017.
79. Interview, Davis.
80. Interview, Gummer.
81. Interview, Tory source.
82. Shipman, *Fall Out*, p. 309.
83. Interview, Tory campaign insider.
84. Interview, Timothy.
85. Interview, Gummer.
86. Interview, Tory campaign insider.
87. Ibid.
88. Interview, May inner circle.
89. Ibid.
90. Interview, Davis.
91. Interview, Tory source.
92. Interview, Hammond.
93. Interview, Tory source.

94. Interview, Milne.
95. Interview, Schneider.
96. Interview, Corbyn.
97. Interview, Tory campaign insider.
98. Alia Middleton, 'Criss-crossing the Country: Did Corbyn and May's Constituency Visits Impact on Their GE17 Performance?', blog, London School of Economics and Political Science, 9 August 2017.
99. Interview, Isaac Levido, January 2023.
100. Interview, Timothy.
101. Interview, Labour HQ insider.
102. '2017 General Election – Marginal Seats Track' reports, C/T Group memos, 26 April–8 June 2017.
103. Interview, Wilkins.
104. Nick Timothy, 'Diary', *The Spectator*, 17 June 2017.
105. Interview, Hill.
106. 'Key Issues from the 2017 Election', produced after the 8 June 2017 election, C/T Group memo.
107. Interview, Tory campaign insider.
108. Interview, Tory source.
109. Nick Timothy, *Remaking One Nation: The Future of Conservatism* (London: Polity, 2020), p. 2.
110. Interview, Tory source.
111. Interview, Hill.
112. Interview, Timothy.

Chapter 6: Regicide and Renewal

1. Interview, Johnson inner circle.
2. Ibid.
3. Tim Shipman, 'Sedgefield Fell, and they Erupted into Song – Things Can Only Get Better!', *Sunday Times*, 15 December 2019.
4. Harry Cole, 'Boris Johnson's Shock 'n' Awe', *Mail on Sunday*, 15 December 2019.
5. Interview, Jacob Rees-Mogg, April 2023.
6. Interview, Johnson inner circle.
7. Anecdote told by Michael Crick, Channel 4 political correspondent, in May 2016 in a *Radio Times* article, quoted in Jasper Jackson, 'Michael Crick: Boris and Cameron "Wrestled Over Papers Like Schoolboys"', *Guardian*, 17 May 2016.

8. Interview, Johnson inner circle.
9. Before 2019 the last UK general election to take place in November, December or January was in 1935.
10. Interview, David Davis, January 2023.
11. Interview, Gavin Williamson, April 2023.
12. Ibid.
13. Interview, Nick Timothy, December 2022.
14. Ibid.
15. Interview, Fiona Hill, March 2023.
16. Ben Riley-Smith, 'Exclusive: How Theresa May Poked Fun at the Size of Donald Trump's Hands', *Daily Telegraph*, 7 February 2017.
17. Interview, Chris Wilkins, March 2023.
18. Interview, David Lidington, March 2023.
19. Interview, Damian Green, March 2023
20. Interview, May Cabinet minister.
21. Interview, Lidington.
22. Interview, Katie Perrior, March 2023.
23. Harry Cole, 'Theresa May Threatens to Exterminate Boris Johnson in Brutal Public Slap Down', *Sun*, 3 November 2016.
24. Interview, Lidington.
25. Interview, Will Walden, January 2023.
26. Theresa May, appearance before the 1922 Committee, House of Commons, 12 June 2017.
27. 'PM words following Chequers', Downing Street press release, 6 July 2018.
28. Interview, Davis.
29. Interview, Tory source.
30. Interview, Rees-Mogg.
31. Interview, Michael Gove, April 2023.
32. Interview, Julian Smith, April 2023.
33. Interview, Gavin Barwell, April 2023.
34. Ibid.
35. Interview, Lord Frost, April 2023.
36. Interview, Johnson Cabinet minister.
37. Interview, Johnson inner circle.
38. Ibid.
39. Ibid.
40. Interview, Eddie Lister, January 2023.
41. Interview, Johnson inner circle.
42. Interview, Frost.

43. Interviews, Johnson inner circle.
44. Ibid.
45. Interviews, Johnson leadership campaign sources.
46. Boris Johnson spokesperson, July 2023.
47. Interview, Johnson inner circle.
48. Ibid.
49. Interview, Tory source.
50. Interview, Steve Baker, April 2023.
51. Ibid.
52. Mark Francois, *Spartan Victory: The Inside Story of the Battle for Brexit* (independently published, 2021), p. 194.
53. Interview, David Canzini, March 2023.
54. Interview, Sir Graham Brady, April 2023.
55. David Cameron, *For the Record* (London: William Collins, 2019), p. 235.
56. UK Parliament, 'Register of Members' Financial Interests, as at 1 October 2018', https://publications.parliament.uk/pa/cm/cmregmem /181001/181001.pdf
57. Interview, Johnson inner circle.
58. Ibid.
59. Interview, Downing Street insider.
60. Historic polling averages data is captured in the 'National Parliament Voting Intention', Politico, https://www.politico.eu/europe-poll-of-polls/united-kingdom/
61. Interview, Johnson inner circle.
62. Ibid.
63. Interview, Baker.
64. Interview, Sir Graham Brady.
65. Interview, Theresa Villiers, April 2023.
66. Interview, Baker.
67. Interview, Canzini.
68. Interview, Barwell.
69. Interview, May Cabinet minister.
70. Ibid.
71. Interviews, May inner circle.
72. Interview, Julian Smith, March 2023.
73. Interview, Eurosceptic Tory source.
74. Interview, Barwell.
75. Interview, Tory source.
76. Interview, Rees-Mogg.
77. Ibid.

78. Ibid.
79. Interview, Grant Shapps, January 2023.
80. Interview, Tory source.
81. Interview, Gove.
82. Interview, Sajid Javid, April 2023.
83. Interview, Rory Stewart, April 2023.
84. Interview, European Research Group source.
85. Interview, Baker.
86. Interview, Tory source.
87. Ibid.
88. Interview, Johnson inner circle.
89. Interview, Oliver Lewis, April 2023.
90. Interview, Baker.
91. Boris Johnson spokesperson
92. Interview, Johnson inner circle.
93. Interview, Tory source.
94. Interview, Lister.
95. Ibid.
96. Interview, Johnson inner circle.
97. Interview, Tory source.
98. Interview, Johnson inner circle.
99. Interviews, Johnson inner circle.
100. Ibid.
101. Interview, Johnson Cabinet minister.
102. Interview, Johnson inner circle.
103. Interview, Gove.
104. Ibid.
105. Interview, Lewis.
106. Ibid.
107. Interviews, Johnson inner circle.
108. Interview, Lord Frost, April 2023.
109. Interview, ibid.: interview, Lewis.
110. Interview, Johnson inner circle.
111. Boris Johnson, Conservative Party conference speech, Manchester, 2 October 2019.
112. Interview, Isaac Levido, April 2023.
113. Ibid.
114. Ibid.
115. Interview, senior Tory campaign source.
116. Interview, Tory source.

117. Interview, senior Tory campaign source.
118. Ibid.
119. Interview, Johnson inner circle.
120. Interview, senior Tory campaign source.
121. Ibid.
122. Ibid.
123. Interview, Nigel Farage, February 2023.
124. Interview, Treasury source.
125. Interview, Jeremy Corbyn, July 2023.
126. Interview, Levido.
127. Shipman, 'Sedgefield Fell, and they Erupted into Song'.
128. Interview, Tory source.

Chapter 7: Squandered Opportunities

1. Interviews, Johnson inner circle.
2. Interview, Cleo Watson, April 2023.
3. Video seen by the author of the Downing Street event on 31 January 2020.
4. 'Coronavirus: Two Cases Confirmed in UK', BBC online, 31 January 2020.
5. 'Coronavirus: How the UK Dealt With Its First Covid Case', BBC online.
6. Interview, Watson.
7. Interview, Watson.
8. Interview, Downing Street insider.
9. Interview, Eddie Lister, January 2023.
10. Ibid.
11. Boris Johnson, televised statement on Covid-19 announcing lockdown, 23 March 2020.
12. Official government Covid-19 data, https://coronavirus.data.gov.uk/
13. Ibid.
14. 'Public Spending During the Covid-19 Pandemic', House of Commons Library briefing paper, 26 April 2023, https://commonslibrary.parliament.uk/research-briefings/cbp-9309/
15. Interviews, Johnson Cabinet ministers and Johnson inner circle.
16. Interview, Downing Street insider.
17. Interview, Lister.

18. Interview, Nadhim Zahawi, May 2023.
19. Interview, Henry Cook, April 2023.
20. Interview, Michael Gove, April 2023.
21. Interview, Jacob Rees-Mogg, April 2023.
22. Interview, Baroness Evans, April 2023.
23. Ibid.
24. Interview, Priti Patel, April 2023.
25. Interview, Lord Frost, April 2023.
26. Interview, Lister.
27. Interview, Patel.
28. Interview, Johnson inner circle.
29. Interview, Patel.
30. Interview, Downing Street insider.
31. Interview, Johnson inner circle.
32. David Wooding, 'Boris' Covid Hell: Boris Johnson Reveals Doctors Prepared to Announce His Death as He Battled Coronavirus', *Sun on Sunday*, 2 May 2020.
33. Ibid.
34. Interview, Lister.
35. Ibid.
36. Ibid.
37. Wooding, 'Boris' Covid Hell'.
38. Interview, Johnson friend.
39. Interview, Lister.
40. Interview, Johnson inner circle.
41. Interview, Lister.
42. Interview, Lucia Hodgson, April 2023.
43. Interview, Theresa Villiers, April 2023.
44. Interview, Rees-Mogg.
45. Interview, Downing Street insider.
46. Ibid.
47. Ibid.
48. Ben Riley-Smith, 'Guto Harri on Life at No 10 with Boris Johnson', *Daily Telegraph*, 13 May 2023.
49. Interview, Tory source.
50. Interview, Johnson inner circle.
51. Interview, Downing Street source.
52. Boris Johnson, 'Labour Should Listen to the Mayor in *Jaws*', *Daily Telegraph*, 4 December 2003.
53. Interview, Johnson inner circle.

54. Interview, May Cabinet minister.
55. Ibid.
56. Interview, Baroness Evans, April 2023; interview, Nicky Morgan, April 2023.
57. Interview, Johnson inner circle.
58. Interview, Downing Street insider.
59. Ibid.
60. Ibid.
61. Interview, Johnson Cabinet minister.
62. Ibid.
63. Ibid.
64. Interview, Baroness Evans.
65. Interview, Johnson Cabinet minister.
66. Interview, Gove.
67. Interviews, Johnson Cabinet ministers.
68. Interview, Lister.
69. Boris Johnson spokesperson, issued to the author after approach for comment on aspects of reporting, July 2023.
70. Interview, Johnson inner circle.
71. Interview, Brandon Lewis, April 2023.
72. Interview, Downing Street insider.
73. Interview, Johnson inner circle.
74. Ibid.
75. Interview, Patel.
76. Interview, Rees-Mogg.
77. Interview, Frost.
78. Interview, senior health department source.
79. Interview, senior education department source.
80. Interview, Tory source.
81. Interview, Villiers.
82. Interview, Frost.
83. Interview, Baroness Evans.
84. Boris Johnson, Lifetime Skills Guarantee speech, Downing Street, 29 September 2020.
85. The Lifelong Learning (Higher Education Fee Limits) Bill was tabled on 1 February 2023.
86. Interview, senior Ministry of Justice source.
87. 'A Fixed Link between Great Britain and Northern Ireland: Technical Feasibility', November 2021, https://assets.publishing.service.gov.uk/government/uploads/system/uploads/attachment_data/file/1035650/

a-fixed-link-between-great-britain-and-northern-ireland-technical-feasibility.pdf; government spending statistics put 'total managed expenditure for 2020/21' at £1,115 billion, https://www.gov.uk/government/statistics/public-spending-statistics-release-november-2021/public-spending-statistics-november-2021

88. Interview, Johnson Cabinet minister.
89. Interview, Downing Street insider.
90. Interview, senior Treasury source.
91. Interview, Downing Street insider.
92. Interview, senior Treasury source.
93. Boris Johnson spokesperson.
94. Interview, senior Treasury source.
95. Ibid.
96. Ibid.
97. Interviews, Downing Street insiders.
98. Interview, Johnson inner circle.
99. Ibid.
100. Interview, Sajid Javid, April 2023.
101. Interview, Johnson campaign source.
102. Ibid.
103. Ibid.
104. Interview, Downing Street insider.
105. Carrie Johnson spokesperson, July 2023.
106. Interview, Johnson campaign source.
107. Ibid.
108. Interview, Downing Street insider.
109. Ibid.
110. Interview, Johnson inner circle.
111. Interview, Downing Street insider.
112. Carrie Johnson spokesperson.
113. Dominic Cummings, appearance before the Commons Health and Social Care Committee and Commons Science and Technology Committee, House of Commons, 26 May 2021.
114. Interview, Downing Street insider.
115. Interview, Frost.
116. Interview, Baroness Evans.
117. Interview, Downing Street insider.
118. Interview, Lister.
119. Interview, Johnson friend.
120. Interview, Downing Street insider.

121. Ibid.
122. Ibid.
123. Interview, Matthew Elliott, February 2023.
124. *Dominic Cummings: The Interview*, with Laura Kuenssberg, BBC 2, 20 July 2021.
125. Interview, Downing Street insider.
126. Ibid.
127. Interview, Lister.
128. Interview, Downing Street insider.
129. Interview, Johnson inner circle.
130. Interview, Downing Street insider.
131. Interview, Johnson inner circle.
132. Interview, Downing Street insider.
133. Interview, Johnson inner circle.
134. Ibid.
135. Interview, Tory source.
136. Interview, Johnson inner circle.
137. Interview, senior Treasury source.

Chapter 8: Downfall

1. Interview, Johnson inner circle. The quotes come from a source who was with Boris Johnson in the aftermath of the news dropping. Other sources confirmed the thrust of Johnson's reaction.
2. Ibid.
3. Ibid.
4. A YouGov poll for Sky News asked 1,005 Tory members who should replace Boris Johnson if he stepped down. The results, published on 9 January 2022, had Rishi Sunak on top with 33 per cent of the vote, followed by Liz Truss on 25 per cent, https://news.sky.com/story/nearly-half-of-conservative-members-think-rishi-sunak-would-make-better-party-leader-than-boris-johnson-poll-12512455
5. Interview, Javid and Sunak allies.
6. Sajid Javid tweet, 6.02 p.m., 5 July 2022, https://twitter.com/sajid-javid/status/1544366218789937152
7. Rishi Sunak tweet, 6.11 p.m., 5 July 2022, https://twitter.com/RishiSunak/status/1544368323625947137
8. Metropolitan Police press release, 'Met's Investigation into Alleged Breaches of Covid Regulations, Op Hillman, concludes', 19 May 2022.

9. Interview, Nadhim Zahawi, May 2023.
10. Interview, Brandon Lewis, April 2023.
11. Interview, Grant Shapps, January 2023.
12. Interview, Priti Patel, April 2023.
13. Interviews, Treasury senior source and Tory source.
14. Interview, Michael Gove, April 2023.
15. Boris Johnson, Downing Street resignation speech, 7 July 2022.
16. 'National Parliament Voting Intention', Politico, https://www.politico.eu/europe-poll-of-polls/united-kingdom/
17. Boris Johnson, Conservative Party conference speech, 6 October 2021, Manchester Central.
18. Interview, David Canzini, June 2023.
19. 'National Parliament Voting Intention'.
20. Report into Owen Paterson, House of Commons Committee on Standards, 26 October 2021.
21. Interview, Jacob Rees-Mogg, May 2023.
22. 'Tories lose North Shropshire Seat They Held for 115 Years', BBC News, 17 December 2021.
23. Taylor Gee and Zack Stanton, '46 Political Scandals That Were "Worse than Watergate"', *Politico Magazine*, 1 February 2018.
24. Cabinet Office, 'Investigation Into Alleged Gatherings on Government Premises during Covid restrictions – Update', 31 January 2022.
25. Boris Johnson, oral evidence given to the House of Commons Privileges Committee, 22 March 2023.
26. Cabinet Office, 'Findings of Second Permanent Secretary's Investigation into Alleged Gatherings on Government Premises during Covid Restrictions', 25 May 2022.
27. Ibid.
28. Ibid.
29. Steven Swinford and Oliver Wright, 'Rishi Sunak Settles in as Downing St's Captain Sensible', *The Times*, 20 June 2020.
30. Pippa Crerar, 'Boris Johnson "Broke Covid Lockdown Rules" with Downing Street Parties at Xmas', *Daily Mirror*, 30 November 2021.
31. 'Downing Street Staff Shown Joking in Leaked Recording about Christmas Party they Later Denied', *ITV News*, 10 December 2021; Paul Brand, 'Email Proves Downing Street Staff Held Drinks Party at Height of Lockdown', ITV online, 10 January 2022.
32. Tony Diver and Ben Riley-Smith, 'Parties Held at No 10 as Her Majesty Mourned', *Daily Telegraph*, 14 January 2022.
33. 'Core Evidence Bundle Materials: Material to Be Relied Upon by

the Committee of Privileges and Rt Hon Boris Johnson MP in the Oral Evidence Session of the Committee on 22 March 2023', 22 March 2023.

34. Ibid.

35. Boris Johnson, Prime Minister's Questions, House of Commons, 8 December 2021.

36. Metropolitan Police press release, 'Met's Investigation into Alleged Breaches of Covid Regulations, Op Hillman, Concludes', 19 May 2022.

37. Interview, Johnson inner circle.

38. Ibid.

39. Past discussion with Tory MP.

40. Interview, CCHQ source.

41. Interview, Johnson inner circle.

42. Dominic Penna and Matthew Robinson, 'Full List of Tories Who Have Called for Boris Johnson to Resign Over Partygate and Pincher', *Daily Telegraph*, 7 July 2022.

43. Interview, 1922 Committee executive.

44. Ben Riley-Smith and Gordon Rayner, 'A Weekend is a Long Time in Politics: How the Knives Came Out for Boris', *Daily Telegraph*, 6 June 2022.

45. Boris Johnson, BBC News interview, 6 June 2022.

46. 'Tories Lose North Shropshire Seat They Held for 115 Years', BBC online, 17 December 2021.

47. 'Local Elections 2022: Results and Analysis', House of Commons library briefing paper, 13 May 2022, https://commonslibrary.parliament. uk/research-briefings/cbp-9545/

48. Interview, Johnson inner circle.

49. Ibid.

50. Interviews, ibid.

51. Interview, Sunak inner circle.

52. Boris Johnson, Downing Street steps speech, 24 July 2019.

53. Interviews, government insider.

54. Interview, senior Treasury source.

55. Interview, Sunak inner circle.

56. Interview, government insider.

57. Ibid.

58. Interview, Johnson inner circle.

59. Ibid.

60. Interview, government insider.

61. Jonathan Rose and Greg Heffer, 'Just how long HAS Rishi been plotting to take No 10?', Mail Online, 8 July 2022.

62. Interview, Tory source.

63. Ibid.

64. Ibid.

65. Interview, Treasury source.

66. Interview, Johnson inner circle.

67. Harry Yorke, 'Liz Truss: Promises of Low Tax and Defence Spending Launch Her Into Third Place', *Sunday Times*, 10 July 2022.

68. Liz Truss tweet, 9.14 p.m., 12 January 2022, https://twitter.com/trussliz/status/1481374158202228736?lang=en

69. Rishi Sunak tweet, 8.11 p.m., 12 January 2022, https://twitter.com/RishiSunak/status/1481358087286108169?s=20

70. Interview, Sunak inner circle.

71. Boris Johnson, House of Commons, 31 January 2022.

72. Rishi Sunak, Downing Street press conference, 3 February 2022.

73. Interview, Simon Clarke, May 2023.

74. Interview, Tory source.

75. Guto Harri, 'An Orgy of Pain', *Unprecedented* podcast, 11 May 2023.

76. Interviews, Johnson inner circle.

77. Interview, Johnson Cabinet minister.

78. Interviews, Johnson inner circle.

79. Interview, Sunak inner circle.

80. Interviews, Johnson inner circle.

81. Ibid.

82. Ibid.

83. Interview, Sunak inner circle.

84. Interviews, Tory sources.

85. The nickname has dull origins: the final letter was once left off his first name.

86. Interviews, Johnson inner circle and Sunak inner circle.

87. Interview, Johnson inner circle

88. Ibid.

89. Interview, Sunak inner circle.

90. Interview, Jake Berry, May 2023.

91. Anna Isaac, 'Operation Save Big Dog: Boris Johnson Draws Up Plan for Officials to Quit Over Partygate So He Can Keep Job', *Independent*, 14 January 2022.

92. Alex Story, 'You will Go Far in the Tories . . . Let Me Slip Into Something More Comfortable', *Mail on Sunday*, 4 November 2017.

93. Sebastian Payne, *The Fall of Boris Johnson: The Full Story* (London: Macmillan, 2022), p. 155.

94. Chris Pincher, letter to the prime minister, 30 June 2022.

95. Dominic Cummings tweet, 1.23 p.m., 2 July 2022, https://twitter.com/Dominic2306/status/1543208854325977088

96. Commons Committee on Standards report into Chris Pincher, 6 July 2023.

97. Interview, Johnson inner circle.

98. Interviews, ibid.

99. Interview, Tory source.

100. Interview, Johnson inner circle.

101. Interview, Gove.

102. Ibid.

103. Interview, Nigel Adams, May 2023.

104. Interview, Johnson inner circle.

105. Commons Liaison Committee, 'Oral Evidence: The Work of the Prime Minister', 6 July 2022.

106. Interview, Tory source.

107. Interview, Zahawi.

108. Nadhim Zahawi tweet, 8.43 a.m., 7 July 2022, https://twitter.com/nadhimzahawi/status/1544950219657330688

109. Interview, Patel.

110. Interview, Dominic Raab, July 2023.

111. Interview, Treasury insider.

112. Interview, Tory source.

113. Interviews, Johnson inner circle.

114. Interview, Gove.

115. Image in the photographs section of this book.

116. Interview, Johnson Cabinet minister.

117. Ibid.

118. Interview, Johnson inner circle.

119. Ibid.

120. Ibid.

121. Ibid.

122. Interview, Tory source.

123. Interview, Johnson inner circle.

124. Original Boris Johnson resignation speech draft, shared with the author.

125. Ibid.

126. Boris Johnson, Downing Street resignation speech, 7 July 2022.

127. Interview, former Conservative Party leader.

Chapter 9: Forty-Nine Days

1. Interview, Kwasi Kwarteng, May 2023.
2. Interviews, Number 10 and Treasury insiders.
3. Interview, Tory source.
4. Kwasi Kwarteng, BBC News interview, 13 October 2022, https://www.bbc.co.uk/news/uk-politics-63244805
5. Interview, Treasury insider.
6. Interview, Kwarteng.
7. Steven Swinford, political editor of *The Times*, broke the news on Twitter at 11.28 a.m.
8. Interview, Kwarteng.
9. Ibid.
10. Ibid.
11. Ibid.
12. Jeremy Hunt told the story at a British Chambers of Commerce event on 17 May 2023: 'I got a text message saying "This is Liz Truss. Please call," and I thought this is going to be a hoax and I was actually on a weekend away with my wife in Brussels. I said I can't believe these hoaxes, but we keep thinking I'm going to get caught out. And we went down and had a lovely breakfast downstairs. And finally I was called by a former special adviser who said, "No, I think Liz Truss really is trying to get in touch with you."'
13. Interview, Kwarteng.
14. Interview, Foreign Office insider.
15. Interview, Liz Truss, April 2023.
16. Interviews, Truss inner circle.
17. Ibid.
18. Interview, Foreign Office source.
19. Interview, Ranil Jayawardena, May 2023.
20. Interview, Adam Jones, May 2023.
21. Interviews, Truss inner circle
22. Interview, Truss inner circle.
23. Interview, Mark Fullbrook, May 2023.
24. Ibid.
25. Ibid.
26. Ibid.
27. Ibid.

28. Interviews, Truss inner circle.
29. Ibid.
30. Ibid.
31. Interview, Sunak ministerial ally.
32. Interview, Truss inner circle.
33. Harry Cole and James Heale, *Out of the Blue: The Inside Story of the Unexpected Rise and Rapid Fall of Liz Truss* (London: HarperCollins, 2022), p. 265.
34. ITV Tory leadership debate, 18 July 2022.
35. Interview, Tory source.
36. Interviews, Truss inner circle.
37. Ibid.
38. Ibid.
39. Interview, senior Truss campaign source.
40. Liz Truss won 81,326 votes from Tory Party members to Rishi Sunak's 60,399, meaning she won the leadership with 57.4 per cent of the vote to his 42.6 per cent.
41. Interview, Tory source.
42. Interviews, Truss inner circle.
43. Ibid.
44. Ibid.
45. Interview, Jones.
46. Ibid.
47. Ibid.
48. Interview, Asa Bennett, May 2023.
49. Interviews, Truss inner circle.
50. Ibid.
51. Ibid.
52. Ben Riley-Smith, 'Liz Truss: I'm the Insurgent Candidate in the Tory Leadership Race', *Daily Telegraph*, 22 July 2022.
53. Interview, Jones, May 2023.
54. 'The Lady's for Turning, Right from CND to Conservative', *The Times*, 9 June 2012.
55. Liz Truss, interview with Nick Robinson on the BBC's *Political Thinking*, September 2021.
56. Liz Truss, Conservative Party conference speech, ICC Birmingham, 5 October 2022.
57. Interview, Truss inner circle.
58. Ibid.
59. Interview, Jason Stein, May 2023.

60. Interview, Truss inner circle.
61. Interview, Kwarteng.
62. Interview, Truss.
63. 'Liz Truss's Big Gamble', BBC Radio 4, 3 December 2022.
64. Interviews, Truss Cabinet ministers.
65. Interview, Truss inner circle.
66. Interview, Simon Clarke, May 2023.
67. Interview, Truss inner circle.
68. Interview, senior Truss campaign source.
69. Interview, Fullbrook.
70. George Parker and Sebastian Payne, 'Truss Rejects "Handouts" in Favour of Tax Cuts to Help Households', *Financial Times*, 5 August 2022.
71. 'The Growth Plan 2022', Treasury, p. 25, https://assets.publishing. service.gov.uk/government/uploads/system/uploads/attachment_data/ file/1105989/CCS207_CCS0822/46402-001_SECURE_HMT_Autumn _Statement_2022_BOOK_Web_Accessible.pdf
72. Interview, Clarke.
73. Memo on tax cuts written by Jacob Rees-Mogg for Liz Truss's Tory leadership campaign, summer 2022.
74. Excerpts of document collected by Chris Philp shared with the author.
75. Interview, Chris Philp, July 2023.
76. The formal appointment of the prime minister by the monarch is known as the 'kissing of the hands' ceremony.
77. Liz Truss, Downing Street steps speech, 6 September 2022.
78. Interview, Treasury insider.
79. Interview, Kwarteng.
80. Ibid.
81. Interview, Treasury insider.
82. Interview, Truss minister.
83. Interview, Truss Cabinet minister.
84. Interview, Truss inner circle.
85. Cole and Heale, *Out of the Blue*, p. 164.
86. Interview, Kwarteng.
87. Interview, Truss Cabinet minister.
88. Interview, Kwarteng.
89. A YouGov poll, 8 September 2022, found 80 per cent of respondents supported the energy price guarantee, 10 per cent opposed it and 10 per cent did not know.

90. Interview, Truss inner circle.
91. Interview, Truss Cabinet minister.
92. Interview, Treasury insider.
93. Interview, Truss inner circle.
94. Ibid.
95. Ibid.
96. Ibid.
97. Interview, Truss Cabinet minister.
98. Interview, Kwarteng.
99. Interview, Truss.
100. Interview, Treasury insider.
101. Kwasi Kwarteng, Growth Plan 2022 speech, House of Commons, 23 September 2022.
102. 'The Growth Plan 2022', p. 11.
103. Kwarteng, Growth Plan 2022 speech.
104. 'The Growth Plan 2022', p. 26.
105. Tim Shipman, Harry Yorke and Caroline Wheeler, '"Biscotti Mini-Budget" Exposes Gulf Between Liz Truss and Keir Starmer – and More Tax Cuts Are on the Cards', *Sunday Times*, 24 September 2022.
106. Interview, Fullbrook.
107. Interview, Iain Carter, May 2023.
108. Interview, Jones, May 2023.
109. Interviews, Truss inner circle.
110. Ibid.
111. Ibid.
112. Interview, Truss inner circle.
113. Interview, Tory source.
114. Front page headlines on the *Daily Mail*, *Daily Telegraph* and *Daily Express*, 24 September 2022.
115. 'Stakeholder Reaction: The Growth Plan – Overall Package', Treasury press release sent via email, 23 September 2022, 3.32 p.m.
116. Chris Philp tweet (later deleted), 10.17 a.m., 23 September 2022.
117. Kwasi Kwarteng, *Sunday with Laura Kuenssberg*, BBC One, 25 September 2022.
118. Interviews, Truss inner circle and Treasury insider.
119. Interview, Treasury insider.
120. Interview, Kwarteng.
121. Interview, Nadhim Zahawi, May 2023.
122. Interview, Treasury insider.

123. Ibid.
124. Richard Partington, 'UK Government Bonds: Why Are Yields Rising and Why Does it Matter?', *Guardian*, 27 September 2022.
125. Richard Partington, 'Bank Confirms Pension Funds Almost Collapsed amid Market Meltdown', *Guardian*, 6 October 2022.
126. 'After U-turn, Britain's Economy Still Paying for Truss's Growth Plan', Reuters, 17 October 2022.
127. 'Bank of England Announces Gilt Market Operation', Bank of England press release, 28 September 2022.
128. Interviews, Truss inner circle and Treasury insiders.
129. Interviews, Truss inner circle.
130. Interview, Truss inner circle.
131. Contemporaneous note, Number 10 meeting, 29 September 2022.
132. Julian Smith tweet, 3.33 p.m., 23 September 2022, https://twitter.com/JulianSmithUK/status/1573319566872150020
133. Interviews, Truss inner circle.
134. Michael Gove, *Sunday with Laura Kuenssberg*, BBC One, 2 October 2022.
135. Interview, senior Downing Street source.
136. Interview, government whip.
137. Interview, Jake Berry, May 2023.
138. Interview, Clarke.
139. Interview, Truss inner circle.
140. Interview, Kwarteng.
141. Ibid.
142. Interview, Clarke.
143. Interviews, government sources.
144. Interviews, Treasury insiders.
145. Interview, government source.
146. Interview, Treasury insider.
147. Interview, Truss inner circle.
148. Interview, Treasury insider.
149. Ibid.
150. Ibid.
151. Interview, Truss inner circle.
152. Ibid.
153. Ibid.
154. Interview, Tory source.
155. Interview, Truss inner circle.

156. Interviews, Truss inner circle.
157. Interview, Truss inner circle.
158. Ibid.
159. Interview, Zahawi.
160. Interview, Treasury insider.
161. Interviews, Downing Street sources.
162. Interview, Downing Street source.
163. Interview, senior Downing Street figure.
164. Ibid.
165. Interview, Truss inner circle.
166. Ibid.
167. Interview, Wendy Morton, May 2023; interview, Craig Whittaker, May 2023.
168. Message shared with the author.
169. Interviews, Downing Street insiders and Morton.
170. Messages shared with the author.
171. Ibid.
172. Interviews, Truss inner circle.
173. Graham Stuart, House of Commons, 19 October 2022.
174. Interview, Graham Stuart, May 2023.
175. Interview, Tory source.
176. Stuart, House of Commons.
177. Interview, Morton.
178. Messages seen by the author.
179. Interview, government whip.
180. Interview, Jacob Rees-Mogg, May 2023.
181. Interviews, Tory MPs.
182. 'Report for Mr Speaker: Investigation into Events outside the "No" Lobby on 19 October. Report Prepared by the Serjeant-at-Arms, the Clerk of the Journals and the Clerk of the Liaison Committee', 1 November 2022, https://www.parliament.uk/globalassets/investigation-report-for-19-october-2022.pdf
183. Interview, Morton.
184. Remarks reported on the evening and accuracy confirmed by Craig Whittaker.
185. Clip from Germany's public-service broadcaster ARD.
186. Interview, Tory source.
187. Ibid.
188. Interviews, Truss inner circle.
189. Interviews, Morton and Whittaker.

190. WhatsApp message sent to UK political reporters, 1.33 a.m., 20 October 2022.
191. Interview, Truss inner circle.
192. Interview, Jones.
193. Interview, Kwarteng.

Chapter 10: Comeback Kid

1. Interview, Tory sources.
2. Interview, Tory source.
3. Interviews, Johnson inner circle and Sunak inner circle.
4. Ibid.
5. Ibid.
6. Interview, Downing Street source.
7. Interview, Sunak inner circle.
8. Interview, Dominic Raab, July 2023.
9. Interview, Sunak campaign source.
10. Interview, Sunak inner circle.
11. Ibid.
12. Katy Balls, 'The Polite Radical: Rishi Sunak on Economic Repair, Migrants and Faith', *The Spectator*, 17 December 2022.
13. Interview, Tory source.
14. Rishi Sunak, interview with Piers Morgan, TalkTV, 2 February 2023.
15. Interview, Raab.
16. Ibid.
17. Interview, Sunak ally.
18. Interview, Jake Berry, June 2023.
19. Contemporaneous note dated 20 October 2022 written by Jake Berry and seen by the author.
20. Interview, Berry.
21. Senior Treasury source, July 2023.
22. Boris Johnson, press statement, 23 October 2022.
23. Interview, Bob Blackman, July 2023.
24. Ibid.
25. Interview, Sunak inner circle.
26. Interviews, Sunak inner circle.
27. Ibid.

28. Ibid.

29. Interview, Sunak inner circle.

30. Caroline Wheeler and Tim Shipman, 'Rishi Sunak Interview: My Wife Definitely Drinks . . . It Massively Irritates Her That I Don't', *Sunday Times*, 6 August 2022.

31. Interview, Sunak inner circle.

32. Ibid.

33. Interviews, Sunak inner circle.

34. Rishi Sunak made the choice in an interview with Darren McCaffrey of GB News on 15 November 2022.

35. Interview, Sunak inner circle.

36. Interview, Treasury insider.

37. Ibid.

38. Interview, Sunak inner circle.

39. The clip made the headlines on 2 March 2021 when it was newly unearthed online.

40. Interview, Sunak inner circle.

41. Interview, Treasury insider.

42. Rebecca Speare-Cole, 'Chancellor Rishi Sunak Poses for Pre-Budget Photo with £180 "Smart Mug"', *Evening Standard*, 8 July 2020.

43. Pippa Crerar, 'Rishi Sunak Seen Using Erasable-Ink Pens on Official Documents and in Meetings', *Guardian*, 27 June 2023.

44. Saman Javed, 'Rishi Sunak's Morning Routine: 6am Peloton, Britney Spears and a Pain au Chocolat', *Independent*, 26 October 2022.

45. Interview, former Tory chancellor.

46. Kat Lay, 'Fit for Office? Rishi Sunak Runs Northallerton 10k', *The Times*, 29 May 2023.

47. Interview, Treasury insider.

48. Ibid.

49. Rishi Sunak, interview, *Test Match Special*, BBC Radio, 1 July 2023.

50. Ibid.

51. Ibid.

52. Interview, Sunak inner circle.

53. Ibid.

54. Patrick Daly, 'Rishi Sunak's Proud Hindu Religion and What he's Said about his Faith', *Daily Mirror*, 24 October 2022.

55. Interview, Sunak ally.
56. Ibid.
57. Rishi Sunak, interview, *Test Match Special*.
58. Interviews, Sunak inner circle.
59. Interview, Raab.
60. Interview, Treasury insider.
61. Ibid.
62. Interview, Tory source.
63. Interview, Sunak inner circle.
64. Interview, Tory source.
65. Interviews, Sunak inner circle.
66. Ibid.
67. Interview, Treasury insider.
68. Harry Cole, 'Lay Off My Missus: My Wife Loves her Country Just Like I Love Mine, says Rishi Sunak as he Defends Millionaire Spouse over Tax Row "Smears"', *Sun*, 7 April 2022.
69. Interview, Treasury insider.
70. Interview, Sunak ally.
71. Interview, senior Sunak campaign source.
72. Interview, Sunak inner circle.
73. Gabriel Pogrund, 'No 10 Refuses to Endorse Gavin Williamson as Threatening Texts Revealed', *Sunday Times*, 5 November 2022.
74. Sir Gavin Williamson tweet, 8.11 p.m., 8 November 2022, https://twitter.com/GavinWilliamson/status/1590074499889696768?s=20
75. Jeremy Hunt, Autumn Statement speech, House of Commons, 17 November 2022.
76. Interview, Sunak inner circle.
77. Rishi Sunak speech, 2012 London Olympic Park site, 4 January 2023.
78. Rishi Sunak, interview with Ben Riley-Smith for the *Daily Telegraph*, 5 June 2023. Part of the full unpublished transcript.
79. Ibid.
80. Interview, Sunak Cabinet minister.
81. Interview, Sunak inner circle.
82. Rishi Sunak, Downing Street steps speech, 25 October 2022.
83. Dominic Raab, 'The People of Britain Will Pay the Price for This Kafkaesque Saga', *Daily Telegraph*, 21 April 2023.
84. Interview, Tory source.
85. Interviews, Johnson inner circle.
86. Interview, Johnson ally.

87. Interview, Raab.
88. Interview, Cameron Cabinet minister.
89. Interview, Sunak inner circle.
90. Boris Johnson, press statement, 9 June 2023.
91. Ibid.

Chapter 11: Wipeout

1. Interview, Sunak inner circle.
2. Ibid.
3. Ibid.
4. Ibid.
5. Ibid.
6. Ibid.
7. Ibid.
8. Ibid.
9. Ibid.
10. Ibid.
11. Ibid.
12. Ibid.
13. Ibid.
14. Ibid.
15. Ibid.
16. Rishi Sunak's five priorities for office were outlined in a speech given in London's Queen Elizabeth Olympic Park on 4 January 2023. They were: halving inflation by the end of 2023; growing the economy; reducing government debt; cutting NHS waiting lists; and stopping the boats carrying migrants across the English Channel.
17. Rishi Sunak, speech to the Conservative Party annual conference, Manchester, 4 October 2023.
18. Rishi Sunak, when asked by a TV reporter about the timing of the general election, 4 January 2024.
19. Interview, Sunak inner circle.
20. Ibid.
21. Ibid.
22. Ibid.
23. Ibid.
24. Interview, veteran Tory; interview, senior Reform source.

25. Interview, Tory source.
26. Ibid.
27. Interview, Sunak inner circle.
28. Interview, Tory source.
29. Ibid.
30. Ibid.
31. Interview, Downing Street insider.
32. Interview, Tory source.
33. Interviews, Sunak inner circle.
34. Interview, Tory source.
35. Interviews, Sunak inner circle.
36. Interviews, Tory sources.
37. Ibid.
38. Ibid.
39. Interview, Tory Cabinet minister.
40. Interview, David Cameron ally.
41. Interview, Tory source.
42. Ibid.
43. Ibid.
44. Interview, Boris Johnson ally.
45. Interview, Sunak inner circle.
46. Ibid.
47. Ibid.
48. Ibid.
49. Interview, Tory Cabinet minister.
50. Ibid.
51. Nigel Farage, press conference, London, 3 June 2024.
52. Conversation, veteran Tory MP, February 2024.
53. Politico poll tracker: https://www.politico.eu/europe-poll-of-polls/united-kingdom
54. Interview, Nigel Farage, July 2024.
55. Interview, Richard Tice, July 2024; interview, Nigel Farage, July 2024.
56. Interview, Reform source.
57. Interview, veteran Tory strategist.
58. Interview, Nigel Farage, July 2024.
59. Interview, Tory campaign source.
60. Interview, Nigel Farage, July 2024.
61. Interview, Sunak inner circle.
62. Ibid.

63. Interview, Nigel Farage, July 2024.
64. Interview, Richard Tice, July 2024.
65. Interviews, Tory sources.
66. Interview, Sunak inner circle.
67. Interview, veteran Tory strategist.
68. Interview, Tory campaign source.
69. Ibid.
70. Interview, Number 10 insider.
71. Interview, Labour campaign source.
72. Ibid.
73. Ibid.
74. Interview, Liberal Democrat campaign source.
75. Conversation, Liberal Democrat campaign source.
76. Interview, Liberal Democrat campaign source.
77. Comments heard by the author shouted by the crowd in Clacton, 4 June 2024.
78. Interview, Tory source.
79. Interview, Sunak inner circle.
80. Rishi Sunak, BBC TV debate with Keir Starmer, 26 June 2024.
81. Interview, Tory campaign source.
82. Rishi Sunak, speech for the eightieth anniversary of D-Day at the British Normandy Memorial, France, 6 June 2024.
83. Front page, *Daily Mirror*, 7 June 2024.
84. Interviews, Sunak inner circle.
85. Ibid.
86. Ibid.
87. Rishi Sunak, message on his official Twitter/X account, 7.45 a.m., 7 June 2024, https://x.com/RishiSunak/status/1798969474466623902
88. Interview, Tory source.
89. Unofficial poster created by Ben Golik, creative director at Uncommon Creative Studio.
90. Interview, Tory campaign source.
91. Ibid.
92. Ibid.
93. Interview, Foreign Office source.
94. Interview, senior Foreign Office insider.
95. Ibid.
96. Interview, Downing Street insider.
97. Interview, senior Foreign Office insider.
98. Interview, Sunak inner circle.

99. Interview, Tory source.
100. Interview, Number 10 insider.
101. Pippa Crerar, 'Rishi Sunak Aide Placed Bet on Election Date Days Before Announcement', *Guardian*, 12 June 2024.
102. Ibid.
103. 'Tory Candidate Tells BBC Election Bet Was "Huge Error of Judgement"', BBC online, 13 June 2024.
104. Interview, Sunak inner circle.
105. Ibid.
106. Rishi Sunak, Downing Street speech on becoming prime minister, 25 October 2022.
107. Interview, Tory campaign source.
108. Ibid.
109. Tory strategy note, 'GE2024 – Mid-Campaign Strategic Imperatives', 10 June 2024.
110. Ibid.
111. Ibid.
112. Interview, Tory campaign source.
113. Ibid.
114. Interview, Sunak inner circle.
115. Ibid.
116. Ibid.
117. Interview, Liberal Democrat campaign source.
118. Interview, Labour campaign source.
119. Rishi Sunak, Downing Street resignation speech, 5 July 2024.
120. Interviews, Number 10 insiders; interview, Labour campaign source.

Conclusion

1. Tony Blair, written comments to the author, June 2023.
2. Interview, George Osborne, July 2023.
3. Interview, Lord Howard, July 2023.
4. Ibid.

Index